FINANCIAL DEVELOPMENT AND ECONOMIC GROWTH

This volume brings together a collection of theoretical and empirical findings on aspects of financial development and economic growth in developing countries. The book is divided into two parts. The first identifies and analyses the major theoretical issues using examples, where possible, from developing countries to show how these work in practice. This section addresses a wide range of topical issues, including endogenous growth and investment. The second part looks at the implications for financial policy in developing countries. Empirical evidence is again drawn from across a broad range of developing countries and regions.

Niels Hermes is a Post-doctorate Research Fellow in the Department of Economics at Groningen University, The Netherlands. His recent work has been directed at analysing the role of domestic finance markets in the process of economic development. Previously, he has also done research into the causes and consequences of the international debt crisis and of capital flight.

Robert Lensink is Assistant Professor in Economics, also at Groningen University. His area of specialisation is economic development, and he has made special reference to the effects of financial flows on developing countries. His two most recent books are *Structural Adjustments in Sub-Saharan Africa* (Longman) and (with Kanhaya Gupta) *Financial Liberalization and Investment* (Routledge).

ROUTLEDGE STUDIES IN DEVELOPMENT ECONOMICS

FINANCIAL DEVELOPMENT AND ECONOMIC GROWTH

Theory and experiences from developing countries

*Edited by Niels Hermes
and Robert Lensink*

London and New York

Learning Resources
Centre

1243413 6 1

First published 1996
by Routledge
11 New Fetter Lane, London EC4P 4EE

Reprinted 1999, 2001

Routledge is an imprint of the Taylor & Francis Group

Simultaneously published in the USA and Canada
by Routledge
29 West 35th Street, New York, NY 10001

Typeset in Times by
Solidus (Bristol) Limited
Printed and bound in Great Britain by
Intype London Ltd

British Library Cataloguing in Publication Data
A catalogue record for this book is available from the British Library

Library of Congress Cataloguing in Publication Data
Financial development and economic growth: theory and experiences
from developing countries / edited by Niels Hermes and Robert Lensink.
   p.   cm. – (Routledge studies in development economics, ISSN
1359-7884; no. 6)
Includes bibliographical references and index.
1. Finance–Developing countries–Case studies.   2. Monetary
policy–Developing countries–Case studies.   3. Developing
countries–Economic conditions–Case studies.   I. Hermes, N.
(Niels)   II. Lensink, Robert.   III. Series.
         HG195.F5348   1996
332′.09172′4–dc20   95-25781
                                                          CIP

ISBN 0–415–13392–0

CONTENTS

CONTENTS

CONTENTS

Part 2 Issues on financial policies in developing countries

CONTENTS

FIGURES

FIGURES

TABLES

CONTRIBUTORS

George C. Abbott, *University of Glasgow, Glasgow*
Bruno Amable, *INRA and CEPREMAP, Ivry-sur-Seine and Paris, respectively*
Jean Claude Berthélemy, *OECD Development Centre, Paris*
Jean-Bernard Chatelain, *CEPII, Paris*
Asli Demirgüç-Kunt, *The World Bank, Washington, DC*
Maxwell J. Fry, *University of Birmingham, Birmingham*
Kanhaya L. Gupta, *University of Alberta, Edmonton*
Thomas Hellmann, *Stanford University, Stanford*
Niels Hermes, *University of Groningen, Groningen*
Ingmar van Herpt, *Free University, Amsterdam*
Robert Lensink, *University of Groningen, Groningen*
Ross Levine, *The World Bank, Washington, DC*
Kevin Murdock, *Stanford University, Stanford*
Victor Murinde, *Birmingham Business School, University of Birmingham*
Matthew O. Odedokun, *University of Ilorin, Ilorin*
Gilles Saint-Paul, *DELTA, Paris*
Joseph Stiglitz, *Washington, DC*
Aristomene Varoudakis, *University Robert Schuman, Strasbourg*
Hans Visser, *Free University, Amsterdam*

PREFACE

This volume contains papers presented at the workshop on 'Financial Development and Economic Growth: Theory and Experiences from Developing Economies' at the University of Groningen, The Netherlands, 7–9 December 1994. Participants at the workshop included policy makers and researchers from both developing and developed economies. All authors and other participants are gratefully acknowledged for their very stimulating contributions during the workshop.

A special thank you is due to a number of persons and institutions who substantially contributed to the success of the workshop. First, F. Baneke, Steven Brakman, Hans van Ees, Harry Garretsen, Henk de Haan, Jakob de Haan, Catrinus Jepma, Gerard Kuper, Ger Lanjouw, Frans van Loon, Bert Scholtens and Elmer Sterken for their willingness to act as discussants and chairpersons. Second, Daan van Soest, Marianne van den Bergh and Mark Thissen for their administrative assistance during the workshop. Third, Rients Abma for his willingness to read the entire manuscript and to check for all kind of errors and for his help during the workshop. Finally, the ABN/AMRO Bank, BEON Pensioen-en Vermogensbeheer NV, the ING Bank, the Ministry of Foreign Affairs, the Ministry of Economic Affairs, the Groningen Universiteits fonds and the Economic Faculty of the University of Groningen for their financial support.

Niels Hermes
Robert Lensink

INTRODUCTION

Niels Hermes and Robert Lensink

Since the publication of the seminal works of McKinnon (1973) and Shaw (1973) the relationship between domestic financial markets and economic growth in developing countries has become a prominent issue on the agenda of academic researchers interested in development economics. Particularly during the 1980s, it attracted strong interest in policy circles, which has been stimulated to an important extent by the adverse experiences of the international debt crisis, which broke out in August 1982 with the Mexican debt moratorium. The debt crisis and the related domestic economic stagnation in many less developed countries emphasised the importance of mobilising domestic financial resources, instead of being dependent on financial inflows, to finance economic growth. With large external debts, developing countries appeared to be very vulnerable to outside economic shocks.

In brief, the importance of financial markets in the process of economic growth can be clarified by pointing out the functions and services they provide. First, financial markets create an accepted medium of exchange, which facilitates trade among economic agents, and which contributes to increased specialisation in the economy. Second, they provide various services related to stimulating the volume of savings and transferring these savings to the most efficient investment projects. Obviously, then, financial markets do make a valuable contribution to economic growth.

Issues such as the preconditions of financial development, and questions related to how to design and organise financial institutions and markets, as well as how to design financial reform increasingly came to the fore in academic as well as in policy circles. It became widely acknowledged that economic growth without well-developed domestic financial markets would be detrimental to the longer run growth prospects of developing countries. This view was underlined by the World Bank study of 1989 on this issue (World Bank, 1989). As a reaction, several developing countries designed and carried out economic reform programmes during the 1980s, in which financial market reforms received a prominent role.

The increased attention from both academics and policy makers for the

1

importance of financial markets in economic development has been further stimulated by the political developments in Eastern Europe during the late 1980s and early 1990s. The radical change from socialism to capitalism that these countries carried through, led to questions with respect to what is the most appropriate way of designing financial markets, as these markets were virtually absent during socialism. In particular, these countries were interested in knowing how to set up efficient financial institutions and regulation. This directed research towards evaluating the function and design of financial markets in both developed and developing countries.

Since the issue of the relationship between financial markets and economic growth is of central importance in the recent discussions on development economics, it may be useful to provide an overview of the contents of modern theoretical and empirical literature on this subject. This volume presents a fairly complete survey of recent theoretical and empirical contributions with respect to the role of finance in economic development. Furthermore, it provides in-depth analyses of policy experiences of developing countries with respect to financial markets' ability to influence the process of economic development. Such an overview is not only useful from an academic point of view, it may also provide valuable information to policy makers for tackling pressing questions about how to design financial market policies in practice.

The volume is divided into two main parts. Part I (Chapters 2–7) contains original contributions on the theory of the relationship between financial development and economic growth. Moreover, this part contains new empirical evidence on this relationship. Part II (Chapters 8–14) presents new theoretical contributions as well as case studies on the issue of government policies towards financial markets. These various contributions are preceded by a survey of the existing literature on the issue of the role of financial markets and financial market policies in the process of economic growth, by Jean Claude Berthélemy and Aristomene Varoudakis (Chapter 1).

Part I opens with a contribution from Gilles Saint-Paul (Chapter 2), who presents a model which explains financial development as being triggered by an unusual increase in the demand for financial services. Such increases may come from a higher level of public debt, or from technological innovations associated with increasing returns to scale (dams, railroads, etc.), which can only be funded by putting together large amounts of savings. He relates this model to the historical experiences of financial development in England, France and Eastern Europe.

Bruno Amable and Jean-Bernard Chatelain (Chapter 3) explore the effects on growth of credit constraints experienced by firms and coming from incentive problems. In the context of an endogenous growth model driven by capital accumulation, any constraint on the level of investment of firms will lower the macroeconomic growth rate. The extent of these credit constraints is related to the level of net worth of firms. In general, higher net worth will increase the willingness of creditors to lend, since higher net worth reduces the incentive-compatibility constraints. One of the interesting outcomes of their model is that institutional arrangements through public intervention may soften the incentive problems, which would have a positive growth effect.

Jean Claude Berthélemy and Aristomene Varoudakis (Chapter 4) present an endogenous growth model, which exhibits multiple steady state equilibria due to reciprocal interactions between the financial and real sectors in the economy. The model shows that depending on the nature of the steady state, there may exist a poverty trap in which the financial sector 'disappears' and where the economy stagnates, or endogenous economic growth may be positive and financial intermediation follows a normal development path. They support their model by testing empirically the existence of multiple steady states linked to the initial state of financial development in a cross-section of 95 developed and developing countries. Moreover, to analyse more thoroughly the influence of specific financial policies on growth experiences of countries, they give an account of the dynamics of the underlying cumulative processes for two country case studies: Taiwan and Senegal.

Victor Murinde (Chapter 5) provides both a theoretical and empirical investigation of the relationship between financial markets and economic growth. First, he presents an endogenous growth model in which growth derives from the behaviour of economic agents in markets for credit, bonds and shares. Second, he estimates the model using the Zellner procedure for a group of seven Pacific Basin countries. The empirical investigation is further extended by using growth accounting exercises as proposed by Dowrick (1992) and by extending the analysis of the role of stock markets as suggested by Atje and Jovanovic (1993). In particular, the empirical analysis points out that stock market development is importantly linked to economic growth.

Matthew Odedokun (Chapter 6) provides an in-depth empirical analysis of the relationship between financial development and the efficiency of investment, proxied by the incremental output–capital ratio. For his analysis, he constructs a wide range of alternative indicators for financial intermediation, government intervention in the financial sector, interest rates, exchange rates and inflation. His findings show that financial intermediation (measured in terms of flow variables) is positively related to investment efficiency. Government intervention appears to be negatively related to efficiency, however. He also finds that policies of real exchange rate appreciations, as well as high inflation are adversely related to investment efficiency. The relation between interest rates and efficiency remains undetermined in his analysis.

Maxwell Fry (Chapter 7) investigates the role financial conditions have played in producing the virtuous circles of high saving, investment, output growth and export growth in a sample of Pacific Basin countries during the past few decades. High saving and investment stimulate output growth and export growth. In turn, high growth raises saving and investment levels. Fry finds that the relatively undistorted nature of both financial and foreign exchange markets in these countries has been important to raise their saving, investment, output and export levels over a long period of time, contributing to the by now well-known Asian miracle.

Turning to Part II of the volume, Ross Levine (Chapter 8) opens with a discussion of the various reasons advanced in favour of government intervention in and regulation of financial markets. Such policies may make important contributions to creating better functioning financial systems, which in turn may induce higher economic growth. Levine contends that intervention and/or regulation may be growth enhancing in the presence of pervasive market failures, but admits that interventions themselves may at times cause or aggravate other market failures. To clarify under what circumstances intervention may be useful, he proposes a checklist for evaluating financial policies with respect to how they affect financial stability and the possibility of contagion, screening and monitoring of financial intermediaries by the private and public sector, screening and monitoring of firms by financial intermediaries, competition among financial institutions, and the existence of incomplete or missing financial markets or contracts. Such a checklist may be very helpful in discussions about the usefulness and the contents of financial sector policies.

Kanhaya Gupta and Robert Lensink (Chapter 9) develop a simulation model to examine the effects of interest rate deregulation on private investment under different assumptions with respect to the behaviour of the private sector. In particular, the model they present enables them to analyse the outcomes of interest deregulation taking into account the existence of informal financial markets, the role of foreign aid and the implications of existing budget deficits. The model specification they use includes a portfolio selection model which is integrated with the consumption–savings decision, and which includes the informal credit market as separate from the formal banking sector, and lets the budget deficit be determined endogenously, as well as treating inflation as an endogenous variable.

In the next chapter Thomas Hellmann, Kevin Murdock and Joseph Stiglitz develop models of government intervention in financial markets in which the government creates rent opportunities, but leaves it to the actions of private agents to reap the potential benefits of these rents. Such an approach – referred to as *financial restraint* – may stimulate private agents to take actions that increase social welfare to levels above those that would have been obtained under a free market system. In particular, they focus on interventionist policies aiming at enhancing deposit mobilisation. One model discusses the individual bank's problem of expropriating the benefits of investing in the opening of a new branch in a new catchment to increase its deposit base. Hellmann, Murdock and Stiglitz show that granting a first-mover bank (temporary) exclusive rights over the new catchment, i.e. by limiting competition, enables this bank to extract the benefits of its investment, which under certain conditions raises social welfare. A second model shows that modest deposit rate controls, which create a positive interest rate margin, stimulate banks to invest in convincing households to hold their wealth as deposits. The latter policy is efficient only if financial markets are in sufficiently low states of depth. At higher levels of financial deepening the benefits of increased deposit mobilisation are more than offset by the costs of disintermediation.

Asli Demirgüç-Kunt and Ross Levine (Chapter 11) discuss the relationship between the initial state and reform of the financial system on the one hand, and public enterprise reform on the other hand. Based on detailed information of nine country case studies, they find that private enterprise reform is more successful in countries with initially relatively well-developed financial systems. Moreover, they find that private enterprise reform is implemented much more successfully if such a reform is supplemented by substantial and well-designed financial sector reforms. However, they underline the fact that the causal relationship between the two kinds of reforms runs in both directions, and that exogenous factors are important in determining the ultimate outcome of both reforms.

In Chapter 12, Hans Visser and Ingmar van Herpt discuss the experiences with financial liberalisation and its impact on the instability of the financial system in the case of Chile during the 1970s and early 1980s. Next, they compare these experiences with what has happened in Indonesia since the government implemented a financial liberalisation programme in the early 1980s. Has Indonesia avoided the policy failures made by the Chilean policy makers during earlier years? Although both countries' experiences show differences, they appear to have had the common experience of financial fragility after financial liberalisation. In both countries implementation of prudential regulation and supervision has been a major problem. While in Chile this – combined with the *de facto* full deposit insurance guarantee provided by the government – contributed to triggering a deep financial crisis, in Indonesia major crises have been avoided until recently. In general, the two countries' experiences show contrasts with respect to the swiftness of carrying out financial liberalisation. Whereas the Chilean policy makers chose to liberalise the markets very radically, the Indonesian government followed a more cautious reform path, which may have been one of the most important reasons why financial crises have not yet occurred on a wide scale.

Niels Hermes (Chapter 13) offers an empirical analysis of the effects of financial reforms on the process of financial intermediation in the case of Chile during 1983–1992. To investigate this issue, the analysis uses balance sheet data of a sample of over 200 Chilean firms. Based on this kind of information, he describes the changing patterns of capital structures and investment choices of these firms. The empirical investigation of these changes may provide evidence whether or not the financial reforms have contributed to reducing market imperfections in financial markets. Moreover, it allows us to evaluate whether or not these reforms have influenced the

5

efficiency of resource allocation through financial intermediation. The findings appear to provide weak evidence for the hypothesis that the Chilean financial reforms during the 1980s contributed to reducing market imperfections and to improving the allocative efficiency of financial markets.

In the final chapter, George Abbott provides a survey of the financial policies, instruments, structures and institutions the CARICOM countries have used recently to enhance resource mobilisation. Abbott argues that, notwithstanding the policy efforts, effective mobilisation in these countries has been disappointing. Basically, this outcome is due to the fact that financial operations occur on a small scale and that too large a number of markets and institutions operate in too thin markets. He concludes that the CARICOM countries should strive for closer cooperation and coordination of their financial market policies at the regional level.

REFERENCES

Atje, R. and B. Jovanovic (1993), 'Stock Markets and Development', *European Economic Review*, 37, pp. 632–40.

Dowrick, S. (1992), 'Technological Catch Up and Diverging Incomes: Patterns of Economic Growth 1960–1988', *The Economic Journal*, 102, pp. 600–10.

McKinnon, R. I. (1973), *Money and Capital in Economic Development*, Washington, DC: The Brookings Institution.

Shaw, E. S. (1973), *Financial Deepening and Economic Development*, New York: Oxford University Press.

World Bank (1989), *World Development Report 1989, Financial Systems and Development*, Oxford: Oxford University Press.

1

MODELS OF FINANCIAL DEVELOPMENT AND GROWTH

A survey of recent literature[1]

Jean Claude Berthélemy and Aristomene Varoudakis

INTRODUCTION

A number of recent studies have used the endogenous growth theory to show the existence of a close association between the level of financial sector development and long-run growth. A positive association between financial development and growth has been well documented since the pioneering statistical work of Goldsmith (1969). In practice, however, governments in developing countries failed to recognise – until at least the end of the 1970s – the need to strengthen the financial system and to set up conditions favourable to financial development. During the 1950s to 1970s, the financial sector was used as an instrument to finance massively interventionist policies based on the development of key industrial sectors which were supposedly 'engines of growth'. These policies mainly took the form of directed credit allocation according to government objectives, and provision of cheap credit (by way of interest rate control and subsidisation) to the alleged key sectors of economic development. Furthermore, repression of the financial system through high reserve requirements and interest-rate controls proved to be an easy source of revenue to governments which lacked efficient instruments of taxation and were running persistent budget deficits.

The external debt crisis clearly showed the importance of relying on a well-functioning financial system to be able to mobilise internal resources in order to finance economic development. Therefore, during the last 10 years, many developing countries undertook programmes of financial liberalisation, aimed at removing various policy-induced distortions that limited the development of the financial sector. However, providing sufficient internal finance for investment is not the only aim of financial sector development policies. Most developing countries are engaged in structural adjustment programmes to correct the deficiencies caused by initial import substitution strategies. Implementation of such programmes involves removal of protectionist measures. They are slow to implement and they typically involve

7

high costs in terms of lost output in the absence of a well-functioning financial system which could smoothly reallocate capital according to comparative advantage. Moreover, it is important that market signals be correctly transmitted, which implies among other policy measures a removal of financial system distortions, which led to parallel capital and foreign exchange markets.

All of these policy-linked reasons account for the considerable recent revival of interest in the analysis of the influence of financial development and financial sector policies on long-run economic growth. In this chapter we provide a broad survey of recent research in an endogenous growth perspective, which shows the possible contribution of financial sector development to long-run growth. In fact, financial systems perform two main functions. On the one hand, they ensure the working of an efficient system of payments. On the other hand, they mobilise savings and improve savings allocation to investment. The first section of this chapter looks at the way these functions of the financial system can contribute to growth.[2] The level of economic development may, however, also influence the development and structure of the financial system. This interdependence is examined in the second section. The third section investigates the effects on growth of the 'natural' imperfections of the financial system (imperfect competition, information asymmetries) and of the distortions which arise from financial repression policies. The fourth section deals with the role of the structure of the financial system, with particular emphasis on the respective advantages of financial markets and bank-based intermediation. The fifth section concludes and points out some possible directions for further research.

FINANCIAL INSTITUTIONS, THE ALLOCATION OF RESOURCES AND GROWTH

The payments system

It is probably true to say that the major contribution of a financial system to growth comes from the setting up of an efficient and adaptable system of payments. A reliable means of exchange is a necessary condition for growth. In cases where no such system exists, prohibitive transactions costs cancel out any productivity gains linked to the division of labour and the beginning of some sort of economic growth. Payments systems adapt alongside and interactively with economic growth. By definition, economic growth implies not only sustained productivity gains but also a maintained opening up of new markets and an ongoing diversification of products. The increasing complexity of exchanges brings with it a growing monetisation of the economies, which becomes necessary in order to sustain the volume of economic activity. This in turn leads to a secular trend towards a slowdown in the money velocity as has been experienced by most developed economies (Friedman and Schwartz, 1982).

Simultaneously, the need to reduce the opportunity cost of holding money brings with it a steady movement of the system of payments towards credit relations managed by banking intermediaries. This trend is reinforced by technical advances which reduce the information costs linked to such use of credit and which make it easier to create financial assets substitutable for traditional monetary assets. This is initially reflected in the secular increase in the weight of financial activities in GDP – along with the percentage of employment in the financial sector – which is associated with economic development (Kuznets, 1971). The advances in intermediation technology can counteract, from a certain stage onwards, the trend towards a slowdown in the velocity of narrow money aggregates. This reduction seems to be confirmed, however, for the wide money aggregates which cover more sophisticated financial assets, whose high cost of use means that they only become accessible beyond a certain level of economic development (see Ireland, 1994). This positive link up between per capita GDP and the degree of monetisation of the economy (or the ratio of the financial intermediaries' assets/GDP) was stressed in initial studies on financial development and growth. Goldsmith (1969), in his international comparative study of 36 countries over a period of a century, was even able to demonstrate that periods of strong growth coincided with accelerated financial development.

Mobilisation of savings

The existence of financial markets and/or banking intermediaries can lead to a better mobilisation of available savings by making the agglomeration of existing financial resources in the economy easier. This means that more efficient technologies can be used which require an initially high level of investment. By exploiting such non-convexities in investment opportunities, financial intermediaries can provide savers with a relatively higher yield, while also contributing directly to a rise in capital productivity and a corresponding speeding up of growth.

Moreover, this process of resource agglomeration enables financial intermediaries to diversify the risks associated with individual investment projects and to offer savers higher expected yields (see the section beginning on p. 10). The rise in expected returns and the diversification of risks encourages financial savings rather than real assets investment with low return (such as consumer durables). Such a reorientation of savings can in turn reinforce the deepening of the financial system even further. On the other hand, substitution and income effects linked to the rise in expected investment returns have an *a priori* undetermined net effect on the rate of savings. Higher yields increase current consumption opportunity costs in terms of future consumption and encourage agents to transfer more resources to the future. At the same time, higher yields enable agents to realise a higher volume of future consumption for a given level of current consumption, which may in turn lead to a decrease in the rate of savings. As a result, improved mobilisation of savings resulting from the development of an intermediation system could conceptually have either a positive or a negative net effect on the economy's long-run growth rate.

In addition, the development of financial intermediation can contribute to the loosening of the liquidity constraints which economic agents frequently face when planning their life cycle intertemporal consumption. Jappelli and Pagano (1994) have looked into the incidence of liquidity constraints in a three-period overlapping-generations model, where agents borrow to finance their consumption when they are young and have no income. Later on, when they receive income, they repay their contracted debts, while at the same time saving to finance consumption during retirement. If borrowing is not readily available during the first stage, agents will find it difficult to smooth their consumption over time. This leads to an increase in the resources transferred from their most active period to retirement; in other words, to a higher rate of savings in the economy. Consequently, were liquidity constraints to be relaxed, the savings rate could fall, which could have a negative effect on the accumulation of capital and growth.

The positive relation between liquidity constraints and the savings rate has been confirmed empirically by Jappelli and Pagano on a sample consisting of OECD member countries and some non-member countries. However, any positive effect from liquidity constraints on the growth rate is based on the assumption that productivity gains are only linked to externalities in the accumulation of physical capital. But as De Gregorio (1993a) suggests, even if liquidity constraints encourage saving, they can also have a negative effect on growth. This will be the case if growth stems from the accumulation of human capital, since the borrowing possibilities for households during schooling would be reduced. It has also been demonstrated (Azariadis and Drazen, 1990; Becker *et al.*, 1990) that the accumulation of human capital may give rise to multiple equilibria of endogenous growth if the private return on human capital investment is positively related to the collective level of educative development. The existence of liquidity constraints resulting from the under-development of the financial system could then, through the influence of externalities, make the selection of a 'low equilibrium' with weak growth more likely, which corresponds to a poverty trap situation (De Gregorio, 1993b).

Improving the allocation of resources

Mobilising sufficient resources for investment is certainly a necessary condition to any economic take-off. Nevertheless, the quality of their allocation to the various investment projects is an equally important factor of growth. The inherent difficulties involved in resource allocation – when faced with productivity risks and insufficient information on the return on investment projects and entrepreneur's skills – create strong incentives for the setting up of financial intermediation structures.

Existing theoretical work has identified various mechanisms to explain the positive incidence of financial intermediation on capital productivity and growth. It is interesting to analyse these mechanisms in relation to the inherent difficulties involved in resource allocation for investment which in turn give rise to financial intermediation activities. Table 1.1 illustrates a cross reading of existing work on the basis of these two criteria. The intermediation activities analysed can be carried out either by banks or financial markets. The

Table 1.1 Financial intermediation and the allocation of resources

Factors leading to the setting up of financial institutions	*Possible influences on the rate of growth*			
	Increase in resources invested in productive capital	Technological specialisation	Elimination of premature liquidation of capital	Increase in productive efficiency
Diversification of risks (productivity or demand shocks)	Levine (1991) Levine (1992a) Obstfeld (1994) Greenwood and Jovanovic (1990)	Saint-Paul (1992)		
Management of liquidity risks	Bencivenga and Smith (1991) Levine (1991) Levine (1992a)		Levine (1991)	
Evaluation of projects and entrepreneurs				King and Levine (1993a) Greenwood and Jovanovic (1990) Levine (1992a)

respective advantages of the two systems lie in other criteria which will be looked at later on.

The return on investment projects is subject not only to productivity risks, resulting from imperfect technological know-how, but also to risks linked to the intensity of future product demand. Productivity (or demand) risks can have two types of adverse effects on the allocation of resources:

- first, they discourage investment by risk-averse economic agents. Potential investors tend to hold a considerable share of their personal wealth in the form of liquid assets which are not risky but less productive.
- second, agents tend to make inefficient technological choices, since return on investment risks can be overcome by technological diversification, at the expense of specialisation and productivity improvement.

The first type of effect can be seen in the models proposed by Levine (1991; 1992a). The existence of productivity risks favours the emergence of stock markets or banking intermediaries which enable agents to diversify their investments. Risk diversification is direct in the case of the stock market. It is indirect in the case of banking intermediaries who, thanks to the widespread diversification of their own portfolio, are in a position to offer depositors a guaranteed return on their investments. The possibility of risk diversification encourages agents to hold (directly, or indirectly through banks) a greater share of their personal wealth in the form of productive capital. This in turn contributes directly to the acceleration of growth. Obstfeld (1994) provides an analysis of the same effect, in connection with the integration of international capital markets, assuming that more risky technologies have a higher expected yield. Promoting the integration of capital markets makes it possible for the investors in every country to diversify their high risk investments at the international level. This means that more resources will be allocated to these types of investment which stimulate global growth.

The model proposed by Saint-Paul (1992) highlights the effects of investment return risks on technological choices. Improving productivity implies selecting more specialised technology, which makes agents more vulnerable to profitability shocks arising from, for example, unforeseen variations in demand. When no financial markets exist, these shocks can be diversified through 'technological flexibility' which means choosing less specialised, and therefore less productive, technologies. The development of financial markets enables agents to reduce such risks through the diversification of their investments, while at the same time choosing more productive and specialised technology. From this point of view, developing financial markets seems even more attractive, especially as the opportunity cost (in terms of productivity loss) involved in flexible technology is high. Saint-Paul (1993) uses the same approach to look at the problem of dual technology often found in developing countries, in relation to the level of development of the financial sector. Technological dualism can also be interpreted as a form of technological risk diversification, when it is impossible to diversify productive risks in the modern sector effectively because financial markets are underdeveloped.

A second factor which plays a role in the setting up of financial institutions is the presence of liquidity risks. These are due to the fact that some productive investments are highly illiquid, in the sense that any premature sale of these assets implies a heavy cutback in their yield. In the three-period overlapping-generation models studied by Bencivenga and Smith (1991) and by Levine (1991; 1992a), consumers have a choice between liquid investments with low yield and illiquid investments whose yield is only realised after two periods. When such an investment is liquidated after only one period, the yield is less than that of the liquid asset. This is due to a certain irreversibility of investments made in the real sector. In the case of such investments, a considerable period of time is required before the technologies involved become really operational and can generate profits. After making the initial investment, some consumers may then be subject to liquidity shocks which are not publicly observable and which are not, therefore, covered by insurance markets. They are then forced to cash in their productive investments prematurely, which in turn has a negative effect on their well-being compared with what would have happened if they had opted for liquid investments instead.[3] The risk of being submitted to such a shock creates a demand for liquidity which puts investors off productive but illiquid assets.

The establishment of financial institutions can mitigate these risks as they allow agents who have experienced such shocks to carry out direct or indirect exchanges with other agents who do not find themselves obliged to liquidate their productive assets. These exchanges can be defined as indirect in the case of banks. These intermediaries are also subject to liquidity risks to the extent that depositors who are experiencing liquidity shortages are obliged to make withdrawals. However, because of the law of large numbers – and as depositors do not all experience liquidity shocks at the same time – the exposure of banks to liquidity risks is lower than that of individual consumers. As a result, banks are able to maintain a smaller share of their portfolio in the form of liquid assets than are individual consumers. The setting up of financial intermediaries therefore makes it possible for the economy as a whole to manage these liquidity risks more efficiently. This in turn leads to a rise in the percentage of resources invested in productive capital which brings with it an acceleration of economic growth.

Liquidity risks can also be managed directly through the setting up of a stock market (Levine, 1991). The stock market provides consumers who have been subjected to liquidity shocks with a means of exchanging investments with other agents who have not experienced such a shock and who wish to increase the share of their wealth which is in the form of productive assets. Being able to exchange securities without being obliged to liquidate productive assets prematurely, encourages agents to hold more of their wealth in the form of productive investments. Levine (1991) suggests that the private efficiency of the accumulation of human capital may be positively influenced – through an externality – by the average amount of resources invested in corporate structures. This externality is justified by assuming that investments in physical capital not only improve skills in the firm through their public good character but also by the encouragement of human interactions which can add to the training process. Premature liquidation of productive investments may therefore, through this external effect, slow down human capital accumulation. Consequently, financial institutions, by providing better management of liquidity risks, also have a positive effect on growth through this channel.

A third factor influencing the setting up of financial intermediaries has to do with monitoring the competence of entrepreneurs and/or the return on investment. Lack of such information is particularly critical in cases where innovative technology, which could conceivably lead to productivity gains, is present but not yet completely under control. According to Levine (1992a) and King and Levine (1993a), the return on investment projects is also subject to influence from other factors besides the productivity risks that can be diversified by financial intermediaries. These additional factors result either from the intrinsic quality of the projects or from the skills of the entrepreneurs in charge of them. In other words, despite the diversification of productivity risks, there is still a positive probability of investing in non-profitable projects which is inversely correlated to the quantity of information available on the quality of investment projects.[4] Monitoring the various available projects necessarily involves assessment, the global cost of which consists essentially of fixed costs. When such fixed costs are sufficiently high, they tend to discourage private investors from carrying out such research for themselves. This in turn increases the probability of investing in a bad risk project, reduces the productive efficiency of investment and has a negative effect on economic growth.

The existence of such fixed costs acts as an incentive to set up specialised institutions to gather and process information on investment projects. When such information is collected for a large number of investors, financial intermediaries can spread the fixed costs among all the investors involved. This cost breakdown means that more evaluations can be carried out, which in turn reduces the chances of investing in bad risk projects. Investment projects are therefore more productive and this has an independent positive effect on growth. It should be remembered that this effect is operational even if the fraction of the resources invested in productive assets is constant. In other words, it remains operational even when growth is not linked to productivity gains arising from the accumulation of capital (Romer, 1986), but only to those resulting from technological innovations (Grossman and Helpman, 1991).[5]

Greenwood and Jovanovic (1990) have analysed monitoring from a

14

slightly different viewpoint. Agents are supposed to have the choice between a low productivity investment which involves no risk and a high-yield risky investment, which is subject to a technological shock. This shock consists of one idiosyncratic component and one 'systemic' component which is common to all technologies. Unless they pay a monitoring fee, private investors can only observe the composite shock which affects their own investment. A financial intermediation system can also be seen as a sort of network linking various economic agents and easing the transmission of information on the return of individual investment projects. By observing the yields from various private projects, financial intermediaries can extract information about the systemic shock which will affect projects as a whole.

Therefore, while the setting up of a network necessarily implies the payment of a fixed cost by each individual investor, creating such a network is still an attractive option as the information which then becomes available enables financial intermediaries to guarantee higher yields thanks to improved allocation of resources:

- first, thanks to a more informed and accurate breakdown of shocks, financial intermediaries can direct investment towards projects which are relatively more profitable.
- second, monitoring the systemic shock enables agents to better diversify the risks intrinsic in private projects. This can lead to an increase in the share of resources invested in productive but risky projects (first column of Table 1.1), thus also contributing to an acceleration of growth.

The empirical relevance of financial development in growth analysis

A number of recent studies have tried to assess empirically the importance of these theoretical links between the development of the financial system and economic growth. The first hurdle they come up against is the working out of adequate indicators for the amount of financial services which are produced in the economy. Computing synthetic financial development indicators is an extremely difficult task due to the diversity of services involved (system of payments, agglomeration of resources, risk diversification and management, monitoring and project evaluation) and the public good character of some of them (system of payments, project assessment). It is further complicated by the diversity of agents and institutions involved in financial intermediation activities (finance markets, banks and savings institutions, insurance companies).

In a series of studies, King and Levine (1993a, b, c) and Levine (1992a) carried out tests using proxies for some of the services produced by the financial system, as well as for the structure of these services. They worked out three main indicators:

(a) the liquid liabilities of financial intermediaries (measured in practice by broad monetary aggregates M3 or M2) as a percentage of GDP. This is in fact an indicator of the relative size of the financial system which is supposed to correlate positively with the volume of financial services provided by that system.

(b) the relative shares of commercial banks and the central bank in total credit outstanding. This indicator of the structure of the financial system highlights the fact that commercial banks have a definite advantage over the central bank concerning risk diversification services, the management of liquidity risks and information monitoring.

(c) the relative amounts of loans granted to the private and the public sector (central administration, local governments, state-owned companies) by the banking system. This indicator is used to demonstrate that a banking system which contents itself with collecting savings to allocate them essentially towards the public sector is not likely to convey resources effectively towards productive investment.

Empirical tests looked at the correlation of these indicators both with the level of economic development (GDP per capita at the beginning of the 1970s and the end of the 1980s) and with the growth rate over the period 1960–1989. The composition of the samples varied between 80 and 90 countries. The results effectively demonstrate a significant correlation between the three indicators and the level of economic development. The most powerful tests examine the significance of these indicators, used as control variables in regressions for international differences in the real output growth rates, the capital stock growth rates and the investment/GDP ratio. These indicators are measured at the beginning of the estimation period to correct any simultaneity bias which could arise, given that a reverse causality exists between financial development and growth (see next section).

The results obtained demonstrate that those countries which initially had a relatively well-established financial system (indicator (a)), later on experienced a relatively higher growth in per capita GDP and also showed a higher investment/GDP ratio. On the other hand, while indicators (b) and (c) had a significant effect on the investment/GDP ratio, their effect on growth was difficult to detect. In addition, as found by Levine and Zervos (1993), extending the study carried out by Levine and Renelt (1992), the initial size of the financial system indicator had a positive effect on growth, robust to changes in the control variables of the regression. King and Levine's results have been confirmed recently by Atje and Javanovic (1994), who took a measure of the fraction of private sector capital stock which is intermediated by banks or by the stock market as their financial development indicator. Their sample consists of 75 countries and the initial value of this indicator exerts a highly significant positive effect on growth rates in the 1980s.

Such econometric results doubtless corroborate the idea that the develop-

16

ment of the financial system can have a causal effect on economic growth.[6] However, two findings suggest that this evidence should be interpreted with care. First of all, even when initial financial development indicators are incorporated into regressions in growth rates, they cannot wholly explain the weak growth performance in some specific country groups. It is particularly striking that in the regressions estimated by King and Levine (1993a, b, c), the dummy variable for African countries consistently appears with a significant negative sign. Second, their estimates are based on the conventional assumption of linearity in the relationship between financial development and growth. This relationship can, however, be non-linear, in so far as two-way causalities link the two phenomena. Such non-linear aspects bring threshold effects into play in the process of economic growth which could possibly explain why certain groups of countries remain stuck in a slow growth equilibrium.

INTERACTIONS BETWEEN THE DEVELOPMENT OF THE FINANCIAL SYSTEM AND GROWTH

Causality and the endogenous development of financial institutions

Where traditional theories insist on the passive role of the financial system which merely adapts itself to the financing needs of the economy's real sector and fits in with the autonomous development of that sector, contemporary theories put forward the idea that financial development has a causal influence on growth. Patrick (1966) worked out a useful reference framework for the study of such causal relationships,[7] where he proposes a distinction between the 'supply-leading approach' and the 'demand-following approach' to financial development. 'Demand-following' financial development appears as a consequence of the development of the real sector. This implies a continuous widening of markets and a growing product differentiation which makes necessary more efficient risk diversification as well as better control of transactions costs. This type of financial development therefore plays a more permissive role in the growth process. On the other hand, 'supply-leading' financial development precedes demand for financial services and can have an autonomous positive incidence on growth. Its role is essentially to mobilise the resources blocked in the traditional sector, transfer them to the modern sector which is capable of promoting growth, and ensure they are used to finance the most dynamic projects. The hypothesis put forward by Patrick (1966) is that 'supply-leading' financial development dominates the early stages of economic development, especially as it makes it possible to finance investments which embody technological innovations more effectively. Once the economic development process has reached maturity, 'demand-following' financial development takes over. In addition, the wider the gap with developed countries, the more likely it is that a developing country will follow the 'supply-leading' financial development model, as demonstrated by the findings of Gerschenkron (1962) and by the experience of countries which experienced late industrialisation such as Japan. Gupta (1984) and Jung (1986) tested the relevance of this hypothesis by subjecting it to Granger causality tests. Gupta, using a small size sample, had favourable results, whereas Jung came up with more nuanced results from a sample of 56 developed and developing countries. More specifically, the tests bore out the hypothesis of 'sequential causality' as stated by Patrick when narrowly defined monetisation indicators were used to assess the degree of financial development. However, they did not provide a means of distinguishing between developed and developing countries, from the standpoint of the direction of causalities, when the ratio of widely defined liquid assets GDP was used as an indicator of financial development.

Patrick's hypothesis is of interest as it highlights the two-way causality which may exist between financial development and growth. It is also incomplete, however, as it does not take the complementarity of the two phenomena into account. While 'supply-leading' financial development can in fact speed up economic growth, 'demand-following' financial development is not just a passive adaptation of the financial system to the development requirements of the real sector. On the contrary, real growth enables the financial system to accomplish its own autonomous evolution, since the sustained increase in real income provides the means to set up a costly and increasingly sophisticated financial intermediation.

If, as has been suggested by Greenwood and Jovanovic (1990) and Levine (1992b) – based on earlier work done by Townsend (1983) – the organisation of financial intermediation networks is expensive, there may be a circular relationship between real growth and the development of the financial sector. Economic growth renders the development of intermediation systems profitable and, at the same time, the establishment of such systems helps speed up growth in the real sector and the structural transformation of the economy. As stressed by Levine (1992b), economic growth even influences the type of financial intermediation systems that the economy can afford. When real income per capita is low, the economy will select 'simple' forms of financial intermediaries whose main purpose will be to mobilise savings, diversify productivity risks and manage liquidity risks. The rise in per capita income enables the economy to develop more 'sophisticated' financial intermediaries, whose functioning will be correspondingly more costly as they will be involved in monitoring investment projects and the identification of the most cost-effective innovations.[8]

In so far as the costs for building intermediation networks are fixed costs, the reciprocity between financial development and growth can give rise to threshold effects. Economies will only choose to develop a particular type of intermediation system when they have passed a certain threshold in terms of income per capita as it is only then that they will begin to reap the benefits of the financial system's positive effect on growth. In the studies mentioned earlier, these critical income thresholds are considered to be exogenous. However, their presence raises the possibility of the existence of two types of 'circular relationships' between financial development and growth.

- First, a 'virtuous' pattern where the high income level supports the adequate development of the financial system which, in turn, provides the prospect for further growth.
- Second, an underdevelopment trap where a low income level makes the development of a financial system impossible, which in turn blocks the allocation of resources to investment and weakens growth.

The possibility that multiple equilibria exist means that the critical thresholds for economic development and the development of the financial system which characterise them are in reality endogenous. It is therefore vital to be able to identify them, to ensure that adequate policies with regard to the financial system can be implemented.

The possibility of multiple equilibria

Saint-Paul (1992) has analysed a mechanism which could give rise to multiple equilibria in financial and economic development (see also Table 1.1). When financial institutions are inadequately developed, risk diversification is carried out through the selection of less specialised – and therefore less productive – technologies. However, the reduction in risk which is brought about by technological flexibility weakens the incentive to develop financial markets – or banking intermediation networks – that involve fixed costs. This can lead to a 'low equilibrium' where the underdevelopment of the financial system leads to an inefficient productive structure which in turn justifies the absence of financial development. On the other hand, the existence of a developed financial system encourages the selection of more specialised and also more productive technologies. The resulting increase in risk justifies the existence of a developed financial system despite the cost involved. The two equilibria can 'co-exist' (multiple equilibria) if incomes are high enough to avoid the fixed costs linked to the development of the financial system being prohibitive. In this way, economic growth may ensure the transition from a 'low equilibrium' to a 'high equilibrium', on condition that revenue is within this critical income zone. Differences in real income per capita can therefore last over the long term between countries which have exactly the same growth potential, depending on the period when they moved from a 'low' to a 'high' equilibrium with a corresponding normal development of financial institutions.

Zilibotti (1994) has looked at a second factor which could also account for multiple equilibria, along with 'thick' market externalities. The basic idea is that capital productivity depends positively on the amount of intermediated resources, while the cost of intermediation depends on the size of the financial market – in other words, on the capital stock which is potentially available for intermediation. An economy with a capital stock that is over a certain threshold will have a 'thick' financial market, which in turn means lower intermediation costs (through a wider spread of fixed costs). This encourages firms to use more intermediated resources, improving capital productivity and maintaining the pace of growth. On the other hand, an economy which does not have much available capital (and therefore has a 'thin' financial market) will have to carry higher costs of financial intermediation, preventing investors from using the possibilities of intermediated investment. This justifies the small size of the financial market and prevents growth from taking off.

Berthélemy and Varoudakis (1994, see also this volume, Chapter 4) have examined a mechanism that involves reciprocal externalities between the real and the financial sector, in an imperfect competition setting where financial intermediation displays an opportunity cost in terms of real resources.

THE CONSEQUENCES OF IMPERFECTIONS IN THE FINANCIAL SYSTEM AND OF FINANCIAL REPRESSION

The 'natural' imperfections of the financial system

The positive effects of the development of the financial system on growth can be mitigated by a number of natural imperfections which interfere with its functioning. Such imperfections arise from the information-intensive functions performed by the finance system.

First, the activities of gathering and processing information on investment projects generally involve fixed costs. This creates a natural trend towards imperfect competition (market segmentation) in so far as it would not be efficient for each individual investor to try to monitor – and to pay the corresponding fixed costs of – all the existing projects in the economy. Second, contrary to the assumption of the previous models, savers (lenders) and investors (borrowers) are generally not the same agents. This creates a problem of information asymmetries since borrowers generally have access to more information than lenders on the quality and the chances of success of investment projects. Under these circumstances, the functioning of the financial markets would be characterised by adverse selection (and adverse incentives) phenomena which could give rise to equilibria with rationing.

Sussman (1993) has studied the effects of imperfect competition in the banking sector on growth, within the framework of a spatial model of monopolistic competition. Firms are subject to productivity risks. They are financed by banks under conditions of asymmetrical information with regard to technological shocks. Banks can acquire such information at some cost, which depends inversely on their geographical distance from the firms. Under these circumstances, the level of economic development can have a positive influence, through the effects of competition and specialisation, on financial intermediation costs. An increase in the capital stock to be intermediated implies a corresponding increase in the size of the financial market and in the number of banks (through entry effects). Each bank then works on a narrower segment of the market, which allows it to concentrate particularly on the firms nearest to it and cut monitoring costs. Increased competition in the banking sector therefore implies a reduction in the costs of financial intermediation and can have a positive effect on growth by encouraging, for example, savings through a rise in net yields.[9] The inverse link between the level of economic development (GDP per capita) and financial intermediation margins has been empirically confirmed by Sussman (1993) for a sample of 64 countries.[10] Working with a smaller sample of 21 OECD countries, Artus (1995) has demonstrated that the degree of concentration in the banking sector had a negative effect on the growth rate.

However, as has already been noted by Stiglitz (1994), competition in the banking sector can prove to be a double-edged sword. The compression in intermediation margins resulting from increased competition necessarily involves an erosion in profits which in turn makes the banking system more vulnerable as it increases its exposure to insolvency. Unlike other business sectors, insolvency in the banking sector can have widespread repercussions on the rest of the economy as it may involve a fall in the volume of loans granted to the real sector. In addition, when a bank goes bankrupt, the information it has collected on its particular market segments is definitively lost. This can lead to intensified borrower rationing. Such effects can strangle economic growth, producing the opposite effect to the traditionally positive influence of a fall in intermediation margins. It would therefore seem relevant to accept that an 'optimal' degree of banking competition exists with respect to growth maximisation.

The existence of investment projects with different levels of risk creates a well-known problem of adverse selection in the credit market when interest rates rise: as the least risky projects stand the best chances of reaching their objectives and of being able to support the extra interest charges, their expected return decreases much more than that of the riskier projects. Lower-risk investors get out of the market earlier (by directing their funds towards safe assets), increasing the proportion of risky projects among potential investments. Furthermore, the existence of information asymmetries and of monitoring costs for investment projects justifies the use of debt contracts. In cases of adverse selection, the use of debt contracts brings about an equilibrium involving credit rationing (Williamson, 1987). This is equivalent to a means of project self-selection, which minimises the risks borne by lenders and optimises the expected yield from their investments.

Bencivenga and Smith (1993) have examined an overlapping-generations endogenous growth model where there are two types of investors, each using technologies which involve different risks. Credit rationing for low risk investors arises from information asymmetries and its degree is determined in conjunction with the equilibrium growth rate. This model highlights an inverse relationship between the intensity of credit rationing and growth, since credit rationing holds back investments which would normally create positive external effects on capital productivity (Romer, 1986).[11]

With this type of approach, any increase in risk differences of investment projects is likely to exacerbate the problem of adverse selection and, consequently, intensify credit rationing. Improvements in 'superior' technology which help reduce the risks of the least risky projects even further can, under certain conditions, have a negative effect on growth because of intensified credit rationing. On the other hand, improvements in 'inferior' technology, where risks are higher, can have a positive influence by reducing credit rationing. Analogous results obtain with regard to government intervention in credit markets, in the form of subsidised investment projects. Global subsidies, given to projects as a whole, can attenuate the problem of adverse selection as they improve expected return for risky projects in a relatively higher proportion. They can therefore have a positive effect on growth by limiting credit rationing. Selective subsidies, usually reserved for the least risky projects, can, on the other hand, have a negative effect on growth as they widen the differences of expected return on investment.

In an asymmetrical information framework, the emergence of banking intermediaries can be explained by the existence of comparative advantages in terms of costs of project monitoring. Boyd and Smith (1992) have studied a model with segmented financial markets, where monitoring costs increase in relation to the distance from the project location. By collecting deposits from all areas and by specialising in the financing of nearby projects, banking intermediaries can narrow differences in credit rationing between localities. Regulation can render such efficiency gains impossible, for example, where limits are set for the geographical zones where banks can operate, particularly with regard to deposit collection (however, see below for a different point of view). In turn, more efficient allocation of capital brings about an increase in its productivity, which raises growth.

Financial repression and the liberalisation of the financial system

Government intervention in the financial system can reach far beyond the subsidising of loans or the regulation of banking activities. In developing countries particularly, it often takes the form of financial repression. McKinnon (1973) defines all policies and regulations which prevent financial intermediaries from operating at a level in accordance with their technological potential as forms of financial repression.

The most common financial repression practices are forms of implicit taxation of financial intermediaries such as:

(a) low-yield required reserves
(b) ceilings on lending or deposit interest rates
(c) inflation tax on monetary assets.

The extent of such implicit taxation can be measured approximately by the savings in interest payments that the government can make on the required reserves held by banks, on its domestic debt which benefits from the ceiling on interest rates and on the amount of unremunerated money balances – subject to the inflation tax – put in circulation, thanks to a monopoly on issuing money instead of interest-bearing public debt.

Fry (1993) has put forward a figure of almost 2.8 per cent of GDP for the inflation tax alone for a sample of 26 developing countries. In addition, estimates by Giovannini and De Melo (1993) put the implicit fiscal revenue provided by financial repression in the form of ceilings on interest rates – coupled with capital controls – at about 1.8 per cent of GDP for a sample of 22 developing countries.[12] The size of these sums, in comparison with the fiscal revenue generated by explicit taxation, provides a possible explanation as to why financial repression is often used as a source of tax revenue, having the added advantage of being more flexible than formal tax legislation.

Alongside these fiscal gains, financial repression also generates costs which can be divided into three categories:

(a) costs in terms of efficiency resulting from distortions in interest rates. Ceilings on deposit interest rates for banks limit the volume of intermediated funds and give rise to an artificial increase in the cost of credit. The same effect is produced by the imposition of high ratios of required reserves which add to the cost of financial intermediation. Ceilings on lending interest rates give rise to credit rationing.
(b) costs which arise from the dissuasive effect which low interest rates can have on savings – as pointed out by McKinnon (1973) and Shaw (1973). This cost even has a cumulative effect since the decrease in savings compromises growth prospects.
(c) costs arising from the limitation of the expansion of the financial sector that chronic compression of interest rates generates. On the one hand, for a given amount of savings, the artificial ceiling on interest rates leads to financial disintermediation which in turn reduces the size of the banking sector in the economy. On the other hand, a reduction in savings is synonymous with a reduction in the size of the financial market which prevents individual banks from taking advantage of economies of scale associated with the fixed costs involved in intermediation. The cutback in the size of the financial sector and the reduced efficiency of the financial intermediation process can also negatively affect growth for the reasons

already mentioned concerning the efficiency of resource allocation to investment.

The negative incidence of financial repression on the long-run growth rate has been empirically confirmed by Roubini and Sala-i-Martin (1992a) for a sample of 52 countries. They demonstrated that the incorporation of a financial repression indicator into growth equations explains the particularly weak performance of Latin American countries in terms of conditional convergence with other economies.

Despite the costs linked to efficient resource allocation and growth, the use of financial repression policies can be justified on grounds of macroeconomic policy. When there are no neutral taxes, the theory of optimal taxation calls for the setting of different types of taxation so as to balance their marginal costs. As Roubini and Sala-i-Martin (1992b) have shown, even if the marginal cost of financial repression is high, it can become comparable to that of explicit taxation if the fiscal system is highly inefficient, producing extensive tax evasion. When the extent of tax evasion is such that even at the optimal level of taxation (which maximises fiscal revenue) government expenditure is not covered, a certain degree of financial repression may seem preferable. Additional fiscal revenue may come from the savings generated – through interest rates controls – on the interest payments on public debt. Other additional income may come from the widening of the inflation tax base linked to the artificial increase in the monetary base (high required reserves; increase in transaction balances due to the inefficiency of the banking system). Bencivenga and Smith (1992) put forward a similar argument – a sort of 'second best solution': where there is a budgetary deficit which must be monetised, an optimal compromise can perhaps be found between the losses in terms of efficiency in the allocation of resources and the widening of the inflation tax base resulting from financial repression in the form of high required reserves. The higher the budget deficit, the more financial repression policies will be considered optimal. This bears out the viewpoint put forward by McKinnon (1982) who stressed the priority in timing of controlling the budget deficit over liberalisation of the financial system.

The experience of the Latin American countries which carried out programmes of financial liberalisation (Argentina, Chile, Uruguay) suggests in fact that the chances of success for such programmes in conditions of macroeconomic instability are slim.[13] In cases where inflation is high and unstable – usually due to an uncontrolled budget deficit – the deregulation of interest rates can bring about a rise in real interest rates. This can have a recessionary effect on economic activity in the short run and can also render the banking sector vulnerable. The elimination of capital controls which comes with the deregulation of interest rates can, under these conditions, lead to a marked real exchange rate appreciation. This may in turn strangle activity in the tradable goods sector even more and eventually lead to balance of payments crises. A liberalisation strategy then becomes unsustainable, so that the economies concerned are more or less obliged to revert to their former financial repression policies.

Besides these considerations, the effectiveness of financial liberalisation as a 'miracle cure' for slow, economic growth is debatable when looked at from the viewpoint of financial market functioning. As stressed by Stiglitz (1994), a rise in interest rates can lead to adverse selection and adverse incentives phenomena which intensify equilibrium credit rationing. A 'moderate' degree of financial repression – avoiding negative interest rates which definitely discourage savings – can improve the risk attributes of investment projects as a whole. This may attenuate credit rationing which, as has already been stated, is not conducive to growth.

A further argument in favour of 'financial restraint' policies is put forward by Hellmann *et al.* (1994, see Chapter 10 of this volume). In their view, because of the public good character of information on the profitability of deposit market entry by individual banks and the fixed costs associated with it (advertising campaigns, etc.), competitive banking equilibrium will be characterised by underprovision of financial services. This makes room for 'mild' policies of financial restraint which may involve restricting entry in some geographical areas or moderately limiting deposit rates at below competitive equilibrium levels. The main idea consists in creating rent opportunities in the financial sector (as opposed to extracting rents from it through financial repression) that enhance incentives for financial deepening and deposit mobilisation.

In addition, 'structuralist' arguments (Van Wijnbergen, 1983) set out the possibility that financial liberalisation simply means that intermediated finance is substituted for informal finance – which emerged in several developing countries as a response to financial repression policies. As the informal sector is not subject to the cost generated by required reserves and has an advantage in terms of risk monitoring for local markets, it may be more efficient in the financing of short term projects than the formal intermediation sector (see World Bank, 1989, Chapter 8 for a more detailed analysis). Nevertheless, as Bencivenga and Smith (1992) have shown, financial liberalisation is still probably a better option, given the considerable comparative advantages of the formal intermediation sector in the areas of productivity risk diversification and management of liquidity risks.

STRUCTURE OF THE FINANCIAL SYSTEM AND ECONOMIC GROWTH

Relative importance of financial markets and banking intermediaries

To know whether the comparative development of financial markets (equity and bond markets) and banks can influence economic growth has long been a hotly debated question – to date unresolved – in economic theory. The debate is constantly been fed by successful – yet at the same time contrasted – experiences in terms of economic development in those countries which first concentrated on financial markets (the United Kingdom, the United States) and those which instead gave priority to universal banks (Germany, Japan). Despite their different routes, industrialised countries would appear to have more or less converged towards a common model of corporate finance. As demonstrated by the international comparison study carried out by Mayer (1990), covering the period 1970–1985, internal funds supplied the major share of the financing for investment in developed countries (two thirds on average). The relative share of external funds in the form of shares and bonds is quite small in all these countries. It is systematically less than 10 per cent of investment spending and can even go into negative figures – on the basis of net operations – in some cases (United Kingdom) due to the incidence of takeovers and restructuring operations in the corporate sector. The contribution from the markets is relatively higher in the United States where it is around 13 per cent on average.

The role of financial markets in the financing of investment has, however, been much more decisive in some countries when they were at less advanced stages in their economic development. The estimates given by Allen (1993) show that in the United Kingdom the financial markets contributed between 25 per cent and 33 per cent to the financing of capital formation during the second half of the nineteenth century and the beginning of the twentieth (essentially with connection to the financing of the expansion of the railways). It is interesting to note that recently observed trends in certain developing countries (at the middle income level) are very different from those currently found in developed countries. Based on the estimates reported by Singh (1992), the contribution from outside sources to the financing of capital formation in the 1980s was well over 50 per cent (even reaching 90 per cent in Korea for the biggest firms), with a significant share coming from the stock market.

The lack of long time series – for a significant number of countries – on the relative importance of different sources of funding, makes it difficult to test directly the incidence of the financial structure on growth. Atje and Jovanovic (1993) succeeded in obtaining favourable results for the hypothesis that the development of the stock market has a positive effect on growth for a sample of 72 countries, but over quite a short period (1980–1988), which does not really seem representative of long term trends. They used an indicator not of the relative importance of financial markets and banking intermediaries, but of the level of stock market development (volume of transactions/capitalisation of the market). Moreover, the estimated effects seem rather fragile given the absence of other explanatory variables which are generally significant in conditional convergence regressions. The incidence of the financial structure on growth is very probably much more complex, since the respective advantages of markets and banks can be correlated with the level of economic development and the technological characteristics of the economies.

The comparative advantages of financial markets and banking intermediaries

The weak share of the stock market in the financing of investment can be explained, first, by the relative drawbacks of equity financing compared with financing by debt contracts, and second, by the comparative advantages of banking intermediaries in the management of such contracts. As Gale and Hellwig (1985) have shown, when problems of productivity risks, information asymmetries and costly monitoring exist, debt contracts with fixed repayment dates will always be favoured over financing by shares with periodic reimbursements through dividends – which are subject to productivity shocks. Monitoring costs are reduced to a minimum with debt contracts because they are only incurred in cases of insolvency, while financing through shares implies continuous monitoring.

Given the optimality of debt contracts to finance investment, banking intermediaries have an advantage over the stock markets (bond markets) as they can be more efficient in terms of information gathering and monitoring costs. While it may not be optimal for individual investors to undertake expensive monitoring, banks have the possibility of minimising such costs by spreading them over several lenders. Second, the dispersion of stock holding on the market and the public good character of the information collected on firms create a free-rider problem when it comes to the payment of monitoring costs. With their large and diversified investment portfolio, banking intermediaries can guarantee a yield for their deposits and can commit themselves credibly to monitoring the return of the projects (Diamond, 1984).

The informational advantage of banks in the external financing of investment is an important argument in favour of the development of the banking system from the point of view of supporting the accumulation of capital. Nevertheless, it does not establish the superiority of banks once and for all compared with financial markets. After all, both types of financial institutions are also active in other areas such as:

27

(a) the diversification of investment risks and the management of liquidity risks,
(b) the implementation of monitoring mechanisms which improve resource management,
(c) the evaluation of the return on productive activities, which contributes to the efficient allocation of resources to investment.

Managing all these activities effectively makes it possible to speed up growth through the mechanisms which have already been examined. As far as the direct or indirect diversification of risks is concerned, the financial markets do not seem to have a decisive advantage over banks.

The monitoring of productive resources management is performed by financial markets through mergers and acquisitions. In the case of oligopolistic firms, where the market cannot guarantee the selection process, this mechanism can effectively create enough incentives for management discipline. However, as noted by Singh (1992), it can also interfere with the selection of investment projects. On the one hand it may generate investments that are not really productive, where the objective is simply to create an effect of size as a form of protection against hostile takeover bids. On the other hand, it may also give rise to a tendency towards 'short termism'. This reduces the attractiveness of long term projects which eventually generate more externalities that increase capital productivity and sustain economic growth.

These potential disadvantages are not found in financial systems based on universal banks (as in Germany and Japan). As they own shares in the capital of firms and are represented on their management boards, universal banks may have an advantage in the restructuring of firms compared with a takeover market-based mechanism (see Benston, 1994). These advantages consist in a reduction in both transactions costs and possible distortions in the quality of investment. Moreover, a share in the company's capital – which is equivalent to profit (and loss) sharing – can attenuate the problems of information asymmetries and shareholder/lender conflicts which limit in a sub-optimal way the debt/equity capital ratio in a financial market system. Studies on the profitability of firms suggest that direct representation of banks in company management structures is likely to encourage more management discipline than is found in a market-based supervision system.

Financial markets may have an advantage over banks in the area of activity evaluation, which acts as a sort of guide for allocating resources towards investment. This type of assessment is also carried out by banks, needless to say, but less often; generally only when new loans are being negotiated. However, as Allen (1993) pointed out, such monitoring procedures by banks could be optimal in competitive environments, where production lags are relatively short and when technical progress is slow. The presence of a great number of firms in a competitive market makes it possible to carry out many 'trial runs' to test the cost-effectiveness of the technologies used. The circulation of this information helps form a consensus on the optimal technology and the probability distribution of its returns. Nevertheless, at more advanced stages of economic development, the exploitation of economies of scale and the continuous differentiation of products brings the market naturally to imperfectly competitive structures. In addition, production lags are considerably longer and technical progress much more rapid. Under these conditions, a consensus on the evaluation of productive activities is no longer possible and monitoring modes through banks are often quite unadapted as guides to the optimal allocation of resources. Financial markets can then play an important and positive role as they, unlike banks, assess the assets of companies regularly and, through monitoring, aggregate the information and the opinions of many agents in the field.

To sum up: even if, for reasons of informational efficiency in the management and monitoring of debt contracts, the external financing of capital formation through banks would appear to be the optimal solution, the development of stock markets is vital for the most efficient allocation of resources towards investment, especially when technologies are still imperfectly controlled and competition is not perfect. This means that financial markets should be developed at the same time as the banking system in those countries which are on the cusp of technical progress, in connection with those sectors which show strong tendencies towards imperfect competition. This was the case in the United Kingdom during the first half of the nineteenth century, at the time of the first industrial revolution and the development of the railways, as well as in the United States during the second industrial revolution at the end of the nineteenth century and the beginning of the twentieth. On the other hand, the development of the banking system (with probably some advantage for the universal banking system) should precede the development of financial markets in developing countries which are in the process of catching up with developed countries (as was the case with Germany or Japan in the nineteenth century). This development phase is essentially based on specialisation in well-tested technologies and depends on firms operating in markets that are fairly competitive. The development of banks is then able to provide better backup for the allocation of resources to investment and growth.

CONCLUSION

There is by now an extensive theoretical – as well as empirical – literature which forcefully highlights the possibility of a causal influence of financial development on long-run economic growth. The mechanisms emphasised by these studies rely on the premise that financial development helps to improve the efficiency of the allocation of savings to investment. The possibility of choosing more productive investments involves: improved management of liquidity risks; more efficient diversification of investors' portfolios; and improved information on the efficiency of various investment projects and/or investors' abilities. This factor is then integrated into an endogenous growth model where any increase in capital productivity has a positive effect on the economy's long-run rate of growth.

Our review of recent theoretical work on financial development and endogenous growth points out at least four issues which, to our minds, warrant further theoretical and empirical development. First, in the presence of threshold effects, linear estimates of the effect of financial development on growth may be quite misleading. Once this possibility is recognised, one should attempt to identify such critical thresholds and assess the dynamics of the different growth regimes they define. Some progress in this direction is made by Berthélemy and Varoudakis (1994, this volume, Chapter 4). These threshold effects considerably strengthen the case against policies of financial repression which appear to exert some kind of hysteresis effects on economic growth. Financial repression policies not only distort the allocative efficiency of the financial system but greatly impede its development as well. They increase therefore the likelihood of the economy being trapped into a 'low equilibrium' with slow growth and an under-developed financial system. Consequently, a subsequent reversal of financial repression policies may be completely ineffective in so far as the economy remains stuck below some critical threshold of financial development which ensures convergence to the high-growth equilibrium.

Second, more theoretical and empirical work is needed on the growth incidence of competition in banking. Typically, a higher level of competition in banking leads to lower financial intermediation margins and faster growth. However, it also increases the exposure of banks to insolvency, which may lead to intensified credit rationing with adverse effects on growth. Would there exist, therefore, an 'optimal degree of competition' in banking with respect to long-run growth? Third, a lot of work remains to be done on the comparative effects of different financial intermediation systems (market-based, universal banking, specialised banks) on growth, as well as on the reverse causation exerted by economic growth on the kind of financial structures the economy can implement. Finally, the possible existence of different growth regimes, depending on the initial level of financial development, raises the question of the appropriate sequence of policy reform. As is well known from the normative theory of economic policy, in second-best situations where some optimality conditions are not fulfilled – as for instance when a financial development threshold is binding – appropriate policies in other areas may be quite different from those usually advocated in first-best situations without distortions.

NOTES

1 This chapter originated as a paper produced in the context of a research programme of the OECD Development Centre on 'Financial Systems, Resource Allocation and Growth'. Comments by the participants in the 'Workshop on Financial Development and Growth' at the University of Groningen are gratefully acknowledged.
2 For a synthetic approach to this question, see also Pagano (1993) and World Bank (1989), Chapter 2.
3 This type of model was initially studied by Diamond and Dybvig (1983).
4 In the present context no differentiation is made between savers and investors. We therefore set aside the problems resulting from asymmetrical information on project quality (see the section beginning on p. 20).
5 The relative importance of these two sources of growth has recently been re-examined by King and Levine (1994).
6 Results along the same lines were also found by Ghani (1992) and by Hermes and Lensink (1993).
7 See also St Hill (1992) for a synthesis of the work done in this field with special reference to developing country experience.
8 Saint-Paul (1994) has put forward the idea that the existence of a large public debt can help financial development, as it cuts down the cost of setting up intermediation networks through learning effects.
9 Analogous effects from competition in the banking sector have been analysed by Zilibotti (1994) and Berthélemy and Varoudakis (1994).
10 These results have been extended recently by Sussman and Zeira (1995) using US cross-state data.
11 Greenwald *et al.* (1990) came up with similar results using a model where firms are subject to financing restrictions in the stock market.
12 Chamley and Honohan (1990) have provided analogous estimates for some Sub-Saharan African countries.
13 For a more detailed analysis, see World Bank (1989), Chapter 9, and Fry (1988).

REFERENCES

Allen, F. (1993), 'Stock Markets and Resource Allocation', in C. Mayer and X. Vives (eds) *Capital Markets and Financial Intermediation*, Cambridge: Cambridge University Press, pp. 81–108.

Artus, P. (1995), 'Mode de financement de l'investissement et croissance' (Financing of Investment and Growth), *Revue Economique*, 46, pp. 169–94.

Atje, R. and B. Jovanovic (1993), 'Stock Markets and Development', *European Economic Review*, 37, pp. 632–40.

—— (1994), 'Finance and Development', unpublished paper, New York University.

Azariadis, C. and A. Drazen (1990), 'Threshold Externalities in Economic Development', *Quarterly Journal of Economics*, 105, pp. 501–26.

Becker, G.S., K.M. Murphy and R. Tamura (1990), 'Human Capital, Fertility, and Economic Growth', *Journal of Political Economy*, 98, Supplement, pp. 12–37.

Bencivenga, V.R. and B.D. Smith (1991), 'Financial Intermediation and Endogenous Growth', *Review of Economic Studies*, 58, pp. 195–209.

—— (1992), 'Deficits, Inflation, and the Banking System in Developing Countries: the Optimal Degree of Financial Repression', *Oxford Economic Papers*, 44, pp. 767–90.

31

—— (1993), 'Some Consequences of Credit Rationing in an Endogenous Growth Model', *Journal of Economic Dynamics and Control*, 17, pp. 97–122.

Benston, G.J. (1994), 'Universal Banking', *Journal of Economic Perspectives*, 8, pp. 121–43.

Berthélemy, J.C. and A. Varoudakis (1994), 'Intermédiation financière et croissance endogène' (Financial Intermediation and Endogenous Growth), *Revue Economique*, 45, pp. 737–50.

Boyd, J.H. and B.D. Smith (1992), 'Intermediation and the Equilibrium Allocation of Investment Capital: Implications for Economic Development', *Journal of Monetary Economics*, 30, pp. 409–32.

Chamley, C. and P. Honohan (1990), 'Taxation of Financial Intermediation: Measurement Principles and Application to Five African Countries', *Working Paper*, No. 421, World Bank.

De Gregorio, J. (1993a), 'Savings, Growth and Capital Market Imperfections: the Case of Borrowing Constraints', *Working Paper*, No. 93/31, International Monetary Fund.

—— (1993b), 'Credit Markets and Stagnation in an Endogenous Growth Model', *Working Paper*, No. 93/72, International Monetary Fund.

Diamond, D. (1984), 'Financial Intermediation and Delegated Monitoring', *Review of Economic Studies*, 51, pp. 393–414.

Diamond, D. and P. Dybvig (1983), 'Bank Runs, Deposit Insurance, and Liquidity', *Journal of Political Economy*, 85, pp. 191–206.

Friedman, M. and A.J. Schwartz (1982), *Monetary Trends in the United States and the United Kingdom*, Chicago: University of Chicago Press.

Fry, M.J. (1988), *Money, Interest, and Banking in Economic Development*, Baltimore: The Johns Hopkins University Press.

—— (1993), 'Financial Repression and Economic Growth', *Working Paper*, No. 93-07, International Finance Group, University of Birmingham.

Gale, D. and M. Hellwig (1985), 'Incentive-Compatible Debt Contracts: The One-Period Problem', *Review of Economic Studies*, 52, pp. 647–63.

Gerschenkron, A. (1962), *Economic Backwardness in Historical Perspective – A Book of Essays*, Cambridge, Mass.: Harvard University Press.

Ghani, E. (1992), 'How Financial Markets Affect Long-Run Growth, A Cross-Country Study', *Working Paper*, No. 843, World Bank.

Giovannini, A. and M. De Melo (1993), 'Government Revenue from Financial Repression', *American Economic Review*, 83, pp. 953–63.

Goldsmith, R.W. (1969), *Financial Structure and Development*, New Haven: Yale University Press.

Greenwald, B.C., M. Kohn and J.E. Stiglitz (1990), 'Financial Market Imperfections and Productivity Growth', *Journal of Economic Behavior and Organization*, 13, pp. 321–45.

Greenwood, J. and B. Jovanovic (1990), 'Financial Development, Growth, and the Distribution of Income', *Journal of Political Economy*, 98, pp. 1076–107.

Grossman, G.M. and E. Helpman (1991), *Innovation and Growth in the Global Economy*, Cambridge, Mass.: MIT Press.

Gupta, K.L. (1984), *Finance and Economic Growth in Developing Countries*, London: Croom Helm.

Hellmann, T., K. Murdock and J.E. Stiglitz (1994), 'Deposit Mobilization under Financial Restraint', paper presented at the workshop on 'Financial Development and Economic Growth', University of Groningen, 7–9 December 1994.

Hermes, N. and R. Lensink (1993), 'The Financial Sector and Its Influence on Economic Growth: Evidence from 14 Latin American Countries, 1963–1989',

Research Memorandum, No. 531, University of Groningen.

Ireland, P.N. (1994), 'Economic Growth, Financial Evolution, and the Long-run Behavior of Velocity', *Journal of Economic Dynamics and Control*, 18, pp. 815–48.

Jappelli, T. and M. Pagano (1994), 'Saving, Growth, and Liquidity Constraints', *Quarterly Journal of Economics*, 109, pp. 83–109.

Jung, W.S. (1986), 'Financial Development and Economic Growth: International Evidence', *Economic Development and Cultural Change*, 34, pp. 333–46.

King, R.G. and R. Levine (1993a), 'Finance, Entrepreneurship and Growth: Theory and Evidence', *Journal of Monetary Economics*, 32, pp. 513–42.

—— (1993b), 'Finance and Growth: Schumpeter Might Be Right', *Quarterly Journal of Economics*, 108, pp. 717–37.

—— (1993c), 'Financial Intermediation and Economic Development', in C. Mayer and X. Vives (eds) *Capital Markets and Financial Intermediation*, Cambridge: Cambridge University Press, pp. 156–89.

—— (1994), 'Capital Fundamentalism, Economic Development, and Economic Growth', *Carnegie–Rochester Conference Series on Public Policy*, 40, pp. 259–92.

Kuznets, S. (1971), *Economic Growth of Nations*, Cambridge: Belknap Press.

Levine, R. (1991), 'Stock Markets, Growth, and Tax Policy', *Journal of Finance*, 46, pp. 1445–65.

—— (1992a), 'Financial Intermediary Services and Growth', *Journal of Japanese and International Economies*, 6, pp. 383–405.

—— (1992b), 'Financial Structures and Economic Development', *Working Paper*, No. 849, World Bank.

Levine, R. and D. Renelt (1992), 'A Sensitivity Analysis of Cross-Country Growth Regressions', *American Economic Review*, 82, pp. 942–63.

Levine, R. and S. Zervos (1993), 'Looking at the Facts: What we Know about Policy and Growth from Cross-Country Analysis', *American Economic Review*, 83, pp. 426–30.

McKinnon, R.I. (1973), *Money and Capital in Economic Development*, Washington DC: The Brookings Institution.

—— (1982), 'The Order of Economic Liberalization: Lessons from Chile and Argentina', *Carnegie–Rochester Conference Series on Public Policy*, 17, pp. 159–86.

Mayer, C. (1990), 'Financial Systems, Corporate Finance, and Economic Development', in R.G. Hubbard (ed.) *Asymmetric Information, Corporate Finance, and Investment*, NBER, Chicago: Chicago University Press, pp. 307–32.

Obstfeld, M. (1994), 'Risk-Taking, Global Diversification, and Growth', *American Economic Review*, 84, pp. 1310–29.

Pagano, M. (1993), 'Financial Markets and Growth: An Overview', *European Economic Review*, 37, pp. 613–22.

Patrick, H.T. (1966), 'Financial Development and Economic Growth in Under-developed Countries', *Economic Development and Cultural Change*, 14, pp. 174–89.

Romer, P.M. (1986), 'Increasing Returns and Long-Run Growth', *Journal of Political Economy*, 94, pp. 1002–37.

Roubini, N. and X. Sala-i-Martin (1992a), 'Financial Repression and Economic Growth', *Journal of Development Economics*, 39, pp. 5–30.

—— (1992b), 'A Growth Model of Inflation, Tax Evasion, and Financial Repression', *Working Paper*, No. 4062, National Bureau of Economic Research.

Saint-Paul, G. (1992), 'Technological Choice, Financial Markets and Economic

Development', *European Economic Review*, 36, pp. 763–81.

——— (1993), 'Technological Dualism, Incomplete Financial Markets and Economic Development', *Journal of International Trade and Economic Development*, 2, pp. 13–26.

——— (1994), 'La dette publique comme moteur du développement financier', (Public Debt as a Financial Development Device), *Revue Economique*, 45, pp. 767–73.

St Hill, R.L. (1992), 'Stages of Banking and Economic Development', *Savings and Development*, 16, pp. 5–21.

Shaw, E.S. (1973), *Financial Deepening in Economic Development*, New York: Oxford University Press.

Singh, A. (1992), 'The Stock-Market and Economic Development: Should Developing Countries Encourage Stock-Markets?', *Discussion Paper*, No. 49, UNCTAD.

Stiglitz, J.E. (1994), 'The Role of the State in Financial Markets', *The World Bank Economic Review*, 8, pp. 19–52.

Sussman, O. (1993), 'A Theory of Financial Development', in A. Giovannini (ed.) *Finance and Development: Issues and Experience*, Cambridge: Cambridge University Press, pp. 29–57.

Sussman, O. and J. Zeira (1995), 'Banking and Development', *Discussion Paper*, No. 1127, Centre for Economic Policy Research.

Townsend, R.M. (1983), 'Financial Structure and Economic Activity', *American Economic Review*, 73, pp. 895–911.

Van Wijnbergen, S. (1983), 'Interest Rate Management in LDCs', *Journal of Monetary Economics*, 12, pp. 443–52.

Williamson, S.D. (1987), 'Costly Monitoring, Loan Contracts, and Equilibrium Credit Rationing', *Quarterly Journal of Economics*, 102, pp. 135–45.

World Bank (1989), *World Development Report 1989*, Washington DC: World Bank.

Zilibotti, F. (1994), 'Endogenous Growth and Intermediation in an "Archipelago" Economy', *Economic Journal*, 103, pp. 462–73.

Part I

THEORETICAL AND EMPIRICAL ISSUES IN FINANCIAL DEVELOPMENT AND ECONOMIC GROWTH

2

DEMAND-DRIVEN FINANCIAL DEVELOPMENT[1]

Gilles Saint-Paul

INTRODUCTION

That financial development is important for growth and capital accumulation is now well recognized. A better financial market makes the allocation of savings to investment more efficient and may increase savings if it is positively correlated with their returns. Empirical evidence on the impact of financial development on real activity is reasonably robust and convincing (Goldsmith, 1969; McKinnon, 1973; Fry, 1988, 1993; King and Levine, 1993).

This paper is interested in the following question: 'Why is it that financial development can be high or low depending on which country or time period we look at, and what are the factors that trigger such financial development?'

We start from the observation that there can be complementarities between financial development and real development, and that these complementarities may keep the economy at an equilibrium with both insufficient financial and real development. These externalities can come from increasing returns in the financial technology, externalities of financial development on technological choice – these are discussed in Saint-Paul (1992a, b) – or thin market externalities in security markets (Pagano, 1993). If externalities are important, then financial development can be thought of as the economy shifting from one equilibrium to another. Such a shift may be triggered by transitory exogenous factors which render financial instruments more valuable. Once these factors have disappeared, the financial sector remains.

The historical record seems to suggest that such transitory events play an important role in financial development. Hence, the creation of the Bank of England and the subsequent British 'financial revolution' was triggered by the treasury's needs to finance wars in the late seventeenth century. Financial development in France was achieved in the nineteenth century as industrial tycoons needed to develop banks in order to fund large infrastructure projects such as railroads. More recently, financial markets have developed in Eastern Europe because of the large volume of capital transactions required by massive privatisation programmes.

In all three instances, financial development is driven by 'demand', i.e. a need to bring together large amounts of savings. In this paper we discuss the role of demand factors in financial development using a simple macro-economic model.

The rest of the chapter is organised as follows: the first section describes the three experiences of financial development in England, France, and Eastern Europe. The second section develops a model which allows us to analyse the role of these demand factors – particularly public debt – in providing financial infrastructure.

STRATEGIES FOR FINANCIAL DEVELOPMENT

The English model: the role of public debt

According to some economic historians (for example Dickson, 1967; Kindleberger, 1984), the industrial revolution in England was preceded by a 'financial revolution' which set up the structure of the English financial system for a long time.

The key event which triggered that financial revolution was the founding of the Bank of England in 1694. The Bank of England was founded in order to finance the large budget deficits that were generated by the Nine Years' War with France. Therefore, British public debt, while reducing the amount of saving available for productive capital accumulation,[2] had positive effects on the country's financial infrastructure. The founding of the Bank of England was followed by the development of private banks and capital markets. As North and Weingast (1989) report, the operations of the Bank of England and trade in public debt generated positive externalities on the development of financial instruments for the funding of private investment. A stock market developed to trade the exchequer bills, the ancestors of treasury bills. In addition to the Bank of England, companies such as the South Sea Company or the East India Company were actively engaged in the trading of government bonds, and were themselves joint stock companies whose shares were also traded on the stock market, thus increasing the depth of that market. The private activities of the Bank of England included the discounting of private bills, which greatly contributed to the liquidity and credibility of the financial system, as well as drawing accounts.

Another important aspect of the English experience is that the founding of the Bank of England was reinforced by the enhanced credibility of government debt, which was brought about by the institutional changes after the 'Great Revolution'. According to North and Weingast (1989), while the Crown had discretionary power over fiscal policy prior to the Revolution, afterwards parliament could tightly monitor the details of government expenditure and even had a right of veto on them. This institutional change clearly embodied a commitment to fiscal restraint when the time came to repay the debt, since government finance was then controlled by the holders of the debt. As a result, despite the four-fold increase in government debt due to the war, interest rates actually fell.

The English experience is therefore suggestive that an increase in the government's borrowing requirement may exert positive spillovers on the country's financial infrastructure, provided the adequate level of credibility is embodied into the institutions.

French and German financial development in the nineteenth century

If we compare financial development in France with the British experience, we see that in France it lagged by at least one century: while financial intermediaries had always existed since the middle ages to deal with government borrowing, the lack of credibility of this government and its reputation for capital levies and financial repression prevented government borrowing from playing a leading role in financial development – the British scenario. France had to wait until the Juillet Monarchy (1830–1848) and the Second Empire (1852–1870) to see business-friendly governments, as opposed to England which started having them after the Revolution (1689).

While the Bank of France was created by Napoleon in 1800 – more than a century after the Bank of England – it did not have the same impact as its English counterpart on the country's financial development. It suffered from the traditional lack of credibility of French national debt and consequently had difficulties selling its shares – contrary to the Bank of England which had been unexpectedly successful in that respect. While merchant banking also existed prior to 1850, there were no marked improvements in the French financial sector until the Second Empire. One can however notice the creation of new financial intermediaries such as Laffitte's Caisse Générale du Commerce et de l'Industrie and Delessert's Compagnie Royale d'Assurances Maritimes. These intermediaries were set up with the purpose of financing large industrial projects and Laffitte and Delessert were both bankers and industrial entrepreneurs.

The reign of Napoleon III saw the emergence of many big banks in France, some of them still in existence and playing a major role in French financial infrastructure. Interestingly, it was the existence of large investment projects – in particular the railways – which motivated the creation of many of these banks. This was made possible, in particular, by the existence of close connections between bankers, high-ranking civil servants and industrial tycoons. Such close connections can still be observed in the culture of the modern French elites.

The clearest example of a financial intermediary mostly engaged in financing large investment projects was the Crédit Mobilier of the Pereire brothers, which was motivated by the financing of the railways in which it played a key role, under the protection of Napoleon III. According to

Cameron (1967), the Crédit Mobilier was the 'forerunner of the great "mixed banks" that became characteristic of Continental Europe in the latter part of the nineteenth century'. While the Crédit Mobilier eventually failed, it was the model for many financial institutions across continental Europe.

One should also mention the Crédit Foncier de France, which helped to finance Paris's reconstruction (under the auspices of the famous Baron Haussman) and other public works, the Crédit Industriel et Commercial, the Crédit Lyonnais and the Société Générale.[3]

Large investment projects not only triggered the development of banking, but also of stock markets. According to Cameron (1967), banks were insufficient as providers of funds to the industry, and because of the large scale and lumpiness of the investments to be made, firms had a large interest in issuing shares. Securities markets, however, were, as in England, complements rather than substitutes for banks. Consortia of banks were needed to underwrite the share issues of large infrastructure projects, and banks such as the Crédit Mobilier were acting as intermediaries between small shareholders and the firms to which they had lent money or that they controlled.

Investment projects played an even greater role in the development of the German financial infrastructure, of which banking is a major component. The Darmstadter Bank, for example, created during the 1850s, was modelled after the Crédit Mobilier, with which it was associated, and had the explicit goal of financing long term investment (see Kemp, 1978). These banks not only played a key role in the industrialisation process, but also favoured the development of further financial instruments such as stocks. As Kemp writes:

> Credit banks on similar principles were founded in ... Germany during the following decade.... These banks also undertook the usual banking services for customers and they were less interested in holding large stock of industrial shares than in encouraging the sale of such shares over their own counters. This was increasingly possible as railways were floated and industrial firms adopted the joint stock form of organisation.
>
> German investment banking ... provided an alternative model to that of Britain.... It obviated the need for the slow build-up of capital by small firms, and, by making it possible to raise large amounts of capital, enabled big plants embodying the latest techniques to be established from the start.
>
> (Kemp, 1978)

We therefore conclude this section by noting that while public debt was favourable to financial development in England, it was harmful for it in France. What triggered financial development in France and the rest of continental Europe was the large need for funds and intermediation services generated by large infrastructure projects in the nineteenth century.

Large-scale privatisation and financial development in Eastern Europe

Eastern Europe entered its transition with both goods markets and financial markets to be developed. Interestingly, there were strong complementarities between the two, as privatisation was needed for creating goods markets, and financial markets were needed to enforce privatisation. As a result, countries such as Bulgaria, Romania, or, to a lesser extent, Poland, which had a slow or non-existent privatisation programme also had an underdeveloped financial market, while more advanced countries such as the Czech Republic, Hungary and Russia had both greater financial development and more successful privatisation.

The parallel development of financial markets and privatisation projects in the Czech Republic is, in that respect, quite telling. This experience is described in detail in, for example, Mejstrik *et al.* (1994). Privatisation favoured the development of such financial intermediaries as the investment privatisation funds (IPFs). These funds not only arose as a response to privatisation, but actually played a key role in its success. In January 1993, the voucher programme had been undersubscribed, as only 2 million Czechs had bought vouchers, compared to an expected 5 million. That figure was boosted to 8.5 million as a response to the advertising campaigns of the mutual funds. While these funds were making excessive promises, they played a key role in fostering the privatisation programme because they offered the consumer what was hoped to be an optimally diversified portfolio of shares in newly privatised firms. In the end, the investment funds collected 72 per cent of all vouchers in circulation. The episode illustrates how the timing of privatisation is closely connected with the timing of financial development.

Another dimension of financial development in the Czech Republic is the Prague Stock Exchange (PSE), which was opened in April 1993. This stock exchange started with nine securities, and turnover remained quite low up to October, when it exploded. The stock market grew rapidly because it was fuelled by shares from privatised companies. The number of traded companies has now risen to over 1,000. Another, parallel, system of trading, the RM system, was created for small vouchers owners, with lower entry costs and a lower trading frequency (twice a month).

Although Mejstrik *et al.* (1994) write that 'Illiquidity continues to plague the capital market. Despite substantial capital flows from foreign investors, the market remains largely under-capitalized; the Czech population is simply unaccustomed to investing', it is clear that the privatisation strategy has generated a large demand for financial services and therefore favoured a level of financial development which is quite respectable by the standards of the region. As an element of comparison, the Warsaw stock exchange only has 28 shares being traded (see Nivet, 1994).

GILLES SAINT-PAUL

A MACROECONOMIC MODEL

Let us consider a simple model of endogenous growth and endogenous financial development where the latter is driven by the demand for loans.

Basic equations

Time is continuous (as in the Blanchard, 1985 overlapping generations model), and we assume savers have access to a storage technology which yields a constant exogenous return ρ. We assume the economy is constantly in a regime where only part of total savings is intermediated, so that the rate of return paid to intermediated savings must be equal to ρ.

There are two sectors: a production sector, which uses capital and labour, and a financial sector, which uses only labour. Labour is freely allocated across the two sectors. The government and the private sector have access to savings through financial intermediaries. The interest charged by financial intermediaries is, at any point in time t, $r_t > \rho$. The intermediation margin $r_t - \rho$ pays for the cost of financial intermediation.

The production sector has a constant returns technology with a Romer-type externality generating constant aggregate returns to capital:

$$y_t = F(K_t, L_t, \bar{K}_t) \tag{1}$$

where $\bar{K}_t = K_t$ describes the effect of the externality and the two following equations hold:

$$F(\lambda K_t, \lambda L_t, K_t) = \lambda F(K_t, L_t, K_t); \forall \lambda \geq 0 \tag{2}$$

$$F(\lambda K_t, L_t, \lambda K_t) = \lambda F(K_t, L_t, K_t); \forall \lambda \geq 0 \tag{3}$$

The latter equation implies, since $\bar{K}_t = K_t$, that the aggregate production function can be written as $F(K_t, L_t, \bar{K}_t) = K_t G(L_t)$.

Labour and capital are paid their private marginal product which yields, using homogeneity:

$$w_t = \partial F/\partial L = K_t G'(L_t) \tag{4}$$

The depreciation rate of capital is δ. Accordingly, the first order condition for the marginal product of capital is:

$$r_t + \delta = \partial F/\partial K = G(L_t) - LG'(L_t) \tag{5}$$

We now turn to the financial sector. At each date t, the financial sector is described by its productivity B_t. B_t is the quantity of savings that can be

42

processed by one unit of labour in the financial sector. Assuming perfect labour mobility between the financial and production sectors, the following arbitrage condition must hold:

$$w_t = B_t[r_t - \rho] \tag{6}$$

Condition (6) means that the revenue generated by one unit of labour in the financial sector, which is equal to the RHS, must be equal to the wage.

We normalise total labour force to 1. Let z_t be employment in the financial sector. Then $L_t = 1 - z_t$. The total level of savings intermediated is equal to $S_t = B_t z_t$. This must be equal to the sum of gross investment and emissions of public debt:

$$B_t z_t = \dot{K}_t + \delta K_t + \dot{D}_t \tag{7}$$

where D_t is the outstanding stock of public debt. Last, we assume that there is a learning-by-doing process in the financial sector: more financial activity today increases tomorrow's financial development:

$$\dot{B}_t = (a + bz_t)B_t \tag{8}$$

Short-run equilibrium

In the short run, interest rates, wages, and the allocation of labour are determined by equations (4), (5) and (6). Eliminating wages from the system, we see that equilibrium is determined by the following two equations:

$$B_t[r_t - \rho] = K_t G'(1 - z_t) \tag{9}$$

$$r_t + \delta = G(1 - z_t) - (1 - z_t)G'(1 - z_t) \tag{10}$$

Figure 2.1 shows how equilibrium is determined in the (z_t, r_t) plane. The downward sloping locus PP is given by equation (10). It tells us that when more people work in the financial sector, the marginal product of capital falls, due to the fact that the labour input in the production function is smaller. The FF locus (equation (9)), means that a higher interest rate drives up, through the intermediation margin, the wage in the financial sectors, which attracts labour in that sector.

As illustrated in Figure 2.1, an increase in K_t/B_t generates an upward shift of FF and a fall in the equilibrium value of z_t. This is simply because it is associated with a rise in the productivity of labour in the productive sector relative to the financial sector.

43

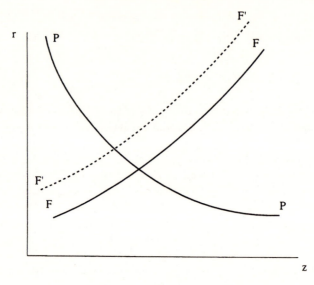

Figure 2.1 Equilibrium determination in the short run

Therefore, in the remainder of the analysis, we shall use a reduced form to describe the effect of K_t/B_t on z_t:

$$z_t = h(K_t/B_t) \tag{11}$$

Long-run equilibrium growth and convergence

We now turn to the determination of long-run growth. To do so, we make the following assumption on the management of public debt: we assume that the government maintains the ratio between public debt and the private capital stock equal to a constant d.

The two state variables governing the system are the capital stock K_t and the level of financial productivity B_t. Plugging (11) into (7) one may write:

$$\frac{\dot{K_t}}{K_t} = \frac{h(k_t)/k_t - \dot{d_t} - \delta}{1 + d_t} \tag{12}$$

where $k_t = K_t/B_t$ and $d_t = D_t/K_t$. Similarly (8) can be rewritten:

$$\frac{\dot{B_t}}{B_t} = a + bh(k_t) \tag{13}$$

44

Subtracting (13) from (12) we can get an evolution equation for k_t:

$$\frac{\dot{k}_t}{k_t} = \frac{h(k_t)/k_t - \dot{d}_t - \delta}{1 + d_t} - (a + bh(k_t)) \tag{14}$$

Let us now consider what happens when d_t is set equal to a constant d. In principle, the RHS of (14) may change signs several times. That is, there can be multiple long-run steady states. The intuition for multiple equilibria is as follows: a reduction in k triggers labour reallocation toward the financial sector. If learning effects are very strong in the financial sector, such shift will further increase B relative to K, thus generating further reductions in k.

However, for a smooth enough specification of $h(.)$, this will not happen. Figure 2.2a shows the dynamics of k when h is isoelastic: $h(k) = Ak^{-\alpha}$. The economy then converges to a unique balanced growth path.

How is the growth rate determined in equilibrium? K and B grow at the same rate g. Using (13) one can see that the growth rate satisfies $g = a + bh(k)$. *The growth rate is therefore a decreasing function of k, i.e. an increasing function of z.* A higher proportion of the workforce must be employed in the financial sector to sustain a higher growth rate: the productivity of the financial sector, which is driven by learning-by-doing, must keep up with growth in the productive sector.

Higher government indebtedness has, in this model, a positive effect on long-run growth because it draws more labour into the financial sector. As

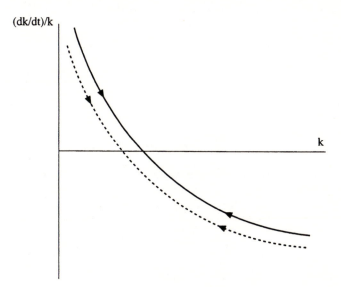

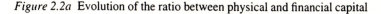

Figure 2.2a Evolution of the ratio between physical and financial capital

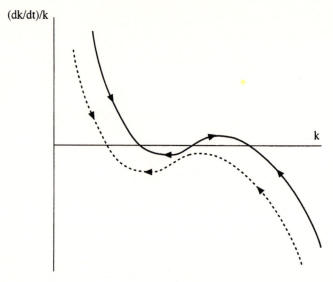

Figure 2.2b Evolution of the ratio between physical and financial capital, multiple equilibria

illustrated in Figure 2.2a, an increase in d shifts the $\dot{k}/k$ locus downwards around equilibrium. Therefore, the equilibrium value of k falls: more people work in the financial sector, and growth is faster.

When multiple equilibria are present, as in Figure 2.2b, an increase in public debt can have large impacts on growth and financial development by shifting the economy from a low-finance equilibrium to a high-finance equilibrium. Furthermore, the economy may stay forever at the high equilibrium, even when the rise in public debt is temporary.

Note that by assuming that not all desired savings are intermediated, we have ruled out any crowding-out effects of debt on physical capital accumulation in the long run. Reintroducing these crowding-out effects would generate an ambiguous impact of d on g, since the crowding-out effect would run counter to the financial effect.

Dynamics

Although there are no crowding-out effects in the long run, in the short run increases in public debt are associated with a drop in capital accumulation. A permanent increase in the debt capital ratio therefore depresses and then increases capital.

To assess the magnitudes of these effects, we have run numerical simulations. We have used an isoelastic specification for h, $h(k) = Ak^{-\alpha}$. The typical response of the capital stock to a permanent increase in the debt/capital

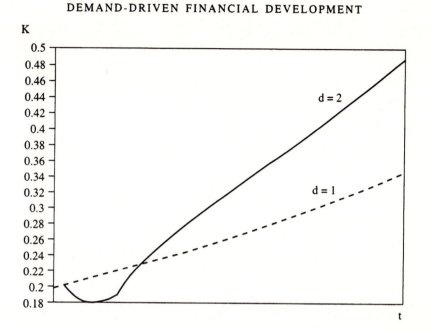

Figure 2.3 Response of the capital stock to a permanent increase in public debt

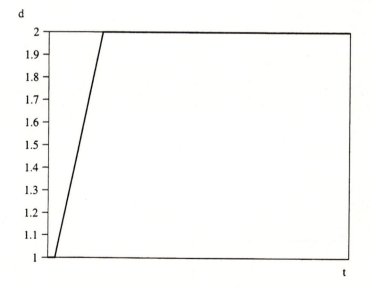

Figure 2.4 Corresponding evolution of public debt

B

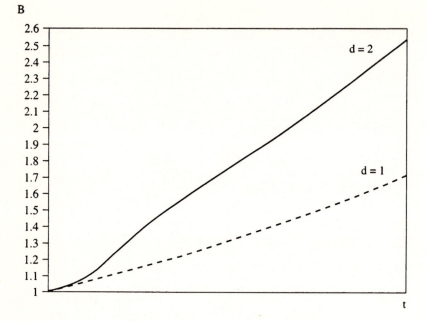

Figure 2.5 Response of financial capital

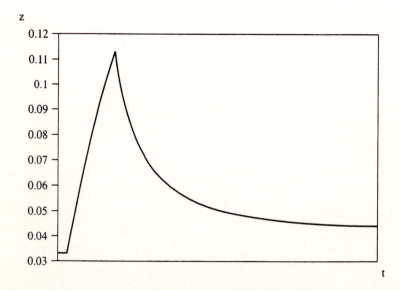

Figure 2.6 Response of financial employment

ratio is illustrated in Figure 2.3. This figure has been drawn for the following set of parameter values: $a = 0$, $b = 1$, $A = 10^{-5}$, $\alpha = 5$, $\delta = 0.1$. The economy starts in a steady state with a debt/capital ratio equal to $d = 1$, implying a growth rate of 3.2 per cent (and 3.2 per cent of the workforce in the financial sector). d then steadily rises to 2 in 2.5 years (Figure 2.4) and stays there thereafter. As shown in Figure 2.3, the capital stock first falls and then rises, to overtake quickly its previous path. It eventually converges to a growth path at a rate of 4.3 per cent a year. Figures 2.5 and 2.6 show the response of the degree of financial development B_t and the share of financial employment z_t, respectively. z_t overshoots its long-run value since a lot of financial activity is needed, relative to the size of the economy, when d_t picks up.

The length of time after which the benefits of the increase in public debt are felt depends on the elasticity of h. For $\alpha = 0.5$, the effect of doubling d on the rate of growth is very small (0.2 per cent), so that it takes several decades for k_t to overtake its previous path.

We also have simulated the impact of *temporary* increases in the debt/capital ratio. For a wide range of values of α, the long-run effect on the capital stock is strictly positive, more so when α is larger.

The model can be applied without modification to the case of large-scale privatisation, since a reduction in state-owned assets is equivalent to an increase in public debt.

Extension: the role of large investment projects

A very simple extension of the model can be made to capture the impact of large investment projects on financial development – the 'French model'. For this, just assume that the net increment in the capital stock, $\dot{K}_t$, consists of a continuum of individual 'projects', which yield the same rate of return (equal to the marginal product of capital r_t), but have different 'sizes'. Assume that the entrepreneurs who undertake these projects have a fixed amount $\bar{s}$ of personal savings. Let $\Phi(i)$ be the cumulative distribution of investment sizes i. The opportunity cost of undertaking the project if its size is less than $\bar{s}$ is equal to the return on the storage technology, ρ. Since in equilibrium one has $r_t > \rho$, entrepreneurs with project sizes less than $\bar{s}$ will not go to the financial market and undertake their project. Hence, a proportion $\phi = 1 - \Phi(\bar{s})$ of the projects will be intermediated. Therefore, the equilibrium condition (7) for financial intermediation can now be written, abstracting from public debt:

$$B_t z_t = \phi \dot{K}_t + \delta K_t \tag{15}$$

The accumulation equation for capital is now:

$$\frac{\dot{K}_t}{K_t} = \frac{h(k_t)/k_t - \delta}{\phi} \tag{16}$$

Finally, the evolution of k_t is now given by:

$$\frac{\dot{k}_t}{k_t} = \frac{h(k_t)/k_t - \delta}{\phi} - (a + bh(k_t)) \tag{17}$$

Comparing (17) with (14), we see that ϕ plays exactly the same role as d. An increase in the proportion of large-scale projects will thicken the upper tail of the distribution of i, thus increasing ϕ. This increases the demand for financial intermediation, thus drawing resources into the financial sector, which is beneficial for financial development and long-run growth.

As in the case of public debt, there is a crowding-out effect, but it is both weaker and of a different nature. In the case of public debt, the crowding-out effect comes from the fact that public debt increases the proportion of workers in the financial sector who process (unproductive) government bonds, thus reducing the amount of financial intermediation, given the size of the financial sector, available for processing transactions in productive assets. In the case of large projects, an increase in their share in total investment opportunities

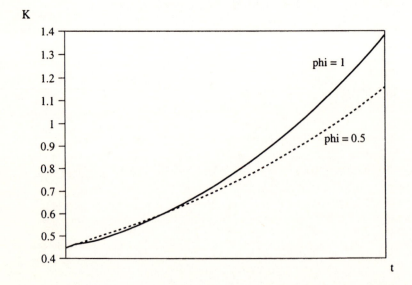

Figure 2.7 Response of the capital stock to a permanent increase in the share of projects intermediated

increases the demand for financial intermediation; to restore equilibrium, capital accumulation must fall, but it is now productive assets which crowd out each other, so that the short-run effect is much less damaging to growth.

Dynamic simulations confirm these views. Figure 2.7 shows the response of the capital stock to an increase in ϕ from 0.5 to 1. The parameters are the same as in the previous section, except for $A = 0.001$ and there is no government debt. The economy starts with a steady state with a growth rate of 5.7 per cent, and eventually reaches a steady state with a growth rate of 7.3 per cent. The transitional period where capital is below its pre-change trend is much shorter than in the previous exercise.

NOTES

1 This chapter originated as a paper prepared for the Conference on Financial Development and Growth, Groningen, December 1994, and the 'Macroeconomics of Privatization' project workshop, Bologna, January 1995. I am grateful to the European Community for financial support under a PHARE-ACE grant. I thank Irena Grosfeld for helpful suggestions.
2 That such crowding out was indeed prevalent at the time is the subject of considerable controversy among historians, for capital markets were much less integrated and developed than now. See Heim and Mirowski (1987), for example. In our model, that form of crowding out is somewhat ruled out by the assumption of a perfectly elastic supply for funds at a required rate of return equal to ρ.
3 A description of the experience of French banks in the nineteenth century can be found in Born (1983).

REFERENCES

Blanchard, O. (1985), 'Debt, Deficits, and Finite Horizons', *Journal of Political Economy*, 93, pp. 223–47.

Born, K.E. (1983), *International Banking in the 19th and 20th Centuries*, New York: St Martin's Press.

Cameron, R. (1967), *Banking in the Early Stages of Industrialization*, New York: Oxford University Press.

Dickson, P.G.M. (1967), *The Financial Revolution in England*, Aldershot: Gregg Revivals.

Fry, M.J. (1988), *Money, Interest and Banking in Economic Development*, Baltimore: The Johns Hopkins University Press.

———— (1993), 'Financial Repression and Economic Growth', *Working Paper*, No. 93-07, International Finance Group, University of Birmingham.

Goldsmith, R.W. (1969), *Financial Structure and Development*, New Haven: Yale University Press.

Heim, C. and P. Mirowski (1987), 'Interest rates and crowding out during Britain's Industrial Revolution', *Journal of Economic History*, 47, pp. 117–39.

Kemp, T. (1978), *Historical Patterns of Industrialization*, London: Longman.

Kindleberger, C.P. (1984), *A Financial History of Western Europe*, London: Allen & Unwin.

King, R.G. and R. Levine (1993), 'Finance and Growth: Schumpeter Might be Right', *Quarterly Journal of Economics*, 108, pp. 717–37.

McKinnon, R.I. (1973), *Money and Capital in Economic Development*, Washington DC: The Brookings Institution.

Mejstrik, M., R. Lastovicka and A. Marcincin (1994), 'Privatization and Opening the Capital Market in the Czech and Slovak Republics', mimeo, CERGE, Prague: Charles University.

Nivet, J.F. (1994), 'The Warsaw Stock Market', mimeo, DELTA.

North, D. and B. Weingast (1989), 'Constitution and Commitment: The Evolution of Institutions Governing Public Choice in Seventeenth Century England', *Journal of Economic History*, 49, pp. 803–32.

Pagano, M. (1993), 'The Flotation of Companies on the Stock Market: A Coordination Failure Model', *European Economic Review*, 37, pp. 1101–25.

Saint-Paul, G. (1992a), 'Technological Choice, Financial Markets, and Economic Development', *European Economic Review*, 36, pp. 763–81.

—— (1992b), 'Technological Dualism, Incomplete Financial Markets, and Economic Development', *Journal of International Trade and Economic Development*, 2, pp. 13–26.

3

ENDOGENOUS GROWTH WITH FINANCIAL CONSTRAINT[1]

Bruno Amable and Jean-Bernard Chatelain

INTRODUCTION

A recent literature has focused on the effects of financial development on growth (Bencivenga and Smith, 1991; Greenwood and Jovanovic, 1990 and Saint-Paul, 1992, *inter alia*).[2] Aside from potential increases in the savings rate, the existence of financial intermediation allows a more efficient use of resources by an improved allocation of credit compared to a situation of individual financial autarchy. For instance, the existence of credit markets permits a diversification of idiosyncratic risk, stemming either from liquidity preference or technological specificities. Moreover, financial intermediaries have an information-gathering aspect which should promote an efficient credit allocation. However, the influence of financial factors on growth are not limited to such aspects. Bencivenga and Smith (1993) have focused on the importance of financial market imperfections on growth. Faced with an adverse selection problem, lenders' optimal reaction may lead them to ration credit. This puts a limit on the attainable growth rate of the economy. In the model of Bencivenga and Smith, policies designed to reduce credit rationing by guaranteeing some loans, promote growth, so that there is room for some public intervention. Asymmetric information between borrower and lender leads also to incentive problems in financial relationships and may result in credit rationing.

This chapter presents a model of endogenous growth where private investors are subject to a particular type of credit rationing, which determines an 'optimal' financial structure of the firm. The motivation of our study stems from empirical work on investment such as Fazzari *et al.* (1988), who show that the level of investment of finance-constrained firms is negatively influenced by the amount of debt service and depends positively on current cash flows. In a context of endogenous growth driven by capital accumulation, any constraints on the level of investment of firms will have macroeconomic consequences on the level of the growth rate. One can then have a growth path limited by the availability of external funds to firms and their capacity to accumulate internal funds.

We consider an asymmetric information problem between lenders and borrowers. To overcome this problem, an optimal financial contract is chosen, so that an endogenously determined debt/equity ratio limits the stock of capital of the firm. In the model, the growth of internal funds net of the debt service determines investment which itself determines the growth of the economy. If we follow a definition given by Cohen (1993), a debt overhang problem appears when the debt-service crowds out investment, which is the focus of our chapter. This finance-constrained growth regime may describe the private sector of an economy which suffers from a high level of the interest rate. Thus, from a *static* incentive problem (cheating on ex-ante investment in soft capital) comes a lower debt/capital ratio and hence a lower level of investment. The debt service increases with the interest rate, so that a *dynamic* debt overhang problem is present. These two effects of a rise of the interest rate lower the growth rate.

The growth of each individual firm is defined by the growth of internal equity, once debt repayments have been made. Contrary to Bencivenga and Smith (1993)[3] and most of the literature on endogenous growth and finance, it is not assumed here that all investment is credit financed. Firms use both internal and external finance for their investments, and their access to external finance is restricted by their amount of wealth because of the information asymmetries existing on the financial market. Internal finance is indeed an important source of funds for corporations and in many countries the dominant one. Mayer (1988, 1991) shows that non-financial firms mostly use internal finance for their investments, of which only a small part is financed by debt or new equity. Retained profits and net worth affect investment since a higher net worth makes it easier to fulfil the incentive-compatibility constraints, making creditors more willing to lend. Hence, financial constraints will determine the growth of capital of the individual firm.

The aggregate rate of growth is derived taking into account the randomness of production for each individual. A firm is managed by succeeding generations of individuals. Each firm follows its own path so that firms differ with respect to their internal wealth.

This chapter proceeds as follows. The first section describes the model used throughout the paper. The first part of this section presents the production function of individual firms. There exist two uses of capital, one being the source of the informational problem that leads to credit rationing. Production is subject to uncertainty. The latter part of the section presents the behaviour of the agents that live for one period and split their income between consumption and bequests, the latter allowing for the continuation of the firm from generation to generation. The financial contract that is acceptable by both borrowers and lenders, i.e. the incentive-compatible contract, is introduced on pp. 57–61. This is followed by a concluding section.

THE MODEL

The utility function

Agents live only for one period, have one offspring and are identical in all respects, except their wealth. They run their own individual firm, collect the returns from their assets, consume and die at the end of the period. All individuals are risk-neutral and, as in Banerjee and Newman (1993) and Aghion and Bolton (1993), an individual's utility depends on consumption C and bequests B so that the latter are a linear function of end of period wealth. More precisely, a fraction δ of available income is consumed and a fraction $1 - \delta$ is given to the offspring; Cobb-Douglas preferences, subject to a budget constraint, give this result. This specification is a very simple formalisation of bequeathing behaviour. It may be noted that the offspring's utility does not enter directly in the parent's utility function. Only the bequest itself enters the utility function. In this model, intergenerational transfers will generate long-run growth. The wealth of the individual firm (the internal equity) can be accumulated over time through retained earnings. More precisely, the entrepreneur provides bequests to her or his offspring, making possible the continuation of the firm. Bequests could then be understood as retained earnings for an individual company.

At the start of her or his life, the agent inherits a positive amount of wealth. It will be supposed that a (small) positive fraction s of this wealth is not available for investment in the individual firm. Instead, this wealth will be invested in the safe asset and the agent will have the disposition of it at the end of her or his life for consumption and bequests. One might think of this part of the wealth as a mandatory insurance imposed by the government for instance, as individual agents are risk-neutral.[4] The existence of this fraction s of the wealth will guarantee that every agent has a strictly positive available income at the end of her or his life, which means that their consumption is strictly positive, as well as their bequests. This condition thus prevents individuals from going totally bankrupt.[5] Accordingly, each individual will inherit a strictly positive amount of wealth.

The production function

The model considers the case of a small economy that has to borrow abroad, taking the world interest rate r as given. There is a continuum of individuals on [0, 1]. Each individual lives for one period during which she or he operates her or his own private business. At the end of the period, each individual collects her or his net income and divides it between consumption and bequests. Each agent has one offspring, so the economy has a fixed-size population of succeeding generations.

Agents have access to a common technology. This technology uses private capital, being uses of the output good whose price is taken as numéraire. Capital entirely depreciates after one period. Private capital may be split between 'hard' and 'soft' capital. As in Gertler and Hubbard (1988), technology is risky, making output random. 'Hard' capital may be thought of as machinery or structures, i.e. traditional investment goods. On the other hand, 'soft' capital refers to any type of input which improves the likelihood that a given level of hard capital input will generate a 'good' productivity realisation. One may think for instance of investment in organisational competence, an important aspect of microeconomic competitiveness. One may, to some extent, also associate with soft capital some research and development expenditures. In this case, these expenditures will not explicitly help to discover new products, since only one good exists in the economy, but one may consider that 'soft' capital will help the firm to keep in touch with the market trends, for instance. However, contrary to the most common conception of research and development, soft capital expenditures are not cumulative. They are not used to discover new knowledge which can be added to previously discovered scientific principles.

y is the output of an individual firm, k its level of privately provided 'hard' capital and h the level of 'soft', intangible or organisational capital. Private productivity $a(h, u)$ is a function of a random event (denoted by a stochastic variable u) and of 'soft' capital investment (denoted h). h is decided before the random event. The ex-post production function is defined as (the time index t will be suppressed where there is no ambiguity):

$$y = a(h, u) f(k) \tag{1}$$

Following Gertler and Hubbard (1988), the random 'private' productivity model is kept as simple as possible, allowing for a moral hazard problem. u is a two state stochastic variable ($u = g$ for a good state and $u = b$ for a bad state). The probability of a bad state of nature is n^b, the probability of a good state of nature is $\pi^g (= 1 - \pi^b)$. h has a discontinuous positive effect on productivity when soft capital is used over a certain proportion of the hard capital in activity.

The random 'effort' or 'productivity' function $a(h, u)$ takes different values according to the realisation of the state of nature u and the amount of soft capital invested (the hidden action):

hidden action	private productivity in the bad state of nature	private productivity in the good state of nature
if $h < \beta k$	$a(h, u) = \theta$	$a(h, u) = \theta$
if $h \geq \beta k$	$a(h, u) = \theta$	$a(h, u) = 1$

with $0 < \beta, 0 < \theta < 1$.

Here, investing in soft capital increases productivity in case of a good outcome. For example, if u is a demand shock, ex-ante expenditure in the flexibility of organisation or in inventories management makes it possible to increase the speed of production to meet this demand. This function $a(h, u)$ could also be written such that h directly affects the distribution of the random term affecting productivity. For example, maintenance expenditures lower the probability of a bad state such as a breakdown of a machine. Such a setting implies the possibility of a moral hazard. If ever observation costs of intangible investment are prohibitive, it will not be possible for outsiders to discern ex-post whether a low productivity result is due to idiosyncratic risk (being unlucky) or to a diversion of funds or inputs invested ex-ante. The random term is assumed to be independently distributed across individuals and through time. With the assumptions made above concerning the impact of soft capital, a firm will either use βk units of soft capital or none at all.

The production function considered here is:

$$f(k) = A\,k \tag{2}$$

K is the aggregate level of private capital. In the production function above, individual production y features constant returns to scale from private input k.

The incentive-compatible contract

The existence of two types of capital is at the root of the information asymmetry. It is supposed that lenders cannot observe perfectly how a firm allocates the borrowed funds. Hard capital expenditures are observable by outsiders, but expenditures on soft capital are not. The quantity of equipment or structures that a firm owns are relatively easy to measure, but the efforts put into organisation, rationalisation, maintenance, stock control, research and development etc., are much more difficult to assess. Only a well-informed insider can evaluate precisely the amount of effort put into such inputs. This creates an incentive problem. A borrower is tempted to divert funds intended for soft capital investment to her or his own profit. The interest of the lender is to devise an incentive constraint so that the borrower does not divert funds for her or his own profit. When the incentive constraint is binding, the loss of productivity induced by under-investment in soft capital would imply a drop in the borrower's profits which would not be offset from the gains from cheating. Therefore under such a constraint, the borrower always invests in soft capital.

Although this diversion of funds can take various forms, such as the personal consumption of inputs inside the company, we will keep the problem simple and assume that these funds may be invested in a safe asset and earn a gross return equal to the world interest rate. With no funds invested in soft capital, the productivity realisation is certain to be bad. When repaying the debt, the entrepreneur will blame bad results on the bad state of affairs, pretending to have invested all funds so as to ensure a positive probability of a good state.

Rational lenders recognise the incentive problem and only accept financial contracts that eliminate the incentive to divert funds. It is supposed that there is perfect competition on the international financial market, so that financial intermediaries, which incur no costs from their activities, cannot make profits from lending. If an individual has inherited w from her or his parent, a fraction $(1 - s)$ of this wealth is freely available to the individual to pursue her or his own investment project. In addition to the inherited wealth, the individual may expect future profits from the activity of her or his firm, augmenting the collaterisable net wealth. If it is profitable to borrow, i.e. if the return to the firm's activity exceeds the safe return, the individual will want to invest a certain amount of (hard) capital k, and thus borrow an amount d: $d = (1 + \beta)k - (1 - s)w$.

The contract then specifies the amount borrowed d and repayments $R^g d$ in the event of a good output realisation, and $R^b d$ when the bad productivity state occurs. The contract is designed so as to be acceptable by both borrower and lender. It thus maximises the firm's expected profits, guaranteeing a return to the lender at least equal to the safe return on the international financial market and taking account of the incentive problem. Indeed, the contract must provide the individual with the incentive to invest in soft capital rather than invest part of the firm's capital for his or her exclusive benefit. Therefore, the incentive-compatibility constraint must be such that the return to an 'honest' activity exceeds the gains from diverting funds.

The optimal financial contract is designed so as to maximise the firm's expected profits, net of debt repayments:

$$(R^g d, R^b d, k) \in ArgMax \left[(\pi^g + \theta \pi^b)Ak - (\pi^g R^g + \pi^b R^b)d \right] + sRw \quad (3)$$

guaranteeing the competitive intermediary an expected return equal to that of the safe asset on the world financial market ($R = 1 + r$, r being the world interest rate):

$$(\pi^b R^b + \pi^g R^g)d = Rd \quad (4)$$

The contract must also take account of the incentive-compatibility constraint denoting $\pi = \pi^g + \theta\pi^b$:

$$[\pi Ak - (\pi^b R^b + \pi^g R^g)d] + sRw \geq [\theta Ak - R^b d + R\beta k] + sRw \quad (5)$$

The agent's temptation to divert funds is lowered when repayments in the event of a bad state increase. However, the amount that a firm can repay is limited by its net wealth. Therefore, some 'limited liability' conditions put limits on the amounts that a firm has to repay either after a good productivity realisation or a bad one.

$$\theta Ak - R^b d \geq 0 \tag{6}$$

$$Ak - R^g d \geq 0 \tag{7}$$

If productivity A is not too high (see Appendix, equation (27)), the incentive constraint is binding and investment and financial decisions are not independent. Under a certain threshold for A, the economy is not productive enough to warrant investment and growth considering the interest factor R as given. Above another threshold, the economy is so productive that incentive problems vanish. The borrower would not have any interest in diverting funds outside of their productive use because such funds would be put to better use inside the firm. Since we are not interested in either of these cases, we will limit ourselves to the consideration of values for A between the two thresholds defined precisely in the Appendix.

As shown in the Appendix, the limited liability constraint in the case of a bad productivity state is binding too. It is indeed desirable in this case to raise repayments as much as possible so as to deter the agent from diverting capital. Following this, the incentive constraint provides a limit to the amount of funds a firm can borrow. The firm is credit rationed according to its initial wealth, so that a firm's investment depends on its wealth:

$$k = \frac{(1 - s)w}{1 + 2\beta - \pi \dfrac{A}{R}} \tag{8}$$

and all firms will face the same repayment interest rates R^g and R^b. One may note that credit rationing is all the more stringent when the fraction of unobservable 'soft' capital β is high. On the other hand, a higher level of productivity A lowers the credit constraint. This incentive-compatibility condition can also be written as an optimal financial structure:

$$d = \left(\pi \frac{A}{R} - \beta\right)k \tag{9}$$

This result follows the intuition. The lender accepts a higher leverage for the higher the productivity level, the lower the real interest rate and the lesser the asymmetric information.

Note that a 'not incentive-compatible contract' is possible. In that case, the entrepreneur maximises profits and diverts funds. The lenders are fully aware of this, know that the bad state of nature is certain and take it into account when charging the interest rate. The level of capital implied by this contract is lower than that of the incentive-compatible contract, while the profits for the entrepreneur are lower too. Because of perfect competition on the financial side, the situation where this contract is proposed is not stable. An intermediary proposing the incentive-compatible contract will attract all the entrepreneurs, and all the other intermediaries will follow.

Debt-overhang aggregate growth

Incentives are provided to agents so that they do not divert funds away from productive activity. From the law of large numbers, a fraction π^b of all firms will experience a bad productivity state, while a fraction π^g will experience a good productivity state. Firms' profits will differ accordingly, and so will consumption and bequests. The evolution of wealth must be differentiated according to whether the parent firm has had a good or a bad productivity realisation. For an agent living at time t whose parent firm has had a bad productivity state, the level of initial wealth w_t is:

$$w_t = (1 - \delta) \{ sRw_{t-1} + [\theta A_{t-1}k_{t-1} - R^b d_{t-1}] \} \tag{10}$$

w_{t-1} is the level of initial wealth of the parent. w_t is the amount of wealth that the agent inherits. It is a fraction $(1 - \delta)$ of the parent's available income at the end of period t–1. This income is the sum of the amount of initial wealth which has not been used in the investment project, augmented with the interest, and the profits coming from the activity of the firm. For agents whose parent firm has experienced a good productivity state, the initial wealth level is:

$$w_t = (1 - \delta) \{ sRw_{t-1} + [A_{t-1}k_{t-1} - R^g d_{t-1}] \} \tag{11}$$

The equations for the evolution of wealth are linear in w_{t-1}. It is thus possible to aggregate across individuals, appealing to the law of large numbers, and derive the expression for total aggregate initial wealth without bothering about the distribution of wealth. We denote with a capital letter the aggregate levels of debt, wealth and capital. Total initial wealth is then:

$$W_t = (1 - \delta) \{ sRW_{t-1} + [(\pi^b \theta + \pi^g) A_{t-1}K_{t-1} - (\pi^b R^b + \pi^g R^g)D_{t-1}] \} \tag{12}$$

Aggregating in a similar way the incentive-compatibility constraint gives:

$$\pi A_{t-1}K_{t-1} - RD_{t-1} = R\beta K_{t-1} \tag{13}$$

so that:

$$W_t = (1 - \delta)\{sRW_{t-1} + R\beta K_{t-1}\} \qquad (14)$$

since

$$K_{t-1} = \frac{1 - s}{1 + 2\beta - \pi\dfrac{A}{R}} W_{t-1} \qquad (15)$$

The evolution of the aggregate capital stock is described by:

$$\left(1 + 2\beta - \pi\frac{A}{R}\right) K_t = (1 - \delta)\left[sR\left(1 + 2\beta - \pi\frac{A}{R}\right) + (1 - s)R\beta \right] K_{t-1} \quad (16)$$

The growth rate of the economy j is:

$$1 + j = (1 - \delta)\left[sR + \frac{(1 - s)R\beta}{1 + 2\beta - \pi\dfrac{A}{R}} \right] \qquad (17)$$

Because of the limit on the private debt/equity ratio derived from the optimal financial contract, the growth rate differs from what could be obtained with other endogenous growth models in the literature. For s small enough, the growth rate depends negatively on the interest rate for two reasons:

- higher interest charges limit the net profits and thus the accumulation of firms' wealth (dynamic effect)
- a higher interest rate limits the amount of external finance lent to the firm because of the constraints imposed by the incentive-compatible contract (static effect).

The growth rate depends negatively on the extent of the asymmetric information, and, as in standard endogenous growth models, positively on the expected productivity of investment and the saving rate $(1 - \delta)$.

CONCLUSION

This paper has presented a model of endogenous growth with imperfect financial intermediaries. The agents have a finite life, and a bequest motive that makes possible a sustainable long-run growth. Asymmetric information implies that private investment depends on firms' internal net worth and is credit-rationed. The rate of growth of the economy depends on the level of the world interest rate and the efficiency of financial markets.

The debt-overhang model, understood as a limit to growth coming from the burden of interest repayment, concerns here the private firms whose access to finance is determined by an optimal debt/equity ratio coming from a moral hazard problem. The growth of firms depends on bequests of dynastic entrepreneurs, i.e. 'individual firms' savings net of debt-interest repayments. The debt-overhang problem specified here is different from repudiation models on sovereign debt based on the cost of the repudiation hypothesis.[6]

Institutional arrangements that would result in a softening of the incentive problems would have a positive effect on growth. For instance, a public intervention that would result in a lower β would be growth enhancing because the credit rationing would be less stringent. This would alter the financial structure of the firm in favour of debt, which would increase the level of capital and the growth rate of the economy.

A public intervention could have some influence on the level of the interest rate, by means of monetary or budgetary policy, in order to avoid excessively high interest rates which worsen the private debt-overhang problem and put a limit to growth for some time. Second, public intervention may be helpful in smoothing the asymmetric information problem. If the government can invest directly in some sort of public capital which increases private productivity, such as education, then under certain conditions there may be lower needs for private investment in soft capital and thus less incentive problems.

APPENDIX

The optimal contract

The optimal financial contract is designed so as to maximise the firm's expected profits, net of taxes and debt repayments:

$$Max[(\pi^g + \theta\pi^b)Ak - (\pi^g R^g + \pi^b R^b)d] + sRw \qquad (18)$$

guaranteeing the competitive intermediary an expected return equal to that of the safe asset on the world financial market ($R = 1 + r$, r being the world interest rate):

$$(\pi^b R^b + \pi^g R^g)d = R[(1 + \beta)k - (1 - s)w] \qquad (19)$$

The contract must also take account of the incentive-compatibility constraint:

$$[\pi Ak - (\pi^b R^b + \pi^g R^g)d] + sRw \geq [\theta Ak - R^b d + R\beta k] + sRw \qquad (20)$$

and it must also satisfy the 'limited liability' constraints, both in the bad and the good productivity states:

$$\theta Ak - R^b d \geq 0 \qquad (21)$$

$$Ak - R^g d \geq 0 \qquad (22)$$

With λ2, λ3 and λ4 the coefficients associated respectively to the zero-profit condition for the financial intermediary, the incentive-compatibility constraint and the limited liability constraints for the bad and good states, and taking the zero-profit condition for banks, one must have:

$$\frac{\partial \mathcal{L}}{\partial k} = [\pi A - R(1 + \beta)] + \lambda_2 [\pi A - R(1 + \beta) - \theta A - R\beta]$$

$$+ \lambda_3 \theta A + \lambda_4 A \qquad (23)$$

$$= 0$$

$$\frac{\partial \mathcal{L}}{\partial R^b} = \lambda_2 - \lambda_3 = 0 \qquad (24)$$

$$\frac{\partial \mathcal{L}}{\partial R^g} = \lambda_4 = 0 \qquad (25)$$

This last equation indicates that the limited liability constraint is never binding in the good productivity state. However,

$$\lambda_2 = -\frac{\pi A - R(1 + \beta)}{\pi A - R(1 + 2\beta)} \qquad (26)$$

a sufficient condition for λ_2 to be strictly positive is:

$$\frac{R(1 + \beta)}{\pi} < A < \frac{R(1 + 2\beta)}{\pi} \qquad (27)$$

The first inequality states that the marginal productivity of private investment exceeds the cost of capital. The second inequality ensures that private firms will always be credit constrained. This condition is supposed to hold so that:

$$\frac{R\,(1\,+\,\beta)}{\pi} < \bar{A}_0 \le A \le \bar{A}_1 < \frac{R\,(1\,+\,2\beta)}{\pi} \tag{28}$$

Following this, the incentive constraint is always binding. Likewise, one has:

$$\theta A k - R^b d = 0 \tag{29}$$

If the incentive-compatibility constraint is binding, then the limited liability constraint in the bad productivity state is also binding, the agents must repay their whole gross profits to the lender. The incentive constraint becomes:

$$\pi A k - R d = R \beta k \tag{30}$$

since the balance sheet equation of the firm is:

$$(1 + \beta)k = d + (1 - s)w \tag{31}$$

one obtains a debt/capital ratio:

$$d = \left(\pi \frac{A}{R} - \beta \right) k \tag{32}$$

which can also be expressed as a wealth constraint on investment:

$$k = \frac{(1 - s)w}{1 + 2\beta - \pi \dfrac{A}{R}} \tag{33}$$

The formulas above indicate that the ratios d/k, d/w and k/w are identical for all firms. Interest rates R^g and R^b are also the same for all firms. Whatever its initial wealth, a firm can borrow at the same conditions (i.e. respecting the same ratios) as any other firm.

NOTES

1 This chapter has benefited from comments from Gerard Kuper, Robert Lensink and Niels Hermes.
2 See Pagano (1993) for a survey.

3 We will not stress the liquidity risk emphasised in Bencivenga and Smith (1991) nor its possible influence on investment and growth.

4 See Akerlof and Dickens (1982) for an argument in favour of a compulsory old age insurance. One could also think of a 'Stone-Geary' type of utility function, with a minimal level of bequest. Under the form specified here, it is as if the agent chose to bequeath her or his offspring a mimimal level of income proportional to her or his own wealth.

5 This assumption is necessary in the very long run for the aggregation to be performed under the law of large numbers so that the population of agents does not decrease to zero.

6 See Cohen (1993) for references.

REFERENCES

Aghion, P. and P. Bolton (1993), 'A Theory of Trickle-Down Growth and Development with Debt-Overhang', *Discussion Paper*, No. 170, LSE Financial Markets Group.

Akerlof, G. and W. Dickens (1982), 'The Economic Consequences of Cognitive Dissonance', *American Economic Review*, 72, pp. 307–19.

Banerjee, A. and A. Newman (1993), 'Occupational Choice and the Process of Development', *Journal of Political Economy*, 101, pp. 274–98.

Bencivenga, V. and B. Smith (1991), 'Financial Intermediation and Endogenous Growth', *Review of Economic Studies*, 58, pp. 195–209.

——— (1993), 'Some Consequences of Credit Rationing in an Endogenous Growth Model', *Journal of Economic Dynamics and Control*, 17, pp. 97–122.

Cohen, D. (1993), 'Low Investment and Large LDC Debt in the 1980s', *American Economic Review*, 83, pp. 437–49.

Fazzari, S.M., R.G. Hubbard and B.C. Petersen (1988), 'Financing Constraint and Corporate Investment', *Brookings Papers on Economic Activity*, 19, pp. 141–95.

Gertler, M. and R.G. Hubbard (1988), 'Financial Factors in Business Fluctuations', *Working Paper*, No. 2758, National Bureau of Economic Research.

Greenwood, J. and B. Jovanovic (1990), 'Financial Development, Growth, and the Distribution of Income', *Journal of Political Economy*, 98, pp. 1076–107.

Mayer, C. (1988), 'New Issues in Corporate Finance', *European Economic Review*, 32, pp. 1167–83.

——— (1991), 'Financial Systems, Corporate Finance, and Economic Development', in R.G. Hubbard (ed.) *Asymmetric Information, Corporate Finance, and Investment*, Chicago: University of Chicago Press, pp. 307–32.

Pagano, M. (1993), 'Financial Markets and Growth: An Overview', *European Economic Review*, 37, pp. 613–22.

Saint-Paul, G. (1992), 'Technological Choice, Financial Markets and Economic Development', *European Economic Review*, 36, pp. 763–81.

4

FINANCIAL DEVELOPMENT, POLICY AND ECONOMIC GROWTH[1]

Jean Claude Berthélemy and Aristomene Varoudakis

INTRODUCTION

The existence of a correlation between financial development and economic growth has been very well documented in the recent literature.[2] However, such a relationship is much more complex than assumed in linear regressions put forward by, for example, King and Levine (1993). In particular, the causality between financial development and growth is rather unclear. As soon as we consider a two-way causation, it becomes impossible to derive any lesson, from a policy design point of view, from such results.

A simple response to this criticism is to test the effect of initial financial development on growth. Although valid, this answer is too simple. From a theoretical point of view, a two-way positive causation between financial development and growth may very well lead to multiple equilibria. In such a case, estimating a linear equation might be misleading, because different countries, or a single country at different periods, might exhibit different growth behaviours, depending on the specific equilibrium towards which they converge.

In this chapter, we show theoretically and empirically the possible existence of multiple equilibria, as well as its consequences for the assessment of the relationship which may exist between financial development and growth. Through this exercise, we show that financial development policies might have very different consequences depending on the initial context of the economy. Moreover, we demonstrate that the effect of other policies depends as well on financial development.

In the first part we present a theoretical model of endogenous growth with reciprocal interactions between the real and the financial sectors of the economy, which lead to multiple steady state equilibria. One of these steady states leads to a poverty trap in which the financial sector disappears and the economy stagnates. A second steady state is characterised by positive

66

endogenous growth and a normal development of financial intermediation activities.

In the second part of the chapter we examine whether this result of multiple steady states linked to the initial level of financial development is supported by cross-country data on economic growth.

Although quite definite, the results that we obtain remain rather theoretical, and a deeper analysis is necessary to understand how specific financial policies influence the growth achievements of a country. This requires a case by case investigation, taking account of history as well as specific institutional aspects. The cross-country econometric exercise does not describe well the dynamics of the underlying cumulative processes, nor the role played by specific financial sector policies. A summary account is given in the third part of this chapter on such case studies, for two countries which represent polar cases: Taiwan and Senegal.

A THEORETICAL MODEL OF FINANCIAL INTERMEDIATION AND GROWTH

The aim of the theoretical model we develop in this part is to make a more in-depth theoretical analysis of the interaction between financial development and real growth. We study an endogenous growth model in which learning-by-doing externalities in the real sector form the source for long-run growth. In performing its intermediation functions, the financial sector[3] uses real resources, which present an opportunity cost in terms of production. Furthermore, the financial sector operates in a monopolistic competition framework. The aim of competition is to collect household savings. In our model, the size of the financial sector has a negative influence on the concentration and margins of financial intermediation through the number of banks that compete for the market.

In our framework there is a reciprocal externality between the banking sector and the real sector that may lead to multiple equilibria. Growth in the real sector causes the financial market to expand, therefore increasing banking competition and efficiency. In return, the development of the banking sector raises the net yield of savings and enhances capital accumulation and growth. The first section below presents the theoretical model. Its multiple steady state properties are studied in the second section.

Modelling interactions between the real and the financial sectors

The consumers

Consumers have an infinite time horizon and they supply labour inelastically. Demographic growth is disregarded and total population is normalised to 1. Consumers hold claims on financial intermediaries (V) whose real yield is r.

They also possess a non-intermediated productive asset – called human capital (H) in what follows – that they rent out to businesses. The real rate of interest (r) is equal to the *net* marginal productivity of capital, defined after adjusting for financial intermediation costs. The rate of return on the non-intermediated asset (human capital) is r_h. It is accepted that the accumulation of the non-intermediated asset does not imply a specific technology, since the model does not focus on the accumulation of human capital as an 'engine of growth'.[4] Consumers therefore accumulate capital 'in the widest sense' – $A = V + H$ – in accordance with their budget constraint. This obviously comes down to supposing that deposits with financial intermediaries and human capital are perfect substitutes from the standpoint of individual consumers. Furthermore, we assume perfect forecasting and an instantaneous iso-elastic utility function. The representative consumer's optimisation programme is:

$$\max_{C_t} u_0 = \int_0^\infty \frac{C_t^{1-\sigma} - 1}{1 - \sigma} e^{-\rho t} \, dt \tag{1a}$$

$$s.c. \ \dot{A}_t = r(A_t - H_t) + w - C_t + r_h H_t \tag{1b}$$

ρ is the pure rate of time preference; w is the real wage rate, which – assuming perfect mobility of labour – is common to the real sector and the financial intermediation sector; and C is consumption in real terms. From this is deduced the usual Keynes–Ramsey condition and the condition of equality of yields on the two assets held by consumers:

$$\frac{\dot{C}_t}{C_t} = \frac{1}{\sigma}(r - \rho) \tag{2a}$$

$$r_h = r \tag{2b}$$

The firms

Firms are symmetrical and possess a technology with constant returns to scale with respect to physical capital (K), human capital (H) and *efficient* units of labour (uE). For reasons of analytical tractability we assume a Cobb–Douglas aggregate production function:

$$Y = AK^\alpha H^\beta (uE)^{1-\alpha-\beta} \tag{3}$$

A proportion u of the work force is employed in the real sector. Physical capital K is *intermediated* by the financial sector. Therefore, this capital aggregate takes into account the improvement in the allocation of savings to investment brought about by financial intermediaries. Technical progress is endogenised following Romer's (1986) model. The efficiency of labour therefore depends – through an externality – on the aggregate stock of capital $(E = K)$.[5]

Profit maximisation by the representative firm implies the following conditions:

$$\alpha u^{1-\alpha-\beta} A \left(\frac{K}{H} \right)^{-\beta} = R = r(1 + i) \qquad (4a)$$

$$\beta u^{1-\alpha-\beta} A \left(\frac{K}{H} \right)^{1-\beta} = r_h = r \qquad (4b)$$

$$(1 - \alpha - \beta) u^{-\alpha-\beta} A \left(\frac{K}{H} \right)^{-\beta} \cdot K = w \qquad (4c)$$

where R is the interest rate in the market for bank credit. We can define $R = (1 + i)r$, where i denotes the margin of financial intermediation.

The financial intermediaries

We model the financial sector in a Cournotian *monopolistic competition* framework with n symmetrical banks. The aim of the competition is to collect savings from households. Banks are confronted with a savings supply function whose instantaneous elasticity with respect to the interest rate is $1/\sigma$ – as implied by the iso-elastic form of the household utility function given in (1a). It is assumed that each bank maximises its profit at a given point in time, considering that the volume of savings collected by the $n - 1$ other banks remains unchanged. In the absence of information asymmetries or other imperfections, the banks have no way of influencing the interest rate on the credit market, which is necessarily equal to the marginal productivity of intermediated capital denoted by (4a). However, each bank knows that its behaviour will influence the yield on investment r and therefore $1 + i$, given the savings supply function and R. The analysis of the behaviour of individual banks is based on the assumption of unchanged behaviour in future periods.

Turning now to financial intermediation technology, it is assumed that the amount of investments intermediated by each bank j represents a fraction ϕ_j of the current savings that it collects[6] – given the financial intermediation margin. This fraction depends on the quantity of real resources used by the bank. Denoting by v_j the level of employment in the representative bank, we assume that $\phi_j = \phi_j(v_j)$, where $\phi'_j > 0$. Since the banks are symmetrical, $v_j = (1 - u)/n$ in a steady state. At the individual-bank level and the aggregate level we get:

$$\dot{K}_j = \phi_j \cdot S_j \Rightarrow \dot{K} = \phi \cdot S \tag{5}$$

where $S = Y - C$ and $\phi = \phi\left(\dfrac{1 - u}{n}\right)$; $\phi' > 0$.

Obviously, the financial intermediation technology (5) implies the existence of increasing returns to scale, at the level of individual banks, with respect to savings S_j and employment v_j. This could be justified by the presence of learning-by-doing effects in financial intermediation activities, affecting the productivity of labour in the banking sector. These effects are assumed to be internal to individual banks, in accordance with our framework of imperfect competition in banking. Such learning-by-doing effects could presumably be linked to the scale of operations of each bank – that is, to the size of the financial market (volume of savings) divided by the number of banks.[7] This 'natural' externality, exerted from the real sector on the financial sector, establishes an interaction between the two sectors of the economy and is an original feature of the model.

The present value of the bank's profit, linked to its current intermediation activities, is expressed as follows:

$$\pi_j = (1 + i)\phi_j(v_j)S_j - v_jw - S_j \tag{6}$$

Profit maximisation by bank j implies, first, $\partial\pi_j/\partial S_j = 0$. Noting that the elasticity $(\partial S/\partial r) \cdot (r/S) = 1/\sigma$ and that $S_j = S/n$, $\phi_j = \phi((1 - u)/n)$ holds in a symmetrical equilibrium, we get from this condition the financial intermediation margin as follows:

$$\frac{R}{r} = 1 + i = \frac{1}{\left(1 - \dfrac{\sigma}{n}\right)\phi} \tag{7}$$

The equilibrium intermediation margin depends on the intensity of competition in the financial sector, expressed by the number n of banks. A reduction in n implies an increase in $1 + i$, given the value of ϕ. Furthermore, the more interest-rate inelastic the savings supply function, the higher the margin of financial intermediation.

The second condition for profit-maximisation by banks ($\partial\pi_j/\partial v_j = 0$) implies equalising marginal labour productivity to the real wage rate. At a symmetrical equilibrium, this condition is written as follows:

$$w = (1 + i)\phi' \frac{S}{n} \tag{8}$$

This result shows that the real sector exerts an *external effect* on the financial sector via the determination of the savings flow S. The larger the size of the financial market – i.e. the higher the amount of household savings – the higher the labour productivity in banks.

Furthermore, under the usual free entry assumption, the long-run equilibrium in the banking sector is characterised by zero profits. Setting $\pi = 0$ in function (6) and combining with condition (8) above, we get:

$$1 + i = \frac{1}{[\phi - ((1 - u)/n)\phi']} = \frac{1}{(1 - \epsilon)\phi} \tag{9}$$

In this equation, ϵ is the elasticity of the savings intermediation coefficient (ϕ) with respect to employment at the bank level. Lastly, the combination of (9) with (7) results in:

$$\frac{\sigma}{n} = \frac{\phi'}{\phi} \cdot \frac{1 - u}{n} = \epsilon \tag{10}$$

This relationship between the number of banks and ϵ determines n in relation to the size of the financial sector $1 - u$. As a matter of fact, a *positive* relationship is often observed (especially from cross-country data) between the development level of the financial sector and the degree of banking competition. Countries in which the development of the financial sector has been repressed, usually have highly oligopolistic banking systems. On the other hand, the banking system is substantially more competitive in financially developed countries.[8] Therefore, to take into account this aspect of the real world, it is assumed that the elasticity in the right-hand side of (10) is *decreasing* with respect to $(1 - u)/n$. According then to condition (10), an increase in n makes it necessary to have a reduction in ϵ. This implies a rise in $(1 - u)/n$, which can only happen if $1 - u$ increases.

The development of the financial sector $(1 - u)$ will therefore be followed by an increase in banking competition (n), the size of the individual banks $((1 - u)/n)$ and the savings intermediation coefficient ϕ. Equation (9) shows that an increase in the size of the financial sector (rise in $1 - u$), which produces an increase in ϕ and a fall in ϵ, implies a *reduction* in the cost of financial

71

intermediation (drop in $1 + i$) through an intensification of competition in the banking sector (rise in n). The decrease in the financial intermediation margin leads in turn to an *increase* in the real interest rate paid to consumers, $r = R/(1 + i)$, given the marginal productivity of intermediated capital.

Endogenous growth and multiple steady states

This section studies the economy's equilibrium outlined above and shows the possibility for multiple steady state equilibria to exist. At the origin of this multiple steady states result is the interaction between the positive external effect of real sector savings on bank productivity and the imperfect competition mechanisms in the banking sector. In order to illustrate this possibility, we consider first a situation in which the financial sector is under-developed. This results in a weak banking competition and thus a high financial intermediation margin. This in turn implies a decrease in the net interest rate r paid to households and therefore – according to the Keynes–Ramsey condition – a low steady state growth rate in the long run. The low return on savings reduces the flow of household savings supplied to banks. In turn, the small size of the financial market implies low marginal labour productivity in the banking sector. Since the real wage rate must be equated in both sectors, the low labour productivity in this sector justifies the low level of employment and therefore the under-development of the banking sector. Consequently, the economy can stay trapped in a low equilibrium with insufficient financial sector development and low growth. Nevertheless, a high equilibrium can also exist in which the high development level of the financial sector strengthens banking competition. This leads to relatively low intermediation margins and a high level of net real interest rates paid to households, a high growth rate, a strong incentive to save and a large financial market. This has positive repercussions on marginal labour productivity in the financial sector and justifies a high level of employment there.

Put more formally, by equalising the real wage rate in the real and financial sectors – equations (4c) and (8) – we get:

$$\frac{S}{K} = (1 - \epsilon)\frac{n\phi}{\phi'}(1 - \alpha - \beta)u^{-\alpha-\beta}A\left(\frac{K}{H}\right)^{-\beta} \tag{11}$$

The capital accumulation equation $\dot{K} = \phi S$ can then be used to compute the capital growth rate, $g = \dot{K}/K = \phi(S/K)$. Combining with (11) above and using z to denote the physical capital–human capital ratio (K/H), we obtain:

$$g = \phi^2(1 - \epsilon)\frac{n}{\phi'}(1 - \alpha - \beta)u^{-\alpha-\beta}Az^{-\beta} \tag{12}$$

So the complete model is made up of the Keynes–Ramsey condition (2a), the two profit-maximisation conditions (4a) and (4b), equation (9) – implying $1 + i = 1/[(1 - \epsilon)\phi]$ –, equation (10) $s/n = \epsilon$, and the capital accumulation equation (12). At a long-run equilibrium, u and n would be constant and therefore $\dot{K}/K = \dot{Y}/Y = \dot{C}/C = g$. When steady state equilibrium exists, these six equations determine six endogenous variables: the growth rate (g), the net return on savings (r), the financial intermediation margin (i), the allocation of labour to the real sector and the financial sector (u), the number of banks (n), and the physical capital-to-human capital ratio $(z = K/H)$. The stationary value of z is obtained from (4a) and (4b):

$$z = \frac{\alpha}{\beta}(1 - \epsilon)\phi \tag{13}$$

As ϵ is a decreasing function of ϕ, the z ratio *increases* with the size of the financial sector, i.e. with $1 - u$. Combining (13), (4a) and (9), the Keynes–Ramsey condition (2a) and the capital accumulation equation (12) can be written:

$$g = \frac{1}{\sigma}\left[\alpha u^{1-\alpha-\beta}A\left(\frac{\beta}{\alpha}\right)(1 - \epsilon)^{1-\beta}\phi^{1-\beta} - \rho\right] \tag{14}$$

$$g = \phi^{1-\beta}\frac{(1 - \epsilon)^{1-\beta}}{\epsilon}(1 - \alpha - \beta)\frac{(1 - u)}{u^{\alpha+\beta}}A\left(\frac{\beta}{\alpha}\right)^{\beta} \tag{15}$$

The system made up of these two equations and the $n = \sigma/\epsilon$ condition allows us to determine simultaneously the long-run, steady state growth rate (g), the allocation of labour to the two sectors (u) and the number of banks (n).

This long-run equilibrium is more easily depicted with the help of a diagram. First of all, consider the Keynes–Ramsey condition (14). This equation shows that the development of the financial sector (reduction in u) has *two opposing effects* on the long-run growth rate. On the one hand, the reduction in the percentage of the workforce employed in the real sector lowers the marginal productivity of capital (R) and therefore the real interest rate paid to consumers $r = R/(1 + i)$. This direct effect will have a negative influence on economic growth, as shown by equation (2a). On the other hand, the development of the financial sector lowers the capital intermediation cost

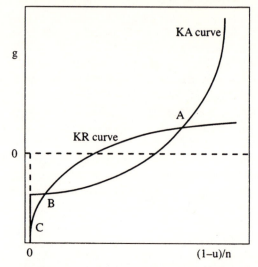

Figure 4.1 The capital accumulation and Keynes–Ramsey condition curves

through both the size effect (increase in ϕ) and the competition effect (increase in n). This implies a rise in the return on savings. This effect runs counter to the first effect and has a positive influence on the rate of economic growth. The Keynes–Ramsey condition is therefore illustrated by the concave curve in Figure 4.1 (KR curve).[9,10] When $u = 1$, we get $g = \{\alpha^{1-\beta}\beta^\beta A[1 - \epsilon(0)]^{1-\beta}\phi(0)^{1-\beta} - \rho\}/\sigma$. This corresponds to the steady state growth rate in the absence of financial intermediation, which is in all likelihood negative. In fact, in a situation of 'financial autarky', the coefficient for the allocation of savings to investment is low whereas elasticity ϵ is high.

Now consider equation (15), expressing capital accumulation (KA curve). A reduction in the size of the financial sector (increase in u) leads to a drop in coefficient ϕ and a rise in elasticity ϵ. Consequently, g clearly decreases with u. The capital accumulation equation is therefore depicted by a falling curve, which asymptotically approaches the vertical axis. Figure 4.1 illustrates the possibility of two interior solutions corresponding to points A and B, in addition to the steady state corresponding to point C where there is no financial intermediation activity. Point C corresponds to a poverty trap. It is a steady state because, in the absence of labour in the financial sector ($u = 1$), the condition concerning the equalisation of wage rates in the two sectors has no reason to hold. The KA curve is therefore extended by the vertical segment $u = 1$. Equilibrium A is the stable one among the two interior solutions. To the left of point A, the real sector employs a relatively small part of the workforce since the marginal productivity of labour in this area is high (it is infinite when $u = 0$); the wage rate is higher in the real sector and the workforce tends to shift over to this sector.

This multiple equilibria result and the stability properties of points A and C representing the high-growth equilibrium (A) and the low-growth equilibrium (C), have significant implications as regards the possibility for the economy to take off. If the economy is to reach a long-run equilibrium with positive growth, the size of the financial intermediation sector has to exceed the critical threshold $1 - u^*$, which corresponds to the unstable equilibrium illustrated by point B. Therefore, if the development of the financial sector is initially weak, the economic growth process will be impeded, the financial sector will tend to shrink and the economy will converge to equilibrium C with no financial intermediation activity and negative growth.

THE ECONOMETRIC MODEL

In this part we study the empirical scope of the result concerning the existence of multiple endogenous growth equilibria in connection with the financial sector's initial level of development, using cross-country data on economic growth. This amounts to searching for groups of countries subject to different long-run growth regimes, depending on their position with respect to a financial development threshold. For the sake of completeness, this search of multiple equilibria is not based only on a financial development criteria. Multiple endogenous growth equilibria do not arise only from interaction between the financial sector and the rest of the economy. They may also appear in connection with the accumulation of human capital, in so far as the return to human capital accumulation is positively related to the economy's educational development.[11] We therefore attempted to take account of this possibility in the econometric model by separating the threshold effects arising from educational development from those which are in all likelihood attributable to financial development. Our search for such groups follows the general methodology of convergence studies and takes account of the possibility that statistical data might be generated by local convergence processes, rather than by a process of global convergence across economies. Such 'convergence clubs' are identified using the methodology put forward by Durlauf and Johnson (1992), by studying the stability of a β-convergence equation according to different sorting criteria for the entire sample of countries.

The first section presents the econometric model based on the β-convergence equation. In the second section we present some tests of the hypothesis of a sample split in connection with financial development and educational development. The third section identifies the 'convergence clubs' and studies their growth properties.

The econometric global convergence equation

We start with a β-convergence equation analogous to those estimated by Mankiw *et al.* (1992) and Barro and Sala-i-Martin (1992) in their studies on conditional convergence. For a given country, the relation concerning the gradual adjustment of y towards its long-run equilibrium is written as:[12]

$$\frac{d}{dt}\ln(y) = \lambda(\ln(y_i^*) - \ln(y)); 0 < \lambda < 1 \tag{16}$$

where y_i^* is the long-run equilibrium level of real income per unit of human capital associated with each one of the two equilibria determined in the preceding section.

By integrating this relation over a time interval $(0,T)$, setting $\ln(y_t) = \ln(Y_t) - \ln(H_t)$ and also setting $\ln(H_T) - \ln(H_0) = g_i^*T$, where g_i^* is a country's i steady state growth rate, the usual β-convergence equation is obtained:

$$\ln(Y_T) - \ln(Y_0) = (1 - e^{-\lambda T})\ln(H_0) - (1 - e^{-\lambda T})\ln(Y_0)$$

$$+ [g_i^*T + (1 - e^{-\lambda T})\ln(y_i^*)] \tag{17}$$

The negative association between $\ln(Y_0)$ and $\ln(Y_T) - \ln(Y_0)$ reflects convergence which is conditional on a set of control variables, determining the steady state growth rate and the equilibrium level of real income per unit of human capital. According to existing theoretical models and empirical evidence (see Levine and Zervos, 1993), possible control variables are government expenditures, variables proxying financial development, the degree of openness of the economy, and even the degree of political stability.

It should be noted, however, that with multiple endogenous growth equilibria the relationship between these control variables and the steady state growth rate (or the equilibrium value of y) is not necessarily linear. Therefore, a very different long-run growth rate g_i^* might correspond to a given level of a control variable, depending on whether the economy is converging to a high growth or to a low growth steady state equilibrium. In other words, equation (17) can be unstable across the entire sample of countries, making statistical search for global convergence inappropriate. Hence the reason for our econometric approach, which consists in analysing the stability of the β-convergence equation (17) across the entire sample with respect to two criteria: the initial level of development of the financial sector, and the initial level of educational development.

Our econometric specification of the convergence equation (17) is close in spirit to the equations estimated by Barro (1991).[13] In accordance with the equations already estimated by King and Levine (1993), our conditional convergence equation incorporates an indicator of the initial development level of the financial sector as an explanatory variable, measured by the ratio of money plus quasi-money to GDP (*MY*). In keeping with previous studies, our econometric equation uses the secondary school enrolment rate in the early 1960s as a proxy for the initial stock of human capital (*LSEC*). Furthermore, we use a measure of the degree of openness as an additional control variable for cross-country differences in long-run growth (OPEN). Openness is measured by the ratio of imports plus exports to GDP. Finally (in keeping mainly with Barro, 1991), we add as control variables for steady state growth:

(a) government consumption expenditures as a percentage of GDP (GOV);
(b) an indicator of political instability made up of the total number of coups d'état and revolutions over the period under examination (REVC); and
(c) a dummy variable which catches the positive effect of oil production on the average GDP growth rate (OIL).

The precise definition of the variables used in the estimation and data sources are given in the Appendix.

The results obtained with OLS are as follows (the *t* statistics in absolute value are given in brackets):[14]

$$LY_{i,1985} - LY_{i,1960} = 1{,}071 - 0{,}321LY_{i,1960} + 0{,}256LSEC_{i,1960} - 1{,}288GOV_i -$$
$$\phantom{LY_{i,1985} - LY_{i,1960} = } (5.34) \quad (4.53) \qquad\quad (4.36) \qquad\qquad (1.89)$$

$$- 0{,}312REVC_i + 0{,}244OIL_i + 0{,}269OPEN_i + 0{,}602MY_{i,1960} \qquad (18)$$
$$ (2.14) \qquad\quad (2.16) \qquad (2.94) \qquad\qquad (2.84)$$

$\bar{R}^2 = 0.438;$ SER $= 0.336;$ n. obs. 95

Skewness $= -0.42$ Kurtosis $= 3.31$ Jarque-Bera Normality test $= 3.17$

All estimated parameters have the expected signs and are significant, with the exception of the coefficient for government expenditure. The negative coefficient associated with the initial level of per capita GDP is similar to that estimated by Mankiw *et al.* (1992) and seemingly indicates the existence of a global convergence tendency across national economies. The strong influence of $MY_{i,1960}$ on the growth rate confirms King and Levine's (1993) well-known results. The finding of a positive influence of openness on long-run growth is in accordance with recent evidence on this subject.[15]

The global convergence hypothesis implies the structural stability of this equation across the entire sample of countries. Testing the multiple steady states hypothesis with respect to the development of the financial sector against the null hypothesis of global convergence of national economies amounts, therefore, to analysing the stability of the parameters in the estimated equation (18) across groups of countries with different initial financial development levels. The same applies to threshold effects associated with educational development.

Stability tests and break points identification

In order to examine the structural stability of regression (18) on the basis of an initial financial development criterion, we first sorted the entire sample of 95 countries[16] in decreasing order according to $MY_{i,1960}$. Successive F-tests on stability (Chow tests) were then carried out on the entire sample by moving the sample's break point forward by one observation each time. The results suggest that the previously estimated equation is unstable, with a significant break point of the sample at a level of the financial development indicator somewhere between 18.4 per cent and 20.5 per cent. This supports the assumption of a convergence process based on the existence of multiple steady states.

Looking for a clustering with respect to $MY_{i,1960}$ only may, however, imply a specification error, due to the possibility of threshold effects in connection with the accumulation of human capital. Because of the positive association between the financial sector's development level and the level of education, the structural instability observed above might in fact reflect an influence exerted by the level of education. Moreover, given the virtual importance of human capital as a driving force of economic growth, the threshold effects associated with the level of education might have the 'priority' over the threshold effects connected with the development of the financial sector. In other words, the development of the financial sector might initiate a growth process only after the accumulation of human capital has passed a certain threshold, ensuring a minimal return on productive investments. In view of these observations, we made another stability test of the convergence equation (18) by looking for break points with respect to the initial level of education, following the same procedure as for the case of financial development. The data clearly reveal the existence of one (or more) break point(s) in connection with the initial level of human capital accumulation, for levels of secondary school enrolment somewhere between 3 per cent and 11 per cent.

Given these results, the next step is to combine threshold effects associated with $MY_{i,1960}$ and $SEC_{i,1960}$, so as to be able to construct a 'convergence-tree diagram'. These convergence trees define groups of countries which share the

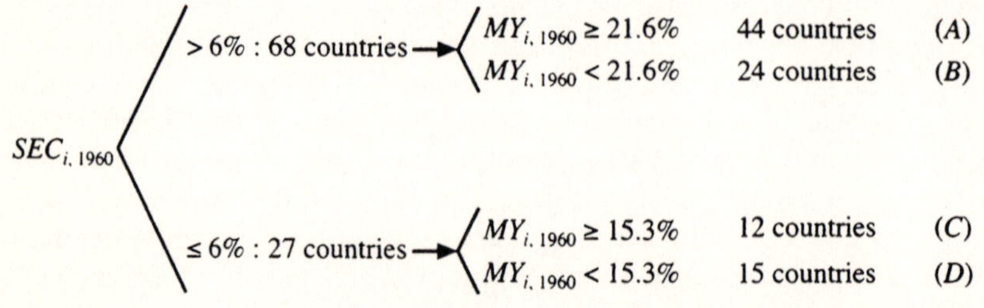

$SEC_{i,1960}$

$> 6\%$: 68 countries $\rightarrow$
$MY_{i,1960} \geq 21.6\%$ 44 countries   (A)
$MY_{i,1960} < 21.6\%$ 24 countries   (B)

$\leq 6\%$: 27 countries $\rightarrow$
$MY_{i,1960} \geq 15.3\%$ 12 countries   (C)
$MY_{i,1960} < 15.3\%$ 15 countries   (D)

Figure 4.2 Convergence-tree diagram

same growth behaviour. The method used to locate the nodes of the tree is documented in Berthélemy and Varoudakis (1995). Through this method, we identify a double clustering of the sample, based first on education and second on financial development, as shown in Figure 4.2.

Growth behaviour of convergence clubs

Parameter estimates

We have re-estimated the growth equation with a specific vector of parameters for each country group. All parameters are estimated in a single equation, but each independent variable is multiplied by dummies corresponding to the definition of our country groups. Through this method, we provide a consistent appraisal of the parameters and of their structural changes according to our clustering. After having skipped non-significant parameters, we obtain the estimates reported in Table 4.1.

Table 4.1 exhibits a number of original results which prove the relevance of our method. First of all the effect of the initial financial development changes drastically from one cluster to the other. In countries with well-developed financial systems, increasing the size of the financial sector effectively improves growth performances; on the contrary, in countries

Table 4.1 Regression with parameters differentiated by cluster
(dependent variable: $LY_{1985} - LY_{1960}$)

Country group/ independent variable	A	B	C	D
LY_{1960}	−0.38	−0.60	−0.49	−0.69
	(4.3)	(3.8)	(6.6)	(5.9)
MY	0.46	−2.40	5.05	−4.83
	(2.4)	(1.9)	(6.8)	(2.5)
LSEC	0.34	–	–	0.24
	(3.7)			(2.5)
GOV	−1.99	3.91	−5.35	2.89
	(2.5)	(5.4)	(5.8)	(1.9)
OPEN	0.28	−1.21	1.00	0.45
	(4.0)	(6.0)	(6.3)	(3.9)
REVC	–	−0.64	−1.59	–
		(3.5)	(7.4)	
OIL	–	0.31	0.67	0.72
		(3.3)	(10.2)	(2.8)
Intercept	1.41	1.14	−0.49	0.24
	(5.3)	(3.3)	(1.9)	(1.0)

Note: Adjusted R^2 = 0.74; SER = 0.23; Skewness = 0.11; Kurtosis = 3.92; Jarque-Bera Normality test = 0.17; In brackets: Student's t-statistics

which have a poorly developed financial system, a marginal increase of its size reduces growth performances. This result is consistent with the existence of a threshold effect related to financial development. Its interpretation is rather straightforward in our analytical framework: if the financial development is insufficient, increasing the size of the financial sector implies consumption of more resources in this sector, without significant improvement in capital mobilisation and efficiency, which are obtained only after a certain threshold is passed.

Second, we observe that education has a significant positive impact on growth principally in the group of relatively well-developed countries (A), indicating again a threshold effect. It seems to have a positive effect also in the poorest cluster (D), but this effect is not quite robust.

Third, the effect of government expenditure is positive for financially developed countries (clusters A and C), and negative for the others. Again, this result has a reasonable explanation in our framework. In the absence of a well-developed financial sector, the state sector may play a strategic role. Promoting economic growth requires the financing of long term and risky investment. Such investments cannot be financed by the market in the absence of a strong financial sector. Moreover, if savings are not well mobilised by the financial system, the state can substitute to it through collecting forced savings via taxation. It has also been observed that a privatisation policy may fail in the absence of a well-functioning financial sector. Demirgüç-Kunt and Levine (Chapter 11 of this volume) show such a result in a study covering ten experiences: Korea, Mexico, Chile in the 1980s and the Philippines, with reasonably well-developed financial sectors and successful public enterprise reforms, on one hand, and Chile in the 1970s, Egypt, Turkey, India, Senegal and Ghana with opposite performances on the other hand.

Last but not least, openness has a positive effect if the financial sector is reasonably well-developed. If not, it may have a negative impact (group B compared to group A), or a smaller effect than in countries with a reasonably well-developed financial sector (group D compared to group C). This result may be interpreted in a similar vein as the previous one. In the absence of a well-developed financial sector, it is difficult to move capital from one sector to the other, and investments tend to be self-financed. In case of trade shocks which affect comparative advantages, the economy reacts as in a specific factor model. Capital is rather immobile among sectors, and then becomes a specific factor. If one sector is positively affected by a shock, other sectors become negatively affected, and the rate of return of capital in these sectors decreases. This increases the probability of enterprise failure in these sectors. In the absence of a financial system which could transfer capital to profitable sectors, this implies capital destruction, and has a negative impact on growth. Such an effect can also be considered in the context of a trade opening policy: previously protected industries are adversely affected, and capital cannot be moved easily to sectors in which the economy has a comparative advantage.

It is clear that, in such a case, the gains from opening are much smaller than in an economy characterised by sectoral capital mobility.

Comparative performance of convergence clubs

In order to check whether the previously identified groups form distinctive 'convergence clubs', it is useful to examine the properties of their respective long-run growth paths. A first analytical approach consists of simply comparing the average performances of these groups over the estimation period from 1960 to 1985. Some useful indicators for this are given in Table 4.2: the average annual growth rate, the average investment ratio and the level of per capita income reached in 1985. We also included information on the initial levels of educational development, financial development, and the average openness degree of the economy.

The clearest split with respect to growth rates appears between groups A and B, comprising countries with sufficient human capital, which are located on either side of the financial development threshold. The same phenomenon can be observed when comparing the investment rates. Moreover, the intuition according to which the investment ratio is endogenously linked to financial development is borne out when the first two groups are compared: A countries have a significantly higher investment ratio than B countries. Nonetheless, there is also a substantial difference in investment ratios between the countries with high (A, B) and the countries with low (C, D) initial educational development. This would suggest that investment could also be influenced by the availability of human capital.

The observed difference in investment ratios between group A and group B countries is sufficient, on an accounting basis, to explain their difference in growth performance. Using a rough estimate of 3 for the capital/output ratio, the 4.2 percentage points increase in the investment ratio – associated with the

Table 4.2 Comparative performances of groups of countries

Group	Growth 1960–1985 (%)	INV/GDP (%)	GDP$_{1985}$,000\$/cap	MY$_{1960}$ (%)	SEC$_{1960}$ (%)	OPEN (%)
A	3.1	22.8	6.1	43.1	37.3	65.8
	>>	>	>>	>>	>>	>>
B	1.7	18.6	2.5	15.9	19.3	49.4
		>	>	<<	>>	
C	1.3	13.8	1.4	20.9	3.2	63.8
			>	>>		
D	0.7	12.6	0.5	10.7	2.4	43.3

Note: >> (>) significantly higher at the 1% (5%) level; << significantly lower at the 1% level

significantly higher level of financial development – exactly accounts for the 1.4 percentage points increase in the annual growth rate of per capita output. Conversely, the 0.4 percentage points difference in growth rates between groups B and C is too small to be accounted for by the 4.8 percentage points rise in the investment ratio, associated with an adequate level of educational development. This could be interpreted as evidence of a lower productivity of investment, due to the lack of a sufficiently developed system of financial intermediation (since B countries are, precisely, located below the financial development threshold).

This evidence suggests that group A is clearly a convergence club, made up of the countries that were, on the whole, on a high-growth path over the 1960–1985 period and had high per capita income at the end of the period. Group B presumably forms a second convergence club, corresponding to a *relative poverty trap*, incorporating countries with sufficient initial human capital to take off, but a financial system lacking in efficiency. This B group contains the vast majority of our sample's Latin American countries, which have a long-standing tradition of implementing financial repression policies. Nevertheless, one country in this group – Korea – is an exception. Korea is renowned for its successful take-off based on a set of suitable policies over the period from 1960 to 1985. One of these policies was moderate financial repression, which enabled capital to be allocated in a relatively efficient way and thereby to accelerate its development (see Stiglitz, 1994). Conversely, our group A actually contains a number of countries (essentially in the Middle East zone) which, although starting with favourable conditions with regard to financial development and education, failed to catch up with advanced OECD countries because of inadequate policies during this period and, presumably, also because of wars.

Group D apparently forms a convergence club around a poverty trap, comprising the countries that initially combine handicaps in the form both of low financial development and absence of human capital. It should be remembered that our econometric results for these countries contain only non-economic variables such as coups d'état or the availability of oil resources to explain growth, which definitely suggests the absence of growth dynamics. Group C is more difficult to characterise, since it contains countries whose take-off could definitely be impeded in so far as the educational development threshold has some priority over financial development. These countries could therefore be in a state of transition, either regressing towards the poverty trap formed by the D group countries, or drawn upwards to the B group (and, then, possibly to the A group) countries. To that end, 'good policies' would certainly be of substantial aid, since growth dynamics in C group countries are significantly influenced by finance, openness, and government spending (see Table 4.1).

CASE STUDIES

It is useful, in order to illustrate the theoretical development above, to look at specific country experiences. The OECD Development Centre has recently conducted a number of case studies on financial systems, resource allocation and economic growth, on which this section is based. Because of space limitation only two countries will be examined here: Taiwan and Senegal.[17] These two countries provide very different experiences over the last three to four decades, almost from total success to total failure. In each of these experiences, the financial sector behaviour, and financial policies, play a significant role.

Taiwan

Taiwan is a good example of a success story, which in the 1960s soon exhibited a virtuous circle of development, with a real GDP growth rate averaging over 8 per cent a year for four decades. Education developed rapidly in the post World War II period so that in the early 1960s educational attainment at the primary and secondary level was reasonably high. In our sample, this country belongs to the first group of countries, with secondary school enrolment rate equal to 27.5 per cent. The human capital stock was not that high in 1960, because the process only started in the 1950s; in terms of years of schooling, the active population had an education level of around three years in Taiwan in 1950. But it was high enough to permit huge progress in this sector, with the help of consistent policies; in 1990, the average number of years of education was around nine. As we shall show below, the financial sector has also played a role in the growth process of this country.

The Taiwanese economy was subject until 1989 to a certain degree of financial repression. Interest rates were controlled by the Central Bank of China (CBC) and set at below market rate level. Consequently, the CBC had to implement a credit rationing policy, which was based on selective credit allocation rules. Within this system, priority was given to export and manufacturing activities. This financial repression apparently has not hampered the economic growth of the Taiwanese economy. On the contrary, the Taiwanese example has been interpreted by Stiglitz (1994) and others as evidence of the existence of an optimal degree of financial repression, which has helped allocate savings to growth generating sectors through a directed credit policy.

From the beginning, the interest rate policy has been cautious and has provided positive incentives to save, and to invest savings in financial assets. Therefore, financial repression has not resulted in a contraction of the volume of activity of the financial sector, which has in fact been able to expand quite rapidly. The M2/GDP ratio was around 26 per cent in the early 1960s, and grew to 76 per cent in the early 1980s. More recently, after the financial liberalisation, this ratio has doubled, to reach 156 per cent in 1991–1993. Other indicators confirm this observation. The number of branches of financial institutions, which was already quite high in the early 1960s (there were 1,359 branches of financial institutions in 1961, i.e. 1.2 per 10,000 persons), grew to 2,830 (1.6 per 10,000 persons) in 1980 and 4,676 (2.3 per 10,000 persons) in 1993.

An important characteristic of the Taiwanese financial system is that it soon became fairly well-developed, in terms of numbers of branches, so that households always had easy access to financial institutions. Also, formal financial institutions, which collect a large share of available household funds, have been subject to a tight prudential control by the financial authorities, so that the safety and stability of the financial system have been quite high. This stability, in itself, may have improved the ability of the financial system to collect the household savings. Finally, the number of branches and the variety of financial institutions have also probably stimulated the competition for savings collection, and this competition may have played a major role as we have shown in our theoretical model.

Notwithstanding this recognised efficiency of the Taiwanese financial system in terms of savings collection, it is generally considered by Taiwanese economists as not very efficient in terms of credit allocation, at least as far as the formal system is concerned. Due to the financial repression policy, banks and other financial intermediaries have been quite conservative in their credit allocation decisions. These decisions have been based on collateral availability criteria rather than on project performance and expected profitability. As a consequence, a major part of credits has been allocated to large public or privately owned companies, while the most dynamic and efficient enterprises in Taiwan have been small and medium size enterprises.

One possible response of enterprises to the defects of financial institutions could have consisted in relying more heavily on capital markets to find financing. However, the domestic financial market was rather narrow until the 1980s, and direct financing, as compared with intermediated financing, played only a small role in the economic growth process. The bond market has always been very thin, due to transaction costs and complicated and slow issuance procedures. At the end of 1993, the volume of issued corporate bonds was less than 1 per cent of the total loans of financial institutions. A stock market was created in 1962, through the Taiwan Stock Exchange Corporation. In the 1980s, incentives were provided to develop this stock market through various tax exemption systems. As a result, a rise in the number of companies having issued stocks has increased steadily in recent years.

In fact, the significant alternative financing device has been the so-called informal financial system. The role of unregulated financing has been essential in credit allocation. During the period 1964–1992, its contribution to total enterprises and household borrowing can be estimated at 28 per cent, and this share was not far from 50 per cent in the early 1960s. As a matter of fact, the informal financial system has never been repressed in any way by the government, which has recognised its utility from the beginning. This informal financial system has therefore been able to provide small investors with financing instruments to which they could not gain access through the formal system, due to credit rationing.

Combined with the directed credit policy favourable to cheaper financing of export activities, this characteristic of the repressed Taiwanese financial system may have had a positive impact on growth. However, it should be stressed that the initial strength of the formal financial system was a necessary condition, to the extent that informal and formal financial systems are interlinked and complement each other.

The economy of Taiwan is therefore a good example of an economy initially endowed with a rather well-developed and diversified financial system, even though the formal financial system has been consistently repressed and has been moderately innovative. This financial system has been very efficient in terms of savings collection and has not been too inefficient in terms of credit allocation, therefore playing a significant role in the economic growth process. In recent years, the financial authorities have taken a step forward, through deregulation and opening to the world capital market; these policy changes have accordingly resulted in a significant development of the financial sector. It is presumably too early to assess their effects on future long-run growth. However, it is interesting to note that in recent years Taiwan has exhibited very high performances in terms of total factor productivity growth; until 1985 its productivity achievements were merely linked to a catch-up effect vis-à-vis the developed world, but it accelerated significantly afterwards. This evolution is due to a structural change in manufacturing production, with the creation of new technological industries such as, for example, the micro-computer industry. Such an endogenous structural adjustment, based on high venture capital investments, could not have appeared in the absence of a dynamic financial sector.

Senegal

Senegal had a very poorly developed education system when it gained independence (1960) and since then it has experienced a heavy demographic pressure (with a population growth rate of around 3 per cent per year) as well as a mismanaged education policy. These two factors have prevented Senegal from achieving good performances in this sector. At its level of GDP per capita, Senegal is still one of the weakest economies in terms of human capital availability. This defect has certainly been the major reason why Senegal has been locked in a poverty trap, characterised by a long-run decline in real GDP per capita.

Other obstacles to development exist in Senegal. One of these obstacles can be found in the marked under-development of the financial sector.

Apparently, Senegal was, at independence, a country where the financial sector was not too under-developed; in fact it figures in our clustering in the third group of countries for which financial development might have played a role in avoiding an absolute poverty trap. But if one looks at the historical evidence, it seems that this was not the case.

First of all, the initial level of the M2/GDP ratio was inflated by the presence, at independence, of a number of European (French) expatriates, with very different behaviour from the Senegalese in terms of financial savings. After the departure of some of these expatriates, the size of the financial sector, as measured by the M2/GDP ratio, declined quite rapidly, from 21 per cent in 1962 to around 13 per cent in 1966 (as compared with the threshold of 17 per cent which defines the boundary between the third and the fourth group of our clustering). Hence, had we decided to fix the initial conditions in 1965 rather than in 1960 in our econometric exercise, the conclusions of our clustering method would have been different for this particular country: it would have belonged to the fourth group.

The M2/GDP ratio does not, in fact, represent the weaknesses of the Senegalese financial system in the 1960s very well. From 1961 to 1973, Senegal had only five banks, four of which were inherited from the colonial period, and these banks operated mainly in Dakar, the capital of the country. In 1964, less than 2 per cent of the population had a bank or postal cheque account. Moreover, apart from the five banks, very few financial services were available. There was no financial market in Senegal. Finally Senegal had, and still has, significant informal financial activities, but these activities were not and are not efficient economically. They consist mainly of small operations by money lenders and rotating credit associations. These financial activities have very little economic development impact since they are oriented more towards consumption financing than towards investment financing. Of course, a major macroeconomic difference from Taiwan is that the Senegalese savings rate is very low; this characteristic bolsters the under-development of the financial sector and its lack of dynamism, in both its formal and informal segments.

Moreover, the banking structure was extremely concentrated, both because of the small number of competing banks and because the interventionist monetary policy implemented by the BCEAO, the regional Central Bank operating within the WAMU (West African Monetary Union) to which Senegal belongs, prevented almost any competition. The monetary policy was based on credit control through rediscount ceilings and liquidity ratios, and the ceilings were allocated to individual banks by a national monetary committee, the decisions of which were generally based on political grounds rather than on economic principles. As a consequence, banks had almost no chance or incentive to compete with each other.

The monetary policy was also characterised, as in other countries, by financial repression, with interest rate control and direction of credit to specific sectors or enterprises. From 1965 to 1985, the real interest rate on deposits was negative most of the time. On average, targeted borrowers also enjoyed negative real interest rates during this period.

In part because of the aforementioned deficiencies, and also because the BCEAO became more independent from France under a new convention with the former colonial power, the monetary policy was changed in 1973–1974, leading to a partial relief of financial repression. This new monetary policy had, for a while, a significant positive impact on Senegalese financial development. For example, the M2/GDP ratio increased to around 30 per cent at the beginning of the 1980s, and the number of banks tripled from five in 1961 to 15 in 1986. The number of bank branches increased from 40 in 1976 to 65 in 1987. Therefore, it seems that real progress had been made towards a deepening of the financial sector. However, this policy was short-lived, for a number of reasons.

First of all, money creation went too far, generating inflationary pressures, so that the central bank decided in 1980 to introduce a bank-by-bank credit ceiling as a further control of overall credit growth. This measure had a negative impact on competition among banks, not only in terms of credit allocation, but also in terms of fund collection, since there was no real money market in which banks could have invested excess liquidities. Second, no serious bank supervision was attempted; while the lack of supervision was not too much of a problem during the 1960s when the credit policy was totally conservative, it has, since then, been a major source of concern. A majority of banks accumulated bad loans and had rapidly deteriorating balance sheets. Third, the government of Senegal embarked at the beginning of the 1970s on a voluntarist policy in the industrial and agricultural sectors. It created a number of public enterprises and agencies, which supported the cost of policy interventions and, in turn, relied heavily on bank credit; in this way, the government indirectly increased monetary financing of its ambitious expenditure policy. Part, if not all, of these enterprises and agencies were poorly managed, so that they had increasing difficulties in paying back their bank loans. As a result of bad loans, eight banks (i.e. half of the banking sector!) became gradually distressed, and seven of them had been dismantled or had stopped operating in 1992.

Therefore, the only attempt to improve financial development in Senegal through reform of monetary policy in 1974 was a total failure. After drastic restructuring, the banking sector is now operating on a small scale, comparable to the situation in 1961; because the size of the Senegalese population has more than doubled since independence, the number of bank branches and other financial intermediaries (including the postal cheque service) per capita has declined. The number of branches of banks and other financial intermediaries is now around 0.2 per 10,000 persons, that is six times less than in Taiwan in 1961. Moreover, the Senegalese financial system offers few services to customers and markedly lacks competition, so that households have very few incentives to increase their financial savings, and enterprises face huge difficulties in obtaining bank loans, even for short term maturities. Because the banking industry has been so severely hit by the crisis of the 1980s, banks have gone back to a very conservative policy, as in the 1960s.

In a context of structural adjustment, these deficiencies of the Senegalese financial sector are very costly, because they create a major obstacle to firms which might want to adapt to the new situation created by the free market, outward oriented, policy. Small and medium size enterprises have many more difficulties than protected and larger enterprises in financing their projects, so that the structure of economic activities can hardly change and adapt itself to the new conditions created by the opening policy. This provides a good example of the possibly negative impact of openness in a financially under-developed economy. As a matter of fact, this incapacity of the modern sector to take advantage of economic opening has been responsible for the failure of the 'New Industrial Policy' launched in 1985 in the context of the structural adjustment policy, which had to be partially abandoned in 1989. This 'New Industrial Policy' had succeeded in driving a number of newly deprotected enterprises to bankruptcy, but had little effect in terms of enterprise creation. One of the main reasons for this lack of response by the private enterprises was their marked difficulty in finding loans, even for short term maturities.

CONCLUDING REMARKS

The interest in looking at interactions between financial development and economic growth has been renewed in recent years by the endogenous growth literature, in which all factors which can improve capital productivity may have an effect on the steady state growth rate of the economy. As a contribution to this literature, we have shown that the introduction of reciprocal interactions between the financial sector and the real sector into a growth model naturally reveals the possibility of multiple steady state equilibria of endogenous growth, characterised by different long-run growth rates.

To test this theoretical framework, it is necessary to go beyond the common exercise which consists in relating the GDP growth rate to an indicator of financial development in a linear equation. If multiple steady state equilibria exist, then the relation between these two variables must be non-linear, and must exhibit some kind of parameter instability. More precisely, each specific steady state equilibrium must be characterised by a specific growth equation. Of course, considerations that go beyond the relations between the financial development and growth need to be introduced. A number of different potential poverty traps have actually been identified in the literature, especially with respect to the accumulation of human capital. Neglecting these alternative sources of poverty traps could lead to an erroneous diagnosis of the reasons for an economy's stagnation or taking off, and consequently to biased estimates of growth equations.

Therefore, to make this kind of theory operational, it is essential to build convergence club tests that accept several possible origins for poverty traps. This is what we have attempted here, by identifying jointly, break points associated with educational development and financial development. Our results show that the former is a pre-condition for growth, while financial under-development may become a particularly severe obstacle to growth in countries where that pre-condition is satisfied. It is also shown that the optimal policies in other sectors, i.e. in our analysis trade policy and government expenditure policy, depend on the absence or presence of a reasonably well-developed financial system. For countries which belong to the financially under-developed categories, economic opening has no positive impact on growth, while government expenditure has a positive effect. These results show that the second-best policies in countries which have not succeeded in developing a financial system might be quite different from the policies usually advocated in a first-best framework.

Obviously, financial policies have an impact on this situation; therefore, in order to be able to pursue optimal policies in other areas it could be advisable to establish as early as possible policies favourable to financial development, which implies in particular avoiding a heavy repression of the financial system. Looking at the sequencing of policies, and at the effect of specific policies vis-à-vis the financial sector needs a more in-depth analysis of country experiences. In this respect, a cross-country econometric exercise cannot be informative enough. The third part of this chapter provided some historical evidence on this matter for two economies, namely Taiwan and Senegal, which have achieved very different economic growth rates in the past, and which have also pursued different, and time varying, financial policies. It is clear from these experiences that misguided financial policies may have an adverse impact on growth, even in a poor country like Senegal.

APPENDIX

List of variables

The countries are denoted by i and the years by t:

$LY_{i,t}$ = log of real per capita GDP.

$MY_{i,t}$ = money supply (broadly defined) as a percentage of nominal GDP.

$LSEC_{i,t}$ = log of the 12- to 17-year-old population's secondary school enrolment rate ($SEC_{i,t}$).

$OPEN_i$ = imports + exports as a percentage of GDP. Average over the period from 1960 to 1985.

GOV_i = government consumption expenditure as a percentage of GDP. Average over the period from 1960 to 1985 or the longest sub-period for which data are available.

$REVC_i$ = average annual number of coups d'état and revolutions over the period from 1960 to 1985.

OIL_i = dummy variable which takes on the value 1 for OPEC countries and some other oil-producing countries and 0 elsewhere.

The data source used (with the exception of the money supply and foreign trade variables) is the Summers and Heston cross-country data base, completed by Barro. The money supply data are taken from the IMF's IFS data base (sum of lines 34 and 35). *OPEN* is also constructed from IFS. Our equation is estimated over a sample of 95 countries, for which data are available on the money supply in the early 1960s. The estimation period runs from 1960 to 1985.

NOTES

1 This chapter originated as a paper produced in the context of a research programme of the OECD Development Centre on 'Financial Systems, Resource Allocation and Growth'. Helpful comments by Henk de Haan and Elmer Sterken are acknowledged.

2 See Berthélemy and Varoudakis (this volume, Chapter 1) for references.

3 In what follows the financial sector is confined to the banking system without making any attempt at analysing the distinct role of the development of stock markets in the growth process. The terms 'banking sector' and 'financial sector' are therefore used interchangeably.

4 For this point, we have adopted the modelling put forward by Barro *et al.* (1992).

5 Recall that the accumulation of the non-intermediated asset we termed human capital is not subject to threshold effects – as would probably be the case with a genuine human capital accumulation technology allowing the private profitability of human capital to increase with the average level of the economy's educational development. In the present context, such threshold effects could be taken into account by assuming that the efficiency coefficient in the production function (A) takes two different values $\bar{A}$ and $\underline{A}$ on both sides of a certain threshold $(H/K)^*$ of the human capital-to-physical capital ratio.

6 A similar formalisation is put forward, at the aggregate level, by Roubini and Sala-i-Martin (1992). They do not, however, endogenise the development of the financial sector.

7 Assume, for instance, that the financial intermediation technology is characterised by constant returns to scale with respect to savings and efficient units of labour: $\dot{K}_j = F(S_j, E \cdot v_j)$. Let $E = \delta S_j$, under the assumption of internal, productivity-enhancing, learning by doing ($\delta > 0$). We then get, $\dot{K}/S_j = F(1, \delta S_j v_j/S_j) = \dot{K}_j = \phi(v_j)S_j$.

8 On this subject, see also Fry (1988), Chapters 10 and 11.

9 The shape of the two curves has been confirmed by a numerical simulation of the model.

10 For illustrative reasons, the size of the financial sector in this figure is measured by $(1-u)/n$, which is an increasing monotonic function of $1-u$.

Table A4.1 List of countries for which data on money supply in early 1960s are available

Group A	Group B	Group C	Group D
Algeria	Argentina	Cameroon	Benin
Australia	Bolivia	Congo	Burundi
Austria	Brazil	Côte d'Ivoire	Ethiopia
Barbados	Chile	Gabon	Haiti
Belgium	Colombia	Gambia	Indonesia
Canada	Costa Rica	Ghana	Malawi
Cyprus	Dominican	Kenya	Mauritania
Denmark	Republic	Madagascar	Nepal
Egypt	Ecuador	Morocco	Niger
Fiji	El Salvador	Saudi Arabia	Nigeria
Finland	Guatemala	Senegal	Rwanda
France	Guyana	Zaire	Sierra Leone
Germany	Honduras		Sudan
Greece	Iran		Togo
Iceland	Israel		Zambia
India	Jamaica		
Iraq	Korea		
Ireland	Mexico		
Italy	Nicaragua		
Japan	Panama		
Jordan	Paraguay		
Malaysia	Peru		
Malta	Philippines		
Mauritius	Turkey		
Myanmar	Venezuela		
Netherlands			
New Zealand			
Norway			
Pakistan			
Portugal			
Singapore			
South Africa			
Spain			
Sri Lanka			
Sweden			
Switzerland			
Syria			
Taiwan			
Thailand			
Trinidad			
Tunisia			
United Kingdom			
United States			
Uruguay			

11   See Azariadis and Drazen (1990); Becker *et al.* (1990).
12   This equation corresponds to the usual log-linear approximation around the stationary equilibrium – see for instance Cohen (1992). The convergence speed λ depends on the production function parameters α and β. Moreover, this β-convergence equation is not incompatible with the possibility of the long-run growth rate being determined endogenously.
13   The equations estimated by Mankiw *et al.* (1992) incorporate the investment-to-GDP ratio as an explanatory variable of long-run growth. This ratio is supposed to approximate the savings rate, which is presumed to be constant. In our modelling, the equilibrium savings rate is an endogenous variable which depends on the level of financial development. The use of the investment-to-GDP ratio as an explanatory variable in (17) might, therefore, be misleading.
14   The standard deviation bias of the parameters, due to the heteroscedastic distribution of the errors, was corrected (in this one and the following regressions) using the White test.
15   See Lee (1993).
16   The complete list of countries is given in the Appendix.
17   The above-mentioned studies have been done by Sébastien Dessus, Jia Dong Shea and Mau Shan Shi (Taiwan), and Jean-Claude Berthélemy, Ann Vourc'h and Abdoulaye Seck (Senegal). Other case studies have been done, or are being done, on Argentina, Brazil, Tunisia and Kenya.

REFERENCES

Azariadis, C. and A. Drazen (1990), 'Threshold Externalities in Economic Development', *Quarterly Journal of Economics*, 105, pp. 501–26.

Barro, R.J. (1991), 'Economic Growth in a Cross Section of Countries', *Quarterly Journal of Economics*, 106, pp. 407–43.

Barro, R.J. and X. Sala-i-Martin (1992), 'Convergence', *Journal of Political Economy*, 100, pp. 223–51.

Barro, R.J., N.G. Mankiw and X. Sala-i-Martin (1992), 'Capital Mobility in Neoclassical Models of Growth', *Working Paper*, No. 4206, National Bureau of Economic Research.

Becker, G.S., K.M. Murphy and R. Tamura (1990), 'Human Capital, Fertility, and Economic Growth', *Journal of Political Economy*, 98, Supplement, pp. 12–37.

Berthélemy, J.C. and A. Varoudakis (1995), 'Thresholds in Financial Development and Economic Growth', *The Manchester School, Supplement*, 63, pp. 70–84.

——— (this volume), 'Models of Financial Development and Endogenous Growth: A Survey of Recent Literature'.

Cohen, D. (1992), 'Tests of the Convergence Hypothesis: A Critical Note', *Discussion Paper*, No. 691, Centre for Economic Policy Research.

Demirgüç-Kunt, A. and R. Levine (this volume), 'The Financial System and Public Enterprise Reforms: Concepts and Cases'.

Durlauf, S.N. and P.A. Johnson (1992), 'Local versus Global Convergence Across National Economies', *Discussion Paper*, No. 131, LSE Financial Markets Group.

Fry, M.J. (1988), *Money, Interest, and Banking in Economic Development*, Baltimore: The Johns Hopkins University Press.

King, R.G. and R. Levine (1993), 'Finance and Growth: Schumpeter Might Be Right', *Quarterly Journal of Economics*, 108, pp. 717–37.

Lee, J.W. (1993), 'International Trade, Distortions, and Long-Run Economic Growth', *IMF Staff Papers*, 40, pp. 299–328.

Levine, R. and S. Zervos (1993), 'Looking at the Facts: What we Know about Policy and Growth from Cross-Country Analysis', *American Economic Review*, 83, pp. 426–30.

Mankiw, G.N., D. Romer and D.N. Weil (1992), 'A Contribution to the Empirics of Economic Growth', *Quarterly Journal of Economics*, 107, pp. 407–37.

Romer, P.M. (1986), 'Increasing Returns and Long-Run Growth', *Journal of Political Economy*, 94, pp. 1002–37.

Roubini, N. and X. Sala-i-Martin (1992), 'A Growth Model of Inflation, Tax Evasion, and Financial Repression', *Working Paper*, No. 4062, National Bureau of Economic Research.

Stiglitz, J.E. (1994), 'The Role of the State in Financial Markets', *World Bank Economic Review*, 8, pp. 19–52.

5

FINANCIAL MARKETS AND ENDOGENOUS GROWTH

An econometric analysis for Pacific Basin countries[1]

Victor Murinde

INTRODUCTION

This chapter proposes and implements simple plausible frameworks for studying jointly some basic elements of endogenous growth that relate to the main aspects of the behaviour of financial markets. In particular, the paper makes several contributions. First, it extends a model of a Lucas (1988), Romer (1989) and Pagano (1993) type endogenous growth economy in order to incorporate the effects of financial markets. It is shown that endogenous growth partly derives from the behaviour of economic agents in the markets for credit (loans), bonds, and stocks (shares). Second, the model is estimated and tested on the fast-growing Pacific Basin countries in a novel application of the Zellner (1962, 1963) procedure in addition to the single equation OLS method. The novelty of the estimation and testing procedures is that we are able to study country-specific as well as cross-country features of financial markets and endogenous growth with reference to Hong Kong, Indonesia, Korea, Malaysia, the Philippines, Singapore and Thailand. Third, we also estimate and test other plausible models that can be regarded as alternatives to our basic model. Specifically, the models considered are the baseline as well as the augmented variants of the Dowrick (1992) growth accounting exercises and the Atje and Jovanovic (1993) model. In general, the country-specific as well as the cross-country evidence obtained sheds light, not only on the endogenous growth phenomena in the Pacific Rim, but also on the contribution of financial markets to the growth process. Finally, the paper offers scope for further research, in particular regarding estimation and testing of models of the King–Levine (1993) variety.[2]

The remainder of this chapter is organised as follows. The first section extends a basic model to incorporate financial markets' effects. Empirical issues and results relating to the model and its plausible alternatives are discussed in the second section, and the third section offers some concluding remarks.

FINANCIAL MARKETS AND ENDOGENOUS GROWTH

Following Pagano (1993), we derive an endogenous growth model of the following form:

$$g_{t+1} = A(I_t/Y_t) - \delta \tag{1}$$

where g = the growth rate at time $t + 1$; A = social marginal productivity of capital; I = investment; Y = income; δ = the rate at which capital depreciates per period. Equation (1) suggests that the growth rate is influenced by the social marginal productivity of capital and the investment–output ratio.[3]

Basing on (1), we aim to model financial market conditions which will enter the endogenous growth model. In general, equilibrium conditions require that gross savings (S_t) equals gross investment (I_t). However, it is reasonable to assume some leakage $(1 - \theta)$ out of the flow of savings during the intermediation process.[4] Hence:

$$\theta S_t = I_t \tag{2}$$

To bring out the details surrounding identity (2), we develop a simple model which adequately captures the main features of financial markets. The main financial markets are the credit (loans) market, the bond market and the stock market. The main participants in the markets are households, non-financial firms, banks, the government, and the overseas sector. The financial markets can be modelled in terms of the supply of and demand for funds or equivalently in terms of the demand for and supply of bonds and/or stocks. The firm (company) and government sectors are net demanders of funds (net suppliers of bonds and/or stocks). The household and overseas sectors are net suppliers of loanable funds and equivalently net demanders of bonds and/or stocks. The analogue is the saving function (for the supply of funds) as well as the investment function (for the demand for funds), as represented in identity (2).

In the light of identity (2), equation (1) can be re-written in steady states as follows:

$$g = A(s\theta) - \delta \tag{3}$$

where $s = S_t/Y_t$. Equation (3) suggests that at steady states, the growth rate is some composite of the social marginal productivity of capital, the proportion of total savings that are transformed into investment, and the savings ratio. In identity form, a re-interpretation of equation (3) can be written as follows:

$$g = \ln\theta + A + \ln s \qquad (4)$$

The idea is that the above identity represents a composite of the three main mechanisms by which financial markets may induce endogenous economic growth. We argue that the financial markets can raise θ, the proportion of savings channelled to investment; they may increase A, the social marginal productivity of capital; they may influence s, the private saving rate. Through these mechanisms, the growth rate of real income per capita rises and the conclusions of endogenous growth are upheld. The first mechanism is particularly important in the process of economic growth. Savings are transformed into investment in such a way that a dollar saved by households (S) generates less than a dollar of investment ($\theta S = I$). Thus, $(1 - \theta)$ represents a fraction that goes to financial markets; for example, the spread between lending and borrowing rate; and commissions and fees to securities and brokers. The leakages of financial resources $(1 - \theta)$ may also reflect the X-inefficiency of the financial markets. As $(1 - \theta)$ diminishes and θ rises, the growth rate of real income per capita increases. The second mechanism predicts that the financial markets increase the productivity of investment by playing an informational role and thus make it possible for economic agents to evaluate alternative investment projects (see Bencivenga and Smith, 1991). In addition, the financial markets make possible the sharing of consumers' liquidity risk through portfolio diversification, which is consistent with Levine (1991) and Saint-Paul (1992). Thus, producers specialise and raise their productivity, thereby increasing growth. In the third mechanism, it is hypothesised that the financial markets can also affect growth by altering the saving rate, S, that is consistent with the target investment – income ratio (I/Y). As the financial markets develop, saving may rise or fall; hence growth can expand or contract.

We consider the behavioural nature of the three variables which underpin the mechanisms in equation (4). First, we posit that the behaviour of θ is influenced by the returns in the bond market and the stock market; hence:

$$\ln\theta = \phi_0 + \phi_1 BR + \phi_2 SR + \mu \qquad (5)$$

where BR = return in the bond market; SR = return in the stock market; and μ = white noise error term. Equation (5) stipulates that the proportion of savings that gets transformed into investment depends on the returns in the bond market as well as the returns in the stock market, because savers aim to invest funds if they can attract high returns.[5] Second, the behaviour of A is directly influenced by the capital–output ratio, hence:

$$\ln A = \lambda_0 + \lambda_1 \ln(K/Y) + \epsilon \qquad (6)$$

where K/Y = capital–output ratio; and ϵ = white noise error term. Equation (6) stipulates that the social marginal productivity of capital is a function of the capital–output ratio. Third, the behaviour of the savings ratio is influenced by the rate of return on deposits and time savings by banks, as follows:

$$\ln s = \tau_0 + \tau_1 MR + u \qquad (7)$$

where MR = the return in the money market; and u = white noise error term. We substitute equations (5), (6) and (7) into (4) to obtain the following reduced form, after some re-arrangement:

$$g = \alpha_0 + \alpha_1(K/Y) + \alpha_2 MR + \alpha_3 BR + \alpha_4 SR + v \qquad (8)$$

where v = white noise error term. In terms of the financial markets, equation (8) relates to the role of the credit market, the bond market and the stock market. The argument is that the saving and investment activities in the financial markets induce economic growth endogenously.

EMPIRICAL ISSUES AND RESULTS

The basic model

We consider the basis for estimating and testing the predictions of the model given in equation (8). The idea is to write an empirical variant of the theoretical model that consists of observable variables which encapsulate the main predictions. The following empirical model is specified:

$$g_t = a_0 + a_1 \ln(I/Y)_t + a_2 MR_t + a_3 BR_t + a_4 SR_t + \epsilon_t \qquad (9)$$

We take g_t to represent the growth rate of real income per capita, as is consistent with the endogenous growth literature. The investment–output ratio (I/Y), rather than the capital–output ratio, is used by approximating the incremental capital stock concept whereby $I_t = K_t - (1 - \delta)K_{t-1}$. After all, the sample countries have more readily available and reliable data on the investment share than on the capital–output ratio. The MR variable is proxied here by the 3-month money market interest rate because this is the rate that ties down the short-run behaviour of savings. We take bond market returns (BR) to represent the bond market effect. The stock market returns variable (SR) represents the stock market effect. The variables are all in real rather than nominal terms. The Appendix explains how the empirical variables were manipulated.

The data set and empirical procedure

The testing ground for this study consists of the rapidly growing economies of the Pacific Basin. Of recent, the financial markets in the Pacific Rim have become the main centre of attention. They have attracted mainstream OECD countries' banks, pension funds, and other money-management outfits.[6] One of the compelling reasons to invest in these financial markets is that they are based on economies which are growing at about 5–10 per cent per year compared with 2.8 per cent in the US and 2.5 per cent in the UK. In addition, manufacturing is shifting from the OECD countries to the Pacific Rim. Our motivation is to investigate the contribution of the financial markets to the phenomenal growth rates that have been experienced by these economies. The sample Pacific Rim countries we consider are Hong Kong, Indonesia, Korea, Malaysia, the Philippines, Singapore and Thailand.

Annual time series data were used spanning the period 1960 to 1993; quarterly data were only available for some of the variables. However, for some of the sample economies the limited time span of data on stock markets meant that the sample period had to be adjusted accordingly during estimation and testing. Most of the data were retrieved from Datastream. Additional data, especially of a demographic nature, were obtained from the ILO (1993) and the United Nations (1992) as well as previous volumes of these publications.

In what follows, we employed two estimation and testing procedures. The first procedure applied the standard ordinary least squares (OLS) to estimate the model on each sample country in a country-specific spirit. To carry out a search process for the lag structure of the model, we tested for the sign and significance of each of the RHS in its current (time t) as well as its one-period lagged (time t–1) form. By deleting the insignificant and perversely signed variables, we were able to obtain a more parsimonious specification of the model that is country-specific. Thus, the approach started with a very general model which was then simplified progressively based on the data available, as suggested by Sargan and Hendry, according to Maddala (1992, p. 3). The interesting aspect of the procedure was that we were able to explore the country-specific growth and financial market experience, as a departure from earlier endogenous growth models which relied on cross-section analysis.

The second procedure applied the Zellner estimation method in order to capture simultaneously country-specific and cross-country experiences. The Zellner method takes the system of 'seemingly unrelated regression equations' (SURE) as a single large equation to be estimated. The idea therefore is to estimate each equation simultaneously on Hong Kong, Indonesia, Korea, Malaysia, the Philippines, Singapore and Thailand. For example, equation (9) has seven variants, but the seven equations are related through the non-zero covariances associated with the error term. Thus, the country-specific (= 7 countries) variants of equation (9) are linked for estimation purposes to reflect the relationship between the error terms. By stacking the N(= 7) observations for Hong Kong (HK), Indonesia (I), Korea (K), Malaysia (M), the Philippines (P), Singapore (S) and Thailand (T), we write the seven variants in vector-matrix notation as follows:

$$
\begin{bmatrix} g_{HK} \\ g_I \\ g_K \\ g_M \\ g_P \\ g_S \\ g_T \end{bmatrix} =
\begin{bmatrix}
Z_{HK} & 0 & 0 & 0 & 0 & 0 & 0 \\
0 & Z_I & 0 & 0 & 0 & 0 & 0 \\
0 & 0 & Z_K & 0 & 0 & 0 & 0 \\
0 & 0 & 0 & Z_M & 0 & 0 & 0 \\
0 & 0 & 0 & 0 & Z_P & 0 & 0 \\
0 & 0 & 0 & 0 & 0 & Z_S & 0 \\
0 & 0 & 0 & 0 & 0 & 0 & Z_T
\end{bmatrix}
\begin{bmatrix} a_{HK} \\ a_I \\ a_K \\ a_M \\ a_P \\ a_S \\ a_T \end{bmatrix} +
\begin{bmatrix} \epsilon_{HK} \\ \epsilon_I \\ \epsilon_K \\ \epsilon_M \\ \epsilon_P \\ \epsilon_S \\ \epsilon_T \end{bmatrix} \quad (10)
$$

where, using the notation C ($=$ country) $= HK, I, K, M, P, S, T$ for Hong Kong, Indonesia, Korea, Malaysia, the Philippines, Singapore and Thailand, respectively; g_c = a vector of dependent variables; Z_c = an NXM matrix of right-hand side variables with M being the number of right hand side variables in equation (9); a_c = an MX1 vector of coefficients; ϵ_c = a vector of regression errors.

The statistical assumptions are that the errors for each country taken separately conform to the standard linear regression model but each country's errors may also be correlated with the contemporaneous errors of the other countries. This is given by the following:

$$E(\epsilon_c \epsilon_c') = \sigma_{cc} I \quad (11)$$

and

$$
E \begin{bmatrix} \epsilon_{HK} \\ \epsilon_I \\ \epsilon_K \\ \epsilon_M \\ \epsilon_P \\ \epsilon_S \\ \epsilon_T \end{bmatrix}
(\epsilon_{HK}' \ \epsilon_I' \ \epsilon_K' \ \epsilon_M' \ \epsilon_P' \ \epsilon_S' \ \epsilon_T') = \Sigma \otimes I \quad (12)
$$

where

$$
\Sigma = \begin{bmatrix}
\sigma_{HKHK} & \sigma_{HKI} & \sigma_{HKK} & \sigma_{HKM} & \sigma_{HKP} & \sigma_{HKS} & \sigma_{HKT} \\
\sigma_{IHK} & \sigma_{II} & \sigma_{IK} & \sigma_{IM} & \sigma_{IP} & \sigma_{IS} & \sigma_{IT} \\
\sigma_{KHK} & \sigma_{KI} & \sigma_{KK} & \sigma_{KM} & \sigma_{KP} & \sigma_{KS} & \sigma_{KT} \\
\sigma_{MHK} & \sigma_{MI} & \sigma_{MK} & \sigma_{MM} & \sigma_{MP} & \sigma_{MS} & \sigma_{MT} \\
\sigma_{PHK} & \sigma_{PI} & \sigma_{PK} & \sigma_{PM} & \sigma_{PP} & \sigma_{PS} & \sigma_{PT} \\
\sigma_{SHK} & \sigma_{SI} & \sigma_{SK} & \sigma_{SM} & \sigma_{SP} & \sigma_{SS} & \sigma_{ST} \\
\sigma_{THK} & \sigma_{TI} & \sigma_{TK} & \sigma_{TM} & \sigma_{TP} & \sigma_{TS} & \sigma_{TT}
\end{bmatrix} \quad (13)
$$

and $\otimes$ is a Kronecker product symbol.

Equation (9) can be written more compactly in obvious notation as follows:

$$g = Za + \epsilon \tag{14}$$

It is possible to estimate this equation directly using the Zellner method. In this case, the estimated coefficients would be given by:

$$a_1 = (Z'(\hat{\Sigma}^{-1} \otimes I)Z)^{-1} (Z'(\hat{\Sigma}^{-1} \otimes I)g) \tag{15}$$

where $\hat{\Sigma}$ is any consistent estimation of Σ.

We can then test the information in the cross-country covariance matrix using the following:

$$N(Ln\sigma_{HKHK} + Ln\sigma_{II} + Ln\sigma_{KK} + Ln\sigma_{PP} + Ln\sigma_{SS} + Ln\sigma_{TT} - Ln|\Sigma^*|) \tag{16}$$

where the σ_{c1c2} are the ordinary least squares residual variances and Σ^* is the Zellner residual covariance matrix. In this problem, the Σ^* is asymptotically distributed as X^2 (7). We also re-estimate each equation by imposing valid restrictions. This enables us to test for the equality of parameters across countries. For example, is the impact of (I/Y) equal across all the seven countries? The restrictions also offer a further increase in efficiency.

If we specify our endogenous growth model as $g = Y_{i\theta i} + X_{i\delta i} + v_i$, then we can compare the determinants of economic growth in all the seven countries by taking the following:

$$g_{HK}(n) = Y_{HK}(n)\theta_{HK} + Y_{HK}(n-1)\mu_{HK} + X_{HK}(n)\delta_{HK}$$
$$+ X_{HK}(n-1)\phi_{HK} + v_{HK}$$

$$\vdots \tag{17}$$

$$g_T(n) = Y_T(n)\theta_T + Y_T(n-1)\mu_T + X_T(n)\delta_T + X_T(n-1)\phi_T + v_T$$

The equality of coefficients across the seven countries in respect of short-run effects may be represented by the following hypotheses, for any j:

$$\begin{aligned}
\theta_{HKj} &= \theta_{Ij} = \theta \dots = \theta_{Tj} \\
\mu_{HKj} &= \mu_{Ij} = \mu \dots = \mu_{Tj} \\
\delta_{HKj} &= \delta_{Ij} = \delta \dots = \delta_{Tj} \\
\phi_{HKj} &= \phi_{Ij} = \phi \dots = \phi_{Tj}
\end{aligned} \tag{18}$$

Restrictions of this kind have the following general form:

$$R\beta = r \tag{19}$$

These restrictions were tested using the following asymptotically valid F-test statistic:

$$F(d, 7N - M) = (R_i\beta_i - r_i)' (R_i S_i R_i')^{-1} (R_i\beta_i - r_i)/d \tag{20}$$

where d is the number of restrictions. We accept the null hypothesis that the restrictions are true, at the 5 per cent level of significance if:

$$F < F^{0.05} (d, 7N - M) \tag{21}$$

An interesting aspect of the endogenous growth story that is captured by our estimation and testing procedure is that, essentially, we recognise that the sample countries have distinct structural differences which endogenously influence their growth rates, but the countries do also have commonalities engendered by the externalities of being in one economic region, such as knowledge and ideas, as is stylised in the new growth theory. In this light, the novelty of using Zellner's procedure is that we are able to estimate equation (9) simultaneously for all the sample countries. Features of the seven economies, that are common on the one hand or distinctive on the other, can be identified by examining the sign, magnitude and significance of the coefficients in the estimated equation. In addition, common but unknown features of the seven economies affect the error terms in the model and these are utilised in Zellner's procedure to improve the efficiency of the estimates. Another novel idea is that pooling the data enables us to obtain more efficient estimates of the coefficients whose signs and magnitudes are at issue in the endogenous growth literature.

Estimation and testing results for the basic model

Table 5.1 reports the country-specific estimation and testing results for the basic model.[7] In general, the diagnostic test results indicate that country-specific estimation results are well-behaved. The independent variables demonstrate high explanatory power on the dependent variable, suggesting that these variables adequately explain the behaviour of the endogenous growth rate of real income per capita; it is also shown that the data statistically fit the model and are consistent with predicted behaviour. It is found that the investment–income ratio significantly induces growth in real income per capita in Malaysia and Thailand only. This finding suggests that the two countries enjoy increasing returns to scale in an endogenous growth sense. However, a significant but inverse relationship is found between the investment–income ratio and the growth rate of real income per capita in

Table 5.1 Country-specific estimation results for the baseline model

Equation (9)	Indonesia	Korea	Malaysia	Philippines	Singapore	Thailand
Constant	.223	.106	.168	.062	−.185	.159
	(5.910)	(3.157)	(6.233)	(2.539)	(−1.794)	(4.616)
$\ln(I/Y)_t$	–	−.086	.086	–	–	.050
		(−2.315)	(5.046)			(2.366)
$\ln(I/Y)_{t-1}$	−.177	–	–	−.076	−.202	–
	(−3.933)			(−11.344)	(−2.469)	
MR_t	–	–	−.740	–	.008	−.008
			(−6.454)		(.735)	(−2.309)
MR_{t-1}	−.074	.038	–	−.151	–	–
	(−6.182)	(1.090)		(−11.516)		
BR_t	−.001	−.098	–	–	−.016	.005
	(−3.433)	(−3.196)			(−.591)	(.913)
BR_{t-1}	–	–	.127	−.602	–	–
			(6.649)	(−16.837)		
SR_t	–	.013	–	–	.061	.019
		(1.384)			(1.676)	(1.008)
SR_{t-1}	.098	–	.011	−.004	–	–
	(2.677)		(1.36)	(−2.125)		
SER	.002	.029	.003	.001	.027	.015
R^2 (adj)	.747	.50	.992	.998	.487	.735
DW	1.583	2.77	2.53	2.488	2.272	1.599

Notes: $\ln(I/Y)_t$ = logarithm of the investment–income ratio; MR = 3-month money market interest rate; BR = bond market return; SR = stock market return; SER = standard error of regression; DW = Durbin–Watson statistic; t-values in parentheses below the estimated coefficients

Indonesia, Korea, the Philippines and Singapore. This finding is at variance with the endogenous growth story with respect to the three Pacific Basin countries.

The money market interest rate variable bears a negative sign and is statistically significant for Indonesia, Malaysia, the Philippines and Thailand. This result suggests that a rise in the money market interest rate may not be consistent with stable growth in real income per capita in the four countries. However, a positive but non-significant relationship is found between the money market interest rate and the growth rate of real income per capita in Korea and Singapore. Overall, therefore, we can generalise that a sharp rise in the money market interest rate can retard or leave unchanged, rather than improve, the growth rate of real income per capita in the sample Pacific Basin economies. It is also found that a positive relationship exists between bond market returns and the growth rate in real income per capita for Malaysia and Thailand only. The relationship is significantly negative for Indonesia, Korea, the Philippines and Singapore. The evidence thus suggests that, except for Malaysia and Thailand, an increase in bond market returns adversely affects

Table 5.2 Zellner estimation results for the baseline model

Equation (9)	Indonesia	Korea	Malaysia	Philippines	Singapore	Thailand
Constant	.201	.115	.172	.072	−.158	.185
	(5.78)	(3.264)	(7.243)	(2.819)	(−2.113)	(5.196)
$\ln(I/Y)_t$	−.163	−.082	.091*	−.085	−.201	.091
	(−4.219)	(−2.719)	(5.672)	(−9.317)	(−2.581)	(5.672)
MR_t	−.115	.065	−.738	−.102	.109	−.009
	(−7.488)	(1.621)	(−7.549)	(−11.850)	(1.076)	(−3.122)
BR_t	−.010*	−.113	.120	−.612	−.010*	.026
	(−5.165)	(−3.847)	(6.923)	(−14.190)	(−5.165)	(1.365)
SR_t	.094	.012	.048*	−.005	.048*	.011
	(3.530)	(2.472)	(2.536)	(−2.847)	(2.536)	(1.355)
R^2 (adj)	.89	.73	.96	.97	.59	.89
DW	1.94	2.01	2.26	2.23	2.00	1.99

Notes: $\ln(I/Y)_t$ = logarithm of the investment–income ratio; MR = 3-month money market interest rate; BR = bond market return; SR = stock market return; DW = Durbin–Watson statistic; t-values in parentheses below the estimated coefficients; *indicates that cross-country equality restrictions were accepted for the respective parameter estimates using the Zellner procedure

the endogenous growth process in the sample Pacific Basin countries. In terms of parameter sign, the predicted role of the stock market in the growth process is borne out by the evidence for all the sample Pacific Rim countries except the Philippines. However, only the estimated coefficients for Indonesia are statistically significant with the predicted sign.

The Zellner estimation and testing results are reported in Table 5.2. Equality restrictions were imposed on some parameters and these were accepted for some countries. The investment ratio is shown to induce growth in real income per capita in Malaysia and Thailand. The two countries accept an aggressive restriction imposed on the parameter estimate for the investment-output ratio. This suggests similarities in the increasing returns to scale enjoyed by those economies in an endogenous growth sense. However, the rest of the sample countries bear a negative and significant relationship between the investment–output ratio and growth in real per capita income.

The Zellner estimation results for the money market interest rate variable are similar to those obtained using the OLS method. The results also indicate a negative relationship between bond market returns and growth in real income per capita for Indonesia, Korea, the Philippines and Singapore. In particular an equality restriction is accepted for Indonesia and Singapore, indicating the common role played by the bond market in these economies. Although the estimates for Malaysia and Thailand do not accept an equality restriction, it is shown that bond market returns may rise consistently with economic growth. The predicted role of the stock market in the growth process is borne out by the evidence for all the sample economies, except the Philippines. An equality restriction is accepted for Malaysia and Singapore, suggesting the common influence of the market on economic growth in these economies.

In general, therefore, both the country-specific and cross-country evidence bring out the crucial importance of the investment–output ratio and (somewhat weakly for the country-specific results) the stock market in the Pacific Basin sample economies. However, the money market effect and the bond market effect are not validated for all the sample economies. Our findings lend weak support to the results in other studies which attribute the phenomenal growth rates of Pacific Rim countries to the emerging financial markets (see, for example, Murinde and Eng, 1994).

Further empirics: growth accounting exercises

Growth theory, old or new, is concerned with investigating the determinants and patterns of the process of economic growth. The motivation is to isolate the factors responsible for differences in growth performance, and identify the variables which can best underpin the existing patterns of growth. We therefore extend this study in order to carry out some growth accounting exercises on the sample economies.[8] We call upon a model used by Dowrick (1992) on a cross-section of 113 countries. To obtain estimates of the growth accounting parameters for each sample economy, we run a regression of GDP growth (y) on initial labour productivity $(\ln (Y/L_0))$,[9] the growth rate of the workforce (W) and the investment rate (INV), thus:

$$y_t = \delta_0 + \delta_1 \ln(Y/L_0)_t + \delta_2 W_t + \delta_3 INV_t + e_{1t} \qquad (22)$$

The hypotheses being tested are associated with the parameters. The first parameter (δ_1) is predicted to bear a negative sign; it measures the extent of technological catch up. Thus, in the above equation, δ_1 is signed to reflect that there is a tendency for multi-factor productivity growth to be inversely related to the initial level of productivity. The coefficient δ_2 estimates the elasticity of output with respect to employment; and δ_3 captures the marginal productivity of gross capital investment.

As in the baseline model, we apply both country-specific estimation and testing procedures as well as the Zellner (1962) method. Cross-country restrictions were imposed, and where plausible, these were retained to show cross-country commonalities. The country-specific results are presented in Table 5.3 while the Zellner-based results are summarised in Table 5.4.

The results in Tables 5.3 and 5.4 suggest that the model is well-behaved empirically and can be used to explain economic growth in the sample Pacific Rim countries. Clearly, for almost all the sample countries nearly 50 per cent of the variance in the growth rate is explained.

Table 5.3 Country-specific estimation results for the growth accounting exercises

Equation (22)	Hong Kong	Indonesia	Korea	Malaysia	Philippines	Singapore	Thailand
Constant	1.412	.014	.137	−.385	−.740	.104	.069
	(3.578)	(.853)	(3.306)	(−3.104)	(−3.082)	(2.143)	(1.245)
$\ln(Y/L_0)_t$	−	.063	−	.055	−	−	.007
		(2.199)		(3.023)			(.397)
$\ln(Y/L_0)_{t-1}$	−0.319	−	−.028	−	−.219	−.014	−
	(−3.612)		(−1.152)		(−3.151)	(−1.000)	
W_t	−	−	.141	.486	−	−	−
			(1.138)	(4.397)			
W_{t-1}	−.049	.079	−	−	−.316	.648	.214
	(−2.016)	(.525)			(−1.236)	(4.518)	(1.516)
INV_t	.960	−	−.175	−	.214	−	.239
	(4.887)		(−1.880)		(2.4420)		(3.759)
INV_{t-1}	−	.0718	−	−.016	−	−.078	−
		(1.452)		(−.371)		(−1.267)	
SER	.022	.0114	.037	.015	.035	.0198	.018
R^2 (adj)	.772	.450	.038	.758	.393	.558	.585
DW	1.546	2.59	1.632	2.461	1.269	1.753	1.626

Notes: Sample period: 1970–1992, annual observations; *t*-values are in parentheses below the estimated coefficients; $\ln(Y/L_0)$ = initial labour productivity; W = the growth of the labour force; INV = investment rate; SER = standard error of regression; DW = Durbin–Watson statistic

The OLS country-specific results show a negative but significant relationship between initial labour productivity (ln (Y/L_0)) and GDP growth (y) for Hong Kong, Korea, the Philippines and Singapore; as predicted, these results show evidence of a technological catch-up. A positive relationship is found for Indonesia, Malaysia and Thailand; contrary to the prediction of the model, these countries do not accept the prediction of technological catch-up.

On the basis of the Zellner cross-country results, cross-country equality restrictions on the parameter estimates are accepted for Hong Kong and Singapore; this suggests that there is common technological catch-up experience shared by these economies. In general, the cross-country parameters estimated for the sample countries (excluding Thailand) range from −0.025 (Korea) to −0.218 (Hong Kong and Singapore). As regards the growth of the workforce (W), the country-specific as well as the cross-country evidence shows strong significance across the whole sample, except for Hong Kong and the Philippines. The elasticity of output with respect to employment is highest in Singapore (0.633) and Malaysia (0.480), while it is lowest in Indonesia (0.092).

As regards the marginal productivity of gross capital investment, the country-specific results for Hong Kong, the Philippines, Indonesia and Thailand show a positive and statistically significant relationship between GDP growth and the investment rate. However, the findings for Korea,

Table 5.4 Zellner estimation results for the growth accounting exercises

Equation (22)	Hong Kong	Indonesia	Korea	Malaysia	Philippines	Singapore	Thailand
Constant	.923	.015	.141	−.374	−.701	.102	.064
	(3.762)	(1.021)	(3.644)	(−3.009)	(−3.659)	(2.816)	(1.622)
$\ln(Y/L_0)_t$	−.218*	.060	−.025	.053	−.216	−.218*	.018
	(−4.003)	(2.310)	(−2.167)	(2.998)	(−3.661)	(−4.003)	(1.172)
W_t	−.051	.092	.130	.480	−.313	.633	.211
	(−2.533)	(.724)	(2.178)	(4.522)	(−5.140)	(4.207)	(−2.032)
INV_t	.906	.091	−.171	−.021*	.213	−.021*	.235
	(4.125)	(1.570)	(−2.004)	(−2.113)	(3.750)	(−2.113)	(4.113)
R^2 (adj)	.79	.55	.69	.86	.78	.79	.49
DW	2.03	2.01	1.96	2.15	2.09	2.08	1.98

Notes: Sample period: 1970–1992, annual observations; $\ln(Y/L_0)$ is the initial labour productivity; W_t is the growth of the labour force; INV_t is the investment rate; DW is the Durbin–Watson statistic; t-values are in parentheses below the estimated coefficients; *indicates that cross-country equality restrictions were accepted for the respective parameter estimates using the Zellner procedure

Malaysia and Singapore do not accept the predicted positive relationship. The Zellner-based evidence suggests that the marginal productivity of gross capital investment is high in Malaysia, Hong Kong, Indonesia, the Philippines and Thailand. In general, the evidence suggests that technological catch-up, the growth of the workforce and the marginal productivity of gross capital investment are important determinants of economic growth in the sample Pacific Basin economies.

We augment equation (22) with a stock market variable, namely the rate of change of the aggregate stock price index (*SP*) in each country, thus:

$$y_t = h_0 + h_1 \ln(Y/L_0)_t + h_2 W_t + h_2 W_t + h_3 INV_t + h_4 SP_t + e_{2t} \qquad (23)$$

We used a conventional F-test to accept or reject the additional variable *SP*. The equation is then estimated in a country-specific spirit and also by using the Zellner procedure. The results are reported in Tables 5.5 and 5.6.[10] In general, the country-specific results of the augmented growth accounting model (Table 5.5) are consistent with those obtained in the baseline growth accounting exercises (Table 5.3). Both the country-specific and cross-country results for the augmented model (equation 23) show that the stock market effect is strongly significant across the whole sample of Pacific Basin countries, except Indonesia and the Philippines. Common stock market effects are found for Hong Kong and Malaysia; and the parameter estimate (0.05) is close to the one obtained for Singapore (0.06). The highest parameter estimates are obtained for Korea and Singapore, which result is consistent with the stock market activity in these countries.

Table 5.5 Country-specific estimation results for the growth accounting model augmented with a stock market effect

Equation (23)	Hong Kong	Indonesia	Korea	Malaysia	Philippines	Singapore	Thailand
Constant	1.179 (4.093)	−.001 (−.373)	.106 (1.955)	.104 (.878)	−1.001 (−3.714)	.068 (1.288)	.099 (2.197)
$\ln(Y/L_0)_t$	–	–	–	.012 (.668)	–	–	.016 (1.225)
$\ln(Y/L_0)_{t-1}$	−.272 (−4.270)	−.026 (−5.307)	−.020 (−.655)	–	−.305 (−3.799)	−.004 (−.280)	–
W_t	–	–	.142 (1.090)	–	–	.34 (2.365)	–
W_{t-1}	−1.899 (−2.715)	.057 (2.655)	–	3.174 (6.795)	−.404 (−1.083)		.240 (2.177)
INV_t	1.013 (7.420)	−.057 (−3.323)	−.070 (−.609)	–	.182 (2.783)	–	.201 (4.069)
INV_{t-1}	–	–	–	−.134 (−3.712)	–	.029 (.508)	–
SP_t	.084 (2.348)	–	.067 (1.778)	–	−.012 (−1.060)	.057 (2.894)	.0298 (2.692)
SP_{t-1}	–	−.002 (−3.805)	–	.042 (3.149)	–	–	–
SER	.015	.177E-03	.038	.0066	.014	.023	.0134
R^2 (adj)	.89	.959	.096	.942	.744	.407	.782
DW	2.315	2.30	1.865	2.462	2.65	2.112	2.480

Notes: Sample period: 1970–1992, annual observations; t-values are in parentheses below the estimated coefficients; $\ln(Y/L_0)$ = initial labour productivity; W = the growth of the labour force; INV = investment rate; SP is the rate of change of the aggregate stock price index; SER = standard error of regression; DW = Durbin–Watson statistic

On the technological catch-up variables, cross-country equality restrictions are accepted for Korea and Malaysia. The influence of the growth of the workforce is shown to be significant across the sample, with cross-country equality restrictions being accepted for Malaysia and Singapore. The investment rate variable yields equal parameter estimates for Indonesia and Korea, and for the Philippines and Thailand; in general, the results are consistent with those earlier obtained in the non-augmented (Dorwick) model. In general, by including the stock market variable, the model is able to explain a higher proportion of the variance in growth rates in the sample economies (0.49 to 0.86 in the baseline model compared to 0.58 to 0.91 in the augmented model). In addition, the influence of technological catch-up, growth of the workforce and the investment rate seem to come out clearly once the stock market effect is integrated into the analysis.

Table 5.6 Zellner estimation results for the growth accounting model augmented with a stock market effect

Equation (23)	Hong Kong	Indonesia	Korea	Malaysia	Philippines	Singapore	Thailand
Constant	.965	−.006	.103	.101	−.960	.61	.100
	(4.248)	(−1.008)	(2.152)	(1.374)	(−3.229)	(1.787)	(2.594)
$\ln(Y/L_0)_t$	−.212	−.021	−.024*	−.024*	−.312	−.010	−.012
	(4.970)	(−6.442)	(−2.713)	(−2.713)	(−3.865)	(−1.542)	(−1.877)
W_t	−.814	.039	.115	.432*	−.391	.432*	.230
	(−3.32)	(2.640)	(1.373)	(5.145)	(−2.008)	(5.145)	(2.818)
INV_t	.904	−.063*	−.063*	−.124	.196*	.023	.196*
	(7.625)	(−3.154)	(−3.154)	(−3.870)	(4.148)	(1.515)	(4.148)
SP_t	.050*	−.006	.063	.050*	−.016	.062	.026
	(3.492)	(−3.904)	(1.914)	(3.492)	(−1.527)	(3.274)	(2.968)
R^2 (adj)	.91	.58	.78	.88	.78	.90	.68
DW	2.01	2.06	2.04	2.03	2.11	2.03	2.24

Notes: Sample period: 1970–1992, annual observations; *t*-values are in parentheses below the estimated coefficients; $\ln(Y/L_0)$ = initial labour productivity; W = the growth of the labour force; INV = investment rate; SP = the rate of change of the aggregate stock price index; DW = Durbin–Watson statistic; *indicates that cross-country equality restrictions were accepted for the respective parameter estimates using the Zellner procedure

Further evidence: the Atje–Jovanovic (AJ) model

We also follow Atje and Jovanovic (1993) to investigate empirically the effect of stock market development on the growth rate of economic activity. The AJ empirical equations can be written as follows:

$$g_t = q_0 + q_1 W_t + q_2 \ln(I/Y)_t + q_3 S_t + v_{1t} \qquad (24)$$

where S is the ratio of the annual value of all stock market trades to GDP; v_{1t} is a white noise error term. To control for the component of growth predicted on the basis of lagged growth, we also used the following equation:

$$g_t = c_0 + c_1 W_t + c_2 \ln(I/Y)_t + c_3 S_t + c_4 g_{t-1} + v_{2t} \qquad (25)$$

The regressions were run for the sample Pacific Basin countries using annual series 1970–1992. The results obtained from estimating the above two equations are reported in Table 5.7 for the country-specific estimates and Table 5.8 for the Zellner-based estimates. It is shown that in all the sample countries, the empirical coefficient of W is large, except for Korea. This result is generally consistent with the earlier findings by Atje and Jovanovic (1993). However, unlike in the previous work, the investment–income variable is statistically significant for almost all the sample economies. It is further found that the stock market variable is important in inducing growth in all the

Table 5.7 Country-specific estimation results: stock markets and endogenous growth in the AJ context

Equation (25)	Hong Kong	Indonesia	Korea	Malaysia	Philippines	Singapore	Thailand
Constant	.108	.018	.021	−.120	−.349	.002	.076
	(3.074)	(6.203)	(.466)	(−2.409)	(−8.290)	(.189)	(1.995)
W_t	.554	1.567	.193	–	.475	.215	–
	(4.089)	(22.053)	(1.228)		(1.592)	(1.193)	
W_{t-1}	–	–	–	.900	–	–	.254
				(5.940)			(1.638)
$\ln(I/Y)_t$	.192	–	–	−.100	–	–	.036
	(2.989)			(−2.119)			(1.627)
$\ln(I/Y)_{t-1}$	–	−.009	.033	–	−.182	−.216	–
		(−9.581)	(10.995)		(−8.801)	(−.756)	
SP_t	.065	−.004	–	–	.053	.0559	.043
	(1.079)	(−3.839)			(7.546)	(2.703)	(2.912)
SP_{t-1}	–	–	−.019	.006	–	–	–
			(−1.461)	(2.044)			
g_{t-1}	.126	.014	.367	.834	.140	.293	.321
	(.539)	(.303)	(1.163)	(1.780)	(1.408)	(1.529)	(1.447)
SER	.026	446E-03	.042	.009	.0097	.024	.019
R^2 (adj)	.654	.91	.50	.90	.96	.44	.59
Durbin-h	−.810	−.279	−.49	–	−1.35	−.57	−.50

Notes: Sample period: 1970–1992, annual observations; t-values are in parentheses below the estimated coefficients; $\ln(I/Y)$ = logarithmic investment–output ratio; W = the growth of the labour force; SP = the ratio of the annual value of all stock market trades to GDP; g_{t-1} = one-year lagged growth of per capita income; SER = standard error of regression; DW = Durbin–Watson statistic

sample economies; specifically the coefficients range from 0.014 to 0.086, suggesting that raising S by a percentage point will raise the growth rate by 0.014 (or 0.086) percentage points in the case of the lower (upper) estimates. Even after including one-period lagged growth, we found that the coefficient of S is still statistically significant. However, the stock market variable for Indonesia changes sign. Basically, in comparison with our earlier results in the baseline models, this finding illustrates what happens when emphasis shifts from broad financial markets (as in the baseline model) to human capital (as BR and MR are excluded in equation 25). In general, the results confirm a large effect of stock markets on economic growth. In terms of policy relevance, the results are encouraging for those countries which aim to develop their stock markets as a means of speeding up their economic growth.

Table 5.8 Zellner estimation results: stock markets and endogenous growth in the AJ context

Equation (25)	Hong Kong	Indonesia	Korea	Malaysia	Philippines	Singapore	Thailand
Constant	.106	.012	.020	−.198	−.342	.001	.072
	(3.650)	(6.198)	(.999)	(−2.416)	(−8.110)	(1.133)	(2.004)
W_t	.408	.824	.275*	.275*	.240	.186	.180
	(5.122)	(22.158)	(4.367)	(4.367)	(1.929)	(1.311)	(2.964)
$\ln(I/Y)_t$	.180	−.112*	.030	−.082	−.112*	−.202	.022
	(3.366)	(−9.508)	(11.524)	(−3.380)	(−9.508)	(−1.265)	(1.841)
SP_t	.086*	−.001	−.022	.014	.050	.086*	.044
	(2.904)	(−3.980)	(−2.542)	(2.486)	(8.520)	(2.904)	(3.210)
g_{t-1}	.112	.010	.302	.613	.134	.203	.302
	(1.100)	(.856)	(1.828)	(2.522)	(1.890)	(2.294)	(2.446)
R^2 (adj)	.72	.76	.88	.78	.70	.79	.58
DW	2.11	2.01	2.24	2.16	2.00	2.02	2.19

Notes: Sample period: 1970–1992, annual observations; *t*-values are in parentheses below the estimated coefficients; $\ln(I/Y)$ = logarithmic investment–output ratio; W = the growth of the labour force; SP = the ratio of the annual value of all stock market trades to GDP; g_{t-1} = one-year lagged growth of per capita income; DW = Durbin–Watson statistic; *indicates that cross-country equality restrictions were accepted for the respective parameter estimates using the Zellner procedure

CONCLUSION

This paper brings together two of the latest innovations in development economics, namely new growth theory and the current interest in financial markets, in order to study the determinants of economic growth. As a starting point, the paper extends a model of a Lucas (1988), Romer (1989) and Pagano (1993) type endogenous growth economy in order to incorporate the effects of financial markets. In the selection of sample countries on which to test the model, the exceptional growth record of the Pacific Basin countries, and the high performance of their financial markets, make the selection of these countries particularly relevant. The model is therefore estimated and tested on Hong Kong, Indonesia, Korea, Malaysia, the Philippines, Singapore and Thailand in a novel application of the Zellner (1962, 1963) procedure in addition to the OLS method. However, the results lend weak support to the model's theoretical prediction that the financial markets have played a significant role in the growth process of these economies; of the three financial markets studied, only the stock market seems to play a significant role.

We extend the study to carry out empirical growth accounting exercises by applying the Dowrick (1992) model in the first instance, and then augmenting the model with a financial market argument. Our initial findings underline the importance of technological catch-up, the growth of the workforce as well as the rate of gross investment in the growth process of the sample Pacific Basin economies. In the subsequent estimates, when the stock market variable is integrated into the analysis, it is found that the stock market effect is important. This result therefore emphasises the role of the stock market, as earlier obtained in the basic endogenous growth model.

We further extend the analysis using the Atje and Jovanovic (1993) endogenous growth model. The model is estimated and tested with and without a lagged endogenous variable. The results confirm that stock markets have a substantial effect on economic growth.

Although it initially uses a baseline AK endogenous growth model and therefore side-steps the stylised optimisation-based and overlapping genera-tions type of analysis, this chapter applies alternative frameworks and a novel estimation and testing procedure that depart from the recent cross-section work. In terms of policy relevance, the results lend support to those countries which aim to develop their stock markets in order to speed up their economic growth.

APPENDIX

Description of variables and data set

The data are drawn from a sample of seven countries: Hong Kong, Indonesia, Korea, Malaysia, the Philippines, Singapore and Thailand. For each country, we retrieved annual as well as quarterly data; we went as far back as the data would permit. Thus, the sample countries, for which empirical evidence is reported, was determined on the basis of data availability rather than any other priors.

g_t = growth rate of real income per capita; let Y be real income (= GDP constant prices), let P be population, then $g_t = \ln (Y/P)_t - \ln (Y/P)_{t-1}$.

$\ln(I/Y)$ = the investment–output ratio, where I is real investment.

MR = the 3-months money market real interest rate.

BR = bond market effect; we considered four proxies, in real terms, namely (i) bond market returns; (ii) interest rate on government bonds; (iii) market value of government bonds; (iv) private sector claims on the (central) government.

SR = stock market effect; we considered two proxies, in real terms, namely a quantity value and a price value, respectively: (i) real stock market value to real income ratio: $SR_t = \ln(SV/GDP)_t$, where SV = real stock market value; (ii) alternatively stock market returns $SP_t = \ln S_t - \ln S_{t-1}$ where S is the stock price index.

y = the real GDP growth rate, i.e. $y = \ln Y_t - \ln Y_{t-1}$ where Y is real GDP (= constant prices).

$\ln(Y/L_0)$ = initial labour productivity; this is computed as follows: let Y be real GDP (constant prices); L_0 be the *mean* of the labour force (employment figures) for the sample period, then compute $\ln(Y/L_0) = \ln Y_t - \ln L_0$.

INV = the real investment rate; this is computed as follows: $\ln (I/Y)_t - \ln (I/Y)_{t-1}$, however, where there are negative values in the data, the investment rate should be taken straight as the investment–income ratio, i.e. (I/Y) – without natural logarithms.

W = the real growth rate of the workforce; let L be employment (= labour); $W = \ln L_t - \ln L_{t-1}$.

SP = the rate of change of the aggregate stock price index; let S be the aggregate stock price index; $SP_t = \ln S_t - \ln S_{t-1}$ (equivalent to definition (ii) of SR; thus SP and SR do not appear in the same equation).

NOTES

1 Constructive criticisms and suggestions on earlier versions of this chapter were received from Niels Hermes, Robert Lensink, Harry Garretsen, Subrata Ghatak, as well as participants in a conference at the University of Leicester (25–26 March 1994), a workshop at the University of Groningen (7–9 December 1994) and a FABER-G seminar at Cardiff Business School. Partial financial support from Cardiff Business School and excellent research assistance from Claire Morgan and Leo Ssebweze are acknowledged. Errors are mine.

2 The main limitation of the baseline model is that it derives from a simple AK structure. The criticism is that we side-step intertemporal optimisation and overlapping generations analysis. However, while these issues fall outside the scope of the theoretical part of the chapter, the extension of the empirical part to other alternative models offers insight into the main current issues in this area.

3 The model in equation (1) incorporates a key argument in the endogenous growth literature namely that $K_t = HK_t + PK_t$, where K = capital, HK = human capital, and PK = physical capital. Investment (I) is then generated from the capital stock in an incremental fashion, i.e. $I_t = K_{t+1} - (1 - \delta)K_t$.

4 Thus, θ denotes the fraction of savings that is actually intermediated into investment, and $(1 - \theta)$ is the fraction of savings that leaks out of intermediation. Assuming a leakage coefficient of 0.1 $(1 - \theta = 0.1; \theta = 0.9)$, 90 per cent of total savings is intermediated into investment, while 10 per cent leaks out of intermediation.

5 We assume that investors are not ultra risk averse; the expected returns in these markets are therefore matched by corresponding risk in a portfolio analysis sense.

6 See Murinde (1994) for a survey of the financial markets in the Pacific Rim.

7 Due to lack of sufficient observations on the bond market effect (BR), Hong Kong is excluded from the results for equation (9).

8 We believe that growth accounting exercises are important in isolating the immediate features and patterns of economic growth in the Pacific Rim economies.

9 See Appendix 1 on the derivation of the empirical counterpart of the initial labour

productivity variable ($\ln (Y/L_0)$). Essentially, L_0 is the mean value of the series obtained as follows:

$$L_0 = (1/N) \sum_{i=0}^{n} L_{t-1}$$

L_0 is then used to scale Y at each time period.

10 It is possible to follow Dowrick and Nguyen (1989, p. 1025) and Dowrick (1992) in using the parameter estimates to decompose observed rates of growth of per capita GDP into four elements: the amount attributable to technological catch-up; the amount due to investment; the amount due to stock market activity; and the amount due to the workforce.

REFERENCES

Atje, R. and B. Jovanovic (1993), 'Stock Markets and Development', *European Economic Review*, 37, pp. 632–40.

Bencivenga, V.R. and B.D. Smith (1991), 'Financial Intermediation and Endogenous Growth', *The Review of Economic Studies*, 58, pp. 195–209.

Dowrick, S. (1992), 'Technological Catch Up and Diverging Incomes: Patterns of Economic Growth 1960–1988', *The Economic Journal*, 102, pp. 600–10.

Dowrick, S. and D. Nguyen (1989), 'OECD Comparative Economic Growth 1950–85: Catch Up and Convergence', *American Economic Review*, 79, pp. 1010–30.

International Labour Office (ILO) (1993), *Yearbook of Labour Statistics*, Geneva: International Labour Office.

King, R.G. and R. Levine (1993), 'Finance and Growth: Schumpeter Might be Right', *Quarterly Journal of Economics*, 108, pp. 717–37.

Levine, R. (1991), 'Stock Markets, Growth and Tax Policy', *The Journal of Finance*, 46, pp. 1445–65.

Lucas, R. (1988), 'On the Mechanics of Economic Development', *Journal of Monetary Economics*, 22, pp. 3–42.

Maddala, G.S. (1992), *Introduction to Econometrics*, second edition, New York: Macmillan.

Murinde, V. (1994), 'Emerging Stock Markets: A Survey of Leading Issues', *Discussion Paper Series in Financial and Banking Economics*, Cardiff Business School, FABER/94/3/1/B.

Murinde, V. and F.S.H. Eng (1994), 'Financial Development and Economic Growth in Singapore: Demand-following or Supply-leading?', *Applied Financial Economics*, 4, pp. 391–404.

Pagano, M. (1993), 'Financial Markets and Growth: An Overview', *European Economic Review*, 37, pp. 613–22.

Romer, P. (1989), 'Capital Accumulation and the Theory of Long Run Growth', in R. Barro (ed.) *Modern Business Cycle Theory*, Cambridge, Mass.: Harvard University Press, pp. 51–127.

Saint-Paul, G. (1992), 'Technological Change, Financial Markets and Economic Developments', *European Economic Review*, 36, pp. 763–81.

United Nations (1992), *Statistical Yearbook for Asia and the Pacific*, Bangkok: UN Economic and Social Commission for Asia and the Pacific.

Zellner, A. (1962), 'An Efficient Method of Estimating Seemingly Unrelated Regression Equations and Tests of Aggregate Bias', *Journal of American Statistical Association*, 57, pp. 348–68.

—— (1963), 'Estimators for Seemingly Unrelated Regression Equations: Some Exact Finite Samples', *Journal of American Statistical Association*, 58, pp. 977–92.

6

FINANCIAL INDICATORS AND ECONOMIC EFFICIENCY IN DEVELOPING COUNTRIES

Matthew O. Odedokun

INTRODUCTION

Financial policies in all ramifications constitute a means for promoting economic growth in developing countries. To best manipulate the financial variables to this end requires a knowledge of whether and how the variables affect growth. In very broad terms, they can be described to influence growth either by changing the quantum of investible resources or by affecting the efficiency of utilisation of a given quantum of resources or both. A few studies have examined the effects that financial variables have on the quantum of investible resources as an indirect way of identifying their effects on growth. A few others have directly related the financial indicators to growth. However, far fewer studies have investigated their effects on the efficiency of resource utilisation and this is one of the reasons which informs the present study, which endeavours to examine this relatively neglected aspect. In addition, we extend our consideration to a broader range of financial variables.

Specifically, the study examines the effects of most macroeconomic variables that are financial in nature on economic efficiency which is, as usual, proxied by the incremental output–capital ratio. Those variables tested for include real interest rate; inflation rate; directed credit schemes; exchange rate policies; financial depth, etc. Annual data over the early 1960s to late 1980s for about 80 developing countries are employed in conducting the tests.

The remaining discussion in this chapter is organised into four sections. In the first, we present a brief survey of the literature and also describe the framework of the study. Further methodological details about the present study are given in the following section, while the empirical results are presented and evaluated in the third. The last section is a summary and conclusion, after which there is an appendix on the data and countries covered by the study.

MATTHEW ODEDOKUN

BRIEF LITERATURE REVIEW AND FRAMEWORK OF THE STUDY

A brief review of the literature

At the theoretical level, various financial policy variables have been postulated as determinants of economic growth. Using the terminologies adopted by Gupta (1987), the theorists can be classified into two categories, viz.: the *financial structuralist* and *financial repressionist* schools. The former comprises those who contend that the quantity of financial variables and its composition affect economic development. Thus, factors like financial deepening (e.g. aggregate financial assets in relation to GDP) and the composition of the aggregate financial variables are posited to be the relevant financial factors on economic growth. Such a position can be traced to the writings of Gurley and Shaw (1960); Goldsmith (1966, 1969); Patrick (1966); and Porter (1966). The financial repressionist school, on the other hand, comprises those who emphasise price variables as the more relevant financial factors on growth. Accordingly, they contend that financial liberalisation in the form of a 'realistic' real interest rate and real exchange rate constitute a way of promoting economic growth, while financial repression, especially in the form of below-equilibrium real interest rate and domestic currency over-valuation, retard growth.[1] This idea is of relatively recent origin and was first put forward by McKinnon (1973) and Shaw (1973), so that it is often referred to as (a part of) the McKinnon–Shaw hypothesis. Without altering the basics, further refinements of the hypothesis are contained in the subsequent theoretical writings of Galbis (1977); Mathieson (1980); Fry (1987); etc. Also, more recently, Greenwood and Jovanovic (1990); Bencivenga and Smith (1991); Levine (1991, 1992); Saint-Paul (1992); Roubini and Sala-i-Martin (1991, 1992); and King and Levine (1993a) have presented various theoretical frameworks that link financial activities or services with steady state growth.

What is common to the structuralist and the repressionist schools, as well as the above mentioned recent group of studies that seek to link financial services with steady state growth, is the idea that the major channel through which financial variables affect economic growth is by enhancing the productive or efficient utilisation of investible resources. This is accomplished through the role of the higher level of financial development (e.g. financial deepening) and also financial liberalisation in facilitating screening of investment projects; migration of funds to more efficient investors, etc.

At the empirical level, a number of tests of the *financial structuralist* hypothesis have been carried out. Some of these use a case study approach of relating the cross-country growth rate with the level of financial development, e.g. McKinnon (1973) and Lanyi and Saracoglu (1983). Others consist of a 'mere' examination of the direction of causation between

116

economic growth and the level of financial intermediation, notable among which are those reported by Fritz (1984); Jung (1986); and Odedokun (1992a). Some others like Wallich (1969); Jao (1976); Wai (1980); Gelb (1989); Lanyi and Saracoglu (1983); and Ghani (1992) adopted the approach of testing for financial intermediation variables (e.g. financial depth and growth of financial variables) in the economic growth equations. Other recent empirical studies that are based on a similar approach include De Gregorio and Guidotti (1992); Gertler and Rose (1991); King and Levine (1993a, 1993b, 1993c); and Roubini and Sala-i-Martin (1991). Some of the major limitations inherent in this approach of including financial intermediation variables in economic growth equations are as we have highlighted in Odedokun (1992b, p. 26). These limitations have recently prompted a direct evaluation of their effects on economic efficiency (rather than on economic growth) by including them as regressors in the equations for incremental output–capital ratio, e.g. Gelb (1989); King and Levine (1992); and Odedokun (1992b). In virtually all the studies, the financial intermediation variables have been found to have positive association with economic growth and/or economic efficiency.

The *financial repressionist* proposition too has received a number of empirical tests. An example is Lanyi and Saracoglu's (1983) case study approach whereby interest rate regimes in various developing countries are classified into real interest rate with positive, slightly negative, and significantly negative values and then this classification is related to economic growth across countries. A similar case study approach has also been reported by Khatekhate (1988) but – unlike in Lanyi and Saracoglu (1983) where a positive relationship was reported – was unable to detect any relationship between the real interest rate and economic growth. Others like Fry (1980); Gelb (1989); Agarwala (1983); Ghani (1992); King and Levine (1992); and Seck and El Nil (1993) adopt the approach of including the real interest rate in economic growth equations and they typically report a positive relationship. But due to many reasons which have been identified by Gelb (1989, pp. 7–9), the likely reverse causation from economic growth to real interest rate poses a problem in identifying the effect of the latter, if any, on the former in such studies. This and similar other econometric problems have encouraged the practice of directly testing for the effect of real interest rate on economic efficiency by relating it to incremental output–capital ratio – instead of or in addition to economic growth. Such studies include those reported by Agarwala (1983); Fry (1979, 1981, 1984); Asian Development Bank (1985); Gelb (1989); King and Levine (1992); and Odedokun (1992b). Most of them have reported a positive association between incremental output–capital ratio and real interest rate. Very few studies, on the other hand, have tested for the other aspect of the *financial repressionist* proposition, viz. concerning the effect of exchange rate valuation either on economic growth or on economic efficiency. The effects of real interest rate have received the greatest empirical attention. All the same, there exists a number of studies on this relatively neglected aspect. For instance, Agarwala (1983) included a measure of exchange rate distortion in his composite index of economic distortions which he relates to both economic growth and incremental output–capital ratio. Gallagher (1991) adopted a similar approach by including a parallel market exchange rate premium as a proxy for exchange rate distortion in the composite 'rent-seeking' variable included in the estimated equation for incremental output–capital ratio. Similarly, Ghani (1992) included the black market exchange rate premium in the estimated economic growth equations. In the same vein, Odedokun (1992b) constructed a dummy variable for real exchange rate distortion that is included as a regressor in the incremental output–capital ratio equations. In virtually all these studies, negative relationships have been reported between the exchange rate distortion index and economic growth or incremental output–capital ratio.

Framework of the present study

The present study is an attempt to explore further the effects of the financial variables, especially by widening the scope of the financial factors tested for. The scope of the test is, however, limited to effects on economic efficiency – rather than being extended to economic growth at large – due to space considerations, coupled with the conceptual and econometric problems of conducting the tests on economic growth directly.

Before we discuss the financial variables considered in the study, we wish to define formally our measure of economic efficiency and state the relationship between it and economic growth. Economic efficiency is conventionally proxied by incremental output–capital ratio (IOCR), defined as a change in output in relation to investment spending.[2] Economic growth, on the other hand, is often measured or defined as the growth rate of total output or real GDP. This is the same notion adopted here. Thus, the relationship between economic growth and efficiency can be described by equation (1) below:

$$dY/Y = (dY/dK)(dK/Y) = IOCR(dK/Y) \qquad (1)$$

where dY/Y = economic growth or rate of change of output; dY/dK = incremental output–capital ratio or IOCR, dY being the incremental output and dK being the investment spending or incremental capital; and dK/Y = the share of investment spending (dK) in total output (Y).

In other words, economic growth is the product of economic efficiency (or IOCR) and the ratio of investment to GDP. Thus, the channels of the effects of financial variables on economic growth have to be through changes in investible resources (dK/Y) or via changes in productiveness or efficiency of the resource utilisation (IOCR) or both. As pointed out earlier, the emphasis of the theory is via efficiency. We are now going to discuss the financial variables whose effects on IOCR are tested for in the study.

Financial intermediation variables

We test for the effects of financial intermediation or development. Because alternative measures do not produce the same or similar results, we report the effects of a wide range of such alternatives. One of these is the ratio of wide money stock M_2 to GDP or M_2/GDP ratio. This is further analysed into the ratio of narrow money stock M_1 to GDP (or M_1/GDP ratio) and the ratio of quasi-money stock or M_2 minus M_1 to GDP – or $(M_2–M_1)$/GDP ratio. In addition, the effects of the growth rate of each of these three ratios, viz.: m_2/gdp; m_1/gdp; and $(m_2–m_1)$/gdp, where the expressions in lower-case letters signify the growth rate of the ratios in the capital letters, are also tested for.[3] Following Gelb (1989), we also express the first-difference of each of these three monetary variables in relation to domestic savings SAV, just as we express them in relation to GDP viz.: ΔM_2/SAV; ΔM_2/GDP; ΔM_1/SAV; ΔM_1/GDP; $(\Delta M_2–\Delta M_1)$/SAV; $(\Delta M_2–\Delta M_1)$/GDP.[4]

By further analysing the wide money stock M_2 into its two components – M_1 and quasi-money stock – in the manner just described, we wish to see whether there is any difference in the effects of the two components on efficiency. This is informed by the fact that while M_1 is basically for facilitating transactions and exchange, quasi-money is primarily supposed to fulfil the role of store of value or the wealth motive, suggesting that the efficiency effect of the former should be greater than that of the latter on *a priori* grounds. To further test for any difference in their effects, we employ the ratio of the former to the latter, i.e. $M_1/(M_2–M_1)$ – and also the growth rate of this ratio, denoted by the expression in lower-case letters, viz.: $m_1/(m_2–m_1)$, as regressors in the equations.

Finally, we also employ a variable from the asset side of the banking system's balance sheet, as opposed to liability-side variables that we have so far been discussing. This is the ratio of outstanding claims on the private sector CR from the banking system to GDP (or CR/GDP ratio). Alternatively, we also experiment with the growth rate of this ratio as well as the flows of the real credit ΔCR in relation to real GDP (i.e. ΔCR/GDP) and also in relation to real domestic investment expenditure, INV (or ΔCR/INV), which roughly indicates the fraction of investment expenditure financed through credit flows from formal financial institutions.[5]

Government borrowing from private financial institutions

It is often contended (e.g. see Fry, 1988) that government borrowing from private financial institutions does not only reduce financial development but also hampers the efficiency of the financial system. Such borrowings take many forms, including compulsory holding of goverment debt instruments and reserve requirements. Thus, we test for the effect of the ratio (GB/TB) of government borrowing from domestic deposit money banks – denoted by GB – to the outstanding claims of the deposit money banking system's total stock of lendings (to both private and public sectors) – denoted by TB. We also test for the effect of growth rate of this ratio, denoted by the expression in lower-case letters: gb/tb. We would expect this to have a negative effect on economic efficiency.

Directed credit schemes

Directed credit policies have often been claimed to affect the efficiency of credit utilisation, e.g. in the World Bank's *World Development Report 1989*, where this occurs and a number of case studies are discussed. However, no previous study – except Odedokun (1992b) – has formally tested for the effect of this factor on economic growth or efficiency, presumably because of the difficulty of identifying a proxy for it. What we do in the present study is to follow the approach adopted in Odedokun (1992b) by proxying the extent or prevalence of directed credit programmes by the development bank lendings in relation to overall economic activity. As it has been pointed out by the World Bank (1989, p. 57), 'development finance institutions have been perhaps the most common means of directing credit'. Specifically, we test for the outstanding stock of lendings to the private sector by the development banking system DEV in relation to GDP, i.e. DEV/GDP ratio. We also test for the growth rate of the DEV/GDP ratio, denoted by dev/gdp, as well as the flow of (i.e. first-difference of) real credit from this banking system ∆DEV in relation to GDP (or ∆DEV/GDP).

Real interest rate

So far, we have been discussing quantity financial variables. We also examine the effects of some price variables. One of these is the real interest rate. As we discussed earlier, virtually all previous studies that test for effects of financial factors on efficiency have included the real interest rate as one of the financial variables considered.

Exchange rate distortion

The few studies that have tested for the effect of exchange rate valuation on economic growth or efficiency do not employ a uniform measure. For instance, a real exchange rate index was employed by Agarwala (1983) in computing a composite distortion index. A black market exchange rate premium was employed instead by Gallagher (1991) and Ghani (1992). However, apart from some other limitations that this proxy tends to have, data on black market exchange rate are not available over many decades for a large number of the countries covered in the present study. Thus, in this study, we follow the approach adopted in Odedokun (1992b), whereby a dummy variable is constructed to serve as a proxy for exchange rate distortion. This dummy variable takes a value of unity if the 'inappropriate' exchange rate policy is adopted and a value of zero otherwise. The 'inappropriate' exchange rate policy is, in turn, characterised as a real appreciation of the currency following a current account deficit in the balance of payments, or a real depreciation following a surplus. That is, in the case of a real appreciation of the domestic currency in the current period (as compared with its value in the previous period) when a current account deficit has just been recorded, or if the currency depreciates in the current period when the country has just recorded a surplus, it is characterised as an 'inappropriate' exchange rate policy. Otherwise, it is 'appropriate'.[6]

Inflation rate

In a way, this is also a financial variable and it may affect economic efficiency directly, quite apart from any effect it may have indirectly by hampering financial intermediation, making the real interest rate negative, and causing the real exchange rate to be 'over-valued'. For example, a high inflation rate may encourage speculative, less-productive or non-productive investment in land and real estate. Thus, as in most other studies that examine effects of financial policies on efficiency, we too test for the effect of the inflation rate and we expect it to have a negative effect.

THE MODEL SPECIFICATION AND DATA

Model specification and estimation

The linear regression equation specified takes the following form:

$$IOCR_{it} = X_{it}\beta + U_{it}(i = 1, \ldots, N; t = 1, \ldots, T) \qquad (2)$$

where IOCR = incremental output–capital ratio; X = matrix of the IOCR determinants discussed earlier; β = vector of the coefficients of X that are to be estimated; U = random error term; N = number of countries included in deriving the estimates; and T = number of periods (in years) covered for each country.

As can be seen from the presence of the time and country subscripts in the above equation, the relationship is to be estimated with panel data – i.e. time-series or annual data pooled across different units or countries. To derive the estimates, we employ the 'fixed-effect technique' of estimating with panel data. This method caters for any inter-country difference in the autonomous component of the dependent variable or IOCR by permitting the intercept terms to vary across countries in the estimation process.

Not all the explanatory variables discussed earlier feature simultaneously in estimating the above equation – only a few are included at a time. One reason for this has to do with the fact that some of the explanatory variables are alternatives or substitutes, e.g. a variable in ratio or level form and its growth rate. Another reason is the prevalence of missing values in respect of the regressors such that simultaneous inclusion of all the regressors would very drastically reduce the total number of observations that would be available for deriving the estimates. There is also the need to minimise the problem arising from intercorrelation among the regressors.

In deriving the estimates, we make sure that the regressors that feature simultaneously in each of the reported equations are not so affected with the multicollinearity problem as to impair the estimates of their coefficients (with the exception of inflation and real interest rates that are inter-correlated and which feature simultaneously in a particular equation reported in Table 6.2 below – this is reported just to highlight a point to which we shall allude later). Interestingly, the inter-correlations among the entire set of regressors (with the exception of the one between the aforementioned inflation and real interest rates) are minimal. This can be inferred intuitively from the matrix of simple correlation coefficients reported in Table 6.1.

Where appropriate, both the contemporaneous and 1-period lagged values of explanatory variables are included simultaneously. This is particularly so in the case of variables that are in growth rate or flow form. Others that are expressed as ratios of GDP or as ratios of one another are not affected by this since their successive values are highly inter-correlated.

In Odedokun (1992b), which can be regarded as the background or working paper version of the present study, 'control variables' in the form of the level and growth of the government expenditure/GDP ratio, level and growth of the export/GDP ratio, etc. were included as additional regressors but were found to have no material effects on the estimates of the coefficients of financial variables. Thus, there is no compelling need for their inclusion in the present study – especially since data on them have many missing values, and therefore their inclusion would substantially reduce the total number of country-year data points that would then be available in deriving the estimates of their coefficients and, hence, of the coefficients of the financial variables that are of interest to us in the present study.

The data, coverage, etc.

Details concerning how the data are measured and the list of countries covered by the study are provided in the appendix. What is done here is simply to summarise and complement the contents of the appendix.

Annual data for 81 developing countries are employed in the study. The

Table 6.1 Mean values of and correlation matrix for key variables

	IOCR	DEV/GDP	dev/gdp	M_2/GDP	m_2/gdp	ΔM_2/GDP	INF	RINT	EXCHDIST
DEV/GDP	-.104	1.000	–	–	–	–	–	–	–
dev/gdp	-.059	.046	1.000	–	–	–	–	–	–
M_2/GDP	-.085	.163	.048	1.000	–	–	–	–	–
m_2/gdp	-.121	.057	.318	.080	1.000	–	–	–	–
ΔM_2/GDP	.200	.063	.224	.398	.686	1.000	–	–	–
INF	-.156	-.051	-.220	-.074	-.323	.292	1.000	–	–
RINT	.121	.100	.194	.127	.363	.382	-.642	1.000	–
EXCHDIST	-.052	.028	-.053	.000	-.013	-.029	.046	-.038	1.000
Mean values	.167	.067	.037	.369	.020	.021	.157	.005	.460

Notes: (i) At significance levels of 1% and 5% respectively, a correlation coefficient is statistically different from zero if its absolute value is up to 0.07 and 0.05 respectively; (ii) The notations are defined as follows: DEV/GDP = development bank lending/GDP ratio; dev/gdp = growth of DEV/GDP; M_2/GDP = stock of banking system's liquid liabilities/GDP ratio; m_2/gdp = growth of M_2/GDP; ΔM_2/GDP = change in real value of the banking system's liquid liabilities/real GDP ratio; INF = inflation rate; RINT = real interest rate; and EXCHDIST = exchange rate distortion

Table 6.2 Empirical results

	(1)	(2)	(3)	(4)	(5)	(6)	(7)	(8)	(9)	(10)	(11)
INF_t	-.221 (-5.7)	-.212 (-6.6)	-.196 (-6.0)	-.195 (-6.0)	-.105 (-2.5)	-.111 (-3.3)	-.225 (-5.7)	-.222 (-6.3)	-.195 (-4.6)	—	-.574 (-4.0)
INF_{t-1}	—	—	—	—	—	—	—	—	-.014 (-0.3)	—	.083 (0.9)
$EXCHDIS_t$	-.021 (-1.3)	-.026 (-1.6)	— (-1.7)	— (-1.7)	-.017 (-1.0)	-.024 (-1.5)	-.025 (-1.5)	-.008 (-0.4)	-.020 (-1.1)	-.032 (-1.9)	-.036 (-2.1)
$EXCHDIS_{t-1}$	—	—	—	—	—	—	—	—	-.020 (-1.1)	.003 (0.2)	-.0001 (-0.04)
GB/TB_t	-.023 (-1.0)	—	—	—	-.041 (-1.8)	—	-.049 (-2.2)	—	—	—	—
$(M_2/GDP)_t$	-.487 (-5.7)	—	—	—	—	—	—	—	—	—	—
$(M_2/GDP)_{t-1}$	—	—	-.266 (-3.2)	—	—	—	—	—	—	—	—
$(M_1/GDP)_t$	—	-.800 (-4.3)	—	—	—	—	—	—	—	—	—
$(M_1/GDP)_{t-1}$	—	—	—	-.113 (-0.6)	—	—	—	—	—	—	—
$(M_2-M_1)/GDP_t$	—	-.441 (-4.5)	—	—	—	—	—	—	—	—	—
$(M_2-M_1)/GDP_{t-1}$	—	—	—	-.320 (-3.1)	—	—	—	—	—	—	—
$M_1/(M_2-M_1)_t$	—	—	—	—	.393 (5.1)	—	—	—	—	—	—
$M_1/(M_2-M_1)_{t-1}$	—	—	—	—	—	.401 (5.5)	—	—	—	—	—

(DEV/GDP)$_t$	—	—	—	—	—	—	—	-.987 (-4.1)	—	—	—
(ΔDEV/GDP)$_t$	—	—	—	—	—	—	—	—	.817 (1.1)	—	—
RINT$_t$	—	—	—	—	—	—	—	—	—	.191 (2.1)	-.199 (-2.1)
Adjusted R²	.048	.054	.032	.033	.072	.072	.029	.056	.052	.059	.075
D.W.	1.58	1.63	1.60	1.60	1.55	1.64	1.59	1.72	1.68	1.57	1.56
K	73	81	81	81	73	81	73	48	48	72	72
N	1,567	1,757	1,738	1,738	1,547	1,738	1,582	982	898	1,155	1,155

Notes: (i) The dependent variable is the incremental output–capital ratio, IOCR; (ii) The t-values are in parentheses below the parameter estimates. At 1%, 5% and 10% levels of significance (using 2-tailed test), a parameter estimate would be statistically significant if its t-value is absolutely up to 2.6, 2.0, and 1.6 respectively; (iii) The D.W., K and N stand for the Durbin–Watson statistic value, number of countries and total number of observations respectively; (iv) The following are the meanings of mnemonics used for the regressors: INF = inflation rate; EXCHDIS = exchange rate distortion dummy variable; GB/TB = ratio of deposit money banks' outstanding claims on the government to their total outstanding claims on the domestic economy; M$_2$/GDP = wide money stock/GDP ratio; M$_1$/GDP = narrow money stock/GDP ratio; (M$_2$–M$_1$)/GDP = quasi-money stock/GDP ratio; M$_1$/(M$_2$–M$_1$) = narrow money stock/quasi-money stock ratio; DEV/GDP = development banking system's outstanding claims on the private sector in relation to GDP; ΔDEV/GDP = flow of lendings from development banking system in relation to GDP; and RINT = real interest rate

periods covered for the countries fall between 1961 and 1989, depending on data availability for each country. No country has less than 10 annual data points, however. The choice of the countries included and the period covered for each included country is solely determined by data availability.

All the data are from the IMF's *International Financial Statistics (IFS) Yearbook*.

EMPIRICAL RESULTS

Presentation of the estimates

The simple correlation coefficients among key regressors are presented in Table 6.1 while the estimates of the equations are reported in Tables 6.2 and 6.3. The estimates of Table 6.3 differ from those of Table 6.2 mainly because the growth rate and first-difference of non-price financial variables feature in Table 6.3, instead of their level-form equivalents in Table 6.2. Further explanatory notes are provided at the foot of each table.

Discussion of the results

As can be seen from both Tables 6.2 and 6.3, the explanatory power of the equations is low for predictive purposes, as evidenced by the low adjusted R^2 values. This has to be due to the heterogeneous nature of the countries covered in the study. On the other hand, the Durbin–Watson statistic values are not so far from 2.0 as to suggest any presence of serial correlation of the residuals. We are now going to evaluate the performance of the specific regressors in the equations, in the same sequence as they were discussed in the second section of this chapter.

Financial intermediation variables

The ratio of money stock to GDP enters all the equations in Table 6.2 with negative coefficients that are also statistically significant, just as the growth rate of the ratio is in Table 6.3. This is so irrespective of whether it is the wide, narrow or quasi-money stock that is being considered – including their 1-period lagged values.[7]

By contrast, the ratio of first-difference of real value of these variables to GDP enters all equations in Table 6.3 with positive and statistically very significant coefficients.[8] This applies to both the current and 1-period lagged values of the variables. The same result is obtained in respect of the variable on the asset side of the banking system's balance sheet – viz.: the first-difference of real stock of claims of the banking system on the private sector in relation to real GDP and in relation to real domestic investment.

Given various notions or concepts of financial deepening and level of

Table 6.3 Further empirical results

	(1)	(2)	(3)	(4)	(5)	(6)	(7)	(8)	(9)	(10)	(11)
INF_t	-.534 (-9.8)	-.357 (-7.0)	-.224 (-5.4)	-.296 (-5.4)	-.487 (-8.9)	-.400 (-7.5)	-.219 (-5.1)	-.202 (-4.7)	-.249 (-6.2)	-.247 (-6.2)	-.265 (-6.5)
INF_{t-1}	.280 (4.5)	.158 (2.7)	-.033 (-0.7)	.227 (3.6)	.277 (4.3)	.258 (4.0)	.113 (2.4)	.093 (2.0)	.058 (1.3)	.060 (1.4)	.054 (1.2)
$EXCHDIS_t$	-.036 (-2.3)	-.033 (-2.1)	-.024 (-1.3)	-.031 (-1.9)	-.036 (-2.2)	-.033 (-2.0)	-.037 (-2.4)	-.038 (-2.4)	-.036 (-2.4)	-.035 (-2.3)	-.037 (-2.4)
$EXCHDIS_{t-1}$	-.040 (-2.5)	-.042 (-2.6)	-.025 (-1.3)	-.039 (-2.4)	-.042 (-2.6)	-.040 (-2.5)	-.030 (-2.0)	-.031 (-2.0)	-.032 (-2.1)	-.032 (-2.1)	-.033 (-2.1)
$(gb/tb)_t$	-.012 (-1.0)	-.013 (-1.1)	—	-.011 (-0.8)	-.011 (-0.8)	—	—	—	—	—	—
$(gb/tb)_{t-1}$	.001 (0.1)	-.012 (-0.9)	—	-.012 (-1.0)	-.004 (-0.3)	—	—	—	—	—	—
$(m_2/gdp)_t$	-.593 (-8.4)	—	—	—	—	—	—	—	—	—	—
$(m_2/gdp)_{t-1}$	.174 (2.4)	—	—	—	—	—	—	—	—	—	—
$(m_1/gdp)_t$	—	—	—	—	-.420 (-6.4)	—	—	—	—	—	—
$(m_1/gdp)_{t-1}$	—	—	—	—	.214 (3.1)	.273 (3.9)	—	—	—	—	—
$(m_2-m_1)/gdp_t$	—	—	—	—	-.002 (-0.1)	—	—	—	—	—	—
$(m_2-m_1)/gdp_{t-1}$	—	—	—	—	-.020 (-0.6)	-.028 (-0.9)	—	—	—	—	—
$m_1/(m_2-m_1)_t$	—	—	—	.272 (1.8)	—	—	.230 (2.4)	—	—	—	—

Table 6.3 (continued)

	A	B	C	D	E	F	G
$m_1/(m_2-m_1)_{t-1}$	—	—	—	—	—	—	—
$(dev/gdp)_t$	-.172 (-3.7)	.297 (1.9)	.421 (4.3)	—	—	—	—
$(dev/gdp)_{t-1}$	-.112 (-2.5)	—	—	—	—	—	—
$(\Delta M_2/GDP)_t$	—	—	1.436 (7.2)	—	—	—	—
$(\Delta M_2/GDP)_{t-1}$	—	—	.776 (3.7)	—	—	—	—
$(\Delta M_2/SAV)_t$	—	—	—	—	—	—	.010 (0.4)
$(\Delta M_1/GDP)_t$	—	1.408 (3.3)	—	1.805 (5.5)	—	—	—
$(\Delta M_1/GDP)_{t-1}$	—	1.091 (2.6)	—	1.359 (4.0)	—	—	—
$(\Delta M_2-\Delta M_1)GDP_t$	—	1.421 (3.4)	—	.996 (3.6)	—	—	—
$(\Delta M_2-\Delta M_1)GDP_{t-1}$	—	.561 (1.3)	—	-.014 (-0.1)	—	—	—
$(\Delta CR/GDP)_t$	—	—	—	—	.442 (3.4)	—	—
$(\Delta CR/GDP)_{t-1}$	—	—	—	—	.188 (1.4)	—	—
$(\Delta CR/INV)_t$	—	—	—	—	—	.108 (4.3)	—

(ΔCR/INV)$_{t-1}$	–	–	–	–	–	–	–	–	–	.043	–
										(1.6)	
Adjusted R^2	.098	.048	.076	.091	.084	.055	.085	.078	.048	.052	.041
D.W.	1.67	1.61	1.68	1.60	1.64	1.64	1.52	1.55	1.50	1.49	1.53
K	73	73	48	73	73	73	81	81	81	81	81
N	1,487	1,491	898	1,465	1,465	1,465	1,657	1,657	1,680	1,680	1,677

Notes: (i) The dependent variable is the incremental output–capital ratio, IOCR; (ii) The t-values are in parentheses below the parameter estimates. At 1%, 5% and 10% levels of significance (using 2-tailed test), a parameter estimate would be statistically significant if its t-value is absolutely up to 2.6, 2.0, and 1.6 respectively; (iii) The D.W., K and N stand for the Durbin–Watson statistic value, number of countries and total number of observations respectively; (iv) The following are the meanings of mnemonics used for the regressors: INF = inflation rate; EXCHDIS = exchange rate distortion dummy variable; and gb/tb = growth rate of the ratio of deposit money banks' claims on the government to their total claims on the domestic economy. Also ΔM$_2$/GDP; ΔM$_1$/GDP; and (ΔM$_2$–ΔM$_1$)/GDP are the ratio of first-difference of real value of wide money stock, narrow money stock, and quasi-money stock in relation to real GDP respectively just as ΔM$_2$/SAV = the corresponding first-difference of wide money stock in relation to domestic savings. Similarly, ΔCR/GDP and ΔCR/INV are the ratio of first-difference of the real value of the banking system's credit to the private sector in relation to real GDP and real investment respectively. The m$_2$/gdp; m$_1$/gdp; (m$_2$–m$_1$)/gdp and dev/gdp respectively stand for the growth rates of wide money stock/GDP ratio; narrow money stock/GDP ratio; quasi-money stock/GDP ratio; and development bank credit to the private sector/GDP ratio

financial development that exist in the literature and in the policy discussion, the above findings should shed light on the most relevant concept for policy to aim at. Specifically, the target that should be promoted is the real flows (or increase in the real value) of the above monetary and credit indicators in relation to the overall economic activities – real GDP or real domestic investment as appropriate. Policies should not simply aim at increasing the ratio of the stock of the monetary or credit items to GDP. This follows from the negative relationship detected between the ratios of the stock items to GDP in a situation whereby the ratios of real flows of the items to real GDP or real investment show a positive association. Because this finding in respect of the effect of money stock/GDP and credit stock/GDP ratios appears rather counter-intuitive, we conducted different sensitivity checks as discussed in the section on pp. 131–32. But the results are invariant, just as when non-financial regressors are added as control variables (as mentioned earlier). As can be seen from Table 6.1, their (level and growth of money stock/GDP ratio) simple correlation coefficients with IOCR are also negative and statistically significant in all cases. A theoretical basis for, or an explanation of, this rather startling empirical finding should be part of the research agenda for future studies. Meanwhile, we can only speculate that the observed negative association might be caused by a yet-to-be-identified 'shock' or factor which would have a negative effect on economic efficiency and, at the same time, a positive effect on the money stock/GDP and credit stock/GDP ratios.

Concerning the relative role of narrow-money and quasi-money stock in relation to GDP, the coefficients of the narrow-money/quasi-money stock ratio – whether current or 1-period lagged value – are positive and significant as reported in Table 6.2. So also are the coefficients of the current and 1-period lagged values of the growth rate of this ratio in Table 6.3. This suggests that narrow-money stock promotes efficiency more than the quasi-money stock.[9] Again, this is a pointer to the appropriate monetary variable to target in order to promote financial deepening that would be most conducive to economic efficiency.

Government borrowing from private financial institutions

As posited, the ratio of the deposit money banking system's claims on the government sector in relation to the system's total domestic credit enters the equations in Table 6.2 with negative coefficients that are also significant in two out of three equations. Although not statistically significant, the coefficients of the growth rate of this ratio are also negative in Table 6.3 results. Thus, on the whole, there is support for the contention that government domination of lending by the private banks does not enhance economic efficiency.

Directed credit scheme

The ratio of development bank claims on the private sector to GDP enters the equation in Table 6.2 with statistically significant negative coefficient. The same holds for the growth rate of this ratio in Table 6.3. This applies to both current and 1-period lagged values.[10] What this suggests is that directed credit – at least, as implemented through development bank lendings – might not enhance efficiency of resource utilisation. This is in line with the recent appraisal of its role in the literature as we pointed out earlier. There is thus a need to revamp the operations of these development institutions to make them enhance economic efficiency.

Real interest rate

As can be seen from the results in Table 6.2, the effect of the real interest rate is not very clear. By including it simultaneously with the inflation rate in the same equation, its coefficient is found to be significantly negative. But by excluding the inflation rate, the coefficient of the real interest rate becomes significantly positive.[11] Thus, on the whole, we are unable to detect a categorical effect of it on economic efficiency. (A further explanation on this finding is given in the last paragraph of p. 132.)

Exchange rate distortion

The coefficients of the proxy for exchange rate distortion – both the current and 1-period lagged values – are negative in all equations and are statistically significant in almost all. This suggests that the policy of a real appreciation of the domestic currency following (or despite) a current account deficit and that of a depreciation in spite of a surplus, hinders economic efficiency.

Inflation rate

The current value of the inflation rate enters all equations with significantly negative coefficients. Although the 1-period lagged value of it enters the equations with positive coefficients in most cases, these coefficients are generally insignificant and, in any case, their values and statistical significance do not match those of the current value of inflation. In other words, the total or overall effect of inflation is negative on economic efficiency. This is in line with *a priori* expectations and previous findings.

Some sensitivity checks

Some sensitivity analyses have been carried out in respect of the results. (The outcomes of this exercise are not presented here, to save space, but are reported in Odedokun, 1992b.) One of these is the partitioning of the entire 1961–1989 period into three sub-periods, viz.: 1961–1973 or pre-oil shock era; 1974–1980; and 1981–1989. The estimates derived for each sub-period (as reported in Table 3 of Odedokun, 1992b) were found to be materially the same as those for the entire 1961–1989 dataset, suggesting temporal stability of the estimates.

Similarly, for the entire 1961–1989 period, estimates were derived for each of four regional groups of countries (viz. Sub Saharan Africa, Asia, Western Hemisphere and the others – comprising North Africa, Middle East and Europe) as reported in Table 4 of Odedokun (1992b). It was found that the results are essentially invariant across the different regions. Also, using the entire dataset, we included regional dummies in deriving the estimates (Table 2 of Odedokun, 1992b). Again, the estimates were found to be basically the same as when the regional dummies were not included.

We also employed a variance component technique of deriving the panel data estimates (as reported in Tables 2 and 3 of Odedokun, 1992b) and found it to yield similar results as those derived through the fixed-effect technique reported here. Thus, the results are not sensitive to the assumption about the country-specific intercept terms that apply to the derivation of panel data estimates. (While the fixed-effect technique only assumes that each country has its own unique intercept, the variance component method further assumes that these intercepts are not correlated with the other regressors.)

Finally, we tested for the effect of outliers and found that, in respect of the real interest rate, the results obtained were affected by excluding outlier values. In their presence, an implausible positive correlation coefficient of almost 1.000 between the real interest rate and each of the nominal interest and inflation rates were now observed and the coefficients of the real interest rate in the estimated IOCR equations assumed negative values. The more the outlier values were dropped, the more significantly positive the coefficients of the real interest rate became. A cut-off figure of below 100 per cent annual nominal interest rate was eventually adopted in deriving the estimates of correlation coefficients between the real interest rate and other variables as presented in Table 6.1. But to adopt this cut-off in deriving the regression results of Table 6.2 would have drastically reduced the number of country-year data points. Thus, we only dropped more extreme or outlier values. Our inability to further reduce the outlier values is a probable explanation of the inconsistency in the observed effect of the real interest rate on efficiency as reported in Table 6.2.

SUMMARY AND CONCLUSION

The study investigates the effects of financial variables on economic efficiency, conventionally measured as the incremental output–capital ratio. Annual data for periods that fall within 1962 and 1989 for 81 developing countries form the basis of the empirical tests. The effects of indicators of financial intermediation; government dominance in financial intermediation, including directed credit schemes; real interest rate; exchange rate valuation; and inflation rates are tested for. Except in the case of the real interest rate, we are able to detect non-ambiguous effects of other variables tested for.

After the usual preamble in the first section, we presented the framework of the study and a brief literature review in the second section. There, we discussed the rationale for the variables whose effects are tested for in the study. These variables are alternative indicators of financial deepening/ development; government domination of what is naturally the private credit markets; directed credit schemes as proxied by development bank lendings; real interest rate; distortionary exchange rate values; and inflation rate. In the third section, we presented the model (regression equation) specified for estimation with the annual data pooled across the countries. The empirical results are presented and evaluated in that section, and the following are the highlights of our findings:

(a) Those indicators of financial depths that are in the form of monetary or credit stock variables in relation to GDP are found to be negatively related to efficiency. By contrast, the indicators of financial development that are in the form of real monetary or credit flow variables in relation to real GDP (or real investment) are found to have strong positive association with economic efficiency. This suggests that the latter indicators should be the better target of financial development policy.

(b) Government domination of what should naturally be regarded as private credit markets is found to hamper efficiency.

(c) A directed credit programme, as proxied by development bank lendings in relation to economic activities, is found to be negatively related to efficiency.

(d) The nature of the data does not permit a detection of a non-ambiguous effect of the real interest rate.

(e) The policy of a real appreciation of the domestic currency following (or despite) a current account deficit and that of depreciating it in spite of a surplus is found to hinder economic efficiency.

(f) The inflation rate too is found to hinder economic efficiency.

APPENDIX: DATA MEASUREMENTS AND THE COUNTRIES STUDIED

The list of countries covered by the study

Algeria, Argentina, Bahrain, Barbados, Benin, Bhutan, Bolivia, Botswana, Brazil, Burkina Faso, Burundi, Cameroon, Cape Verde, Chile, Colombia, Costa Rica, Cyprus, Dominican Republic, Ecuador, Egypt, El Salvador, Fiji,

Ghana, Guatemala, Guyana, Haiti, Honduras, Hungary, India, Indonesia, Iran, Israel, Jamaica, Jordan, Kenya, Korea, Kuwait, Liberia, Libya, Madagascar, Malawi, Malaysia, Malta, Mauritius, Mexico, Morocco, Myanmar, Nepal, Nicaragua, Niger, Nigeria, Oman, Pakistan, Panama, Papua New Guinea, Paraguay, Peru, the Philippines, Rwanda, Saudi Arabia, Senegal, Sierra Leone, Singapore, South Africa, Sri Lanka, Swaziland, Syria, Tanzania, Thailand, Togo, Trinidad and Tobago, Tunisia, Turkey, United Arab Emirates, Uruguay, Venezuela, Yemen, Yugoslavia, Zaire, Zambia, Zimbabwe.

The data

All data are from relevant issues of the IMF's *International Financial Statistics (IFS) Yearbook*.

1   The narrow-money and quasi-money stock are the end-of-year values (lines 34 and 35 of the IFS respectively).
2   The deposit money banks' stock of claims on the public and private sectors as well as the whole banking system's stock of claims on the private sector are the end-of-year values, respectively from lines 22a, 22d and 32d of the IFS. Similarly, the development banks' stock of claims on the private sector is the end-of-year values or line 42d of the IFS.
3   Real interest rate is nominal interest rate minus inflation rate. The nominal interest rate is the deposit rate (line 60L of the IFS) or discount rate (line 60 of the IFS), in the absence of data on deposit rate.
4   Real exchange rate is the domestic currency price of SDR divided by domestic–foreign price ratio, with domestic price being GDP deflator and foreign price being GDP deflator of industrial or OECD countries. This means that upward movement of the real exchange rate represents a real depreciation of the domestic currency. The dummy variable for exchange rate distortion thus takes a value of unity if the product of the first-difference of this real exchange rate (which is positive in the case of a real depreciation) and the 1-period lagged value of current account (which is positive if the surplus is recorded in the preceding year) is negative.
5   Inflation rate is the growth rate of GDP deflator (line 99b.p of the IFS).
6   The dependent variable, IOCR, is the first-difference of real GDP (line 99b.p of the IFS) divided by real gross domestic investment (nominal gross domestic investment or lines 93e plus 93i of the IFS, deflated by GDP deflator).

NOTES

1   Also implicit, but not explicit, in their position is the negative role of the inflation rate on the efficiency of resource utilisation.
2   This conventional measure of efficiency, however, has some limitations. For instance, it is standing for the actual (as opposed to the incremental) output–

capital ratio, based on the questionable assumption that the two are the same. Also, it attributes output changes to investment spending alone. But despite these and other limitations, no better practical alternative measure of economic efficiency has been proposed in the literature – especially given the data limitations for constructing conceptual alternatives in developing countries.

3 There are many reasons for testing for the effects of these variables (and others to be discussed later) in both the level and growth rate forms. For example, policy discussion is generally conducted in terms of the level form of the variables. On the other hand, there is the general tendency for various variables to be intercorrelated when in the level form so that their individual effects become less precise to estimate whereas they become much less intercorrelated when in growth rate form.

4 In all cases, it is the real value of these monetary variables that are first-differenced before expressing them as ratios of real GDP or real savings. Dividing the first-differences of their nominal values with nominal GDP or nominal savings produces a different result – statistically insignificance of their coefficients in the equations.

5 Again, it is the first-difference of the real value of the credit stock that is expressed in relation to real GDP or real investment spending. To express the nominal value of the first-difference in relation to nominal GDP or nominal investment spending produces a different result, which is statistically insignificant.

6 The logic of this is based on the fact that a country that is running current account deficits does not normally need to further appreciate the value of the domestic currency in real terms just as a country having surplus does not normally need to depreciate the value. The preceding (as opposed to the current) period's current account deficit is made the basis of the current period's reaction function of real exchange rate authority because, among other reasons, the present current account balances may simply be reflecting the actual real exchange rate policy currently being pursued.

7 The ratio of the outstanding banking system's claim on the private sector to GDP has a statistically insignificant coefficient, just as has the growth rate of this ratio. Thus, and in view of space constraint, the equations where they feature are not reported.

8 When expressed in relation to domestic savings instead of GDP, their coefficients are still positive but generally lose statistical significance. Thus, only one such equation is reported as we have it in Table 6.3.

9 In view of the negative coefficients of these monetary variables when expressed in relation to GDP, the finding can also be interpreted to mean that narrow-money stock hinders efficiency less than the quasi-money stock.

10 It can be seen from Table 6.2 that the coefficient of the ratio of first-difference of the stock of development bank real credit to real GDP is statistically insignificant.

11 By featuring the real interest rate simultaneously with the inflation rate, we are risking the econometric problem of multicollinearity between the two whereas dropping the inflation rate means that we are risking another econometric problem of error of omitted variables.

REFERENCES

Agarwala, R.K. (1983), 'Price Distortion and Growth in Developing Countries', *World Bank Staff Working Papers*, No. 575, World Bank.
Asian Development Bank (1985), *Improving Domestic Resource Mobilisation*

Through Financial Development, Manila: Asian Development Bank.

Bencivenga, V.R. and B.D. Smith (1991), 'Financial Intermediation and Endogenous Growth', *Review of Economic Studies*, 58, pp. 195–209.

De Gregorio, J. and P.E. Guidotti (1992), 'Financial Development and Economic Growth', mimeo, International Monetary Fund.

Fritz, R.G. (1984), 'Time-series Evidence on the Causal Relationship between Financial Deepening and Economic Development', *Journal of Economic Development*, 9, pp. 91–112.

Fry, M.J. (1979), 'The Cost of Financial Repression in Turkey', *Savings and Development*, 3, pp. 127–35.

—— (1980), 'Saving, Investment, Growth and the Cost of Financial Repression', *World Development*, 8, pp. 317–27.

—— (1981), 'Interest Rates in Asia: An Examination of Interest Rate Policies in Burma, India, Indonesia, Korea, Malaysia, Nepal, Pakistan, the Philippines, Singapore, Sri Lanka, Taiwan and Thailand', International Monetary Fund, Asian Department.

—— (1984), 'Financial Saving, Financial Intermediation and Economic Growth', in *Improving Domestic Resource Mobilization through Financial Development*, Vol. II, Manila: Asian Development Bank.

—— (1987), 'Models of Financially Repressed Developing Economies', *World Development*, 10, pp. 731–50.

—— (1988), *Money, Interest and Banking in Economic Development*, Baltimore: The Johns Hopkins University Press.

Galbis, V. (1977), 'Financial Intermediation and Economic Growth in Less Developed Countries: A Theoretical Approach', *Journal of Development Studies*, 13, pp. 58–72.

Gallagher, M. (1991), *Rent-seeking and Economic Growth*, Boulder, Colorado: Westview Press.

Gelb, A. (1989), 'A Cross-section Analysis of Financial Policies, Efficiency and Growth', *PPR Working Paper WPS*, No. 202, World Bank.

Gertler, M. and A. Rose (1991), 'Finance, Growth, and Public Policy', *World Bank Working Paper*, No. 814, World Bank.

Ghani, E. (1992), 'How Financial Markets Affect Long-run Growth: A Cross-Country Study', *PPR Working Paper WPS*, No. 843, World Bank.

Goldsmith, W. (1966), *The Determinants of Financial Structure*, Paris: OECD.

—— (1969), *Financial Structure and Development*, New Haven: Yale University Press.

Greenwood, J. and B. Jovanovic (1990), 'Financial Development, Growth, and the Distribution of Income', *Journal of Political Economy*, 98, pp. 1076–107.

Gupta, K.L. (1987), 'Aggregate Savings, Financial Intermediation and Interest Rate', *Review of Economics and Statistics*, 69, pp. 303–11.

Gurley, J.G. and E.S. Shaw (1960), *Money in a Theory of Finance*, Washington DC: The Brookings Institution.

International Monetary Fund (IMF), *International Financial Statistics Yearbook*, Washington DC: IMF, various issues.

Jao, Y.C. (1976), 'Financial Deepening and Economic Growth: A Cross-Section Analysis', *Malaysian Economic Review*, 21, pp. 47–58.

Jung, W. (1986), 'Financial Development and Economic Growth: International Evidence', *Economic Development and Cultural Change*, 34, pp. 333–46.

Khatekhate, D.R. (1988), 'Assessing the Impact of Interest Rates in Less Developed Countries', *World Development*, 16, pp. 577–88.

King, R.G. and R. Levine (1992), 'Financial Indicators and Growth in a Cross Section

of Countries', *World Bank Working Paper*, No. 819, Washington DC: World Bank.
—— (1993a) 'Finance, Entrepreneurship, and Growth: Theory and Evidence', *Journal of Monetary Economics*, 32, pp. 513–42.
—— (1993b), 'Financial Intermediation and Economic Development', in C. Mayer and X. Vives (eds) *Capital Markets and Financial Intermediation*, London: Centre for Economic Policy Research, pp. 156–89.
—— (1993c), 'Finance and Growth: Schumpeter Might be Right', *Quarterly Journal of Economics*, 108, pp. 717–38.
Lanyi, A. and R. Saracoglu (1983), 'Interest Rate Policies in Developing Economies', *Occasional Paper*, No. 22, Washington DC: International Monetary Fund.
Levine, R. (1991), 'Stock Markets, Growth, and Tax Policy', *Journal of Finance*, 46, pp. 1445–65.
—— (1992), 'Financial Intermediary Services and Growth', *Journal of Japanese and International Economics*, 6, pp. 383–405.
McKinnon, R.I. (1973), *Money and Capital in Economic Development*, Washington DC: The Brookings Institution.
Mathieson, D.J. (1980), 'Financial Reform and Stabilization Policy in a Developing Economy', *Journal of Development Economics*, 7, pp. 359–95.
Odedokun, M.O. (1992a), 'Supply-leading and Demand-following Relationship between Economic Activities and Development Banking in Developing Countries: An International Evidence', *Singapore Economic Review*, 37, pp. 46–58.
—— (1992b), 'Multi-country Evidence on the Effects of Macroeconomic, Financial and Trade Policies on Efficiency of Resource Utilization in Developing Countries', *IMF Working Paper*, WP/92/53, International Monetary Fund.
Patrick, H.T. (1966), 'Financial Development and Economic Growth in Underdeveloped Countries', *Economic Development and Cultural Change*, 14, pp. 174–89.
Porter, R.C. (1966), 'The Promotion of the Banking Habit and Economic Development', *Journal of Development Studies*, 2, pp. 346–66.
Roubini, N. and X. Sala-i-Martin (1991), 'Financial Development, the Trade Regime, and Economic Growth', *Working Paper*, No. 876, National Bureau of Economic Research.
—— (1992), 'A Growth Model of Inflation, Tax Evasion, and Financial Repression', *Working Paper*, No. 4076, National Bureau of Economic Research.
Saint-Paul, G. (1992), 'Technological Choice, Financial Market and Economic Growth', *European Economic Review*, 36, pp. 763–81.
Seck, D. and Y.H. El Nil (1993), 'Financial Liberalization in Africa', *World Development*, 21, pp. 1867–82.
Shaw, E. (1973), *Financial Deepening in Economic Development*, New York: Oxford University Press.
Wai, Tun U. (1980), *Economic Essays on Developing Countries*, Rockville, Md: Sijthoff and Nordhoff.
Wallich, A. (1969), 'Money and Growth: A Cross-section Analysis', *Journal of Money, Credit, and Banking*, 1, pp. 281–302.
World Bank (1989), *World Development Report 1989*, Washington DC: World Bank.

7

FINANCE AND GROWTH IN PACIFIC BASIN DEVELOPING COUNTRIES[1]

Maxwell J. Fry

INTRODUCTION

To achieve rapid economic growth, the volume and efficiency of investment must be of paramount concern. High and sustainable levels of economic growth require high levels of saving and investment. Growth is also stimulated by export performance. However, the basic prerequisite for any export growth is sustainable output growth. Hence, saving, investment, exports and economic growth are inextricably related to one another.

This chapter examines the role of financial conditions in producing the virtuous circles of high saving, investment, output growth and export growth found in the Pacific Basin. Over the past decade, high rates of economic growth have been accompanied by even higher rates of export growth; saving and investment ratios have also been high in these countries.

In this study I use the real deposit rate of interest and the black market exchange rate premium as proxies for financial repression. Negative real interest rates generally reflect some government-imposed distortion in domestic financial markets (Giovannini and De Melo, 1993). Since governments, using financial repression as a source of revenue, attempt to prevent capital outflows that would erode the tax base, black market exchange rate premia also provide an indicator of financial repression.

After an overview of the relevant macroeconomic characteristics of the Pacific Basin developing market economies in the first section, the chapter investigates the effects of financial conditions on saving and investment behaviour in the second and third sections. Two further sections then examine the effects of financial conditions on export and output growth. The penultimate section presents some simple bivariate relationships that support the general conclusion concerning the relationship between financial repression and economic growth.

THE PACIFIC BASIN DEVELOPING MARKET ECONOMIES IN A GLOBAL PERSPECTIVE

The economic success of Hong Kong, Indonesia, Korea, Malaysia, Singapore, Taiwan and Thailand over the past two or three decades is undisputed. Table 7.1 shows that high rates of economic growth have been accompanied by even higher rates of export growth over the past decade. Table 7.1 also shows that the high savers of the world are to be found in the Pacific Basin. Only in the Asia-Pacific region has saving as a proportion of GNP or GDP risen over the past decade.

The saving ratio of the Asia-Pacific developing countries broke the 30 per cent barrier in 1987 and has hovered around this level since then. It is forecast to remain at about 30 per cent in 1994 and 1995 (IMF, 1994a, p. 174). For the period 1987–1992, the 30 per cent saving ratio in the Asia-Pacific developing countries can be compared with ratios of 21 per cent in the industrial countries, 19 per cent in Africa, 19 per cent in the Middle East and developing Europe and 20 per cent in the developing countries of the Western Hemisphere (IMF, 1994a, pp. 173–74).

While Japan's saving ratio has risen by about 5 percentage points since the mid-1980s, Indonesia's rose by over 10 percentage points and Thailand's increased by over 15 percentage points since 1983. Saving ratios have doubled in both Korea and Singapore since 1971; they also increased substantially in Hong Kong and Taiwan over the period 1971–1987. Since 1987, however, Taiwan's saving ratio has declined from 39 per cent to 29 per cent of GNP.

For the Asia-Pacific developing countries as a whole, investment has risen from 26 to over 30 per cent of GDP in the past decade. Over the period 1987–1992, the Asia-Pacific developing countries achieved an investment ratio of 31 per cent of GDP compared with 21 per cent in the industrial countries, 21 per cent in Africa, 22 per cent in the Middle East and developing Europe and 21 per cent in the developing countries of the Western Hemisphere (IMF, 1994a, pp. 173–74).

Five years ago, the Pacific Basin developing countries were net savers and so net capital exporters. Now, however, this country group absorbs virtually all its saving in increased domestic investment. Hong Kong, Korea, Malaysia, Singapore and Taiwan posted current account surpluses in the period 1986–1988. Thailand's current account was balanced, leaving only Indonesia as a deficit country. By the 1990s the picture had changed: only Hong Kong, Singapore and Taiwan ran current account surpluses, while Hong Kong's and Taiwan's surplus had fallen substantially.

Fairly predictably, the Asia-Pacific region also stands out from the other regions of the world in terms of its rate of economic growth. All other regions of the developing world experienced substantial reductions in their growth rates between the periods 1971–1981 and 1982–1992. Annual average growth

Table 7.1 Output, exports, saving and investment in seven Pacific Basin developing economies, 1982–1992

Country	Real GNP growth rate	Real export growth rate	Saving ratio	Investment ratio
Hong Kong	6.8	16.2	31.0	27.5
Indonesia	6.1	7.6	29.5	32.5
Korea	9.9	10.8	31.8	32.1
Malaysia	6.3	12.6	29.4	33.0
Singapore	6.9	7.5*	44.1	40.9
Taiwan	8.5	11.2	33.1	21.8
Thailand	8.6	16.4	26.0	30.9

Notes: Simple growth rates for real GNP and exports are calculated from the coefficient of time in an estimate of the logarithmic value of the dependent variable, 1982–1992.
*Nominal exports deflated by the GNP deflator

rates fell from 2.9 to 2.8 per cent in the industrial countries, from 2.8 to 2.2 per cent in Africa, from 4.8 to 2.2 per cent in developing Europe,[2] from 5.8 to 3.2 per cent in the Middle East and from 5.1 to 2.0 per cent in the developing countries of the Western Hemisphere. In the developing countries of the Asia-Pacific region, however, growth in real GDP averaged 5.5 per cent over the period 1971–1981, rising to 7.1 per cent over the period 1982–1992 (IMF, 1994b, pp. 152–53).

Superior performance in domestic resource mobilisation is just one of the explanations for the Pacific Basin success story. In addition to higher saving and investment ratios, the developing countries of the Pacific Basin region achieved more efficient use of the factors of production, labour and capital. While the additional output produced by an extra unit of investment between the 1970s and 1980s fell in all other regions of the world, it rose in the Pacific Basin region.

In the Pacific Basin region, as elsewhere, there is a much higher correlation between growth and saving ratios than there is between growth and investment ratios. While causality runs predominantly from growth to saving, it runs both ways, albeit less strongly, in the case of investment. The stronger relationship between growth rates and saving ratios than between growth rates and investment ratios is well illustrated by comparing Singapore and Taiwan. For the past decade, Singapore has posted the highest investment ratio in the Pacific Basin region at 41 per cent of GNP. However, Hong Kong, Korea, Taiwan and Thailand achieved higher growth rates than Singapore. Although Taiwan's saving ratio has been relatively high, Taiwan's investment ratio was only half Singapore's over the past decade. Hence, high growth rates were associated with high saving ratios but not necessarily with high investment ratios. This illustrates the point that at least half of the rate of economic growth is determined by the efficiency with which factors of production are used rather than the quantity of those factors.

Although not immediately apparent, another statistically significant relationship exists between growth rates and the *difference* between national saving and domestic investment ratios. Countries with saving ratios that are higher than their investment ratios have substantially higher growth rates than countries which have higher investment than saving ratios. A high saving–investment balance depreciates the real exchange rate, so stimulating export growth. Since export growth stimulates output growth, this may form the link between the saving–investment balance and output growth. However, this association may also reflect systematic differences in the efficiency of locally and foreign financed investment. One rough measure of investment efficiency is the incremental output/capital ratio (IOCR). Over the past decade, for example, Singapore's IOCR averaged 0.18 compared with Korea's 0.29 and Taiwan's 0.37.

NATIONAL SAVING

My saving function *SNY*, expressed as the ratio of national saving to GNP (both in current prices), is based on a life-cycle model (Mason, 1987). The standard life-cycle saving model has young, income-earning households saving to finance consumption when they become old, non-earning households. Figure 7.1 illustrates these life-cycle patterns of income and consumption. Income $E(a)$ and consumption $C(a)$ of a household aged a are expressed as a fraction of lifetime income.

The simplest life-cycle model assumes that each household consumes all its resources over its lifetime. In such a case, the level of household consumption L over its lifetime

$$L = \int C(a)da \tag{1}$$

is equal to 1.

Even if no household saves over its lifetime, this life-cycle model shows that aggregate saving can still be positive, provided that there is positive growth in aggregate real income. With positive growth, the lifetime resources of young savers exceed those of old dissavers and there will be positive aggregate saving. Because incomes of younger, earning households are higher than were incomes of older, non-earning households, saving exceeds dissaving in the society as a whole.

The aggregate saving ratio is determined by the age profile of the average household's saving: $S(a) = E(a) - C(a)$, and by the lifetime resources that each age group can mobilise. If $V(a)$ is the ratio of lifetime resources of all households aged a to aggregate real income, then $V(a)S(a)$ is the total saving of age group a as a fraction of aggregate real income. The aggregate saving rate s is derived by summing across all age groups:

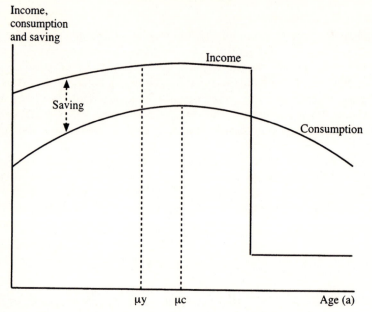

Figure 7.1 Life-cycle patterns of income, consumption and saving

$$s = \int V(a)S(a)da \qquad (2)$$

With steady state growth, $V(a)$ is independent of time and given by

$$V(a) = V(0)e^{-ga} \qquad (3)$$

where $V(0)$ is the ratio of lifetime resources of newly formed households to aggregate real income and g is the rate of growth in aggregate real income. If g is zero,

$$s = V(0)(1 - L) = 0 \qquad (4)$$

All aggregate real income is consumed because $V(a)$ is a constant, L equals 1, and $\int S(a)da$ is $1 - L$.

The lifetime resources $V(a)$ of young savers exceed those of old dissavers and there can be positive aggregate saving when growth in aggregate real income is positive. This is the 'rate-of-growth effect'. The rate-of-growth effect is itself determined by the relationship between income and consumption over the household's lifetime. Mason (1987) shows that the timing of household saving can be defined in terms of the mean ages of consumption

142

μ_c and income μ_y, as shown in Figure 7.1. These are the average ages (weighted by the values of consumption expenditure and income at each age) at which half lifetime consumption and income are reached.

The higher is the rate of economic growth, the richer is the current generation compared to the previous generation. The rate-of-growth effect can be positive only to the extent that households on average accumulate wealth when they are younger in order to dispose of these assets when they are older. In countries where households can borrow against future income, households may have spent more than they have earned, in cumulative terms, for a large part of their lifetime. In this case, the rate-of-growth effect can be negative.

When the restrictive assumption of zero lifetime saving is discarded, the life-cycle model can incorporate a level effect as well as the rate-of-growth effect discussed above. The level effect, which includes the bequest motive for saving, refers to the ratio of lifetime consumption to lifetime income. Any factor that increases this consumption ratio reduces the ratio of lifetime saving to lifetime income. It also reduces the ratio of current saving to current income.

The aggregate saving rate can be represented approximately as a function of g, L, μ_c, and μ_y. All factors that influence the aggregate saving rate must enter through one of these four variables (Fry and Mason, 1982):

$$s \approx -\log(L) + (\mu_c - \mu_y)g \tag{5}$$

Equation (5) allows factors that influence the timing of consumption or income over the life cycle to enter the saving function interactively with the rate of growth in income.

The level of household consumption can be approximated by a log-linear function in a vector of independent variables z:

$$L = e^{-\alpha z} \tag{6}$$

The difference between the mean ages of consumption and income is represented by a linear function in the same vector of independent variables z:

$$\mu_c - \mu_y = \beta z \tag{7}$$

Substituting equations (6) and (7) into equation (5) gives

$$s \approx \alpha z + \beta z g \tag{8}$$

For this study I estimate the following national saving function:

$$SNY = b_{10} + \overset{+}{b}_{11} \widehat{YG} + b_{12}RD^2 + b_{13}BLACK^2$$
$$+ b_{14}\widehat{YG} \cdot RD^2 + b_{15}\widehat{YG} \cdot BLACK^2 + \overset{+}{b}_{16} SNY_{t-1} \tag{9}$$

where *SNY* is the national saving ratio, *YG* is the rate of growth in real GNP (continuously compounded), *RD* is the real deposit rate of interest, and *BLACK* is the black market exchange rate premium measured as 1 + (*PR*/100), where *PR* is the premium expressed in percentage form.

An increase in the real risk-adjusted rate of return on financial assets raises the relative price of current to future consumption. If the substitution effect outweighs the income effect as posited by Olson and Bailey (1981), then the saving ratio rises with an increase in the real interest rates. This implies an increase in the mean age of consumption. Summers (1981) also pinpoints circumstances in which a rise in the rate of interest shifts consumption towards older age, raising the mean age of consumption.

Theoretically, it is possible that the income effect could outweigh the substitution effect, so causing a decline in the mean age of consumption, provided the income elasticity of current consumption substantially exceeds the income elasticity of future consumption. There is, however, no plausible basis for expecting such a preference structure (Olson and Bailey, 1981). The interest rate effect on the mean age of earning is ambiguous but probably negligible. Consequently, one anticipates that a rise in the domestic or foreign real interest rates would increase the rate-of-growth effect.

The real rate of interest also influences the relative price of bequests. Thus a rise in the real rate of interest may reduce the level of lifetime consumption. There is no reason, however, why the elasticity of substitution between present and future consumption should be the same as the elasticity of substitution between present consumption and bequests (Olson and Bailey, 1981).

Any observed association between real interest rates and saving ratios may indicate only that there is substitution between saving embodied in physical goods that are not recorded as investment in the national income accounts, and saving embodied in financial assets that does finance investment as defined by national income accountants (Brown, 1973; Fry, 1978). In an open economy, financial repression may affect *measured* national saving through unambiguous portfolio shifts rather than true saving effects. If illegal capital flight takes place through under-invoicing exports and over-invoicing imports, the measured balance of payments deficit on current account rises when capital flight increases. Since national saving is measured by subtracting the current account deficit from domestic investment, it will fall when the measured current account deficit rises. If such illegal capital flight is influenced in part by relative yields on domestic and foreign financial assets, measured national saving or national saving actually available to finance domestic investment would be affected positively by an increase in the domestic real interest rate. In both these cases, a higher real interest rate may not raise the true saving ratio, but rather free more resources for productive investment. Its true effect may be on the average efficiency of investment, not on its volume. However, this suggests that financial repression would be associated with lower measured national saving ratios.

Referring to work by Calvo and Coricelli (1992), De Gregorio and Guidotti (1993, p. 11) claim that real interest rates are not a good indicator of financial repression or distortion. They suggest that the relationship between real interest rates and economic growth might resemble an inverted *U* curve:

> Very low (and negative) real interest rates tend to cause financial disintermediation and hence tend to reduce growth, as implied by the McKinnon-Shaw hypothesis.... On the other hand, very high real interest rates that do not reflect improved efficiency of investment, but rather a lack of credibility of economic policy or various forms of country risk, are likely to result in a lower level of investment as well as a concentration in excessively risky projects.
>
> (De Gregorio and Guidotti, 1993)

In other words, large negative and large positive real interest rates may well exert the same deleterious effect. De Gregorio and Guidotti abandon real interest rates in favour of domestic credit to the private sector divided by GNP as a measure of financial development.

The De Gregorio–Guidotti effect could also apply to saving behaviour. Very high real interest rates reflecting increased risk and uncertainty could also reduce measured national saving, particularly if the increased domestic risk encourages savers to remove their savings abroad through under- and over-invoicing. I resolve the problem that both very low and very high real interest rates could deter saving, not by abandoning real interest rates, but rather by using the square of the real deposit rate. This ensures that large positive and negative values exert the same effect, presumably negative, on the saving ratio.

My other measure of financial repression, the black market exchange rate premium, may also produce a negative effect on the national saving ratio. It too may reflect country risk and hence the decreased attractiveness of domestic assets. Since virtually all black market exchange rate premia are positive, I used both the level and the square of the black market exchange rate premium in an initial specification search. The estimate reported here uses the square of the black market exchange rate premium since it has a marginally higher explanatory power than its level.

In effect, the saving function derived here is the private sector saving function Snp/Y to which the government saving ratio Sng/Y has been added; Snp is private national saving, Sng is government sector national saving, and Y is GNP. Unfortunately, disaggregated saving data are unavailable for most of the sample countries.[3] In any case, inflation badly distorts the measurement of disaggregated private and public saving because of the failure to account correctly for the inflation tax revenue. Fortunately, however, including components of public saving that are not substitutes for private saving affects only the intercept, provided they are independent of the explanatory variables (Fry and Mason, 1982).

For all the empirical work reported in this chapter, data are taken from *International Financial Statistics*, CD-ROM, the World Bank's *Socio-economic Time-series Access and Retrieval System: World Tables*, and *World Development Report 1991: Supplementary Data*. Since the coefficient of *RD* was not significant when *RD* was entered independently, this term is omitted from the saving estimate for a sample of 16 developing countries (Argentina, Brazil, Chile, Egypt, India, Indonesia, Korea, Malaysia, Mexico, Nigeria, Pakistan, the Philippines, Sri Lanka, Thailand, Turkey and Venezuela) reported below.

The regression method used throughout this study is iterative three-stage least squares which is, asymptotically, full-information maximum likelihood (Johnston, 1984). I estimate the 16 individual country equations for saving, investment, export growth, and output growth as systems of equations with cross-equation equality restrictions on all coefficients except the intercept. Hence, the estimates apply to a representative member of this sample of developing countries.[4] The estimation technique corrects for heteroscedasticity across country equations and exploits contemporaneously correlated disturbances.[5] The estimation period is 1970–1988.[6]

The estimate (297 observations, t statistics in parentheses) for the national saving ratio is:

$$SNY = 0.274\widehat{YG} - 0.055BLACK^2 - 0.538(\widehat{YG} \cdot BLACK^2)$$
$$(1006.809)\ (-141.954)(-90.088)$$

$$- 0.073(\widehat{YG} \cdot RD^2) + 0.820SNY_{t-1}$$
$$(-69.276)(3983.060)$$

$$R^2 = 0.862$$

(10)

It indicates that the national saving ratio in this sample of countries is increased by income growth. However, a higher black market exchange rate premium not only exerts a negative impact on saving through the level effect but also reduces the rate-of-growth effect, as shown by the negative interaction term. The real interest rate also reduces the national saving ratio as it diverges from zero by reducing the rate-of-growth effect. The fourth section of the chapter demonstrates that a higher black market exchange premium and a real exchange rate that diverges from zero also reduce the national saving ratio indirectly by reducing the rate of economic growth.

INVESTMENT

The investment function specified here in terms of the ratio of investment to GNP is based on the flexible accelerator model. Blejer and Khan (1984) describe some of the difficulties of estimating neoclassical investment functions for developing countries. Without data on the capital stock and the return to capital, there is little choice in practice but to use some version of the accelerator model.

The accelerator model has the desired capital stock K^* proportional to real output y:

$$K^* = \alpha y \tag{11}$$

This can be expressed in terms of a desired ratio of net investment to output $(I/Y)^*$:

$$(I/Y)^* = \alpha\gamma \tag{12}$$

where γ is the rate of growth in output denoted YG in the regression equation.

The partial adjustment mechanism specified for the investment *ratio* is somewhat more complicated than the equivalent mechanism for the *level* of investment. Specifically, there could be a lag in achieving the same investment ratio this year as last year if output rose rapidly last year; this year's desired investment *level* will be higher than last year's, despite a constant desired *ratio* of investment to output. To incorporate this adjustment lag, last year's growth rate, γ_{t-1}, can be included as an explanatory variable. In this case, however, the coefficient of γ_{t-1} was insignificant; hence, γ_{t-1} is omitted from the estimate.

The remaining adjustment mechanism allows the actual investment rate to adjust partially in any one period to the difference between the desired investment rate and the investment rate in the previous period:

$$\Delta(I/Y) = \lambda[(I/Y)^* - (I/Y)_{t-1}] \tag{13}$$

or

$$I/Y = \lambda(I/Y)^* + (1 - \lambda)(I/Y)_{t-1} \tag{14}$$

where λ is the coefficient of adjustment.

The flexible accelerator model allows economic conditions to influence the adjustment coefficient λ. Specifically,

$$\lambda = \beta_0 + \left[\frac{\beta_1 z_1 + \beta_2 z_2 + \beta_3 z_3 + \cdots}{(I/Y)^* - (I/Y)_{t-1}} \right] \tag{15}$$

where z_i are the variables that affect λ. Since one of these variables can be an intercept term for the depreciation rate, the flexible accelerator model can be estimated for the gross rather than the net investment ratio.

A simple specification search suggests that, for the 16 developing countries analysed here, the speed of adjustment is influenced by the real interest rate squared but not by the black market exchange rate premium. If the real deposit rate of interest is held below its free-market equilibrium level, the effective (albeit unobservable) real loan rate would rise as the real deposit rate falls. The lower the real deposit rate, the smaller is the volume of saving and hence the higher is the market-clearing loan rate of interest. In such case, the real deposit rate acts as an inverse proxy for the real loan rate and has a positive impact on the investment ratio (Blejer and Khan, 1984). In other words, changes in the real deposit rate trace out movements along the supply (saving) curve rather than along the demand (investment) curve.

In the absence of administrative ceilings, real interest rates are likely to be positive. In such a case, a rise in real deposit rates could be produced by a leftward shift in the supply (saving) curve and a corresponding movement up the demand (investment) curve. The result is a reduction in investment. In other words, a zero real interest rate maximises the investment ratio. Lower real rates imply ceilings that reduce the availability of investible funds. Higher real rates signal distress borrowing not for investment but for survival; loan demand for productive investment is crowded out. The real interest rate squared allows for these non-linear effects on investment.

The investment function derived from this flexible accelerator model is (297 observations):

$$IY = 0.251\widehat{YG} - 1.628RD^2 + 0.692IY_{t-1}$$
$$(32.671) \quad (-11.661) \quad (43.998) \tag{16}$$

$$R^2 = 0.794$$

Evidently, high negative or positive real interest rates reduce the investment ratio.

EXPORT GROWTH

For a small, open, developing economy, export demand is likely to be infinitely elastic. Therefore, export growth in this model is determined from the supply side. The first determinant of export supply, expressed as the rate of growth in exports at constant prices XKG, is the rate of growth in real GNP,

YG, acting as the supply constraint. Since higher investment raises the capacity to export, the ratio of domestic investment to GNP, expressed in constant prices IKY, is included as an additional supply constraint.

The basic price variable in the export equation is the real exchange rate or the relative price of exports to non-traded goods. However, the real exchange rate is itself determined by the saving–investment balance and foreign exchange restrictions. Hence I estimate a quasi reduced-form equation, substituting the gap between national saving and domestic investment as a ratio to GNP (SIY) and the black market exchange rate premium for the real exchange rate.[7] Again, the black market exchange rate premium squared yields somewhat better results than its level (290 observations):

$$XKG = 0.364(\widehat{YG}) + 0.179(\widehat{IY}) + 0.496(\widehat{SIY}) - 0.224(BLACK^2)$$
$$\quad\;\; (5.797) \qquad (3.756) \quad\;\; (11.941) \qquad (-2.846) \qquad\qquad (17)$$

$$R^2 = 0.153$$

As anticipated, the output growth rate, the investment ratio and the saving–investment balance increase export growth, while the black market premium exerts a negative effect.

OUTPUT GROWTH

The effect of export growth on output growth is explored by Feder (1982). Feder argues that there are two channels – higher marginal productivities and externalities – through which rapid export growth can affect the rate of economic growth in excess of the contribution of *net* export growth to GNP. If exports affect the production of non-exports with a constant elasticity θ, the rate of growth in *gross* exports at constant prices XKG captures solely the externality effect, while the rate of growth in exports scaled by the lagged export/GNP ratio $XKGY$ picks up both the differential marginal productivity δ and the externality effects (Feder, 1982): $YG = [\delta/(1 + \delta) - \theta] \cdot XKGY + \theta \cdot XKG$. In fact, only XKG is significant here, implying that $\delta/(1 + \delta) = \theta$.

The standard Harrod–Domar model used in the earlier literature in development economics is based on the assumption of surplus labour. Hence, it can be expressed $Y = \sigma K$, where Y is output, σ is the constant output/capital ratio, and K is the capital stock. Taking first differences and dividing both sides by Y gives the growth rate relationship $\gamma = \sigma(I/Y)$, where γ is the rate of economic growth ($\Delta Y/Y$) and I is investment (ΔK). An increase in the saving–investment ratio, s or I/Y, raises the growth rate γ permanently. For example, with s equal to 0.3 and σ equal to 0.25, the rate of growth is 7.5 per cent. At a saving ratio of 0.4 per cent, the growth rate rises to 10 per cent.

The assumption of constant marginal returns to capital in the early development models was regarded as a serious defect for most of the 1960s and 1970s. However, endogenous growth models developed since the mid-1980s provide a theoretical justification for assuming that the marginal product of capital does not diminish for the economy as a whole. As Krugman (1993, p. 17) notes: 'The basic idea of this literature ... is that there may be external economies to capital accumulation, so that the true elasticity of output with respect to capital greatly exceeds its share of GNP at market prices.' The aggregate production function in a typical endogenous growth model takes the form $Y = K^\alpha X^\beta$, where K is capital, X is some factor like land or labour that has a fixed supply per capita, and $\alpha \geq 1$. The variable K represents a combination of physical capital and knowledge.

To be compatible with the existence of competitive markets, individual firms face declining returns to scale and diminishing marginal productivity of their own capital. However, positive production externalities from the knowledge component or learning process of K, which is a public good, increase returns and raise the marginal productivity of capital at the aggregate level. This is modelled by making the efficiency of an individual firm a function of the aggregate capital stock. For an individual firm using k and x inputs combined with the aggregate stock of knowledge, the production function could take the form $y = K^\phi k^v x^\beta$, where $v + \beta \leq 1$ and $\phi + v = \alpha \geq 1$ (Romer, 1991). In this model, as in the Harrod–Domar model, an increase in the investment ratio raises the growth rate permanently.

Capital as broadly defined in endogenous growth models need not suffer from diminishing marginal returns due to learning-by-doing, human capital, research and development, or public infrastructure. One group of endogenous growth models (Scott, 1989, 1992) sets the elasticity of output with respect to the aggregate capital stock at one, implying increasing returns to capital and labour together. Another group (Lucas, 1988; Romer, 1990) introduces a specific growth factor which raises the total productivity of the other factors of production; one such growth factor is human capital. Empirically, it is much easier to broaden the concept of capital and posit a learning externality than it is to identify and estimate any specific growth factor. All this justifies the inclusion of the investment ratio in an aggregate growth rate function.[8]

Although the marginal product of capital may not suffer diminishing returns, its value could be affected by financial repression. As the World Bank (1989, pp. 29–31) points out:

> Historically, the quality of investment has been at least as important for growth as the quantity. Although the fastest-growing countries had higher rates of investment than the others, empirical studies generally find that less than half the growth in output is attributable to increases in labour and capital. Higher productivity explains the rest. Faster growth, more investment, and greater financial depth all come partly from higher saving. In its own right, however, greater financial depth also contributes to growth by improving the productivity of investment.

An increasing body of evidence suggests that qualitative differences in investment are far more important than quantitative differences in explaining different rates of growth across countries (Fry, 1995, Chapter 8; King and Levine 1993a, 1993b; Roubini and Sala-i-Martin, 1992). These productivity differentials may be caused by trade distortions and financial repression imposed on the economy by government policy (Dollar, 1992; Roubini and Sala-i-Martin, 1991). Therefore, I interact both the black market exchange rate premium *BLACK* and the domestic real interest rate *RD* squared with the investment ratio. In this case the initial specification search indicated that the level rather than the square of the black market exchange rate premium produced better results.

The point made by De Gregorio and Guidotti (1993) that very high real interest rates can be as destructive as very low real rates holds up well in this growth rate estimate. Initially, I estimated the relationship between the rate of economic growth *YG*, the investment ratio *IKY*, the real rate of interest *RD* and the rate of growth in exports at constant prices *XKG* in an equation of the form:

$$YG = \beta_1(IKY) + \beta_2[IKY \cdot (RD + \beta_3) \cdot (RD + \beta_3)] + \beta_4(XKG) \qquad (18)$$

Since the parameter β_3 was not significantly different from zero, although its negative value implies that growth is maximised at some positive real interest rate, I drop it from the estimate reported here. Three-stage iterative least squares estimate is (290 observations):

$$YG = 0.226(\widehat{IKY}) - 0.999(\widehat{IKY} \cdot BLACK) - 0.354(\widehat{IKY} \cdot RD^2)$$
$$(16.850) \qquad (-9.786) \qquad (-11.389)$$
$$+ 0.098(\widehat{XKG}) \qquad\qquad (19)$$
$$(19.691)$$

$$R^2 = 0.202$$

Both the direct effect from equation (19) and the overall effect from the joint simulation of equations (10), (16), (17) and (19) of a rising real interest rate on output growth are illustrated in Figure 7.2.[9] This figure is produced using the mean values of all the explanatory variables with the exception of the real deposit rate of interest. The mean value of the real deposit rate is zero with a standard deviation of 23 per cent. Its minimum value is –83 per cent and its maximum value 221 per cent. Figure 7.2 shows that the relationship between the real interest rate and growth does indeed resemble an inverted *U*. Both very low and very high real interest rates reduce output growth through the effects of such interest rates on investment productivity.

The line P_n in the figure denotes two standard deviations below the mean of all negative interest rates in the Pacific Basin economies, C_n denotes two

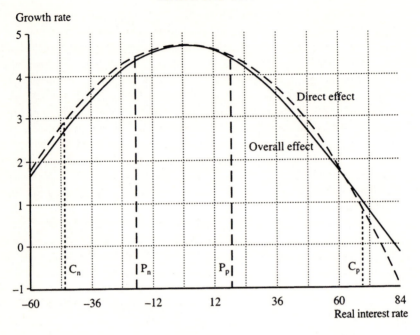

Figure 7.2 Effects of real interest rate on economic growth rate

standard deviations below the mean of all negative interest rates in the remaining 11 countries (the control group), P_p denotes two standard deviations above the mean of all zero or positive interest rates in the Pacific Basin economies, while C_p denotes two standard deviations above the mean of all zero or positive interest rates in the control group countries. Evidently, real interest rates deviated from their growth-maximising level far more in the control group countries than they did in the Pacific Basin economies.

This result is comparable to other estimates of the effect on real interest rates of economic growth. For example, Polak (1989) reports econometric estimates for a sample of 40 developing countries over the period 1965–1985 in which an increase in a negative real interest rate by 10 percentage points raises the rate of economic growth by between 2 and 3 percentage points. He concludes that a reduction in the real interest rate below its equilibrium level by 1 percentage point requires an increase in the investment ratio by 1 percentage point in order to maintain a fixed rate of economic growth. I find similar relationships in various samples of Asian developing economies (Fry, 1991, 1995).

Both the direct effect from equation (19) and the overall effect from the joint simulation of equations (10), (16), (17) and (19) of a rising black market foreign exchange rate premium on output growth are illustrated in Figure 7.3.[10] The growth rate is reduced as the black market exchange rate premium

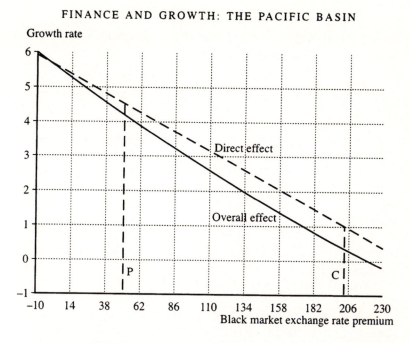

Figure 7.3 Effects of black market premium on economic growth rate

rises through its effect on investment productivity. The mean value of the black market exchange rate premium is 31 per cent with a standard deviation of 63 per cent. Its minimum value is –10 and its maximum value is 639 per cent.

The line *P* denotes two standard deviations above the mean of all zero or positive black market exchange rate premia in the Pacific Basin economies, while *C* denotes two standard deviations above the mean of all zero or positive black market exchange rate premia in the control group of countries. Evidently, black market exchange rate premia tended to be considerably higher in the control group than they were in the Pacific Basin economies.

Over the period 1970–1988, the continuously compounded output growth rate in the Pacific Basin countries averaged 6.2 per cent compared with 3.9 per cent in the control group. Over the same period, the black market exchange rate premium averaged 6.2 per cent in the Pacific Basin countries compared with 42.6 per cent in the control group, while the square of the real interest rate was 10 times greater in the control group than it was in the Pacific Basin. Differences in the distortion measures account for 1.7 of the 2.3 percentage point difference in output growth rates between the Pacific Basin and control group countries. In other words, these two distortions explain approximately three quarters of the difference in output growth rates between these two country groups.

FURTHER SUPPORT FOR THE IMPORTANCE OF FINANCIAL CONDITIONS

While financial instability typically accompanies financial repression, financial stability is a prerequisite for financial development. A realistic exchange rate that deviates little from the equilibrium free-market rate is another essential prerequisite. A crucial condition for financial stability is fiscal discipline; government deficits must be kept under control. The empirical work reported in this paper indicates that financial distortions explain much of the difference in saving and investment ratios as well as export and output growth rates between five Pacific Basin and a control group of 11 other developing countries.

Further support for the importance of financial conditions is provided by the tests of different sample means in Table 7.2. The means of inflation, domestic credit expansion and the proportion of domestic credit expropriated by the government (reflecting fiscal discipline) are all significantly lower in Pacific Basin developing economies than in the control group of developing countries. In contrast, output and export growth rates, as well as the export ratio, are significantly higher in the Pacific Basin developing economies.[11]

Finally, I examine simple relationships between rates of economic growth, inflation, the black market exchange rate premium, the ratio of net domestic credit to the government sector to total domestic credit and the real interest rate squared for the sample countries. Table 7.3 presents these bivariate regression estimates. They yield significantly negative relationships between growth and inflation and between growth and the black market exchange rate premium. On the other hand, they indicate significantly positive relationships

Table 7.2 Sample means for some key macroeconomic variables

Variable	Pacific Basin mean	Control group mean	Difference	SE of difference
YG	6.4	4.1	2.3*	0.5
XKY	32.7	17.2	15.5*	1.7
XKG	9.3	5.1	4.1*	1.7
INF	12.8	27.3	−14.5*	3.5
DDCY	6.1	10.2	−4.1*	0.8
DCG	22.5	34.1	−11.6*	2.8
DCGR	16.6	38.9	−22.4*	4.7

Notes: *YG* = rate of growth in GNP (constant prices, continuously compounded); *XKY* = exports/GNP (constant prices); *XKG* = rate of growth in exports (constant prices, continuously compounded); *INF* = rate of change in GNP deflator (continuously compounded); *DDCY* = change in domestic credit/GNP (current prices); *DCG* = rate of change in domestic credit (continuously compounded); *DCGR* = net domestic credit to government/domestic credit (current prices).
*Significant at 99 per cent confidence level

154

Table 7.3 Bivariate relationships between growth, inflation, and government credit ratios

	Dependent variable	
	YG	INF
INF	−0.037	
	(−5.668)	
BLACK	−0.014	
	(−3.684)	
DCGR		0.060
		(1.973)
RD^2		0.005
		(9.303)

Notes: *YG* = rate of growth in GNP (constant prices, continuously compounded); *INF* = rate of change in GNP deflator (continuously compounded); *BLACK* = black market exchange rate premium; *DCGR* = net domestic credit to government/domestic credit (current prices); *RD* = domestic real interest rate; *t* statistics in parentheses

between inflation and the government credit ratio and between inflation and the squared real interest rate. These results are consistent with the hypotheses that government deficits raise inflation and lower rates of economic growth.[12] The findings of Fry and Lilien (1986), combined with results reported here, are certainly consistent with the hypothesis that greater monetary and fiscal discipline, combined with the absence of financial repression in the Pacific Basin developing economies, have contributed to the higher levels of saving and investment, as well as the higher output and export growth rates in this region.

CONCLUSION

This chapter demonstrates that a reasonably large part of the above-average economic performance of the Pacific Basin developing market economies can be explained by their negligible levels of financial repression, as measured both by the real rate of interest and the black market exchange rate premium. Their relatively undistorted financial and foreign exchange markets have stimulated investment and export growth. High investment and rapid export growth have accelerated economic growth. Higher rates of economic growth and undistorted financial and foreign exchange markets raise both saving and investment ratios. The evidence suggests that financial conditions played an important role in producing the virtuous circles of high saving, investment, output growth and export growth found in the Pacific Basin.

NOTES

1 My thanks go to Jakob de Haan, François de la Vergne and Claude Mathieu for useful comments on parts of this paper. Financial support from the ACE Programme of the European Commission's PHARE Operational Service under contract ACE-92-0615-R entitled 'Adjustment and Growth in Eastern Europe' with the University of Birmingham and from the French Planning Commission under its project on 'Convertibility and Exchange Rate Regimes in East European Countries' at the University of Bordeaux is gratefully acknowledged. *Micro TSP*, version 7.0, was used for all graphics and regressions.

2 The second period here is 1982–1990.

3 Indeed, not even government deficit or government revenue and consumption expenditure data are available for several of the sample countries.

4 Tests were not conducted for the appropriateness of imposing these cross-equation restrictions.

5 The instruments are the exogenous explanatory variables plus lagged domestic credit expansion divided by GNP, the lagged terms of trade and real exchange rate indices in natural logarithms, lagged growth, lagged saving and investment ratios, the public sector borrowing requirement divided by GNP, the world real interest rate, oil price inflation, the rate of growth (continuously compounded) in OECD output, and lagged cumulated *net* foreign liabilities converted into domestic currency and divided by lagged GNP.

6 Shorter periods are used in all estimates for Brazil (1970–1985) and Chile (1970–1984), and in the output and export growth equations for Sri Lanka (1970–1987) and Venezuela (1975–1987).

7 An estimate using the national logarithm of the real exchange rate produces virtually the same results.

8 Endogenous growth models provide a paradox with respect to international capital flows. On the one hand, neoclassical growth models imply that capital flows from the capital-rich countries to capital-poor countries which exhibit higher marginal returns to capital. However, this flow can exert only a small and temporary effect on poor countries' growth rates. Endogenous growth models, on the other hand, provide a much more important role for capital in the growth process. Without diminishing marginal productivity of capital, however, there is no incentive to transfer it from capital-rich to capital-poor countries (Krugman, 1993).

9 The simultaneous equation model also contains identities defining the saving–investment gap and the equivalence of the nominal and real investment ratio.

10 Again, the simultaneous equation model also contains identities defining the saving–investment gap and the equivalence of the nominal and real investment ratio.

11 The variance of inflation is also lower in the Pacific Basin developing economies than in the control group.

12 The variance of inflation also has a significant negative relationship with economic growth.

REFERENCES

Blejer, M.I. and M.S. Khan (1984), 'Government Policy and Private Investment in Developing Countries', *IMF Staff Papers*, 31, pp. 379–403.

Brown, G.T. (1973), *Korean Pricing Policies and Economic Development in the 1960s*, Baltimore: Johns Hopkins University Press.

Calvo, G.A. and F. Coricelli (1992), 'Stagflationary Effects of Stabilization Programs in Reforming Socialist Countries: Enterprise-Side vs. Household-Side Factors', *World Bank Economic Review*, 6, pp. 71–90.

De Gregorio, J. and P.E. Guidotti (1993), 'Financial Development and Economic Growth', mimeo, International Monetary Fund.

Dollar, D. (1992), 'Outward-Oriented Developing Economies Really Do Grow More Rapidly: Evidence from 95 LDCs, 1976–1985', *Economic Development and Cultural Change*, 40, pp. 523–44.

Feder, G. (1982), 'On Exports and Economic Growth', *Journal of Development Economics*, 12, pp. 59–73.

Fry, M.J. (1978), 'Money and Capital or Financial Deepening in Economic Development?', *Journal of Money, Credit and Banking*, 10, pp. 464–75.

———— (1991), 'Domestic Resource Mobilization in Developing Asia: Four Policy Issues', *Asian Development Review*, 9, pp. 15–39.

———— (1995), *Money, Interest, and Banking in Economic Development*, second edn, Baltimore: Johns Hopkins University Press.

Fry, M.J. and D.M. Lilien (1986), 'Monetary Policy Responses to Exogenous Shocks', *American Economic Review*, 76, pp. 79–83.

Fry, M.J. and A. Mason (1982), 'The Variable Rate-of-Growth Effect in the Life-Cycle Saving Model: Children, Capital Inflows, Interest and Growth in a New Specification of the Life-Cycle Model Applied to Seven Asian Developing Countries', *Economic Inquiry*, 20, pp. 426–42.

Giovannini, A. and M. De Melo (1993), 'Government Revenue from Financial Repression', *American Economic Review*, 83, pp. 953–63.

International Monetary Fund (IMF) (1994a), *World Economic Outlook*, May, Washington DC: International Monetary Fund.

———— (1994b), *International Financial Statistics Yearbook*, Washington DC: International Monetary Fund.

Johnston, J. (1984), *Econometric Methods*, third edn, New York: McGraw-Hill.

King, R.G. and R. Levine (1993a), 'Finance and Growth: Schumpeter Might Be Right', *Quarterly Journal of Economics*, 108, pp. 717–37.

———— (1993b), 'Finance, Entrepreneurship, and Growth: Theory and Evidence', *Journal of Monetary Economics*, 32, pp. 513–42.

Krugman, P.R. (1993) 'International Finance and Economic Development', in A. Giovannini (ed.) *Finance and Development: Issues and Experience*, Cambridge: Cambridge University Press, pp. 11–23.

Lucas, R.E., Jr (1988), 'On the Mechanics of Economic Development', *Journal of Monetary Economics*, 22, pp. 3–42.

Mason, A. (1987), 'National Saving Rates and Population Growth: A New Model and New Evidence', in D.G. Johnson and R.D. Lee (eds) *Population Growth and Economic Development: Issues and Evidence*, Madison: University of Wisconsin Press for the National Academy of Sciences, pp. 523–60.

Olson, M. and M.J. Bailey (1981), 'Positive Time Preference', *Journal of Political Economy*, 89, pp. 1–25.

Polak, J.J. (1989), *Financial Policies and Development*, Paris: Development Centre of the Organisation for Economic Co-operation and Development, 1989.

Romer, P.M. (1990), 'Endogenous Technological Change', *Journal of Political Economy*, 98, pp. S71–S102.

———— (1991), 'Increasing Returns and New Developments in the Theory of Growth', in W.A. Barnett, B. Cornet, C. d'Aspermont, J.J. Gabszewicz and A. Mas-Colell (eds) *Equilibrium Theory and Applications: Proceedings of the Sixth International Symposium in Economic Theory and Econometrics*, Cambridge:

Cambridge University Press, pp. 83–110.

Roubini, N. and X. Sala-i-Martin (1991), 'Financial Development, the Trade Regime, and Economic Growth', *Working Paper*, No. 3876, National Bureau of Economic Research.

—— (1992), 'Financial Repression and Economic Growth', *Journal of Development Economics*, 39, pp. 5–30.

Scott, M.F.G. (1989), *A New View of Economic Growth*, Oxford: Clarendon Press.

—— (1992), 'A New Theory of Endogenous Economic Growth', *Oxford Review of Economic Policy*, 8, pp. 29–42.

Summers, L.H. (1981), 'Capital Taxation and Accumulation in a Life Cycle Growth Model', *American Economic Review*, 71, pp. 533–44.

World Bank (1989), *World Development Report 1989*, Washington DC: World Bank.

Part II

ISSUES ON FINANCIAL POLICIES IN DEVELOPING COUNTRIES

8

FINANCIAL SECTOR POLICIES
Analytical framework and research agenda
Ross Levine[1]

INTRODUCTION

Establishing appropriate financial sector policies is of paramount importance to policy makers because financial intermediaries provide services – facilitating transactions and risk management, mobilising and allocating capital, and exerting corporate governance – that are necessary for economic growth.[2] More 'efficient' financial systems provide better financial services, and thereby provide a bigger boost to growth than less efficient financial systems. If inherent characteristics of the market for financial intermediary services suggest that unregulated markets will inadequately supply these crucial services, then governments have a responsibility to consider interventions to improve the provision of financial services. Government policies, however, often play the principal role in reducing the quality of financial services and in obstructing financial development. Consequently, policy makers have the difficult task of enacting interventions that ameliorate market failures, while avoiding government interventions that negatively affect the provision of financial services.

The major purposes of this chapter are to develop a framework for analysing financial sector policy issues, to demonstrate the usefulness of this framework by examining two policies, and to identify important research questions regarding the links between financial sector policies and economic growth. More specifically, I review reasons commonly advanced by economists for government intervention in and regulation of financial markets, use these reasons to develop a five-point checklist for evaluating financial policies, and then use this framework to examine government insurance of financial intermediary liabilities, and official restrictions on the activities of banks. An important by-product of constructing this analytical framework is that it highlights crucial weaknesses in economists' understanding of the ties between financial sector policies and sustained economic development.

手稿

REASONS FOR GOVERNMENT INTERVENTION

This section describes five inherent characteristics of the activities of financial 中间机构 intermediaries that economists frequently argue create a potentially positive role for government intervention in financial markets:[3]

外部性
1 Externalities in failure: contagion;
2 Externalities in monitoring financial institutions;
3 Externalities in appraising and monitoring firms;
4 Imperfect competition;
5 Missing or incomplete markets.

Although the economics profession generally places great confidence in the ability of free, competitive markets, many financial economists argue that free financial markets – financial markets that are unregulated and unrestricted by the government – will not provide good financial services in a stable fashion, so government supervision and regulation of financial market activities can sometimes improve social welfare. Great care must be taken, however, since government interventions and regulations themselves frequently thwart the stable provision of high quality financial services. Thus, this section reviews five market failures commonly discussed in the literature as justifying government involvement and identifies important areas for future research.

Externalities in failure

Description

Probably the most widely cited and accepted reason for government supervision and regulation of financial intermediaries is the fear of contagion: the fear that the failure of one intermediary will cause other intermediaries to fail. Given poor information about the solvency and performance of financial institutions, investors may interpret weakness in one financial institution as a signal of the poor condition of other financial institutions and withdraw their funds from all intermediaries. Individual financial institutions will not consider that their independent actions could trigger broader, systemic failure. Thus, from society's perspective, individual institutions will tend to engage in excessive risk taking. For this reason, many financial analysts argue that government supervisors and regulators should enact policies to ensure the safety and soundness of the financial system.[4]

Effects of contagion on the provision of financial services

Contagion and the fears of contagion can hinder economic development.

• First, contagion directly disrupts economic activity. For example, bank runs cause banks to demand payment of existing loans and slow the

162

issuance of new loans, which, under most plausible conditions,[5] reduces investment, induces bankruptcies, raises unemployment, and slows growth.

- Second, by inducing a contraction in credit and the medium of exchange and by interfering with banking operations, contagion can disrupt a country's payments system and thereby impede all forms of commerce.
- Third, failing financial institutions in a crisis environment will not evaluate firms and monitor managers objectively, or provide risk hedging vehicles as effectively as stable institutions. Thus, resources will be deployed less efficiently than in the absence of systemic financial failure.[6,7]
- Finally, fears of contagion and financial instability reduce confidence in financial intermediaries. The drop in confidence will make resource mobilisation more difficult.

The importance of contagion and financial fragility to economic activity suggests that contagion and financial stability should be part of our select 'checklist' of issues to consider when evaluating financial policies.

Market response to failure externalities

The market will respond to the threat of contagion. Safe intermediaries will try to establish transparent means for communicating their soundness to the public. Established institutions will try to coordinate their actions when a few isolated failures threaten the financial system. Financial intermediaries will be better able to communicate their condition to the public and coordinate in crises if there are standardized, informative, and consolidated financial statements of financial intermediaries, and the financial system is not very fragmented.

Policy implications

Potential policy responses to externalities associated with financial intermediary failure fall into six categories. First, governments can require information disclosure to make it easier for the public to distinguish troubled from safe financial institutions. Second, governments should avoid financial policies that augment the possibility of contagion. For example, evidence from the United States suggests that financial policies encouraged the proliferation of an excessively large number of fragmented, under-diversified banks that are more sensitive to economic shocks; less able to organise private insurance and self-regulatory mechanisms; and less capable of coordinating effectively when problems arise.[8] Third, governments may enact financial policies that seek to encourage prudent risk taking by financial intermediaries. This may include restricting the activities and investments of financial institutions, establishing high-risk based capital requirements, requiring intermediaries to hold portfolios well diversified across different firms, regions and industries, promoting strong liquidity management policies, and even limiting competition to encourage safe practices. Fourth, governments may avoid tax systems that create incentives for high debt–equity ratios which enhance the financial fragility of enterprises. Fifth, governments may develop forward looking contingency plans to minimise the negative consequences of contagion and support private initiatives at coping with potential contagion. Finally, governments may insure investor assets in financial intermediaries to prevent contagion. The crucial research question is which, if any, of these policies will, on net, best reduce the probability of contagion while not creating other problems. Bringing rigorous theoretical and especially empirical work to bear on this question will assist policy makers.

Externalities in monitoring financial institutions

Description

Many financial economists argue that externalities associated with assessing and overseeing financial intermediaries will induce financial market participants to devote too few resources to evaluating and supervising financial intermediaries.[9] It is very costly and time-consuming to research and evaluate the condition and prospects of complex financial intermediaries. Many financial market participants, therefore, will be unwilling or unable to assess financial intermediaries. Instead, many investors will attempt to observe the behaviour of market participants who have carefully researched and evaluated intermediaries and use these observations in making their own investment decisions. Thus, expenditures by one entity on evaluating a financial institution often create benefits for other investors who do not have to pay the research costs. These externalities suggest that unregulated markets will insufficiently monitor and evaluate financial institutions.[10]

This tendency for insufficient monitoring is exacerbated in the case of financial institutions for at least two reasons: one, financial intermediaries frequently have many small creditors (e.g. depositors), so that the incentives for any individual creditor to undertake the expensive monitoring costs are small; and two, it is very costly to evaluate financial intermediaries, so that only very large, sophisticated claim holders would monitor financial institutions. Thus, without government encouragement, many analysts argue that unregulated markets will inadequately monitor financial institutions.

Effects of externality

Insufficient monitoring of financial intermediaries can affect negatively the provision of financial services and stymie economic growth. At the most general level, insufficient monitoring of financial intermediaries will worsen the principal–agent problem of intermediaries. Financial intermediary managers will not act in the best interests of creditors, and financial intermediary services, therefore, will not be appropriately supplied to the economy. At a similarly general level, insufficient monitoring of financial intermediaries may prevent markets and institutions from arising or severely limit their activities. For example, the mutual fund industry in the United States would probably not have blossomed in the last 15 years unless investors could easily compare funds and maintain sufficient confidence in fund behaviour. Thus, poor monitoring of financial intermediaries will tend to reduce the provision of all financial services and also hinder financial innovation.

Given that poor monitoring of intermediaries worsens financial services, I discuss just three particular negative effects of externalities in monitoring financial intermediaries.

- First, insufficient monitoring of financial institutions increases opportunities for financial institutions to fund large owners, managers, or related parties without appraising and monitoring objectively the entity receiving credit. Thus, poorly monitored intermediaries will allocate resources less efficiently.[11]
- Second, insufficient monitoring of financial institutions tends to raise uncertainty about these institutions. This uncertainty will tend to deter investors from entrusting their savings to financial institutions and thereby will hinder capital mobilisation.
- Third, insufficient monitoring of financial intermediaries by the market may encourage concentrated ownership (or the emergence of a few large debt holders) of intermediaries, so that large owners and creditors find it worthwhile to monitor intermediaries. Concentrated ownership of intermediaries may keep intermediaries from growing to optimal size and thereby alter the products offered by them; and create greater incentives and opportunities for financial institutions to behave generously towards large creditors and their related business interests.

Consequently, the effect of financial policies on the incentives for private investors and institutions, as well as on public supervisors and regulators, to evaluate and monitor financial intermediaries must be carefully considered in evaluating and designing financial regulations and policies.

Market response to externality

Unregulated markets may respond to this dearth of creditor monitoring. For example, in the case of banks, small depositors would be wary of putting their savings in banks in which they did not have confidence. Consequently, banks might respond by designing simple, innovative ways to communicate the safety of their portfolios to savers, or by creating capital structures where

165

financial intermediaries have a few large creditors or owners that are respected by the public and are expected to monitor the intermediary objectively. While these mechanisms may enhance monitoring, they are unlikely to eliminate the under-supply of private sector monitoring of financial intermediaries. Uncertainty about the objectivity of large creditors and the information communicated by the bank would in most cases still imply insufficient monitoring of financial institutions.

Policy implications

Governments should create incentives for self-regulatory agencies and private monitoring arrangements and minimise policies that create disincentives for sound monitoring.[12] Legal systems that define and enforce property rights efficiently will help creditors, rating agencies, and other institutions to monitor financial intermediaries while also facilitating the emergence and functioning of self-regulatory bodies. Similarly, sound accounting standards and information disclosure laws will facilitate the ability of the private sector to monitor financial intermediaries.

If self-regulatory and private arrangements do not monitor financial intermediary activities adequately, however, governments should seek to improve private sector monitoring through legal, accounting, and other reforms; review and reform financial sector policies that are impeding or creating disincentives for private sector monitoring of intermediaries; and help monitor financial institutions directly. Governments often set capital adequacy requirements, monitor the asset quality of intermediaries, establish regulations regarding the liquidity of banks, set limits on large exposures, restrict intermediary financing of intermediary managers, owners, or related parties, monitor trading on insider information, and carefully regulate the entry of new participants. Conducting effective supervision and designing appropriate incentives for self-regulation, however, are very difficult. Some of these details will be discussed below. The essential point in the present context is that one critical criterion for evaluating financial policies is how they affect the monitoring of financial institutions. An essential research issue is that economists do not have ways of comparing supervisory and regulatory systems across countries in a way that generates helpful policy guidance.

Externalities in appraising and monitoring firms

Description

Many authors argue that externalities associated with appraising and monitoring firms imply that financial intermediaries will not devote sufficient resources towards researching and overseeing firms. The externalities arise because there are large, fixed costs associated with evaluating, appraising, and monitoring firms and managers, and market participants will attempt to free-ride on the efforts of others. For example, once bank A carefully examines a firm, it is unlikely to share this information with other investors. Nonetheless, other intermediaries and investors can easily observe the actions of bank A and thereby infer the results of its appraisal: if bank A funds the firm, other financial market participants will interpret this as meaning that bank A has a positive view of the firm's future; and if bank A does not fund the firm, market participants will presume that this signifies that bank A's evaluation produced doubts about the firm. Similarly, if bank A funds a firm, other investors will presume that bank A will provide corporate governance. Thus, investors and intermediaries who do not research, evaluate, and monitor will use and benefit from bank A's operations without paying for these services; expenditures by one financial intermediary on selecting firms and monitoring managers create external benefits for other investors and financial intermediaries. The intermediaries that supply these financial services do not receive full compensation for appraising and monitoring firms, since other financial market participants free-ride. If evaluators and monitors received full compensation, they would invest more in evaluating firms and monitoring managers.

Effects of externality on the provision of financial services

An undersupply of evaluation and monitoring services will have negative economic implications by reducing the provision of critical financial services:

- First, if intermediaries devote too few resources to appraising firms and evaluating projects, the financial system will allocate resources less efficiently and economic growth will be correspondingly slower than in the absence of evaluation externalities.
- Second, if intermediaries devote too few resources to evaluating and monitoring firms, the public will be more wary of the soundness of intermediary investments, and intermediaries will therefore find it more difficult to mobilise savings.
- Third, too little monitoring of firm managers will provide management with too much independence from firm creditors. Managers may allocate firm resources based on personal interests rather than long-run firm interests, which would hinder the efficient resource allocation and slow economic development.
- Fourth, to the extent that the principal–agent problem is not mitigated by financial intermediaries, firm ownership may become more concentrated (to ease the principal–agent problem) than it would be in the presence of sufficient monitoring services. This could hurt economic efficiency by

forcing investors to have less diversified portfolios than they would like to hold.

Given the economic importance of financial intermediary evaluation and monitoring of firms, the effects of financial policies and regulations on incentives for intermediaries to research and monitor firms should be part of the 'checklist' of issues to be taken into consideration when evaluating the pros and cons of financial policies.

Market response to externalities

Unregulated markets may create methods for internalising some of the externalities associated with financial intermediary monitoring of firms. For example, a firm may pay higher fees and interest rates to financial intermediaries that carefully monitor the firm if it believes that this monitoring will be observed by financial market participants and thereby enhance the firm's access to capital markets and other intermediaries.[13] Through this market mechanism, intermediaries that carefully evaluate and monitor firms will internalise more of the social benefits of this information-gathering activity and thereby reduce the under-supply of financial intermediary monitoring of firms. Nonetheless, externalities associated with monitoring firms are unlikely to be eliminated, so financial institutions will tend to under-supply evaluation and monitoring services. Even more importantly for the purposes of establishing a useful analytical framework, financial policies may affect the incentives and ability of financial intermediaries to evaluate and monitor firms. Thus, analyses of financial policies should consider the effects of such policies on incentives to monitor firms even in the absence of preexisting externalities.

Policy implications

Two straightforward, though often unachieved, policy strategies for enhancing financial intermediary appraisal and monitoring of firms are worth noting here. First, make it easier for the private sector to evaluate and monitor firms. Information disclosure laws, competent accounting standards, standardised and transparent financial reporting forms, and an efficient corporate legal system that make the ownership, control, and performance of firms more transparent will facilitate the ability of auditors, creditors, rating agencies, and financial intermediaries to evaluate firms. Second, government supervision and regulation can be carefully crafted to encourage sound financial intermediary monitoring of firms. For example, regulators can help ensure that ownership and control of financial intermediaries, non-financial firms, and subsidiaries are transparent to avoid related party transactions and other investments that suffer from conflicts of interest and therefore do not reflect impartial appraisals. Similarly, regulators can help financial intermediaries establish sound credit review policies and sound procedures for monitoring firms so that they detect problems early and have pre-designed methods for coping with emerging problems. More focused research on which financial sector policies and regulations will induce financial intermediaries to monitor enterprises while not creating negative side-effects will advance the research advice that economists can give to policy makers.

Imperfect competition

Description of imperfectly competitive financial markets

Numerous financial analysts argue that financial markets do not behave in a perfectly competitive manner. Since many economists' faith in unregulated markets is based on models of perfect competition, the belief that financial intermediary relationships are not perfectly competitive has led some economists to cite this as an additional rationale for government overview of financial markets (Stiglitz, 1994).

There are large fixed costs associated with evaluating firms and monitoring activities and the information about firms and managers is imperfect and uncertain. Both the cost of obtaining information on firms and the uncertainty surrounding this information create incentives for financial intermediaries to establish long-run relationships with firms; intermediaries will be able to recoup the costs of spending resources to acquire information over long periods, and firms will be able to access cheaper and more secure financing. The cost and imperfect nature of information acquired by financial intermediaries imply that financial markets will operate differently from perfectly competitive markets. Once an intermediary undertakes the costly process of researching a firm, obtaining information on the firm and its market, and establishing a relationship with management, that particular intermediary has a cost advantage relative to other intermediaries in terms of providing credit to that particular firm. Consequently, the specific intermediary can charge higher than marginal cost for credit to that particular firm since other intermediaries would have to spend large fixed costs to research the firm before providing credit. Thus, even if the credit market is contestable, costly and imperfect information makes the credit market imperfectly competitive.

Economic implications

The optimal degree of competition among financial intermediaries is difficult to specify, so the direct economic implications of imperfectly competitive financial markets produced by the high costs of acquiring information on firms are difficult to quantify. Insufficient competition and contestability will reduce the level of financial services offered by markets and also slow the rate of financial innovation. Similarly, to the extent that imperfect competition creates excessively symbiotic links between financial intermediaries and firms, the objectivity with which intermediaries evaluate firms will deteriorate. On the other hand, to the extent that an oligopolistic financial system reflects the build-up and maintenance of long-run relationships that encourage an efficient exchange of information and more complete monitoring, then apparently lax competition will reflect good monitoring of firms. Similarly, excessive competition may provoke risky practices and insufficient attention to acquiring information on firms and monitoring managers.

Policy implications

One mechanism for limiting competition is through 'franchise' value as explained by Caprio and Summers (1996). By restricting entry, officials can create monopoly profits. These monopoly profits increase the value of having a licence – the franchise value – and increase the costs of losing that licence through bankruptcy. Consequently, financial policies that increase franchise value tend to decrease competition while simultaneously decreasing risk taking.

Supervision and regulation need to balance the negative and positive aspects of competition in the financial sector so as to maximise the efficient processing of information, while minimising arrangements that thwart innovation and encourage excessive risk taking. While easy to say and hard to accomplish, it is a balance that should be kept in mind when evaluating financial policies, and it is an area requiring substantial theoretical and empirical research.

Thus, the effect of financial policies on the level of competition should be carefully considered and therefore forms one of our 'checklist' items.

Missing or incomplete markets

Description of informational asymmetries

Financial institutions are in the business of obtaining and processing information and making funding decisions based on this information. Information obtained by intermediaries, however, is imperfect relative to the information known by the person or entity requesting funding. These information asymmetries imply that some financial arrangements will be limited or non-existent – even though these arrangements would exist in the absence of informational asymmetries. Five examples will help clarify this point.

- *Credit rationing 1*: If it is difficult for banks to obtain accurate information about the riskiness of firms, raising interest rates may cause firms with the safest projects to drop out of the loan market, so that the mix of firms demanding loans would become more risky. Thus, raising interest rates may cause an *adverse selection* of firms requesting loans. To mitigate this adverse selection problem, banks may keep interest rates lower than the rate that would clear the market to maintain a safer mix of firms in the pool of firms demanding credit. At this low interest rate, there will be an excess demand for loans by firms, so banks will have to use non-price mechanisms to allocate credit. The adverse selection problem reduces the issuance of loans below what it would be in the absence of asymmetric information.

- *Credit rationing 2*: If it is impossible to monitor the behaviour of firms perfectly, raising interest rates may induce project managers to change their behaviour and undertake riskier projects. To mitigate this *moral hazard* problem, banks may keep interest rates lower than would clear the loan market. Consequently, there will be an excess demand for loans by firms.

- *Equity issuance*: If firm insiders have more information about the firm than outsiders, then the issuance of new shares by insiders will be perceived as a negative signal by outsiders: insiders willing to sell shares to outsiders must think the price is high. This informational asymmetry between insiders and outsiders will discourage the raising of capital through equity issuance and therefore reduce the usefulness of the stock market as a vehicle for raising capital and diversifying risk.

- *Incomplete insurance 1*: Insurance creates incentives for the insured to do less to avoid the insured-against event. If information were fully available and monitoring were costless, the insurance agency could pre-specify a comprehensive, complex list of actions and behaviours for the insured that would eliminate this *moral hazard* problem. However, all actions cannot be monitored. Thus, insurers will provide less than complete insurance to enhance the incentives for the insured to avoid the insured-against event. The result is incomplete insurance because of information asymmetries.

- *Incomplete insurance 2*: Voluntary deposit insurance schemes will be difficult to organise because of informational problems inherent in evaluating and pricing the riskiness of banks. Good banks may not want to join deposit insurance schemes because they are unsure about the asset quality of other banks; good banks do not want to subsidise bad banks and it may be too difficult and costly to evaluate other banks and set risk-based deposit insurance premia. This *adverse selection* problem induces a deterioration of voluntary deposit insurance schemes.

Financial and economic implications

The above examples illustrate cases of incomplete or missing markets that involve a reduction in financial intermediary services – especially risk management services – from the level of services that would exist in the absence of information asymmetries. Thus, savings mobilisation, resource allocation, and risk diversification will be less efficient because of credit rationing and built-in incentives against the raising of capital through stock offerings. Similarly, moral hazard problems created by insurance may imply incomplete insurance markets that yield less risk reduction opportunities. Finally, because of adverse selection problems, certain types of private insurance – like voluntary deposit insurance and other self-regulatory insurance schemes – may be provided at a sub-optimal level.

Consequently, policy makers should consider the effects of financial policies and regulations on the types of financial contracts and services offered by financial markets to the public.[14]

Market response to asymmetric information

Market mechanisms – which rely heavily on the legal infrastructure – can reduce these asymmetries and their negative economic effects. Intermediaries and firms build long-run relationships that facilitate information exchange. The ability to use collateral in loan contracts helps extract information from borrowers that reduces informational asymmetries and expands the availability of financial services. Also, efficient legal systems and registries permit creative financial contracting to service the needs of clients, and sound bankruptcy courts enable intermediaries to seize and dispose of assets of delinquent borrowers quickly and confidently, which further promotes the provision of financial services. Finally, financial systems that allow a single financial intermediary to engage in different financial contracts – like issuing loans and buying equity – may be able to establish relationships with firms that maximise information exchange, thereby reducing the negative effects of asymmetric information. Nonetheless, these informational problems frequently cannot be eliminated. The important policy and research question is: 'Are the problems sufficiently large to justify government involvement and will government intervention itself negatively affect economic performance?'

Policy implications

The last sub-section makes clear that the government can help minimize the negative effects of informational asymmetries by having an efficient court system, effective means of quickly identifying and disposing of collateral, accurate well-functioning property registries, standardised and useful financial and accounting standards, etc. In other words, by supplying the best legal infrastructure possible, governments can help the financial system provide high quality financial services. The government may also take more direct steps to fill perceived missing markets. Thus, many governments form development banks and other means of funnelling credit to areas where the financial system is not voluntarily choosing to finance.

Summary statement on market failures

From a policy perspective, the probable existence and economic importance of market failures suggests a potential role for government. Although the market may produce contractual and financial arrangements that mitigate the negative consequences of the five discussed market failures, the inherent characteristics of financial markets imply that some of these market failures are important in all countries. But it is not clear that the potential positive effects of government intervention outweigh the potential negative repercussions of those same interventions. Analysts should evaluate whether policy changes – on net – aggravate or ameliorate the negative effects of market failures.

INSURANCE OF INVESTOR ASSETS IN FINANCIAL INTERMEDIARIES

Government insurance of financial intermediary liabilities[15]

There are many different ways to organise government insurance. Governments may insure all assets, a percentage of assets, or only relatively small asset holders. The design of insurance schemes may also differ. For example, governments may attempt to charge a market price for the insurance they provide based on the riskiness of particular financial institutions. Or, governments may charge a simple fee that is not market or risk based. Furthermore, governments may require financial institutions to insure themselves with private insurers that are authorised and monitored by the government.

For simplicity, I first discuss complete government insurance in the absence of risk-based premiums, risk-based capital requirements, or private insurance arrangements to get the blunt, first-order effects of government insurance on the five market failures defined above. Below, I broaden the discussion to more sophisticated insurance schemes. It is important to emphasise from the outset, however, that this section does not review comprehensively the design of financial intermediary liability insurance schemes. This section has the more modest objective of identifying a few features associated with insuring saver assets, especially bank deposits.

173

Contagion and financial stability

Insurance of assets in financial intermediaries will tend to reduce the probability that the failure of one institution will spread to other institutions; credible government insurance lowers the probability of contagion. Nonetheless, insurance of intermediary liabilities – especially in conjunction with a low capital–asset ratio – may increase financial fragility by generating incentives and capabilities for excessive risk taking and looting on the part of intermediaries.

Evaluation and monitoring of intermediaries

Insuring investor assets in intermediaries reduces private sector monitoring of financial intermediaries. If investor assets are credibly insured, they will have fewer incentives to monitor the intermediary.

In addition to reducing private sector monitoring of intermediaries, insurance also increases incentives for risk taking by financial intermediaries.[16] For example, the capital strength of banks is a way of signalling wary depositors about the security of the bank. Deposit insurance lowers the benefit of maintaining high capital standards to reassure depositors. Thus, banks with deposit insurance have incentives to reduce capital/asset ratios. Similarly, banks with insured deposits have weaker incentives to signal depositors that the bank is managing interest rate and exchange rate risk well and screening clients more carefully than banks without insured deposits. Furthermore, banks with deposit insurance have greater incentives to lend to riskier clients than banks with no deposit insurance. Bank owners keep most of the benefits from lending to clients with very risky but potentially high return projects, but if the risks do not pay off and the bank fails, some of the losses will be passed to the government insurance fund. This incentive to gamble with insured deposits is intensified as the capital position worsens.

Thus, the combination of greater incentives for financial intermediaries to assume risk and lower incentives for private creditors to monitor financial intermediary behaviour implies that government insurance dramatically augments the need for compensating government actions that intensify monitoring of intermediaries.[17]

Besides increasing incentives and opportunities for excessive risk taking, government insurance – by reducing private sector monitoring of intermediaries – enhances incentives for owners of financial intermediaries to bankrupt the intermediary for profit.[18] If an owner's capital plus expected future long-run profits are less than what the owner can extract from the intermediary through dividend payouts and investments that yield large payments in the short run (with large losses in the future), the owner will extract those short-run profits and let the intermediary go bankrupt in the future. Although governments often enact regulations to restrict this type of behaviour, these regulations are sometimes poorly designed, insufficiently supervised, and ineffectively enforced. As described in great detail in Akerlof and Romer (1993), sometimes the ability to extract short-run profits involves fraud and sometimes lax or inappropriate accounting conventions or regulations permit owners to extract intermediary resources in the short run even though this leads to bankruptcy in the long run. Thus, bankruptcy for profit need not involve breaking the law. Regardless of the mechanisms through which owners may bankrupt intermediaries for profit, this analysis has an important policy implication: government insurance enhances opportunities for bankruptcy for profit by reducing private creditor monitoring of financial institutions and therefore reinforces the desire for policies that strengthen sound assessment and monitoring of insured intermediaries. This monitoring should include maintaining sufficient capital to reduce incentives for bankruptcy for profit as well as assessing asset allocation carefully.[19]

Evaluation and monitoring of firms

Government insurance tends to reduce the intensity with which insured financial intermediaries monitor firms.[20] One way in which intermediaries compete for funds is by having a reputation for carefully monitoring the firms in which they invest. Careful monitoring by the intermediary lowers the probability that the intermediary will experience losses. Thus, in the absence of insurance, safe intermediaries should be able to raise funds less expensively than intermediaries who do not monitor firms intensively. Investors with assets in insured intermediaries, however, are less concerned about losing their savings than if these savings were not insured. Therefore, in the presence of insurance, intermediaries have less of an incentive to monitor firms carefully, invest in a diversified portfolio of relatively safe firms, and communicate this information credibly to savers.

Competition among financial intermediaries

Insurance will also influence the level and form of competition. For example, with deposit insurance, depositors view banks as closer substitutes than without deposit insurance. Banks will compete in terms of services and interest rates, but banks will have fewer incentives to transmit information to depositors about the quality of their loans. In the absence of insurance, however, intermediaries would need to convey information about the quality of their assets to attract investors. Insurance may also change the overall level of competition. For example, in an oligopolistic banking system with a few large, well-established banks that are able to self-regulate each other and self-organise a deposit insurance system that excludes other banks, the introduction of government deposit insurance for all banks may increase the level of competition for deposits in the system. Thus, it is difficult to draw clear conclusions about the effect of government insurance on the level and form of competition.

Incomplete or missing markets

Mandatory government insurance may be a mechanism for overcoming a market failure. As discussed above, incomplete or missing insurance markets often exist because of adverse selection: if the costs of acquiring information and monitoring other intermediaries and designing risk-based insurance fees and capital requirements are very high, safe financial intermediaries may opt out of privately organised, voluntary insurance schemes because they do not want to subsidise more risky intermediaries. The existence of a large number of banks, for example, will tend to aggravate the adverse selection problem by making monitoring of banks and coordinating a voluntary, private insurance system more difficult. Thus, voluntary insurance systems will tend to deteriorate when adverse selection is particularly acute; there will be an incomplete – or missing – market of insurance of financial intermediary liabilities. Mandatory government insurance is one means of coping with this missing markets problem.

Political economy and the fallacy of choice

While lowering the likelihood of contagion, insurance of intermediary liabilities reduces monitoring of insured financial intermediaries and often curtails the intensity with which financial intermediaries assess and monitor firms. These negative consequences have led some analysts to argue that the costs of insuring investor assets in intermediaries are greater than the benefits, and many recommend abolishing or avoiding government organised insurance. Typically, this is not an option.

Given the huge macroeconomic implications of financial failure, governments will act, typically, to prevent individual financial intermediary failures from spreading and becoming systemic failures. Many governments have insured assets when faced with financial failures even in the absence of preexisting commitments and even after stating beforehand that the government would not insure assets in the case of financial failure.

Thus, most governments cannot credibly commit themselves not to interfere in the presence of financial failure. The *belief* by the public that the government insures their investments creates the moral hazard problem; there is a reduced incentive to monitor financial institutions on the part of the public because people expect that the government will insure their assets in the case of failure. Thus, the policy choice between government insurance and no government insurance is generally irrelevant. The more useful concerns are explicit versus implicit insurance, and the level and design of the coverage.

Different societies expect different levels of government insurance. Some societies expect governments to protect the assets of small savers in banks, others expect deeper coverage (e.g. insuring large bank accounts), while some societies expect the government to insure a broader set of institutions (insurance policies, private pension accounts, and even the returns on investment company assets). The extent of the moral hazard problem produced by insurance is a by-product of these expectations and therefore also depends on political and historical ingredients that vary from country to country.

Public expectations about the coverage of government insurance may also change systematically with financial development and even respond to changes in financial policy. Two examples will help illustrate these points. As a country's financial system develops, households may shift their assets out of insured demand deposits into uninsured, relatively unregulated money market mutual funds. As this shift occurs, public expectations concerning government responsibility towards money market mutual funds may change. Specifically, expectations may expand to include money market mutual funds under the umbrella of government insurance. Thus, the 'understanding' between the public and government is critical in designing financial policies because this understanding – or social contract – between the public and the government concerning what saver assets are insured by the government determines the depth and scope of the moral hazard problem.

A second example illustrates that using financial regulation to limit the scope of government insurance is a complex task that mixes economics and sociology. Some analysts propose the creation of 'narrow' banks.[21] These narrow banks would enjoy 100 per cent deposit insurance and would be the only institutions tied to the nation's payments system. These narrow banks would also be very restricted and tightly regulated. They could only make loans that were almost risk free; they would not be permitted to assume interest rate risk; and they would face high capital requirements. Thus, households would have a safe place to save, with correspondingly low returns. If savers sought higher returns, they could invest in uninsured financial institutions. This would limit the moral hazard problem created by insurance since the intermediaries receiving government insurance would be tightly restricted and supervised. One problem with this scheme is that it may not be compatible with public expectations. While in some contexts the population may adjust its expectations of the scope of government insurance to this new regulatory structure, this may not occur in all countries. For example, savers may believe the government would also insure intermediaries that are *not* narrow banks if faced with a financial crisis. This expectation would lower the incentives of private creditors to monitor non-narrow bank financial intermediaries carefully. Thus, the narrow bank scheme may not control the moral hazard problem.

The greater are public expectations of a government safety net, the greater is the need for financial policies that strengthen monitoring of insured intermediaries.

Implicit instead of explicit government sponsored insurance

We now evaluate the relative strengths and weaknesses of explicit versus implicit government sponsored insurance using the five-point framework for studying financial policies.[22] Authorities could forgo a formal, government operated insurance system. Instead, the government could intervene following a financial failure. This 'implicit' insurance has been used in many countries. It must be emphasised, however, that implicit insurance does not avoid the moral hazard problem created by public expectations of government insurance; using implicit instead of explicit insurance does not circumvent the reduction in monitoring of intermediaries by creditors created by public expectations of government insurance. Implicit insurance provides flexibility in terms of the amount and form of protection since preexisting rules and procedures restrict decision making. Nonetheless, on balance, *this section argues that explicit insurance generally has important advantages over implicit insurance.*

Financial stability

Implicit insurance will often not offer the same stability as explicit insurance. Implicit insurance implies ad hoc, unsystematic procedures for coping with failures, does not foster the build-up of an insurance fund that could withstand potential financial crises, and therefore may not significantly enhance public confidence in the safety of their assets.[23]

Monitoring financial intermediaries

Explicit insurance seems to offer greater opportunities and encouragement for governments to enact forward-looking financial policies that bolster private and public sector overview of financial intermediaries, rather than implicit insurance. Although proponents of implicit insurance argue that greater uncertainty concerning government insurance enhances incentives both for private creditors to monitor intermediaries, and intermediaries to form private insurance and self-regulatory bodies, this argument relies on the assumption that uncertainty surrounding the extent and form of government insurance creates positive incentives for private sector monitoring of intermediaries that are greater than the negative incentives for private creditor monitoring of intermediaries generated by expectations of government insurance.

More importantly, under the premise that the public expects the government to insure assets in the presence of a financial crisis, governments will be able to counteract the moral hazard problem created by government insurance to a greater degree than with implicit insurance. By explicitly recognizing a social responsibility to insure some class of saver assets, governments will be able to design and enact forward-looking financial regulations that augment the monitoring of financial intermediaries and enhance financial stability better than could be achieved with an implicit insurance system. For example, governments could use risk-based insurance premia with explicit insurance. Government organised risk-based insurance premia would send confusing signals with implicit insurance. Other forward-looking policies include the building up of an adequate insurance fund, restrictions on insured intermediary activities, coordinated use of self-regulatory bodies, private insurance arrangements, trustworthy rating agencies, and reputable auditing firms to intensify monitoring of financial intermediaries. Moreover, a credible, explicit insurance system may be able to limit public expectations regarding the size and set of financial instruments insured by the government. For example, with explicit insurance and universal banks, it may be possible to limit the government safety net to small checking accounts. It may be impossible to draw this line *ex post* with implicit insurance.

Monitoring firms

As mentioned above, insurance tends to reduce the intensity with which intermediaries monitor firms. Insurance reduces incentives for intermediaries to establish a reputation for carefully monitoring firms, because investors are less concerned about losing their investments. Although choosing explicit or implicit insurance does not appear to affect firm monitoring incentives differentially, explicit government insurance encourages better regulatory strategies. Specifically, in the absence of explicit government insurance, governments may believe there is not a moral hazard problem. Therefore, officials may not design financial policies appropriately, because they will ignore, or insufficiently weigh, the distortions created by expectations of government insurance.

Competition

For similar reasons, explicit insurance may prompt the government to consider raising the franchise value of insured intermediaries. This would reduce risk taking and further work to counterbalance the moral hazard created by government insurance. This would be recommended only if there were sufficient competition to spur innovation and efficient provision of financial services.

Market incompleteness

Finally, in terms of the effects on the availability of financial arrangements, there does not appear to be much difference between explicit and implicit insurance.

Vignettes on private insurance

An alternative or complement to government organised insurance is private insurance. For example, a group of banks could create a deposit insurance fund. If credible, private insurance will limit the probability of contagion, stimulate self-regulation, and encourage financial stability. Private insurance also has advantages with respect to government insurance. Kane (1985, 1989) has noted that, in the United States, government officials are slow to recognise the existence of a problem and also slow to take action to cope with the problem once it is recognised. Kane argues that the interests of government officials often differ from those of taxpayers. Taxpayers want to cope with bank problems in the least expensive way, while government officials want to project a favourable image of their capacity.[24] Government officials, therefore, focus on minimising the number of failures recorded on their watch and assigning the blame for failures to others rather than focusing their energies on expeditiously minimising the aggregate expense to the insurance fund. Private insurance may reduce some of these problems by establishing better incentives for the owners and managers of private insurance funds.

Private insurance funds that eliminate fears of contagion will be difficult to organise, however, for a number of reasons. First, losses in a crisis could be larger than the reserves of the private insurance fund, in which case members would face two difficult options: to inject more capital, which could weaken otherwise healthy institutions and contribute to the contagion; or not to inject more capital, which could reduce public confidence in the private insurance scheme and precipitate a spread of the crisis. Thus, in many cases private insurance may not be sufficiently credible to lower the probability of contagion substantially. Second, if the public still believes that the government ultimately stands behind these private insurers, the public will not evaluate carefully whether the private insurance system has adequate funding and staff. Under these conditions, private insurance will not substitute for government insurance in the case of a sufficiently large financial failure. Governments will still have to choose between implicit and explicit government insurance and the precise form of the insurance system if they choose explicit insurance. Third, as mentioned above, adverse selection problems in participating in voluntary private insurance schemes will hinder the functioning of these voluntary schemes. For example, safe banks may not want to subsidise risky banks and it may be very difficult, complex and costly to set risk-based insurance premiums. Thus, safe banks may opt out of private insurance schemes. With mandatory government insurance, safe banks could not leave the insurance system. Fourth, many countries have large publicly-owned banks, so that organising an effective private insurance fund would be very difficult. Finally, an alternative to having banks form their own private insurance system is to use insurance companies to insure bank deposits. But in most countries the banking system is larger than the insurance industry, so that the insurance industry may not have the capacity to underwrite bank deposits. Also, if an insurance company cancelled the insurance of an individual bank, this would tend to precipitate a run on that bank. Governments may not wish to give private insurers such powers.

Private insurance, therefore, may only work in special cases. Where a few banks have very good historical reputations and have established sound mechanisms for self-regulation, the public may have confidence in their ability to self-regulate, insure deposits, and screen other intermediaries. Using examples from different states in the United States in the 1800s, Calomiris (1989) shows that in states where a few banks created self-insurance organisations with strong self-regulatory powers and where each bank's liability to the insurance fund was *unlimited*, there was much tighter monitoring of banks and many fewer bank failures than in other states.[25]

Instead of viewing private and public insurance as substitutes, Kane (1993) views the two methods of insuring saver assets as complements. He proposes that banks with insured deposits should be required to have insurance with a private company. These private insurance companies would have to be authorised, monitored and reinsured by the government. While not solving all problems, Kane argues that this type of institutional arrangement would make evaluation and monitoring of banks more responsive to market conditions since private insurers – with their financial capital on the line – would have incentives more aligned with those of taxpayers than government supervisors who do not have their financial capital exposed. It is important to note, however, that even in Kane's proposal, the government ultimately stands behind the liabilities of financial institutions.

THE LEGAL ORGANISATION OF FINANCIAL INTERMEDIARIES

Introduction

This section uses the five-point checklist to examine some of the ways in which the permitted legal organisation of financial intermediaries may affect the provision of financial services. Financial intermediaries may be organised in a myriad of ways. For simplicity, consider three cases. First, define 'universal banking' as the case when all financial activities can be performed by a single legal entity. Thus, deposit-taking, loan-making, equity purchasing, securities underwriting, mutual fund management, insurance, etc. can all occur in one legal entity called a universal bank. Second, define a 'financial group' as the case when a holding company owns separately capitalised subsidiaries that perform different financial functions. Thus, banking functions – deposit-taking, loan-issuance, and direct links to the payments system – occur in the 'bank' subsidiary of the holding company, securities underwriting occurs in the investment bank subsidiary, mutual fund operations happen in the mutual fund subsidiary, and insurance practices occur in the insurance subsidiary of the financial group. Third, define 'separate banking' as the case when banking functions must be performed in a separate legal entity called a bank, and all other financial functions must be performed outside of the bank. Thus, deposit-taking, loan-making, and direct links to the payments system occur in the bank. Investment banking, mutual fund management, and insurance operations occur in intermediaries unrelated to the bank. Banks cannot own or be owned by other financial institutions, and large owners of banks cannot own other financial intermediaries in the separate banking model. These three cases allow us to examine how the legal organisation of financial institutions influences the provision of financial services.

Financial stability and contagion

Financial groups and universal banks will tend to be larger than any single financial intermediary in a separate banking system. Thus, failure of a financial group or a universal bank will create larger economic disruptions than failure of a single bank in a separate banking system. While failure of a large financial institution will tend to cause more disruptions than failure of a small financial institution, universal banks and financial groups may be able both to reduce the risk of failure of any individual universal bank or financial group and also reduce the risk of contagion. Contagion may be reduced because a few large universal banks or financial groups may be able to coordinate more effectively when faced with a failure than many small financial intermediaries in a separate banking system.

In terms of the risk of failure of an individual financial institution, broadening financial powers from a separate banking system to a financial group to a universal banking system has ambiguous effects. The ability to engage in a broader set of financial activities may permit greater mechanisms for diversifying geographical, sectoral, interest rate, credit, liquidity, and exchange rate risk. On the other hand, securities trading and investment banking activities tend to be relatively risky. These activities may be particularly risky when combined with banking activities, as will be detailed below.[26] Thus, moving from separate banking to financial groups to universal banking may increase or decrease the likelihood of financial intermediary failure, and the change in financial fragility will depend on the measurement and control of risks that arise from combining different financial functions.

Analysts often propose financial groups as a mechanism for reducing the economic disruptions of the failure of any single financial institution while maximising the benefits from combining different financial functions in a multifaceted group (e.g. loan-making, equity ownership, mutual fund management, securities underwriting, etc.). Proponents argue that failure or weakness of one subsidiary in a financial group may be contained in that subsidiary. Nonetheless, the financial group can coordinate subsidiary activities to enhance the provision of financial services. Thus, financial groups may be safer than universal banks while still capturing the economies of scope and scale fostered by universal banking.

Sceptics of the financial group system, however, argue that the holding company structure will not really insulate the bank subsidiary of a financial group from problems in another subsidiary. If the 'firewalls' are not fireproof – or even very fire repellent – the main advantage of the financial group system would vanish. As Talley (1993a) notes, there are at least three ways in which problems may spread through a financial group. First, creditors of a failing subsidiary may be able to convince the courts to 'pierce the corporate veil' and require other subsidiaries of the financial group to support the failing subsidiary. Second, the holding company may try to support a failing subsidiary with the capital and assets of other subsidiaries even in violation of existing regulations. This support will be difficult to detect and control because subsidiaries of a financial group will interact and transact in many areas, from information processing, to marketing, to coordinating loans, insurance, underwriting, trading, and mutual fund activities. Third, problems in one subsidiary may affect public confidence in other subsidiaries, including the bank. Thus, financial distress in the investment banking subsidiary may reduce confidence in the management and financial conditions of the bank subsidiary and cause depositors to switch their funds to another bank in another financial group. Given that the public is likely to view the financial group as a single entity, banks in a financial group will probably not abandon a failing subsidiary, and contagion may occur within financial groups. Thus, financial groups may not provide the advertised degree of insulation between subsidiaries.

One important complication in moving from a separate banking system to a financial group to a universal banking system is that increasing the linkages between banking and other financial functions may expand the set of financial instruments presumed to be insured by the government. In particular, with a separate banking system, governments may be able to define the set of financial instruments insured by the government more narrowly than with financial groups or universal banks. For example, in a separate banking system, governments may be able to insure bank deposits credibly up to $100,000 but not returns to investments in mutual funds. When all of these financial services are provided by a universal bank, the government may find it difficult to insure credibly only specific financial instruments. As public expectations regarding government insurance of financial instruments spread, private sector monitoring of financial intermediaries will diminish. A decrease in private sector supervision of financial intermediaries will raise financial fragility unless counterbalanced with official actions to intensify the overview of financial intermediary activities.

Financial groups are often suggested as a compromise vehicle. The deposits in the bank subsidiary may enjoy deposit insurance but financial instruments in other subsidiaries do not enjoy government insurance. But, as argued above, the public may view the financial group as a homogeneous entity, and this may make it very difficult to designate only certain financial instruments as government insured.

Monitoring financial intermediaries

Monitoring universal banks and financial groups that mingle different financial functions may be much more difficult than assessing the condition and overseeing the activities of separate financial institutions. Importantly, the complexity of measuring exposure to specific firms, industries, and geographical locations, and of evaluating the riskiness of the intermediary in general may grow more than proportionally as the diversity of functions performed by the intermediary grows. Analysts find it very difficult to measure credit risk, liquidity risk, interest rate risk, exchange rate risk, and the risk and expected return on equity and real estate investments separately. When various financial functions are combined in a universal bank or financial group, assessing the total risk and exposure of an intermediary may prove exceedingly complex. Computing capital standards in light of these measurements will also be difficult and controversial since intermediaries may have very different combinations of the various risk components. Furthermore, broadening financial intermediary powers may encourage the development of larger, more powerful intermediaries. The political influence that will likely accompany this power may also hinder the ability of officials to force full disclosure of information and supervise intermediaries effectively and objectively.

The potential for conflicts of interest and insider manipulations will also grow as one moves from a separate banking system to a financial group system to a universal banking system. Monitoring transactions between the financial intermediary and significant shareholders, directors, officers, and their important and relevant business concerns will be more difficult, since the intermediary will be involved in more transactions and more complex transactions. Similarly, there will be greater opportunities for conflicts of interest. For example, banks with problem loans to a client may try to extricate themselves by underwriting and selling shares to an investment company or trust account run by the bank itself. Or, banks may issue a bridge loan to support a new equity sale being underwritten by the investment banking arm of the bank and thereby use insured deposits to support lucrative but risky investment banking activities.[27]

Financial groups are often proposed as a compromise. The optimistic view holds that financial groups are easier to monitor than universal banks, since each subsidiary can be assessed and monitored individually. A more sceptical view, however, suggests that financial groups are not easier to monitor than universal banks, and the *belief* itself that financial groups are easier to monitor may produce poor monitoring. Regarding the first point, transactions between subsidiaries in a financial group will be difficult to detect and monitor accurately as detailed above. Thus, assessing the risk, asset quality, and capital adequacy of individual subsidiaries without examining the consolidated financial group may be at best difficult and probably misleading. This implies that to gauge the condition and capital adequacy of subsidiaries within a financial group, creditors and supervisors will have to measure the consolidated state of the financial group. The second sceptical point regarding supervision of financial groups is that financial groups may produce a false sense of security. Supervisors may believe that each subsidiary is sufficiently capitalised to support the risk associated with each subsidiary. This belief may stymie a consolidated assessment of the overall condition of the financial group.

Monitoring of firms

Moving from a separate banking system to financial groups to universal banking should have generally positive effects on how the financial system evaluates and monitors firms, though there are reasons for caution. Expanding the array of services provided by a single entity – or related entities within a financial group – may broaden and deepen the relationship between the intermediary and firm and facilitate the flow of information. Also, banks that hold equity in firms and sit on the boards of directors will tend to exert better corporate governance. On the other hand, universal banks and financial groups may have a greater tendency than more narrowly defined institutions to become over-exposed to a few firms and thereby lose their ability to monitor corporations objectively.

Competition

Merging financial functions in financial groups or universal banks should increase competition in the short run but may decrease competition in the longer run. By allowing banks to compete against investment banks, securities companies and insurance companies, universal banks would initially increase competition. Similarly, by allowing banks to form insurance companies and mutual funds within the structure of a financial group, for example, should spur competition in the short run. On the other hand, if economies of scale and scope are important, decompartmentalising financial powers may eventually encourage the consolidation of financial power in the hands of a few large financial groups or universal banks. This consolidation of power could work to reduce competition and contestability. Furthermore, such consolidation would concentrate considerable economic and, therefore, political power in the hands of the few individuals who control these financial groups and universal banks.

Market completeness

With the ability to provide a broader array of financial services, universal banks and financial groups should be better able to service clients than individual financial entities in a separate banking system. With an expanded array of interactions with clients, universal banks and (perhaps to a lesser degree financial groups) should be able to obtain more information about clients. Economies of scope from bundling several services will reduce information acquisition costs. Thus, financial intermediaries that enjoy greater flexibility in performing a broad spectrum of financial functions for clients, should be able to overcome – to a greater degree than compartmentalised financial intermediaries – the informational asymmetries that cause incomplete or missing markets. With more information, financial intermediaries should be able to provide better financial services.

Messages on the legal organisation of financial intermediaries

The analysis yields two helpful messages. First, as banks become more closely linked with other financial intermediaries, either by being associated within financial groups or by being moulded into a single universal bank, it will become increasingly difficult to limit the set of financial instruments that are either implicitly or explicitly insured by the government. The government safety net may extend beyond demand deposits to money market mutual funds and other instruments. The broadening of the social safety net increases the importance of the government spurring sound supervision of financial intermediaries, so that the financial system provides stable high quality financial services. The second message is that as banks become more closely associated with other financial intermediaries, assessing, monitoring, supervising, and regulating the riskiness, performance, and regulatory compliance of financial institutions will become increasingly difficult. These two messages suggest that as banks become more closely tied with other financial intermediaries either within financial groups or in a universal bank, both the difficulty and the importance of effectively monitoring and supervising financial intermediaries rise.

CONCLUSIONS

Economists advance a number of reasons for why free, unregulated financial markets will under-supply growth-promoting financial services. These reasons are often termed 'market failures'. Since economists generally have confidence that unregulated, competitive markets effectively allocate resources and generate improvements in living standards, these market failures form the analytical justification for government interventions in and regulation of financial markets. But, market failures are not sufficient conditions for government action, for such actions may not alleviate the market failure, and the interventions themselves may cause or aggravate other market failures. Thus, financial sector policies must be evaluated and compared in terms of whether they improve or aggravate these five market failures, and researchers must provide insights and tools for deciding whether government interventions in particular circumstances will, on balance, improve or worsen financial services.

This chapter proposed a five-point checklist for evaluating financial policies. Specifically, how will financial policies affect

1 financial stability and the possibility of contagion;
2 private and public sector evaluation and monitoring of financial intermediaries;
3 financial intermediary evaluation and monitoring of firms;
4 the degree of competition among financial institutions; and
5 the spectrum of financial arrangements available to firms and individuals?

Using this checklist, I evaluated two financial policies: insurance of saver assets in financial intermediaries and the powers and activities in which particular financial intermediaries should be allowed to engage. While I believe that this checklist is helpful for organising discussions of financial sector policies, much more rigorous research is required on the links between financial sector policies and the secure provision of financial services.

NOTES

1 I received very helpful suggestions from Herb Baer, Jerry Caprio, Maria Carkovic, Asli Demirgüç-Kunt, Tom Glaessner, Niels Hermes, Robert Lensink, David Scott, Dimitri Vittas, Sara Zervos. The findings, interpretations, and conclusions are my own and should not be attributed to the World Bank, its Board of Directors, its management, staff, or member countries.
2 See King and Levine (1993a,b) and Caprio *et al.* (1994).
3 Any study of the role of government in financial markets owes a great debt to Joseph Stiglitz. This chapter relies heavily on Stiglitz's (1994) review. Consequently, I do not cite all of Professor Stiglitz's contributions which have shaped and guided the study of financial economics, but instead point the reader to Stiglitz (1994) for citations.
4 Note, however, that this is different from ensuring the existence of any individual

financial institution. Individual financial intermediary failures may have very positive repercussions by stimulating better practices in other intermediaries and weeding out relatively poor intermediaries. Also, individual failures may encourage privately organised insurance schemes, self-regulatory organisations, and better monitoring by creditors. The external social costs of an individual financial intermediary failure stem from potential contagion; poor information may induce a failure to spread to otherwise healthy intermediaries.

5 If firms could costlessly identify new channels of finance and if bankruptcy courts costlessly and instantly redeployed assets, then the economic disruptions of contagions would be much smaller.

6 Evidence in the United States suggests that bank failure – or bank distress more generally – harms client firms because of the intrinsic, though non-tradeable, long-run relationships that develop between banks and their customers. Increases in the probability that the bank–borrower relationship will be negatively disrupted reduces the share price of the borrower, while the rescue of a bank expected to fail increases the stock price of client firms. See Slovin *et al.* (1993).

7 The disruptions caused by financial intermediary bankruptcies will be particularly acute and long term because financial intermediaries are primarily involved in the production, assessment, and dissemination of information. This information capital is not as easily sold and transferred in bankruptcy courts as physical capital. Thus, bankruptcy of financial institutions will entail the loss of information. The loss of financial intermediary information on a large scale through bankruptcy will significantly diminish the ability of society to evaluate firms and monitor managers efficiently for an extended period. These arguments should not be used to justify excessive forbearance, however, since insolvent financial institutions with little or no capital at risk will not provide good financial services and will tend to undertake extremely risky and imprudent activities.

8 For example, Calomiris (1989) notes that in the 1800s, many states in the United States prohibited branch banking. This led to the emergence in those states of many, under-diversified banks. The lack of diversification increased exposure to idiosyncratic risk. The large number of banks made it difficult for banks to (a) establish private deposit insurance funds with sound monitoring mechanisms and (b) coordinate effectively when confronted with a drop in depositor confidence. In fact, states with financial policies that restricted branching suffered more banking failures than states with fewer, better diversified banks.

9 The terms 'evaluating' and 'monitoring' should be interpreted broadly to include assessing the quality of management, the performance of the intermediary, the accuracy of disclosed information, the connections between management and firms or other intermediaries, the quality of the business plan, and changes in the character of the intermediary without the consent of creditors.

10 Another way to see that free markets will tend to under-monitor financial intermediaries is to note that to a significant degree, information about the management and solvency of financial institutions is a public good: many people can have this information at the same time and it is difficult to exclude others from using the information. For example, if I know mutual fund A is good, you can know it also without it detracting from what I know; if I invest in mutual fund A and you know that I am well informed, my actions will convey information to you without me telling you. The public good characteristic of monitoring financial institutions suggests that too little monitoring will occur. This example relies on 'you' knowing that 'I' am well informed. If market participants cannot determine easily who is well informed and where the well informed invest, then

the public good characteristic diminishes in importance.

11 Furthermore, poor information about the management and performance of specific financial intermediaries will make it difficult for savers to evaluate and compare financial institutions and funnel their resources to those financial intermediaries best able to allocate capital efficiently.

12 For how to create incentives for self-regulation of securities markets, see Glaessner (1992).

13 In the United States, borrowers experience abnormally positive stock returns when they announce that they have renewed loans with their banks. These abnormal returns do not materialise for non-bank debt (James, 1987; Lummer and McConnell, 1989). This illustrates the importance the market gives to bank monitoring of firms.

14 Caprio (1992) analyses the interactions of financial reform and asymmetric information. He concludes that the long-run relationships that form between financial intermediaries and firms to mitigate informational asymmetries must be carefully considered in designing financial reforms, so that the negative economic implications of asymmetric information are not unnecessarily aggravated by reform.

15 Talley and Mas (1993) provide an excellent analysis of deposit insurance. The discussion here draws liberally from their insights.

16 See Merton (1992).

17 See Dowd (1993).

18 See Akerlof and Romer (1993).

19 Governments can promote better monitoring through a combination of mechanisms. Governments can monitor directly: they can (a) restrict activities and investments, (b) require intermediaries to hold well-diversified portfolios, (c) review the owners, management, and organisation of intermediaries, and (d) use risk-based capital requirements and risk-based insurance premiums to create appropriate incentives for intermediaries. Governments may insure only small investors, which would maintain incentives for large investors to monitor intermediaries. Besides direct government supervision and regulation, governments may require and use audits from internationally reputable accounting firms and assessments by rating agencies to evaluate financial institutions. Furthermore, by increasing the franchise value of insured intermediaries through reduced competition, governments reduce incentives for risk taking and thereby counterbalance enhanced incentives and opportunities for risk taking created by government insurance.

20 Recall, I am assuming that insurance premiums and capital requirements are not risk-based and that regulations and official supervision of intermediaries do not fully compensate for the incentives created by insurance.

21 See the discussion and citations in Talley (1993b).

22 To be precise, no country can have a perfectly explicit deposit insurance scheme. There may, in almost all countries, exist a difference between public expectations of what the government would insure in the case of a crisis and the formal legislation on deposit insurance. By definition, therefore, the implicit part of deposit insurance is the difference between public expectations and explicitly written laws and regulations on deposit insurance. Consequently and formally, this section should be viewed as analysing the positive and negative consequences of writing laws and regulations that more precisely match public expectations.

23 It should also be noted that the public expenditure effects from financial failure can be very large (as the savings and loan experience in the United States

demonstrates). Therefore, building an insurance fund prior to a failure may mitigate the macroeconomic implications of a systemic financial failure.

24　See also Glaessner and Mas (1995) on principal–agent problems in regulatory agencies.

25　Another example is West Germany. In 1966, a purely private consortia of banks formed a mutual-type, deposit insurance fund. The Federal Association of German Commercial Banks organised cross-monitoring of banks to ensure stability of the banking system. In 1976, this purely private insurance fund came under public sector regulation, but administration and monitoring are still organised and conducted by the private Federal Association of German Commercial Banks.

26　Note, however, that empirical evidence suggests that security affiliates' operations of banks did *not* deleteriously affect the soundness of banks in the United States prior to the Glass–Steagall Act of 1933 that legally separated commercial banking from securities operations (White, 1986).

27　See Edwards and Edwards (1991) for examples of the activities of financial and industrial groups in Chile. Also, see Akerlof and Romer (1993).

REFERENCES

Akerlof, G.A. and P.M. Romer (1993), 'Looting: The Economic Underworld of Bankruptcy for Profit', mimeo, University of California.

Calomiris, C.W. (1989), 'Deposit Insurance: Lessons From the Record', *Economic Perspectives*, Federal Reserve Bank of Chicago, May/June, pp. 10–30.

Caprio, G., Jr (1992), 'Policy Uncertainty, Information Asymmetries, and Financial Intermediation', *World Bank Policy Research Working Paper*, No. 853, World Bank.

—— and L.H. Summers (1996, forthcoming), 'Financial Reform: Beyond Laissez Faire', in D. Papadimitriou (ed.) *Financing Prosperity in the 21st Century*, New York: Macmillan Press.

——, I. Atiyas, J.A. Hanson and Associates (1994), *Financial Reform: Theory and Practice*, New York: Cambridge University Press.

Dowd, K. (1993), 'Deposit Insurance: A Skeptical View', *Review*, Federal Reserve Bank of St Louis, January/February, pp. 14–17.

Edwards, S. and A. Cox Edwards (1991), *Monetarism and Liberalization: The Chilean Experiment*, Chicago: University of Chicago Press.

Glaessner, T. (1992), 'External Regulation vs Self-Regulation. What is the Right Mix?: The Perspective of the Emerging Securities Markets of Latin America and the Caribbean', Washington, DC: World Bank manuscript.

Glaessner, T. and I. Mas (1995), 'Incentives and the Resolution of Bank Distress', *World Bank Research Observer*, 10, pp. 53–73.

James, C. (1987), 'Some Evidence on the Uniqueness of Bank Loans', *Journal of Financial Economics*, 19, pp. 217–35.

Kane, E.J. (1985), *The Gathering Crisis in Federal Deposit Insurance*, Cambridge: MIT Press.

—— (1989), 'How Incentive-Incompatible Deposit–Insurance Funds Fail', *Working Paper*, No. 2836, National Bureau of Economic Research.

—— (1993), 'An Agency-Cost and Bonding Paradigm for Analyzing Deposit–Insurance Reform', mimeo, Boston College.

King, R.G. and R. Levine (1993a), 'Finance and Growth: Schumpeter Might Be Right', *Quarterly Journal of Economics*, 108, pp. 717–37.

—— (1993b), 'Finance, Entrepreneurship, and Growth: Theory and Evidence',

Journal of Monetary Economics, 32, pp. 513–42.

Lummer, S.L. and J.J. McConnell (1989), 'Further Evidence on the Bank Lending Process and the Capital Market Response to Bank Loan Agreements', *Journal of Financial Economics*, 25, pp. 99–122.

Merton, R.C. (1992), 'Operation and Regulation in Financial Intermediation: A Functional Perspective', mimeo, Harvard University.

Slovin, M.R., M.E. Sushka and J.A. Polonchek (1993), 'The Value of Bank Durability: Borrowers as Bank Stakeholders', *Journal of Finance*, 48, pp. 247–66.

Stiglitz, J.E. (1994), 'The Role of the State in Financial Markets', *World Bank Economic Review*, 8, pp. 19–52.

Talley, S.H. (1993a), 'Bank Holding Companies: A Better Structure for Conducting Universal Banking?', in D. Vittas (ed.) *Financial Regulation: Changing the Rules of the Game*, Washington DC: World Bank, pp. 321–51.

———— (1993b), 'Are Failproof Banking Systems Feasible? Desirable?', *World Bank Policy Research Working Paper*, No. 1095, World Bank.

Talley, S.H. and I. Mas (1993), 'The Role of Deposit Insurance', in D. Vittas (ed.) *Financial Regulation: Changing the Rules of the Game*, Washington DC: World Bank, pp. 419–38.

White, E.N. (1986), 'Before the Glass–Steagall Act: An Analysis of the Investment Banking Activities of National Banks', *Explorations in Economic History*, 23, pp. 33–45.

9

INTEREST RATE DEREGULATION AND INVESTMENT

A simulation study[1]

Kanhaya L. Gupta and Robert Lensink

INTRODUCTION

There is by now a vast literature, both theoretical and empirical, on the effects of interest rate deregulation on the growth of developing countries. Equally vast is the literature on the effects of foreign aid, the implications of the existence of informal credit markets and the implications of financing budget deficits by alternative sources. However, in virtually no work on the effects of interest rate deregulation are all these different strands brought together. Of course, there are efforts which try to combine one or more of these issues. For example, Van Wijnbergen (1983), and others in the 'structuralists' school, examine the role of informal credit markets, but they pay very little attention to the role of foreign aid, wealth effects, crowding out of private credit by the needs of the government to finance budget deficits, and so on. Morisset (1993) examines the effect of crowding out of private credit caused by the government's budgetary needs and a shift in the private sector's portfolio caused by interest rate deregulation. But he treats budget deficits as being exogenous, ignores the role of foreign aid and informal credit markets and treats savings as being exogenously determined, thus eliminating all indirect effects of deregulation via changes in wealth. Gupta (1993) rectifies some of the shortcomings of Morisset (1993), but still ignores foreign aid and informal credit markets and takes budget deficits as given. Gupta and Lensink (1993) enlarge the model by incorporating informal credit markets. But they leave out foreign aid and treat government deficit as being exogenously given. In a subsequent paper, Gupta and Lensink (1994) bring together the government sector and foreign aid. They explicitly endogenise the budget deficit and examine the effects of interest rate deregulation in the presence of aid under the assumptions of it being exogenous and endogenous. However, in this case, they ignore the informal credit markets. Their analysis is again partial given that the deregulation effects are sensitive to the existence of such markets.

The main reason for the shortcomings of the literature surveyed above is the fact that analytical solutions of more general models are virtually impossible to get. Hence, the attempts to obtain some insights in the presence of specific restrictions on the structures of the economies portrayed. An option which enables us to integrate all of the aspects considered above is, of course, that of a simulation model. This is the aim of this chapter. More specifically, this chapter proposes a model which is solidly based on an integrated model of portfolio allocation and consumption-savings decisions of the private sector with appropriate attention to the underlying adding-up restrictions, which treats budget deficits as being endogenous, explicitly recognising the role of foreign aid as well as the role of informal credit markets. The model will be used to examine the effects of interest rate deregulation under different assumptions with respect to the private sector's behaviour.

The chapter is organised as follows. In the first section we specify and discuss the model; in the second section we discuss the simulation strategy and the parameter values used in the simulations. Some illustrative simulations are reported in the third section, and the chapter is concluded with a brief summary.

THE MODEL

This section presents the main equations of the model.[2] The model consists of four sectors: the private sector, the government sector, the banking sector and an external sector. The list of the notations and definitions of the variables used are given in Table 9.1.

Non-bank private sector

The non-bank private sector is assumed to hold five assets: government bonds, physical capital, deposits of the formal banking sector and those of the informal banking sector and an inflation hedge, say foreign currency.[3] The private sector, which is considered to be credit constrained, receives credit from the formal and the informal banking sectors. All variables are in real terms, unless stated otherwise. The real budget constraint can be derived from column 1 in Table 9.2.

The asset demand equations of the non-bank private sector are derived by using a multivariate adjustment function. For reasons of convenience and since parameters were not available, all cross adjustment coefficients are assumed to be zero. The asset demand equations of the non-bank private sector are then given by:

$$\Delta m = \alpha_1 y_d + \alpha_2 W + \alpha_3 \Delta L_p + \alpha_4 (i_m - \pi^e) - \alpha_5 (i_k - \pi^e)$$

$$- \alpha_6 (i_b - \pi^e) - \alpha_7 (e^e - \pi^e) - \alpha_8 (i_u - \pi^e) + \alpha_9 \Delta L_u - \epsilon_1 m_{-1}$$

(1)

Table 9.1 Notations and definitions used in the model

All variables are in real terms, denoted in domestic currency, unless stated otherwise

---

| Δ | represents change in the value of a variable, i.e., $x = x - x(-1)$. |

ENDOGENOUS VARIABLES

π^e	expected (and actual) rate of domestic inflation
A	foreign aid
b	government bonds
C_p	private consumption
C_g	government consumption
e	exchange rate (an increase represents a depreciation of the home currency)
e^e	expected (and actual) rate of depreciation of the home currency
f	foreign assets
f^*	real foreign assets denoted in foreign prices
i_{lb}	lending rate of the formal banking sector
i_{lu}	lending rate of the informal banking sector
I_g	government investment
imp	imports
imp^*	real imports denoted in foreign prices
IP_g	interest payments of the government
IP_p	interest payments of the formal private banks
IP_u	interest payments of the informal banks
IP_f	interest payments of the foreign sector
k	physical capital of the private sector
k_g	physical capital of the government sector
k_T	total stock of physical capital
L_p	private loans from the formal private banking sector
L_u	private loans from the informal banking sector
L_g	government borrowing from the formal private banking sector
L_{cb}	transfers from the central bank to the government
m	formal bank deposits
p	domestic price level
R	reserves of formal banks
R_u	reserves of informal banks
S_p	private savings
T	government tax revenue
u	informal bank deposits
W	net private wealth
x	exports
y	production
y_d	disposable income
Y^d	aggregate demand
Y^s	aggregate supply

EXOGENOUS VARIABLES

δ	rate of depreciation
π^*	expected (and actual) world rate of inflation
A^*	(real) foreign aid denoted in foreign prices
h_f	the required reserve ratio of the formal banking sector
h_u	reserve ratio of the informal banking sector
i_b	nominal rate of return on bonds
i_m	nominal rate of return on formal bank deposits
i_k	nominal rate of return on private capital
i_u	nominal rate of return on informal bank deposits
p^*	world price level

$$\Delta k = \alpha_{11} y_d + \alpha_{12} W + \alpha_{13} \Delta L_p - \alpha_{14}(i_m - \pi^e) + \alpha_{15}(i_k - \pi^e)$$
$$- \alpha_{16}(i_b - \pi^e) - \alpha_{17}(e^e - \pi^e) - \alpha_{18}(i_u - \pi^e) + \alpha_{19}\Delta L_u - \epsilon_{11} k_{-1} \tag{2}$$

$$\Delta b = \alpha_{21} y_d + \alpha_{22} W + \alpha_{23} \Delta L_p - \alpha_{24}(i_m - \pi^e) - \alpha_{25}(i_k - \pi^e)$$
$$+ \alpha_{26}(i_b - \pi^e) - \alpha_{27}(e^e - \pi^e) - \alpha_{28}(i_u - \pi^e) + \alpha_{29}\Delta L_u - \epsilon_{21} b_{-1} \tag{3}$$

$$\Delta u = \alpha_{51} y_d + \alpha_{52} W + \alpha_{53} \Delta L_p - \alpha_{54}(i_m - \pi^e) - \alpha_{55}(i_k - \pi^e)$$
$$- \alpha_{56}(i_b - \pi^e) - \alpha_{57}(e^e - \pi^e) + \alpha_{58}(i_u - \pi^e) + \alpha_{59}\Delta L_u - \epsilon_{51} u_{-1} \tag{4}$$

The consumption function is given by:

$$\Delta C_p = \alpha_{41} y_d + \alpha_{43} \Delta L_p - \alpha_{44}(i_m - \pi^e) - \alpha_{45}(i_k - \pi^e) - \alpha_{46}(i_b - \pi^e)$$
$$- \alpha_{47}(e^e - \pi^e) - \alpha_{48}(i_u - \pi^e) + \alpha_{49}\Delta L_u + \epsilon_{41} W_{-1} \tag{5}$$

It should be pointed out that all nominal rates of return, except for the expected rate of depreciation, are assumed to be exogenously given, but not the real rates of return since inflation is treated as being endogenously determined (see below). Private savings and wealth are defined as:[4]

$$S_p = y_d - C_p \tag{6}$$

$$W = W_{-1} + S_p - \delta k_{-1} \tag{7}$$

In the simulations the demand for foreign currency is derived from the budget constraint. Therefore, an explicit equation for the demand for foreign currency is not specified.

Finally, disposable income is defined as:

Table 9.2 The accounting framework of the model

	1. PS	2. CB	3. PB	4. UB	5. GS	6. ES	Total
1 Non-financial transactions	$C_p + \Delta k - y_d$		IP_p	IP_u	$C_g + I_g - T + IP_g$	$x - imp + IP_f$	0
2 Bonds	Δb				$-\Delta b$		0
3 Deposits	$\Delta m + \Delta u$		$-\Delta m$	$-\Delta u$			0
4 Foreign assets	Δf				$-A$	$-\Delta f + A$	0
5 Loans	$-\Delta L_p - \Delta L_u$	$\Delta L_{cb} - \Delta R - \Delta R_u$	$\Delta L_p + \Delta L_g + \Delta R$	$\Delta L_u + \Delta R_u$	$-\Delta L_g - \Delta L_{cb}$		0
Total	0	0	0	0	0	0	0

Notes: PS stands for non-bank private sector; CB stands for central bank; PB stands for formal private banks; UB stands for informal private banks; GS stands for government sector; and ES stands for the external sector

$$y_d = y - T + (i_b - \pi^e)b_{-1} + (i_m - \pi^e)m_{-1} + (i_u - \pi^e)u_{-1}$$

$$+ (e^e + \pi^* - \pi^e)f_{-1} - (i_{lb} - \pi^e)L_{p_{-1}} - (i_{lu} - \pi^e)L_{u_{-1}}$$

$$(8)$$

Government sector

The government's expenditure consists of expenditure on consumption, investment and interest payments on outstanding government debt and stock of loans from the formal private banking sector. These expenditures are financed by taxes, by transfers from the central bank, by borrowing from the public (bond issue) and from the private formal banking sector and by foreign aid. The government's budget constraint can be derived from column 5 in Table 9.2.

In this model the supply of government bonds is entirely determined by demand by the private sector. Assuming that transfers from the central bank to the government are exogenous, this means that in the absence of foreign aid, any residual needs for funds to finance a given budget deficit must come from borrowing from the banking sector. In the event that a deposit rate deregulation leads to a reallocation of the private sector's portfolio against government bonds, it must imply an increase in government's demand for bank credit, which, *ceteris paribus*, implies a reduction in the credit available for the private sector.

The government equations are derived by optimising a loss function subject to the budget constraint (see Gupta and Lensink, 1996). The results are:

$$I_g = \eta_1 \Delta k + \eta_2 y_{-1} - \eta_3 C_{g-1} + \beta_2 \left(\frac{ep^*}{p} A^* + \Delta b + \Delta L_{cb} - IP_g \right) \qquad (9)$$

$$C_g = \eta_4 C_{g-1} + \eta_5 y_{-1} - \eta_6 \Delta k + \beta_4 \left(\frac{ep^*}{p} A^* + \Delta b + \Delta L_{cb} - IP_g \right) \qquad (10)$$

$$T = \eta_7 y_{-1} + \eta_8 \Delta k + \eta_9 C_{g-1} - \beta_6 \left(\frac{ep^*}{p} A^* + \Delta b + \Delta L_{cb} - IP_g \right) \qquad (11)$$

Given C_g, I_g, T, Δb, A, ΔL_{cb}, and the net interest payments of the government, IP_g, ΔL_g is determined by the government's real budget constraint. Finally, interest payments are defined as

$$IP_g = (i_{lb} - \pi^e)L_{g-1} + (i_b - \pi^e)b_{-1} - \pi^e L_{cb,-1} \qquad (12)$$

Banking sector

This sector consists of three sub-sectors: the central bank, the formal private banks and the informal credit markets. The formal private bank lends to the non-bank private sector and the government. Liabilities of the formal private bank consist of bank deposits of the non-bank private sector. The informal bank lends only to the non-bank private sector. Liabilities are in the form of informal deposits held by the non-bank private sector. Both types of banks are assumed to hold reserves at the central bank. The budget constraints of the formal private bank, the informal private bank and the central bank are given in columns 3, 4 and 2 of Table 9.2. The supply of formal and informal loans is determined by the budget constraints of the formal and informal banks, respectively.

Reserves of both banking sectors are equal to a fixed percentage of bank deposits, hence:

$$R = h_f m \tag{13}$$

$$R_u = h_u u \tag{14}$$

Taking into account capital gains (losses) on reserves, net real interest payments of both types of banks are specified as:

$$IP_g = (i_m - \pi^e)m_{-1} - (i_{lb} - \pi^e)(L_{p-1} + L_{g-1}) + \pi^e h_f m_{-1} \tag{15}$$

$$IP_u = (i_u - \pi^e)u_{-1} - (i_{iu} - \pi^e)L_{u-1} + \pi^e h_u u_{-1} \tag{16}$$

The lending rates are determined by the zero-profit condition for the banking system (see e.g. Montiel *et al.*, 1993):

$$i_{lb} = (1/(1 - h_f))i_m \tag{17}$$

$$i_{li} = (1/(1 - h_u))i_u \tag{18}$$

The assets of the central bank consist of loans to the government. The liabilities are the reserves of both the formal and the informal bank. Reserves are distributed to the government in the form of a non-interest paying transfer. Note that in contrast to other work in this field, we do not assume that these transfers are only used for unproductive government expenditures, but that they also affect government investment and taxes.

External sector

In rate of change, real exports and real imports denoted in foreign prices are specified as a function of the real exchange rate:

$$\frac{\Delta x}{x_{-1}} = -\eta_{10}(\pi^e - e^e - \pi^*) \tag{19}$$

$$\frac{\Delta imp^*}{imp_{-1}^*} = -\eta_{11}(\pi^e - e^e - \pi^*) \tag{20}$$

Real foreign interest payments, denoted in domestic prices, are defined as

$$IP_f = (e^e + \pi^* - \pi^e)f_{-1} \tag{21}$$

Aggregate demand, aggregate supply, inflation and exchange rates

With private investment, private consumption, government consumption, government investment and imports and exports already determined, we can write aggregate demand as:

$$y^d = C_p + C_g + \Delta k + I_g + x - imp \tag{22}$$

Using a Leontief type technology, aggregate supply is determined by

$$y^s = y = \alpha k_T \tag{23}$$

where

$$k_T = k + k_g \tag{24}$$

The goods market is closed by price changes. We assume that expected (and actual) inflation is determined by the equilibrium condition on the goods market, i.e. from the following condition:

$$y^s = y^d \tag{25}$$

Note that the balance of payments (the budget constraint of the external sector: column 6 in Table 9.2) is automatically in equilibrium in the case where aggregate demand equals aggregate supply and the budget constraints of the other sectors hold. This implies that there are no changes in foreign reserves that might affect domestic money supply.

With respect to the expected devaluation of the exchange rate, we assume that it gradually adjusts to purchasing power parity. This implies:

$$e^e = \eta_{12}(\pi^e - e^e_{-1} - \pi^*) + e^e_{-1} \tag{26}$$

By assuming different values for η_{12} we are now able to simulate with a fixed exchange rate regime, or a flexible exchange rate regime in which exchange rates are formed by purchasing power parity.

THE SIMULATION STRATEGY

The basic purpose of this chapter is to propose a simulation model which can be used to examine the effects of interest rate deregulation on investment. In order to illustrate how the model works we can simulate the model in a variety of ways. However, for reasons of space, we only give a few simulations which shed light on a number of contentious issues in the literature. The specific simulations reported relate to:

The nature of the private sector's portfolio

Here the main contentious point is what would happen if physical capital was a poor substitute for money, in our case for the formal and informal deposits. This, of course, does not rule out the possibility that the deposits may be close substitutes for government bonds and/or the inflation hedge. In many models where only two assets are assumed, namely, capital and money (Sussman, 1991), the issue strictly relates to the degree of substitutability between these two assets. We consider an extreme form of this relationship, namely, the situation in which the two assets are independent of each other in the private sector's portfolio.

Importance of credit constraints

Here, four possibilities clearly present themselves. The first one is that which is embodied in the baseline simulation, where both households and firms are credit constrained. Its opposite extreme is where neither of them is. The other two are intermediate possibilities where either the households or the firms are credit constrained. The effect of an interest rate deregulation when only households (consumption) are (is) credit constrained is examined in this chapter.

Importance of interest rates in stimulating private savings

This is one of the most contentious issues in the literature. We examine this by considering the case where consumption is not at all affected by changes in real interest rates. It is this assumption which virtually all other studies in this area use to justify treating consumption/savings as an exogenous variable.

The importance of wealth effects

In the developing countries, this issue can be analysed along the same lines as for the developed countries. But two points may play a more important role here. The first relates to the importance of internal finance for financing investment in these countries. Given the under-developed nature of the capital markets and even the banking sector in these countries, it is plausible to assume that internal funds would play a more important role than in the developed countries, or, at least, an important one. The second relates to the role of wealth in the consumption function. Here the issue is even more complicated. It is possible to show that in a slow growing economy, wealth will not play a significant role in the consumption–savings decision. The effect of the first possibility is examined in the simulations.

Our model does not address the problem of actual forecasting. The purpose is to set out different cases which are compared with each other. Since data for a number of variables are lacking we could not estimate the entire model. Although most parameters are based on available econometric estimates for Asian developing countries, they do not pertain to a specific country.

We start by presenting the parameters used in the base model. Table 9.3 gives the parameters of the asset demand equations as well as the parameters for private consumption. Estimates with respect to the coefficients in the equation of demand for informal deposits and with respect to the coefficients for informal credit in the asset demand and consumption equations are not available. Admittedly rather ad hoc, we assumed that formal and informal credits affect asset demand and consumption alike. Further, we assume that the composite coefficients have the property of symmetry, i.e. $\alpha_5 = \alpha_{14}$; $\alpha_6 = \alpha_{24}$, etc. The sources of the other coefficients are given in Table 9.3. Table 9.4 presents the parameters for the government equations, the initial values and the exogenous variables. All initial values refer to the group of Asian Developing Countries (IMF, IFS and World Bank, World Tables). Where figures for the whole group of Asian countries are not available, figures for India are used (IMF, IFS). Note that all initial values are given as percentages of GDP (y). Some other assumptions: α in the aggregate supply equation is set at 0.33, η_{10} and η_{11} in the equation for exports and imports are set at 0.60 and –0.85, respectively (based on Marquez, 1990). η_{12} in the exchange rate equation is set at 0. Hence, we simulated with a fixed exchange rate regime.[5]

This chapter takes the following approach: in all simulations we assess the impact of a sustained increase in the nominal return on formal bank deposits (i_m) by 1 percentage point. Results are presented as deviations from the baseline, where i_m has its original value. We start by running a BASE

Table 9.3 Parameters of the asset demand equations and private consumption

F. Deposits	Capital	Bonds	I. Deposits	Consumption
$\alpha_1 = 0.0227$	$\alpha_{11} = 0.0296$	$\alpha_{21} = 0.005$	$\alpha_{51} = 0.0227$	$\alpha_{41} = 0.7$
$\alpha_2 = 0.01$	$\alpha_{12} = 0.2$	$\alpha_{22} = 0.107$	$\alpha_{52} = 0.02$	$\alpha_{43} = 0.255$
$\alpha_3 = 0.2$	$\alpha_{13} = 0.258$	$\alpha_{23} = 0.0351$	$\alpha_{53} = 0.2$	$\alpha_{44} = 0.005$
$\alpha_4 = 0.0412$	$\alpha_{14} = 0.0606$	$\alpha_{24} = 0.0087$	$\alpha_{54} = 0.087$	$\alpha_{45} = 0.005$
$\alpha_5 = 0.0606$	$\alpha_{15} = 0.1$	$\alpha_{25} = 0.002$	$\alpha_{55} = 0.005$	$\alpha_{46} = 0.005$
$\alpha_6 = 0.0087$	$\alpha_{16} = 0.02$	$\alpha_{26} = 0.0429$	$\alpha_{56} = 0$	$\alpha_{47} = 0.255$
$\alpha_7 = 0.0178$	$\alpha_{17} = 0.011$	$\alpha_{27} = 0.018$	$\alpha_{57} = 0.027$	$\alpha_{48} = 0.255$
$\alpha_8 = 0.0087$	$\alpha_{18} = 0.0005$	$\alpha_{28} = 0$	$\alpha_{58} = 0.0412$	$\alpha_{49} = 0.255$
$\alpha_9 = 0.2$	$\alpha_{19} = 0.258$	$\alpha_{29} = 0.0351$	$\alpha_{59} = 0.2$	$\alpha_{49} = 0.015$
$\varepsilon_1 = 0.5$	$\varepsilon_{11} = 0.18$	$\varepsilon_{21} = 0.3$	$\varepsilon_{51} = 0.5$	–

Sources: Morisset (1993); Gupta (1993); Ogawa *et al.* (1994)

SIMULATION. In that case all coefficients have the values as presented above. In addition to this base simulation we present alternative simulations for the cases identified above, which means changes in some of the coefficients in the model. For these simulations also the results are presented as differences from the baseline. Note that the baseline in the alternative simulations differs from the baseline in the base simulation since some coefficients are adjusted.

Since this chapter is primarily concerned with the impact of a financial liberalisation as represented by an increase in the nominal deposit rate on private investment, we decided to present, for the BASE SIMULATION, figures for private investment as well as figures for all endogenous variables entering the equation for private investment. Because private investment as well as income, wealth, inflation and supply of credit are endogenous variables in our model, the causality of the mechanisms is unclear: all variables are simultaneously determined. Nevertheless, the different endogenous variables entering the investment equation may shed some light on the reasons why private investment increases or decreases during the simulation period. We also present figures for government investment and demand for government bonds. The latter variable gives some insight about the crowding-out effect of government demand for formal credit resulting from a portfolio shift of the private sector.

In the BASE SIMULATION, for each time period the variables, except for inflation, are expressed as point elasticities. The first graph presents the interest rate elasticities of the capital stock of the private sector (elascap) and the government sector (elascapg).[6] The second graph presents the interest rate elasticities of formal bank loans to the private sector (elasloanp), the interest rate elasticities of government loans (elasloang) and the interest rate elasticities of informal loans (elasloani). The third, fourth and fifth graphs present the interest rate elasticities of the demand

Table 9.4 Parameters of the government equations, initial values and exogenous variables

G. Inv.	G. Cons.	Taxes	Exog. variables	Exog. variables	Start values	Start values	Start values
$\eta_1 = 0.0$	$\eta_4 = 0.62$	$\eta_7 = 0.08$	$i_m = 0.05$	$A^* = 0.0119$	$f^* = 0.746$	$W = 3$	$b = 0.12$
$\eta_2 = 0.04$	$\eta_5 = 0.03$	$\eta_8 = 0.0$	$i_k = 0.05$	$h_f = 0.05$	$I_p = 0.27$	$k_g = 1$	$m = 0.4$
$\eta_3 = 0.19$	$\eta_6 = 0.0$	$\eta_9 = 0.19$	$i_b = 0.05$	$h_u = 0.05$	$I_u = 0.081$	$k = 2$	$C_g = 0.14$
$\beta_2 = 0.20$	$\beta_4 = 0.35$	$\beta_6 = 0.2$	$i_u = 0.06$	$\delta = 0.05$	$I_g = 0.11$	$u = 0.085$	$y, y_d = 1$
			$p^* = 1$	$n^* = 0$	$imp^* = 0.24$	$x = 0.22$	$p, e, p^* = 1$

Sources: Government consumption, investment and taxes, see the Appendix. With respect to the different assets we take averages for some Asian countries. However, not all data were available. The non-available starting values for the assets are constructed in a way that is consistent with the budget constraints for government bonds (elasbond), net wealth (elaswealth) and disposable income (elasinc), respectively. Finally, the last graph presents the effects of an increase in the deposit rate on inflation. The variable we present (infld) is defined as the increase in the rate of inflation due to a one percentage increase in the deposit rate.

THE SIMULATION RESULTS

The base simulation

We start the analysis by presenting the simulation results for the base model. Figure 9.1 shows that financial liberalisation in our model initially has a negative effect on private capital. However, after 10 years an interest rate deregulation started to have a positive effect on private capital. After 10 simulation periods the interest rate elasticity of private capital is positive and increases during the rest of the simulation period. The figure also shows that the capital stock of the government is negatively affected by a financial liberalisation. This suggests that capital of the private and government sectors are substitutes.

The decrease in the capital stock of the private sector in the first periods is mainly the result of a decline in formal credit available for the private sector, which arises, among other things, from an increase in government's demand for formal credit (see Figure 9.2). Hence, government's demand for credit crowds out the supply of credit to the private sector. The increase in government's demand for formal credit is, for example, caused by a decline in demand for government bonds by the private sector (Figure 9.3). Figure 9.3 also shows that demand for government bonds starts to increase after 15 simulation periods. The continuously rising increase in government's demand for credit then starts to weaken. Also the negative effect of an interest rate deregulation on government capital starts to decline.

An important reason for the increase in the capital stock of the private sector after some simulation periods is the increase in wealth during the simulation period (Figure 9.4) and the positive impact on disposable income (Figure 9.5).

The effect on inflation (Figure 9.6) may seem counter-intuitive when we consider Figure 9.1. However, this is not necessarily so, given that the effect on government's capital accumulation is negative throughout the simulation period and the effect on private capital becomes positive after some simulation periods. And since aggregate demand and aggregate supply are being driven by both private and public investment expenditures, it is not necessarily a surprise that the economy seems to experience excess supply in the first simulation periods, and hence decreasing inflation and later on excess demand and therefore increasing inflation. However, it is important to consider the magnitude of the effect. It is truly very small, so that the

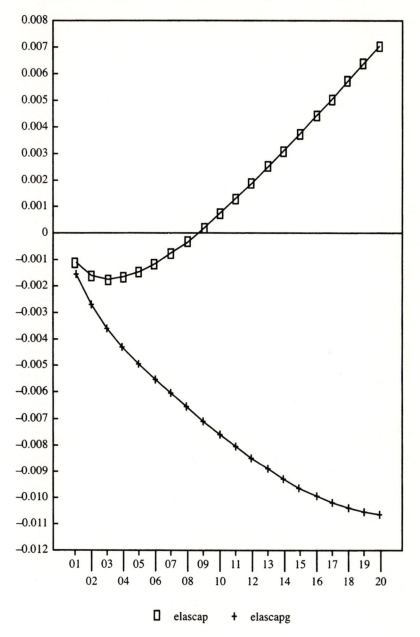

Figure 9.1 Base simulation: effects on capital

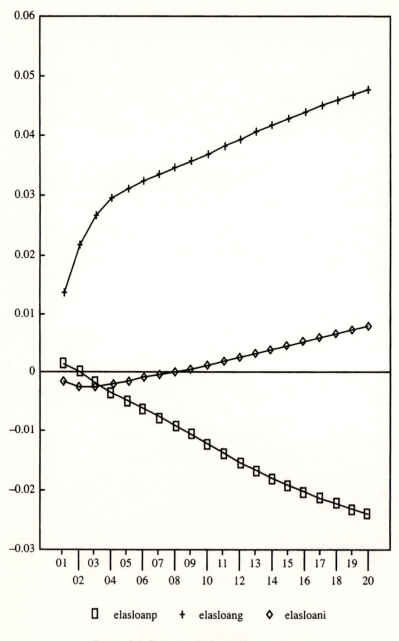

Figure 9.2 Base simulation: effects on loans

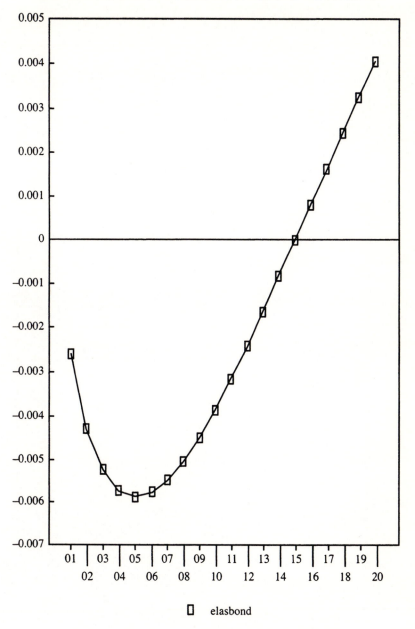

□   elasbond

Figure 9.3 Base simulation: effects on government bonds

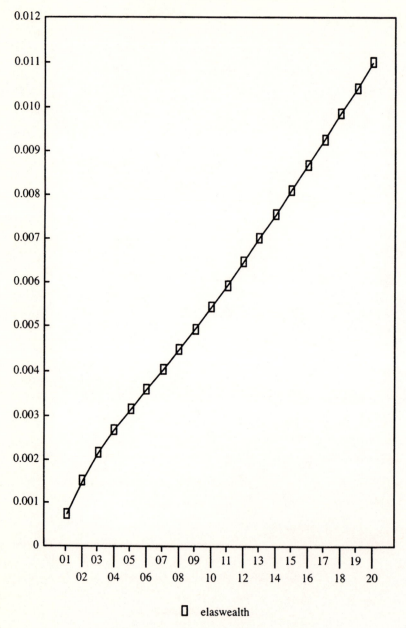

□ elaswealth

Figure 9.4 Base simulation: effects on wealth

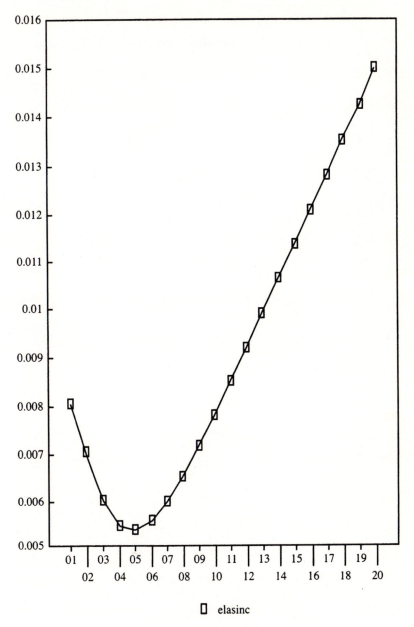

Figure 9.5 Base simulation: effects on income

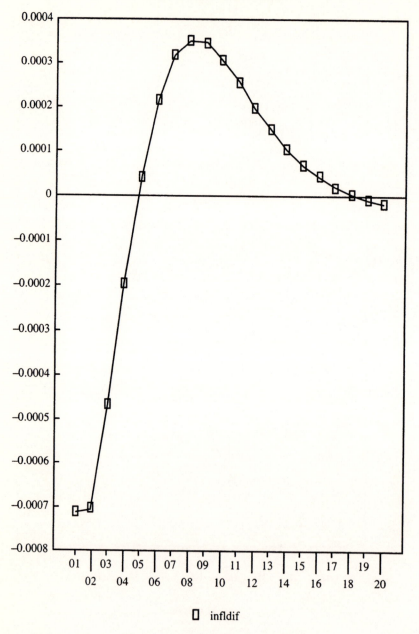

□ infldif

Figure 9.6 Base simulation: effects on inflation

inflationary potential of the interest rate deregulation policy in the base model must be considered rather minor.

The alternative simulations

For the alternative simulations, for reasons of space, we only present differences between the interest rate elasticities of the capital stock of the private sector and the government sector, for the alternative simulation and the base simulation, namely,

$$\text{difcap} = \text{elascap}_a\text{-elascap}_b$$
$$\text{difcapg} = \text{elascapg}_a\text{-elascapg}_b,$$

where the subscript $_a$ denotes alternative simulation and the subscript $_b$ denotes the base simulation. If difcap or difcapg is positive this means that interest rate deregulation in the alternative case has a favourable effect on the elasticity of capital in comparison to the base simulation.

No substitution between deposits and capital

The advocates of the financial liberalisation school, e.g. McKinnon (1973) and Shaw (1973), assume that an increase in deposit rates leads to a portfolio shift out of unproductive assets (cash) into bank deposits. However, this may be a too extreme simplification of reality in developing countries. It is also possible that bank deposits might be close substitutes for productive assets, such as private capital, as well. Clearly, the fact that deposits and private capital are treated as being gross substitutes is one of the reasons why the simulations point to a weak negative effect of financial liberalisation on private capital. In order to assess the implications of substitutability between deposits and private capital, we simulate the effects of financial liberalisation assuming that deposits and private capital are not substitutes. This means that $\alpha_{14} = \alpha_{54} = \alpha_{18} = \alpha_{55} = 0$ in the asset demand equations for the private sector.

The results of this simulation are displayed in Figure 9.7. This figure shows that difcap and difcapg are positive during the whole simulation period. This implies that interest rate deregulation in the case where deposits and capital are not substitutes has a more positive or less negative effect on government and private capital than when deposits and capital are substitutes. This is what we should expect in view of the fact that there is a no direct negative substitution effect on private investment via portfolio adjustment. We can conclude from this that the smaller the degree of substitutability between deposits and capital in the private sector's portfolio, *ceteris paribus*, the greater the effect of interest rate deregulation on private capital accumulation.

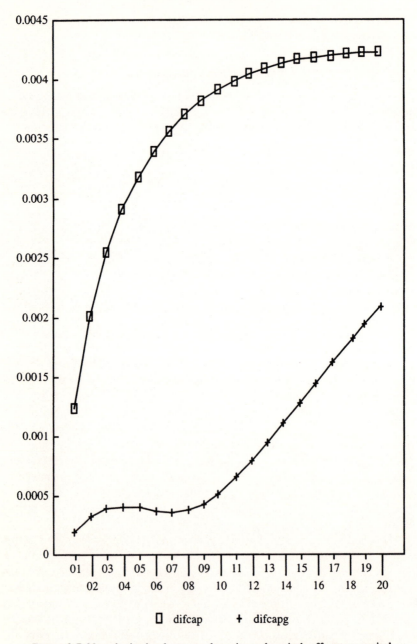

Figure 9.7 No substitution between deposits and capital: effects on capital

Only consumption is credit constrained

This implies that $\alpha_3 = \alpha_9 = \alpha_{13} = \alpha_{19} = \alpha_{23} = \alpha_{29} = \alpha_{53} = \alpha_{59} = 0$ and $\alpha_{43} = \alpha_{49} = 1$ in the asset demand equations for the private sector. Note that the demand for foreign assets is also credit constrained, as can be seen by deriving the adding-up restrictions. The results for this case are shown in Figure 9.8. Figure 9.8 shows that difcap is positive during almost the whole simulation period. This outcome presumably follows from the fact that the negative effects of a decline in formal credit on investment no longer apply. The burden of the crowding-out effect does not fall on investment when only consumption is credit constrained.[7]

Consumption not affected by real interest rates

This implies that $\alpha_{44} = \ldots = \alpha_{48} = 0$ in the equation for private consumption. The outcome of this case is shown in Figure 9.9. Figure 9.9 shows that difcap and difcapg are negative during almost the whole simulation period. Note, however, that the differences between the base simulation and the alternative simulation, as represented in Figure 9.9, are very small. This may well reflect the fact that the real interest rate coefficient in the consumption function is only 0.05, so that its replacement with a value of zero is not likely to make any significant difference. However, it should be noted that the seeming irrelevance of the interest rate sensitivity of consumption–savings does not justify the normal practice of treating savings as being exogenous (Morisset, 1993), because consumption–savings is affected not only by real interest rates but also by a host of other factors, as can readily be seen from our model. What is more, even the real interest rate may have an effect, albeit indirectly.

Lower wealth effect in investment equation

In this simulation it is assumed that the coefficient of net wealth in the investment equation (α_{12}) decreases from 0.2 to 0.15. We did some other simulations with respect to the wealth coefficient as well (see Gupta and Lensink, 1996), but these are, for reasons of space, not reported here. From these simulations it became very clear that a change in the wealth coefficient has important effects on the results. This would clearly suggest that a proper modelling of investment is most important in order to assess the role of financial liberalisation in stimulating private investment.

It can be seen from Figure 9.10 that a small decrease in the wealth coefficient has a relatively negative effect on the elasticity of private capital and government capital with respect to an interest rate deregulation, as compared to the base simulation. The decrease in private capital, however, becomes smaller during the simulation period.

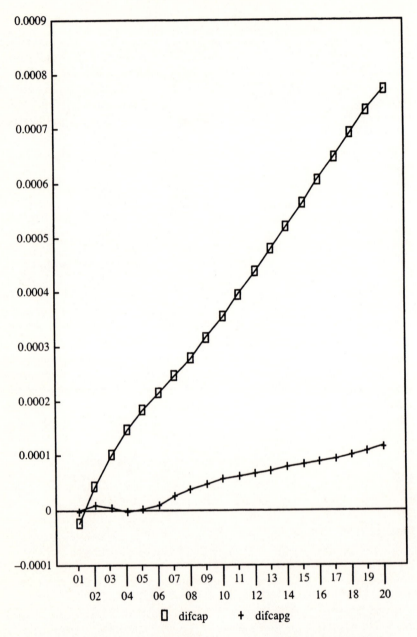

Figure 9.8 Only consumption is credit constrained: effects on capital

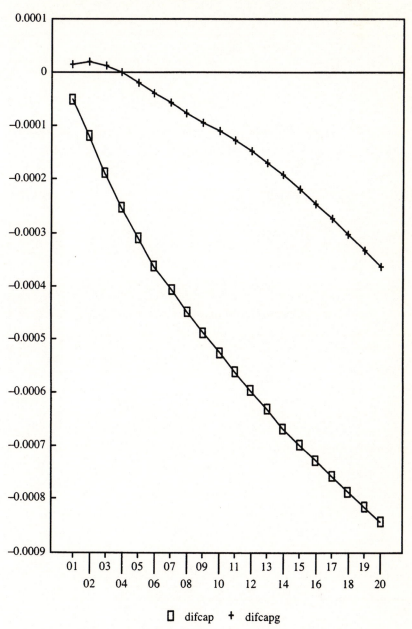

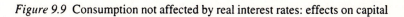

Figure 9.9 Consumption not affected by real interest rates: effects on capital

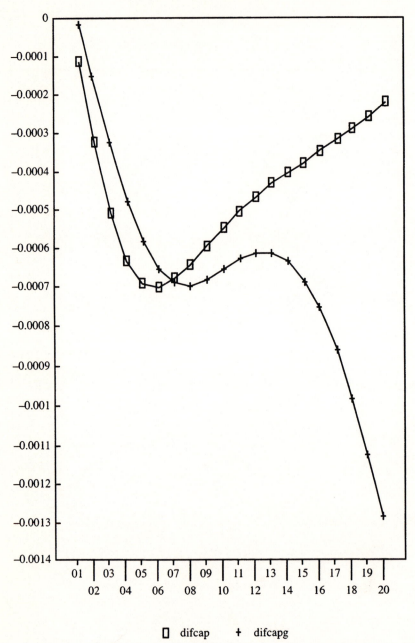

☐ difcap   + difcapg

Figure 9.10 Lower wealth effect: effects on capital

CONCLUDING REMARKS

The aim of this chapter has been to specify a simulation model which can shed light on a number of controversial issues regarding the effect of interest rate deregulation on private investment. Unlike virtually all other works in this area, our specification includes a portfolio selection model which is integrated with the consumption–savings decision, which includes the informal credit market as distinct from the formal banking sector, lets the budget deficit be determined endogenously as well as treating inflation as an endogenous variable. A distinct characteristic of the model is its treatment of interest income and interest burden in the budget constraints of the private and the government sectors. An advantage of our model is that it enables us to examine a variety of channels, hitherto unidentified in the literature, which can impact on the relationship between interest rate deregulation and private investment.

Since we report only a small selection of illustrative simulation examples, it is not possible to comment on the overall effectiveness of financial liberalisation. The presented simulations shed light on a number of issues, though. They show, for example, that under a variety of changes to the private sector's behaviour, the effect of deregulation is relatively robust in so far as the quantitative effect is concerned. It is relatively small, although the direction of the effects is sensitive to some of the specific characteristics of the firm's behaviour towards capital accumulation. The qualitative outcome of our simulations is similar to the findings reported by other researchers in the field, for example, Lewis (1992) for Turkey, Morisset (1993) for Argentina, Montiel *et al.* (1993) from a simulation model and Gupta (1984) for a cross-section of developing countries. These other studies, however, shed little light on the sensitivity issue addressed here.

NOTES

1 This paper was written while K.L. Gupta was a visiting professor at the University of Groningen. It draws heavily from Gupta and Lensink (1996). The authors would like to thank Hans van Ees for very useful comments.
2 See Gupta and Lensink (1996) for a full description of the model.
3 This variable could also represent gold or the stock of land. It may be seen as a composite of highly substitutable assets, which serves as an inflation hedge.
4 Note that normally consumption fixed capital is introduced in the definition of disposable income of the private sector. For pragmatic reasons, however, we decided not to take consumption fixed capital into account in disposable income, but to subtract it from savings in order to calculate the increase in net wealth. Since depreciation is exogenous and assumed to be equal before and after an interest rate deregulation, our assumption does not substantially affect the results.
5 We applied formal stability analysis to a specific version of the model. The model appears to be stable at the knife-edge, meaning that the stability is quite sensitive to rather small changes in some of the parameters.

6 They are defined as follows:

$$\text{elascap} = ((k_{p,a} - k_{p,b})/k_{p,b}) \cdot (i_{m,b}/(i_{m,a} - i_{m,b}))$$
$$\text{elascapg} = ((k_{g,a} - k_{g,b})/k_{g,b}) \cdot (i_{m,b}/(i_{m,a} - i_{m,b})),$$

where $k_{p,a}$ = the stock of physical capital of the private sector after the increase in the deposit rate; $k_{p,b}$ = the stock of physical capital of the private sector before the increase in the deposit rate (the base deposit rate); $k_{g,a}$ = the stock of physical capital of the government sector after the increase in the deposit rate; $k_{g,b}$ = the stock of physical capital of the government sector before the increase in the deposit rate; $i_{m,b}$ = the base deposit rate; $i_{m,a}$ = the deposit rate in the alternative model and hence $i_{m,a} - i_{m,b}$ = the increase in the deposit rate. All other elasticities are defined similarly.

7 In Gupta and Lensink (1996) we present a simulation in which only investment is credit constrained. For this case the effect of an interest rate deregulation on private investment becomes more negative.

REFERENCES

Gupta, K.L. (1984), *Finance and Economic Growth in Developing Countries*, London: Croom Helm.

—— (1993), 'Financial Liberalization, Wealth Effects and Private Investment', *Research Paper*, No. 93-22, University of Alberta.

Gupta, K.L. and R. Lensink (1993), 'Informal Credit Markets, Deregulation and Private Investment', *Research Memorandum*, No. 559, University of Groningen.

—— (1994), 'Financial Liberalization, Foreign Aid and Private and Public Investment', University of Groningen.

—— (1996), *Financial Liberalization and Investment*, London: Routledge.

Lewis, J.D. (1992), 'Financial Repression and Liberalization in a General Equilibrium Model with Financial Markets', *Journal of Policy Modelling*, 14, pp. 135–66.

McKinnon, R.I. (1973), *Money and Capital in Economic Development*, Washington DC: The Brookings Institution.

Marquez, J. (1990), 'Bilateral Trade Statistics', *Review of Economics and Statistics*, 72, pp. 70–77.

Montiel, P.J., P.R. Agénor and N. U. Haque (1993), *Informal Financial Markets in Developing Countries*, Oxford: Blackwell.

Morisset, J. (1993), 'Does Financial Liberalization Really Improve Private Investment in Developing Countries?', *Journal of Development Economics*, 40, pp. 133–50.

Ogawa, K., M. Saito and I. Tokutsu (1994), 'The Flow of Funds Equations of Japanese Non-Financial Firms', *Journal of the Japanese and International Economies*, 8, pp. 72–105.

Shaw, E.S. (1973), *Financial Deepening in Economic Development*, New York: Oxford University Press.

Sussman, O. (1991), 'Macroeconomic Effects of a Tax on Bond Interest Rates', *Journal of Money, Credit and Banking*, 23, pp. 352–66.

Van Wijnbergen, S. (1983), 'Interest Rate Management in LDCs', *Journal of Monetary Economics*, 18, pp. 433–52.

10

DEPOSIT MOBILISATION THROUGH FINANCIAL RESTRAINT[1]

Thomas Hellmann, Kevin Murdock and Joseph Stiglitz

INTRODUCTION

In his seminal work on financial development, Shaw (1973) noted that financial systems in developing countries were mostly characterised by low levels of formal intermediation and a weak institutional structure. Along similar lines, McKinnon (1973) noted that self-intermediation was prevalent in many developing countries.

Since then, discussions of financial development have mainly focused on 'liberalisation', as the lack of financial deepening was normally due to governments extracting rents from the financial sector. The (often explicit) assumption of this discussion was that a competitive financial system with a laissez-faire government would be the desired system. But experiences with liberalisation have provided mixed results. Equally troublesome, some of the fastest-growing economies, such as post-war Japan and more recently several of the East Asian NICs followed a path that was markedly different from the free market solution (cf. Stiglitz, 1993a, b). These events have called into question a simplistic 'free financial markets' paradigm. On the other hand, numerous experiences show that old-fashioned financial repression is not a desirable system either (cf. Fry, 1988a, b),[2] leaving us with the difficult problem of finding appropriate ways to mix governments and markets. In Hellmann *et al.* (1994, 1996) we develop an argument about how governments can enable the private financial markets to work more efficiently. The essence of this approach is that the government creates rent opportunities, but leaves it to private agents to take the actions that capture the benefits of these opportunities. By creating rent opportunities that induce agents to take socially beneficial actions, a better outcome may be achieved than under a free market system with laissez-faire.

In this paper we apply these ideas to the specific issue of deposit mobilisation. This issue is central to the debate on financial deepening. Mobilising deposits is crucial in many developing countries. Domestic funds

219

provide a cheap and reliable source of funds for development, which is of great value for developing countries, especially when the economy has difficulty raising capital in international markets. Yet in many developing countries a considerable amount of savings are not intermediated through the formal sector. In particular, there exists a significant savings potential in the rural (and/or semi-urban) sector in many developing countries (cf. Adams, 1978; Vogel, 1984). One of the reasons for the lack of savings mobilisation is that banks simply do not cater to significant numbers of households. Indeed, in many rural areas banks are entirely absent, and even in urban and semi-urban areas banks do not reach out to a significant proportion of the population.

Since banks in many developing countries have been nationalised, the causes of poor deposit mobilisation are often related to the incentive structure within the public sector.[3] As governments begin to privatise banks, however, we are faced with the question of how private markets are likely to pursue deposit collection. In particular, we need to ask what type of market failures are likely to occur, and what government policies can address these failures.

In this chapter we will develop two models that show the limitations of competitive deposit mobilisation, and derive the policies which may address these problems. In the first model, we consider the investment decision of a bank to open a new branch in a catchment area of unproved quality. If the bank has imperfect information about the profitability of the new catchment, it may have a problem expropriating the benefits of an explorative investment. If the catchment is not profitable, the bank will bear the cost of exploration, but if the catchment is good, other banks will follow suit and compete away profits in the new area. Put differently, there is a market imperfection in that information about the profitability of a catchment becomes public information after entry. In this paper we show that in such a context a limit on competition may be socially beneficial. By granting the first-mover bank (temporary) exclusive rights over its new catchment it can be compensated for the exploration costs. We show that a restriction of competition is in general superior to a policy of subsidisation under competition. We show that if the expected return to entry is not necessarily a monotonic function of the private signal, the government may not be able to induce the efficient entry condition, regardless of the amount of subsidy. By offering an appropriate length to the exclusive rights, the government can always induce efficient entry. And once the exclusive right expires, subsequent entry eliminates the static allocative inefficiency associated with restrictions on competition, indicating that an exclusive right of limited duration is superior to a permanent monopoly position.

The second model is concerned with a situation where banks are already competing in a market for deposits, but where the market is not yet fully penetrated. In particular we examine a situation where a portion of depositors is unfamiliar with the process of depositing their money in banks. This can be because of a lack of information, a general distrust of banks, or the cost of 'monetising' savings.[4] Banks however can invest in 'growing the market'. The idea is that banks become actively engaged in soliciting households to deposit their wealth with banks. This can take a number of forms: a bank may engage in an advertising campaign, it may use business contacts to convince people to monetise their savings and deposit them with banks, or it may offer subscription bonuses to people opening a new account. The effect of such a campaign is to attract new customers that fall in one of two categories. Some customers will have previously deposited their money with a different bank, while others are newly introduced to the banking system. We argue that while campaign investments are in general beneficial through introducing new customers to the banking sector – thus increasing financial depth – they can also become an inefficient form of non-price competition, when attracting customers from one bank to another.

We develop a simple model that allows us to analyse under what circumstances a bank will want to grow the market through an 'educational advertising campaign'. In a competitive equilibrium banks will undertake no investments in growing the market. This is because they are making zero profits on the margin, implying that they will gain no benefits by attracting additional customers. As a result, there are no incentives to deepen market penetration. If the government imposes a deposit rate ceiling, banks make positive profits on the marginal depositor. They will then make positive amounts of campaign investments, thus introducing new customers to the system, as well as competing to draw customers away from each other. We show that as long as the market is in a sufficiently low state of financial depth, lowering the deposit rate from the competitive equilibrium rate will be welfare-enhancing, even when we take into account the effect that lower deposit rates induce some households to substitute out of formal sector deposits. Once the market is sufficiently penetrated however, deposit rate controls are no longer desirable: at that point the gains from increased financial depth are more than offset by the costs of disintermediation.

The two models are an application of the framework discussed in Hellmann *et al.* (1996). The first model illustrates the importance of limitations on competition. Exclusive rights in new catchments ensures that banks which want to deepen their deposit base by opening new branches can appropriate rents from these activities. The second model illustrates the benefits of modest deposit rate controls. A positive margin on attracting new depositors is necessary if banks are to grow the deposit market. The deposit rate control, however, should not be permanent in this model: once financial deepening has occurred, there are inefficiencies due to pricing and non-price competition.

The remainder of this chapter is structured as follows. The first section reviews briefly the main aspects of *financial restraint*; the second section discusses incentives to deposit mobilisation through exclusive rights for new branches; and the third section discusses deposit mobilisation through non-price competition. This is followed by a brief conclusion.

AN OVERVIEW OF FINANCIAL RESTRAINT

Financial restraint is a set of policies designed to improve the efficiency of financial markets. Its two fundamental building blocks are deposit rate control and limitations on the amount of competition in the financial sector. Financial restraint embodies a set of financial policies designed to create rent opportunities that induce agents in the financial sector to engage in beneficial activities that are under-provided in a competitive market. In a related paper, Hellmann, Murdock and Stiglitz (1996) (HMS henceforth), develop a much broader outline of the financial restraint framework. In this section we only highlight the main aspects of the argument developed in that paper.

Our premise is that market failures are pervasive in the financial sector because of imperfect information and other transactions costs (cf. Stiglitz, 1993a).[5] One way to overcome these inefficiencies is for the government to affect the incentive structure in an otherwise private, profit-oriented, financial sector. The government can create rent opportunities, that induce private agents to take actions that are socially beneficial, but would otherwise not have been taken in competitive markets under laissez-faire. Note that this is a fundamentally different approach from the old-fashioned interventionist thinking, where the government undertakes the believed socially beneficial actions itself. By leaving the actions to the private market, the government is effectively 'out-sourcing' them, leaving the efficiency of execution to private agents, and by-passing the numerous inefficiencies that can be expected from direct government action. Note also that this approach differs substantially from that of a government distributing rents. Subsidies and related support programmes are typically not performance-based, and may create greater dependency on the part of subsidised firms, rather than self-sufficiency. When the government creates rent opportunities but then allows profit-maximising firms to pursue those rents, private information is incorporated in allocation decisions and the most efficient firms/banks profit and grow the most.

There is a number of important inefficiencies in the financial market, that governments may want to address through financial restraint. In HMS (1996) we identify three main areas that may be of particular concern to many developing and even developed economies – moral hazard in banking, deposit mobilisation, and asset substitution.

First we argue that moral hazard in banking, and the related problems of bank failures are endemic to a perfectly competitive banking system. Indeed, in HMS (1994) we show that competitive equilibria may have the property that banks gamble with, or even attempt to 'loot', their depositors' money, even in a market regime where there is no deposit insurance and depositors can rationally foresee these actions. As pointed out by Caprio and Summers

(1993), the problem is that banks do not value their 'franchise' enough. The banks' future income streams are not sufficiently high to value their continued operation enough to choose their investment portfolio efficiently. Banks may choose the (privately) optimal investment portfolio to maximise returns in the short run at the possible cost of being closed down thereafter, even if this harms the social return to the portfolio. In HMS (1994) we show that deposit rate controls can provide precisely the franchise value that would induce banks to behave more as long term players. Moreover, restrictions on competition may become necessary to prevent the effect of deposit rate controls being undermined by non-price competition from new entrants and/ or from incumbents.

Second, we argue that financial restraint increases the incentives to invest in deposit mobilisation, and thus to financial deepening. This chapter will focus on this topic.

A third aspect of financial restraint concerns the mitigation of undesirable side effects, in particular the problem that deposit rate controls may lead to asset substitution, where depositors seek out alternative savings vehicles. Restrictions on competing asset markets, such as bond markets or foreign savings instruments, are discussed in HMS (1996).[6] These restrictions perform the role of limiting inefficient reallocation of savings in response to deposit rate control. The reallocation incentives for depositors are increasing as the deposit rate falls, indicating that a limit on the extent of deposit rate control may be desirable.

Having briefly outlined the rationale for financial restraint, it is necessary to clarify the difference between financial restraint and financial repression. The fundamental difference is illustrated by Figure 10.1. In financial repression, the government represses deposit (as well as lending) rates, *in order to finance budget deficits*. The government is using the financial sector to extract rents from the private sector. Not surprisingly, we see under-capitalised banks lacking commercial orientation and often engaging in unsound practices. Moreover, financial repression is associated with high (and volatile) inflation rates, as part of the government's extraction of rents. Under

	Rent extraction	No direct rent extraction	Rent creation
High inflation	Financial repression	Southern cone	
Low inflation		Free markets	Financial restraint

Figure 10.1 Financial repression and financial restraint

Note: *There was some indirect rent extraction from the financial sector through inflation tax

223

financial restraint, however, the government needs to maintain a low inflation environment, where the real interest rate must remain positive and predictable (cf. HMS 1996).[7] Most important, the government does not extract rents from, but creates rents within, the private sector.

Our arguments supporting a regime of financial restraint as a tool to promote financial deepening are theoretically motivated, but they have some empirical roots. In particular they are inspired by the success of a number of East Asian economies, including post-war Japan (see also Stiglitz, 1993b). The creation of rents within the financial sector played an important role in the process of economic development for these countries.

DEPOSIT MOBILISATION THROUGH EXCLUSIVE RIGHTS ON NEW BRANCHES

In this section we describe a model that captures the decision of a profit-maximising bank on whether to open a branch in a previously unserved area. The investment is costly, and the expected return is uncertain due to limited knowledge about the quality of the potential depositors in the area. In a competitive market, the bank has too little incentive to develop a rural branch network because of the public good nature of the information about the quality of the deposit base. If it invests and quality is poor, it loses its investment. If the quality is high, competitive entry limits profits.

If the government offers exclusive rights for banks developing new branches, the private incentives of the bank approach the social optimum, relative to those of a competitive market. The arguments are analogous to the arguments for 'patent protection'. In order to induce sufficient entry, investors need protection from competitors who free-ride on the inventors' investments in information discovery. In the model described herein, it is possible to replicate exactly the social optimum entry condition if the government offers an exclusive right of appropriate length and provides a subsidy equal to a fraction of the fixed cost of entry. Moreover, protection is superior to subsidisation in a competitive market. The amount of the subsidy necessary to induce entry is always less when accompanied by an exclusive right, and a subsidy will not necessarily replicate the efficient entry conditions when the bank is subject to competition immediately after entry. This is because with competition it may be that a bank will choose not to enter a higher quality catchment because it is more likely to face competition after entry.

Description of the model

We consider the bank's decision whether to enter a particular rural catchment area of depositors. In the country, there are many rural catchments of potential depositors. Each catchment can be modelled using a Hotelling framework

224

where households supply one unit of deposit and are distributed with uniform density (D) around a unit circle. All households in a particular catchment have the opportunity to self-intermediate, earning a return on their deposit (s). If a bank opens a branch in their catchment, then depositors may choose to monetise their savings and open an account at the branch. Transacting with the bank is costly, however, when the branch is far from their home. If a household is a distance x from home, the cost of transacting with the bank is bx. Households maximise their net return on savings, so a household will monetise its savings if:

$$r - bx > s \qquad (1)$$

where r is the deposit rate offered by the bank.

Banks maximise profits. They have a fixed cost (per period) of serving a market equal to F. If no bank currently serves a particular catchment, then banks do not observe s. Rather, they know the distribution of s, $G(s, \theta)$ and they observe the signal θ, where

$$G(s, \theta_1) < G(s, \theta_2) \ \forall \ s \ if \ \theta_1 < \theta_2 \qquad (2)$$

Once a bank enters a given market, all banks observe s with certainty.[8] Hence there is a public good aspect associated with entry into new markets.

The structure of competition is shown in Figure 10.2. The bank enters the market, s becomes observable and then a second bank may enter as well. Then banks choose r and deposits are collected and the funds invested. The important aspect here is that if the market is sufficiently attractive (i.e. s is below a critical threshold), then a second bank will enter and compete for deposits. This creates a discontinuity in the expected profits when s falls. Normally, a lower s implies higher profits, but as s crosses below the threshold where competition ensues, profits decrease.

Banks can invest deposits in a competitive lending market where they earn a return L on their funds.[9] This can be thought of as a situation where banks use funds collected in rural areas to support investment in the urban centre. Alternatively, banks may have profitable investment opportunities in the rural catchment. For example, some high expected return projects may not be undertaken because they require (relatively) large capital investments and the

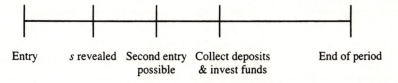

| Entry | s revealed | Second entry possible | Collect deposits & invest funds | End of period |

Figure 10.2 The structure of competition

transaction costs of collecting them through self-intermediation are too great. For the purposes of this analysis, we will abstract from the specifics of the lending allocation, and simply assume banks earn L on their investment. As a consequence, the maximum deposit rate that banks may pay is L. For simplicity, we assume that G has support over $[L - b, L]$.[10] Expected bank profits in the first period are:

$$\pi = \int_{L-b}^{L} (\pi|s)dG(s, \theta) \tag{3}$$

where $\pi|s$ depends on the structure of competition and will be discussed later. After the first period, if the catchment is not profitable (given the structure of competition), the bank will withdraw. We can define $\bar{s}$ by $[(\pi|\bar{s}) = 0]$. If $s < \bar{s}$, then the bank will operate profitably in the catchment for all future periods, effectively providing it with an annuity. Thus the total expected profits from entry are:

$$E(\pi|\theta) = \int_{L-b}^{L} (\pi|s)dG(s, \theta) + \frac{\delta}{1 - \delta} \int_{L-b}^{\bar{s}} (\pi|s)dG(s, \theta) \tag{4}$$

where δ is the discount factor. All banks observe the same signal θ about the distribution of s in a given catchment, but the government does not observe the signal. Part of the goal of policy will thus be determining an efficient mechanism to utilise the private signal to encourage efficient entry into rural catchment areas.

In the following four sub-sections, we will determine the entry conditions that would be used by a social planner to maximise welfare, by a profit-maximising firm guaranteed a monopoly position in the catchment, and by a profit-maximising firm vulnerable to competition from subsequent entry. Our results, presented in the sub-section on p. 233 are based primarily upon the comparison of these three entry conditions.

Socially efficient entry

We will first consider the decision of the hypothetical social planner as to whether entry into a rural catchment is efficient, given the available information. We assume that the social planner (unlike the government) can observe θ. If $s < L$, then for at least some depositors near it, the branch offers higher returns than self-intermediation. The fixed cost F is incurred (in the first period) before the value of s is discovered. Hence, the social planner must trade off the expected gains from monetising savings versus the cost of entry. Before paying the fixed cost in any subsequent period, the gains from monetising the savings must at least cover the fixed cost, defining $s*$ by

$[(W|s*) = 0]$. Expected welfare (where welfare is measured by the total social return to entry) is thus:

$$E(W|\theta) = \int_{L-b}^{L} (W|s)dG(s, \theta) + \frac{\delta}{1 - \delta} \int_{L-b}^{s*} (W|s)dG(s, \theta) \qquad (5)$$

The social planner will offer a rate L to depositors, so that all depositors for whom the social return increases with formal intermediation choose to monetise their savings. Depositors up to a distance $x*$ from the bank will open accounts, where x is defined by:

$$L - bx* = s, \text{ or } x* = \frac{L - s}{b} \qquad (6)$$

All households on each side of the bank up to a distance $x*$ from the branch will choose to open accounts with the bank. Given s, per period welfare from entry is:

$$W|s = 2 \int_{0}^{x*} D(L - s - bx)dx - F \qquad (7a)$$

$$W|s = \frac{D(L - s)^2}{b} - F \qquad (7b)$$

If s is sufficiently high, then the surplus generated from entry is negative (because it fails to cover the fixed cost). The bank will withdraw from the market in the second (and all subsequent periods) when $s > s*$, where

$$(W|s*) = 0 \Rightarrow s* = L - \sqrt{\frac{bF}{D}} = L - \frac{1}{\sqrt{\dfrac{bD}{F}}} b \qquad (8)$$

Entry then is socially efficient when

$$E(W|\theta) = \int_{L-b}^{L} \frac{D(L - s)^2}{b} dG(s, \theta) - F +$$

227

$$\frac{\delta}{1-\delta} \int_{L-b}^{s^*} \left[\frac{D(L-s)^2}{b} - F \right] dG(s, \theta) > 0 \qquad (9)$$

Entry by a monopolist

The monopolist will enter the market when its expected profits, given θ, are positive, or

$$E(\pi^m|\theta) = \int_{L-b}^{L} (\pi^m|s)dG(s, \theta) + \frac{\delta}{1-\delta} \int_{L-b}^{s'''} (\pi^m|s)dG(s, \theta) > 0 \qquad (10)$$

Once the bank observes s, it can choose its profit-maximising deposit rate. The monopolist must trade-off two opposing effects in deciding this deposit rate. When it increases the rate, it can attract a larger number of depositors, but its margin on all depositors it captures then falls. The profit-maximising rate exactly balances these two effects.

Given that it offers a rate r^m, the marginal depositor (at a distance x^m from the bank) will open an account with the bank if:

$$r^m - bx^m = s \ or \ x^m = \frac{r^m - s}{b} \qquad (11)$$

Profits, given s, are then:

$$\pi^m|s = 2 \int_0^{x^m} D(L-r)dx - F \qquad (12a)$$

$$\pi^m|s = \frac{2D(L-r)(r-s)}{b} - F \qquad (12b)$$

The profit-maximising interest rate is thus (from $\dfrac{d\pi^m|s}{dr} = 0$):

$$r^m = \frac{L+s}{2} \qquad (13)$$

giving

228

$$\pi^m | s = \frac{D(L - s)^2}{2b} - F \qquad (14)$$

The monopolist will continue operation in the second and all subsequent periods when $s \leq s^m$ where $s^m \equiv [(\pi^m | s^m) = 0]$, or[11]

$$s^m = L - \sqrt{\frac{2bF}{D}} = L - \frac{\sqrt{2}}{\sqrt{\frac{bD}{F}}} b \qquad (15)$$

The monopolist will enter when

$$E(\pi^m | \theta) = \int_{L-b}^{L} \frac{D(L - s)^2}{2b} dG(s, \theta) - F +$$

$$\frac{\delta}{1 - \delta} \int_{L-b}^{s^m} \left[\frac{D(L - s)^2}{2b} - F \right] dG(s, \theta) > 0 \qquad (16)$$

Entry with the threat of competition

The entry decision of a bank vulnerable to competition is different from those described above in a fundamental way – the revealed value of s determines the structure of competition that the bank faces. If s is sufficiently small,[12] the bank will have to compete for deposits. If, however, the value of s is large in some sense, then the bank will earn monopoly profits. This implies that when s crosses a critical threshold, the structure of competition changes and the profits of the bank fall discontinuously.

Assume for the moment that s is sufficiently small not to affect the pricing decision of either bank. N firms enter the market, spaced evenly around the Hotelling unit circle. A depositor located between two banks, offering rates r_1, r_2, respectively, will choose the first bank when

$$r_1 - bx^c > r_2 - b \left(\frac{1}{N} - x^c \right), \quad or \quad x^c = \frac{r_1 - r_2}{2b} + \frac{1}{2N} \qquad (17)$$

Profits, given s, are then:

$$\pi^c | s = 2 \int_0^{x^c} D(L - r_1) dx - F, \quad if \quad s < L - F \qquad (18a)$$

and

$$\pi^c|s = D(L - r_1)\left(\frac{r_1 - r_2}{b} + \frac{1}{N}\right) - F \tag{18b}$$

Otherwise the profit-maximising interest rate is thus (from $\dfrac{d\pi^c|s}{dr_1} = 0$):

$$r_1 = \frac{1}{2}\left(L + r_2 - \frac{b}{N}\right) \tag{19}$$

Incentives for both banks are symmetric, so the equilibrium interest rate will be:

$$r^c = L - \frac{b}{N} \quad and \quad x^c = \frac{1}{2N} \tag{20}$$

We began by assuming that s does not bind the pricing decision of the bank. Thus, $s < s^c$ where

$$\tag{21a}$$

$$s^c \equiv r^c - bx^c$$

$$s^c = L - \frac{3}{2N}b \tag{21b}$$

We can then determine profits when both banks compete with each other to collect deposits.

$$\pi^c|s = \frac{bD}{N^2} - F \tag{22}$$

Because we are considering a range where s is sufficiently small for banks to compete with each other, it makes sense that s does not impose a binding constraint on either bank's decision. Thus, we should expect that profits under competition are independent of s, as is the case.

For simplicity, we want to limit the analysis to the case where *at most* two banks can enter in a competitive market. We therefore examine the case of $4F \le bD < 8F$.[13] This implies that, when two banks are competing in the market, $\pi^c|s = kF$ with $0 \le k < 1$.

Now let us assume that s creates a binding constraint on the pricing decision of the bank, i.e. $s \geq s^c$. Thus each bank will choose a deposit rate such that its marginal depositor (at a distance $x^d = \dfrac{1}{2N}$ from the bank) will be just indifferent between an account with the bank and self-intermediation.[14] This occurs when

$$r^d = s + \frac{1}{2N} b \tag{23}$$

We can now determine profits under this duopoly-like structure of competition.

$$\pi^d|s = 2 \int_0^{\frac{1}{2N}} D(L - r^d)dx - F \tag{24a}$$

$$\pi^d|s = \frac{D}{N}\left(L - s - \frac{b}{2N} \right) - F \tag{24b}$$

We can show that $s^c < s^d < s^m$, where $s^d \equiv [(\pi^d|s^d) = 0]$; therefore, $(\pi^d|s^c) > 0$ and $(\pi^d|s^m) < 0$. Since $\pi^d|s$ is a continuous function, it must be the case that s^d is at an intermediate point between the two.

The structure of competition as a function of s

The structure of competition depends on the value of s that is revealed. If $s < s^c$, then a second bank enters and the two compete, yielding profits of $\pi^c|s$. When $s^c \leq s \leq s^d$, a second bank enters and they both act like duopolists, earning profits of $\pi^d|s$. If, however, $s > s^d$ then a second bank would lose money if it entered. Thus the incumbent bank knows it has a monopoly position and will earn $\pi^m|s$.

Let us define $\hat{\pi}^s|s$ as the actual profits captured by the incumbent bank as a function of s. Then

$$\hat{\pi}^c|s = \begin{cases} / \ \pi^c|s & \text{when} \quad s < s^c \\ \ \pi^d|s & '' \qquad s^c \leq s \leq s^d \\ \backslash \ \pi^m|s & '' \qquad s > s^d \end{cases} \tag{25}$$

A bank will enter a market based on its signal θ of the quality of the catchment when

$$E(\hat{\pi}^c|\theta) = \int_{L-b}^{L} (\hat{\pi}^c|s)dG(s, \theta) - F + \frac{\delta}{1 - \delta} \int_{L-b}^{s'''} (\hat{\pi}^c|s)dG(s, \theta) > 0 \quad (26)$$

i.e. when its expected profits from entry (given the type of competition it faces as a function of s) are positive.

An important feature of the underlying profit function $(\hat{\pi}^c|s)$ is that it is *not monotonically* decreasing in s. This is because there is a discontinuous increase in realised profits when s increases from s^d to $s^d + \epsilon$. Realised profits are zero when $s = s^d$ (by definition), whereas they are positive when $s = s^d + \epsilon$ (because the structure of competition changes from duopoly to monopoly and $[\pi^m|(s = s^d + \epsilon) > 0]$). We can see the shape of $(\hat{\pi}^c|s)$ in Figure 10.3 below.

Entry incentives and government policy

First-best entry incentives would have banks choose to enter the market whenever expected social welfare from entry is positive. Failing that, it is preferable that the entry decision efficiently utilise available private information about the quality of the catchment area. Specifically, since $G(s, \theta_1) < G(s, \theta_2)$ whenever $\theta_1 < \theta_2$, the private incentive to enter the market should be increasing as θ decreases.

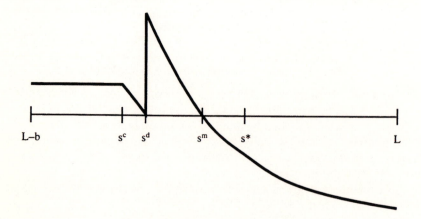

Figure 10.3 Profits under competition

Result 2.1

The incentives to enter are always greater for the monopolist than for the competitive firm, but always less than the social optimum.

Proof: Comparing the expected profits of the monopolist (equation (10)) to that of a competitive firm (equation (26)), we find that

$$E(\pi^m|\theta) - E(\hat{\pi}^c|\theta) = \frac{1}{1-\delta} \; [\int_{L-b}^{s^t} (\pi^m - \pi^c)dG(s,\theta)$$

$$+ \int_{s^t}^{s^d}(\pi^m - \pi^d)dG(s,\theta)] > 0 \tag{27}$$

This result follows directly from the observation that competition can never produce higher profits than monopoly. If this were possible, then the monopolist could just replicate the competitive equilibrium and be better off.

The entry incentives of the monopolist are similarly always less than the social optimum (from equation (5)).

$$E(W|\theta) - E(\pi^m|\theta) = \int_{L-b}^{L} (W - \pi^m)dG(s,\theta) + \frac{\delta}{1-\delta} \; [\int_{L-b}^{s^m} (W - \pi^m)dG(s,\theta)$$

$$+ \int_{s^m}^{s^*} WdG(s,\theta)] > 0 \tag{28}$$

This is because of the allocative inefficiency arising from the monopolist's pricing power. In particular, the monopolist pays a deposit rate of

$r^m = \frac{1}{2}(L + s) < L$. This results in depositors at the fringes of the market

$(x^m < x \leq x^*)$ choosing self-intermediation even though it is socially efficient for them to deposit their funds with the formal financial sector. If the monopolist cannot capture the entire social return, its incentives will be less than the socially efficient level. ☐

Result 2.2

The expected profits for the monopolist are monotonic in θ so that incentives for the monopolist to enter are increasing as θ decreases. Expected profits for the competitive firm are not necessarily monotonic, so that a lower quality signal (higher θ) may give a stronger incentive to enter.

Proof: Expected profits for the monopolist $(E(\pi^m|\theta))$ are increasing as θ decreases because $(\pi^m|s)$ is decreasing in s and $G(s, \theta_1) < G(s, \theta_2)$ $\forall s$ if $\theta_1 < \theta_2$.

The result for the competitive firm is ambiguous because of the truncated nature of its returns. When s is sufficiently small ($s < s^d$), a second bank will enter the market, and the resulting competition will drive profits to a level less than that achieved by the monopolist. From equation (26),

$$E(\hat{\pi}^c|\theta) = \int_{L-b}^{L} (\hat{\pi}^c|s)dG(s, \theta) + \frac{\delta}{1 - \delta}\int_{L-b}^{s^m} (\hat{\pi}^c|s)dG(s, \theta) \qquad (29)$$

We demonstrated in the sub-section on pages 231–32 that $\hat{\pi}^c|s$ is not monotonically decreasing in s. Given that θ represents a shift of first order stochastic dominance in $G(s, \theta)$, we know that $E(\hat{\pi}^c|\theta)$ is not necessarily decreasing in θ. As an example, let us assume that there is a large probability mass at $s = s^d$. A small increase in θ may shift that probability mass to $s = s^d + \epsilon$, resulting in a discontinuous *increase* in $E(\hat{\pi}^c|\theta)$. $\qquad\square$

Result 2.3

Assuming the government knows $G(s, \theta)$, there exists an efficient subsidy $c^m F$ with $c^m < 1$ such that the monopolist has efficient entry incentives. Should the expected profits of the competitive firm be monotonic, then there exists a subsidy $c^c F$ such that entry incentives are efficient. The subsidy for competitive firms must exceed that for the monopolist ($c^c > c^m$). If competitive profits are not monotonic, then the government may not be able to provide the socially efficient incentive with a subsidy.

Proof: Expected welfare [$E(W|\theta)$] is monotonic in θ and always greater than the profits of the monopolist [$(E(\pi^m|\theta)$]. If we define θ^* as the efficient entry signal (i.e. $\theta^* \equiv [(E(W|\theta^*) = 0])$, then the optimal subsidy is:

$$c^m F = -E(\pi^m|\theta^*) \qquad (30)$$

Then the monopolist will enter for all $\theta \le \theta^*$ because

$$E(\pi^m|\theta) + c^m F = E(\pi^m|\theta) - E(\pi^m|\theta^*) \ge 0, \forall\, \theta \le \theta^* \qquad (31)$$

which is the efficient entry condition. Similarly, if competitive profits are monotonic in θ, then we can define the subsidy for the competitive firm as:

$$c^c F = -E(\hat{\pi}^c|\theta^*) \qquad (32)$$

to generate the efficient entry incentives. It will always be more costly for the government to induce efficient entry in the competitive market structure.[15]

$$E(\hat{\pi}^c|\theta^*) < E(\pi^m|\theta^*) \Rightarrow c^c F > c^m F \qquad (33)$$

If the competitive profit is *not* monotonic in θ, then the government may not be able to provide the efficient entry incentive. Non-monotonicity implies that:

$$E(\hat{\pi}^c|\theta_1) < E(\hat{\pi}^c|\theta_2), \quad \text{for some} \quad \theta_1 < \theta_2 \tag{34}$$

In particular, if $E(\hat{\pi}^c|\bar{\theta}) < E(\hat{\pi}^c|\bar{\theta}^*)$, for some $\bar{\theta} < \theta^*$, then the competitive bank will not enter when $\theta = \bar{\theta}$ even with a subsidy of $c^c F$. We have

$$E(\hat{\pi}^c|\bar{\theta}) + c^c F = E(\hat{\pi}^c|\bar{\theta}) - E(\hat{\pi}^c|\theta^*) < 0 \tag{35}$$

□

Result 2.4

If the government offers a full subsidy equal to the fixed cost of entry, entry is excessive. The subsidisation policy fails to utilise private information about the quality of the catchment.

Proof: If the government were to encourage entry by offering a subsidy equal to the total fixed cost, it would generate excessive incentives for entry. From equation (26), the expected profits with the subsidy are:

$$E(\hat{\pi}^c|\theta) + F = \int_{L-b}^{L} [(\hat{\pi}^c|s) + F]dG(s, \theta) + \frac{\delta}{1 - \delta} \int_{L-b}^{s'''} (\hat{\pi}^c|s)dG(s, \theta) > 0, \forall \theta \tag{36}$$

So competitive firms will have an incentive to enter all markets, regardless of their signal of the quality of the catchment. With a complete subsidy of the fixed cost of entry, banks bear no downside risk from entry. □

Result 2.5

If the government grants a sufficiently long exclusive right (of duration T) and offers a subsidy equal to $c^p F$, then the government can induce efficient entry even when the returns under competition are not monotonic in θ. This subsidy is less than that needed by a firm in a completely competitive market but greater than that needed to induce efficient entry by the monopolist (i.e. $c^m < c^p < c^c$). The advantage of an exclusive right with limited duration is that after T periods elapse, the static inefficiency arising due to monopoly power is eliminated by competition.

Proof: If the government offers an exclusive right of T periods to the first entrant, the expected profits to the bank are:

235

$$E(\pi^p|\theta) = \int_{L-b}^{L} (\pi^m|s)dG(s,\theta) + \frac{\delta - \delta^T}{1 - \delta} \int_{L-b}^{s'''} (\pi^m|s)dG(s,\theta)$$

$$+ \frac{\delta^T}{1 - \delta} \int_{L-b}^{s'''} (\hat{\pi}^c|s)dG(s,\theta)$$

(37)

We make the claim that if T is sufficiently long, then the government can induce efficient entry with a subsidy. This is equivalent to the statement that there is no $\tilde{\theta} < \theta^*$ such that $E(\pi^p|\tilde{\theta}) < E(\pi^p|\theta^*)$.

To prove this let us consider the set of all $\bar{\theta} < \theta^*$ for which $E(\hat{\pi}c|\bar{\theta}) < E(\hat{\pi}^c|\theta^*)$. For each of these there exists some $\bar{T}$ for which $E(\pi^p|\bar{\theta}) \geq E(\pi^p|\theta^*)$. We can see this easily in the limiting case where $\bar{T} \to \infty$ because then $E(\pi^p|\bar{\theta}) = E(\pi^m|\bar{\theta})$ and $E(\pi^m|\theta)$ is monotonically decreasing in θ. If T represents the minimum $\bar{T}$ such that this condition is satisfied everywhere, then $E(\pi^p|\theta) \geq E(\pi^p|\theta^*), \forall \theta < \theta^*$.

The government can now offer a subsidy equal to

$$c^pF = -E(\pi^p|\theta^*)$$

(38)

We can see that $c^m < c^p < c^c$ because $E(\pi^m|\theta^*) > E(\pi^p|\theta^*) > E(\pi^c|\theta^*)$.[16] Even though a larger subsidy is necessary to induce efficient entry when the government grants an exclusive right of limited duration, rather than a permanent monopoly to the bank, there are potential social gains from competition in the future. Once the exclusive right expires, entry by a second bank will eliminate the deadweight loss from monopoly power. In particular, if the government has a lower discount rate than that used by the bank in its entry decision, the social gains perceived by the government from entry may outweigh the economic loss from future competition as perceived by the bank. □

DEPOSIT RATE CONTROLS AND FINANCIAL DEPTH

In the previous section we examined the entry decision of banks into new catchment areas. In this section we will look at the related problem of how, in a given market, banks can 'deepen' their market penetration. By financial depth we have a precise concept in mind: a deposit market has not achieved its full depth (i.e. has not been fully penetrated) if there exist households that are not depositing their wealth in banks, even though the deposit rate exceeds the return of their chosen alternative form of investment. This definition reflects the commonly observed phenomena in developing countries that although financial institutions are present, a significant proportion of households does not utilise their services. There may be several reasons for this, including lack of visibility of the banks, lack of knowledge and trust among households about the banks' activities, and switching costs, such as when households hold their wealth in real assets that need to be sold off before their value can be deposited with banks.

In this section we ask the following question: under what circumstances will private profit-maximising banks spend resources to grow the deposit market, i.e. to attract those households that are currently outside the formal system? To increase financial depth, banks can be proactive in a number of ways, ranging from spending resources on improving their infrastructure to actually engaging in promotional campaigns that educate households about the benefits of financial savings. We will summarise these activities as an 'educational advertising campaign'.

In a competitive banking environment, an educational advertising campaign is a tool of non-price competition, in the sense that banks spend resources on attracting new customers using mechanisms other than changes in the deposit rate. We will show that this non-price competition arises only when the government intervenes to place a ceiling on the interest rate banks may offer to depositors. Traditional economic analysis would emphasise the static allocative inefficiency of non-price competition. We emphasise, however, that this non-price competition can be beneficial in an environment characterised by low financial depth. If the campaign reaches households that are already in the financial system it will only induce them to switch among competing banks without creating social value. If, however, it reaches households previously not connected to the system, it creates social returns by increasing financial depth. Deposit rate controls create margins that allow banks to capture some of these social returns. As a consequence they allow for a decentralized solution to the challenge of increasing financial depth.

Description of the model

There are H households that each supply one unit of deposits. Households want to maximise the value of their savings, choosing between putting their wealth either into financial savings or into other uses, that we summarise as 'self-intermediation'. The return to self-intermediation for any particular household is s, where s is privately observed by households. For the entire economy, the distribution of these returns is $G(s)$ with a support $[s_{min}, s^{max}]$. For a given interest rate r, the probability that any particular household will choose to monetise its savings is $G(r)$.

We denote the number of households which are connected to the financial sector by K. We assume that these households will choose between self-intermediation and financial savings on the basis of maximising expected returns. Not all households, however, are connected to the formal financial sector. The remainder of households $(H - K)$ will always self-intermediate, unless reached by an educational advertising campaign. Thus K is a measure of financial depth, ranging from 0 to H.

We assume that there are two banks that compete via Bertrand in the deposit rate.[17] Banks have one further choice variable: they may invest in an educational advertising campaign. This campaign has two effects. First, it introduces to banks households that were previously not connected to the formal financial sector. Once a household has been exposed to an educational campaign, it is inside the financial system. Depending on the deposit rate it may then choose to deposit its wealth or not. Second, a campaign resolves the choice of an indifferent depositor. When two banks offer the same deposit rate, a household contacted by one bank's campaign will go to that bank. If a household has been contacted by both or neither bank, it remains indifferent. If the two banks offer different deposit rates, standard Bertrand competition implies that all depositors will prefer the bank with the higher deposit rate, irrespective of campaigns. Banks cannot price discriminate between depositors previously connected or not, nor between households that were or were not reached by the campaign.

A campaign is costly. If we define c_i as the probability that a household is exposed to the campaign of bank i, then the cost of the campaign is determined by $z(c_i)$, where z satisfies $z(0) = 0$, $z'(c) \geq 0$, $z'(0) = 0$; $z'(1) = \infty$ and $z''(c) > 0$.

Investment under competition

Let L be the expected value of an additional deposit to the bank. L could be the safe rate of return, or it could be the expected return on a lending portfolio. Let r_i be the deposit rate offered by bank i, and let d_i be the quantity of deposits mobilised by bank i. Profits for bank i are then given by:

$$\pi_i = (L - r_i)d_i(r_i, r_{-i}, c_i, c_{-i}) - z(c_i) \tag{39}$$

The number of deposits which the bank captures depends on its deposit rate relative to its competitor and on the total number of households with financial savings (which depends on K, c_i, c_{-i}). Applying the above selection criteria of households, we have

$$d_i(r_i > r_{-i}, c_i, c_{-i}) = [K + (H - K)(c_i + c_{-i} - c_i c_{-i})]G(r_i) \tag{40a}$$

$$d_i(r_i < r_{-i}, c_i, c_{-i}) = 0 \tag{40b}$$

$$d_i(r_i = r_{-i}, c_i, c_{-i}) = [K(0.5 c_i c_{-i} + 0.5(1 - c_i)(1 - c_{-i}) + c_i(1 - c_{-i}))$$
$$+ (H - K)(c_i(1 - c_{-i}) + 0.5 c_i c_{-i})]G(r_i) \tag{40c}$$

Result 3.1

In a competitive equilibrium, banks will earn zero profits ($\pi_i = 0$) and offer deposit rates equal to the lending rate ($r_i = r_{-i} = L$). Banks will make no investments in growing the market, i.e. $c_i = c_{-i} = 0$.

Proof: Suppose that $r_i < L$. Then bank $-i$ will offer a deposit rate of $r_{-i} = r_i + \epsilon$, where ϵ is arbitrarily small. Since $d_i(r_{-i} + \epsilon > r_i) > d_i(r_{-i} = r_i)$ for sufficiently small ϵ, this deviation is always profitable. Thus $r_i = r_{-i} = L$ in equilibrium. Since banks must earn non-negative profits, $c_i = c_{-i} = 0$. $\square$

This result is due to the extreme properties of Bertrand competition. We use it as a convenient benchmark case to argue that if banks have no margin on deposits, they are unwilling to make investments to increase the size of the market. No investments are made in the campaign by either firm and K, the number of households with financial savings, always remains unchanged.

Total social income is thus:

$$I^{FM} = KF(L) + (H - K)E \tag{41}$$

where $E \equiv \int_{-\infty}^{\infty} sdG(s)$ and $F(r) \equiv [LG(r) + \int_{r}^{\infty} sdG(s)]$. E is the expected return under self-intermediation, while $F(r)$ is the expected return with financial intermediation at a deposit rate r. For all $r > s_{min}$, we have $F(r) > E$. $\square$

Investment under financial restraint

Now suppose the government intervenes to place a limit $\underline{r}$ on the deposit rate paid by banks. Both banks will offer $\underline{r}$ and then choose a level of c to maximise their profits. The derivative of the bank's deposits as a function of the size of its campaign is

$$\frac{\partial d_i}{\partial c_i} = [(H - 0.5K) - 0.5(H - K)c_{-i}]G(\underline{r}) \tag{42}$$

so that a bank's first order condition for the optimal choice of c_i is given by

$$Q(\underline{r})[(H - 0.5K) - 0.5(H - K)c_{-i}] - z'(c_i) = 0 \tag{43}$$

where $Q(\underline{r}) \equiv (L - \underline{r})G(\underline{r})$.

Let us define the following conditions:

$$\text{Condition } Q: \frac{\partial Q}{\partial \underline{r}} = (L - \underline{r})g(\underline{r}) - G(\underline{r}) < 0 \qquad (44)$$

$$\text{Condition } Z: z''(c_i) > (H - K)0.5Q(\underline{r}) \; \forall \; c_i \qquad (45)$$

Note that condition Q is always satisfied locally for $\underline{r}$ close to L. Condition Z is easily satisfied by choosing a sufficiently convex cost function.

We can now state:

Result 3.2

Whenever the deposit rate is set to a level $\underline{r} < L$, and assuming condition Z holds, there is a unique stable and symmetric equilibrium, where each bank spends a strictly positive amount of resources on an educational advertising campaign. The equilibrium size of a campaign c_i is a decreasing function of K, an increasing function of H. If condition Q is satisfied (is not satisfied), then c is a decreasing (increasing) function of $\underline{r}$.

Proof: The first term of the first order condition is always strictly positive thus $z' > 0$, and thus $c_i > 0$. Condition Z ensures that the Jacobian matrix is positive definite, guaranteeing a well-behaved equilibrium. The comparative statics are immediate from differentiating the first order condition with the respective variables. □

Result 3.2 establishes the fundamental result that deposit rate controls can induce private banks to invest in growing the market. The bank's incentive to invest in an educational advertising campaign is stronger, the lower the financial depth. The effect of an increase in the deposit rate is two-fold. For higher $\underline{r}$, the margin on deposits decreases for those depositors which the bank successfully captures at a deposit rate of $\underline{r}$, making a campaign less attractive (as reflected by the $G(\underline{r})$ term). More depositors, however, would respond to a campaign at a higher deposit rate, making a campaign more powerful (as reflected by the $(L - \underline{r})g(\underline{r})$ term). If condition Q is satisfied, the first effect dominates, so that the size of the campaign is a decreasing function of the deposit rate. This will always be the case for $\underline{r}$ close to L.

Government policy as a function of financial depth

In an equilibrium with deposit rate controls, banks make positive investment in the campaign of c. This will induce some households previously not connected to the financial sector to open deposit accounts $[(H - K)(2c - c^2)]$ at a cost of $2z(c)$. Total household income under deposit control is then:

$$I = [K + (H - K)(2c - c^2)](F(\underline{r}) + (H - K)(1 - 2c + c^2)E - 2z(c) \qquad (46)$$

The social planner has an indirect control problem of controlling c through $\underline{r}$. There is a trade-off between the benefits of having market growth versus the cost of distorting the deposit rate on the existing depositors. The competitive outcome is an extreme outcome in this trade-off, where $\underline{r} = L$ so that $c = 0$.

We can derive two important results from this maximisation problem.

Result 3.3

There exists a critical level K^*, where $O < K^* < H$, such that for all $K \geq K^*$, L is the optimal deposit rate, and for all K with $K < K^*$ the optimal deposit rate $\underline{r}^*$ lies strictly below L. Moreover, the optimal deposit rate is a non-decreasing function of K.

Proof: See Appendix. □

Result 3.4

For any $K < H$, if the social planner can only control c through the control of $\underline{r}$, the optimal c will be smaller than if the social planner could control c directly.

Proof: See Appendix. □

Result 3.3 has two important parts. First it formally shows that for a significant range of parameters ($K \in [0, K^*]$) deposit rate controls are not only effective in inducing campaigns, but that they are actually optimal for a social planner, despite their costs of disintermediation. In the range $K \in [K^*, H]$ the marginal benefit of introducing further households into the system is not worth the cost of disintermediation.

Second, result 3.3 shows that the optimal level of the deposit rate depends on the level of financial depth. The more rudimentary the financial inter-mediation (i.e. the lower K) the lower the optimal deposit rate. This is a formalisation of a claim we have made (Hellmann *et al.*, 1995) that the optimal amount of financial restraint, such as through deposit rate controls, is a direct function of the level of financial development.

Result 3.4 finally shows that while deposit rate controls can induce private banks to spend some amount of resources on deepening the financial markets, this amount may still be insufficient from a social planner's perspective. A government may therefore want to do more to promote financial deepening. We leave the discussion on the efficiency of such policies to future research.

We have thus shown that competition in deposit rates leads to a situation where banks have no incentives to collect additional deposits. The funda-mental insight is that the incentive to grow the deposit market depends on the margins that banks make on deposits, i.e. the difference between lending and deposit rates. Deposit rate controls ensure that competition will not drive these margins down to zero. They are therefore a powerful instrument to allow private deposit markets to grow.

CONCLUSION

This chapter asks the question under what circumstances banks have incentives to increase their deposit collection efforts. We compare outcomes under a perfectly competitive market with outcomes under financial restraint, i.e. a combination of deposit rate controls and restrictions on competition. In the first model we show that temporary exclusive rights may be an efficient way of inducing banks to open branches in new areas. In the second model we show that deposit rate controls can induce banks to grow the deposit market. Our analysis could be extended in a number of ways. For instance, we have only examined one among several possible forms of non-price competition. It would also be desirable to integrate the two models, in order to develop a life-cycle model of new branches. Beyond these theoretical questions, we also believe that there are interesting institutionally descriptive and empirical questions about when banks actively mobilise deposits, and exactly what activities they undertake for this purpose. Such research could thus contribute to the broader question of what policies may be most effective to promote financial deepening.

APPENDIX

Proof of Result 3.3   We begin by proving the first assertion. The social planner never wants to set the deposit rate above L, as no bank would be willing to collect deposits. The first derivative of I w.r.t. $\underline{r}$ is given by $\dfrac{\partial I}{\partial \underline{r}} + \dfrac{\partial I}{\partial c}\dfrac{\partial c}{\partial \underline{r}}$,

where $\dfrac{\partial I}{\partial c} = 2[(H - K)(1 - c)(F(\underline{r}) - E) - z']$ and

$\dfrac{\partial I}{\partial \underline{r}} = \dfrac{\partial F(\underline{r})}{\partial \underline{r}}[K + (H - K)(2c - c^2)$. Evaluating this at $K = 0$ and $\underline{r} = L$ yields

$\dfrac{\partial I}{\partial c} = 2H(F(L) - E) > 0, \dfrac{\partial c}{\partial \underline{r}} < 0$ (since condition Q is always satisfied near L)

and $\dfrac{\partial I}{\partial \underline{r}} = 0$, implying that I is decreasing in $\underline{r}$ near L. This implies that in a

neighbourhood of $K = 0$, the optimal deposit rate is always lower than L. Consider next the case of $K = H$. We immediately recognise that any

campaign only wastes social resources (i.e. I is always a decreasing function of c, as the only term is $-2z(c)$). It follows that $r = L$ optimal. Finally, consider the derivative of I w.r.t. r in the neighbourhood of $r = L$ and $K = H$, which is given by $H\,\dfrac{\partial F(L)}{\partial r} > 0$. It follows that not just at $K = H$, but also in a neighbourhood of $K = H$, the optimal deposit rate is L. Combining these two results, we can conclude that there exists K^*, with $0 < K^* < H$, so that for all K smaller than K^*, a reduction in the deposit rate increases social income.

To prove the second assertion, suppose first that condition Q is always satisfied. Consider $\dfrac{\partial I}{\partial K} = (1 - c)^2[F(r) - E]$,

so that $\dfrac{\partial^2 I}{\partial K \partial r} = 2(1 - c)[F(r) - E](-\dfrac{\partial c}{\partial r}) + (1 - c)^2\,\dfrac{\partial F(r)}{\partial r}$, which is positive, establishing that I is supermodular in r and K (cf. Milgrom and Roberts, 1990). It follows that the optimal choice r is non-decreasing in K.

If condition Q is not satisfied everywhere, then it is possible that c increases with r. The optimal choice of r, however, will never occur at a point where this is true. This is because for every c_1 and r_1, where condition Q is violated, there exists another $r_2 > r_1$, so that c_1 is chosen at both r_2 and r_1. This can be deduced from the fact that $c(r)$ is continuous, is decreasing (increasing) in r whenever condition Q is (not) satisfied, and satisfies $c(r) = 0$ at $r = L$. The social planner will always choose r_2 over r_1 to implement c_1, as this involves less disintermediation. We can therefore rephrase the social planner's maximisation problems over the following restricted domain of deposit rates: $r \in [s_{min} \cdot L]$ and condition Q is satisfied at r. I is supermodular over this domain, and we obtain again that the optimal choice of r is a non-decreasing function of K.

Proof of Result 3.4   In the direct control problem, the social planner would set $\dfrac{\partial I}{\partial c} = 0$, which involves $c > 0$ whenever $K < H$. If $K^* < K < H$ no resources are spent on campaigns in the indirect control problem. If $K \leq K^*$, we have seen in the previous proof that for any optimal choice of r we have $\dfrac{\partial c}{\partial r} < 0$. From the first-order condition of choosing the optimal r, we have

$\dfrac{\partial I}{\partial c} = \dfrac{\partial I}{\partial \underline{r}} \bigg/ \left(-\dfrac{\partial c}{\partial \underline{r}} \right) > 0$. Again, the amount of resources spent on a campaign

are less than in the direct control problem.

NOTES

1 This chapter originated as a paper prepared for the workshop *Financial Development and Economic Growth: Theory and Experiences from Developing Economies*, held at the University of Groningen, the Netherlands on 7–9 December 1994. It represents the views of the authors and does not necessarily represent that of any organisation with which they are or have been affiliated.

2 Empirical results show that economic growth is strongly correlated with financial deepening (cf. King and Levine, 1993) but that economic growth is not monotonically related to interest rates, once interest rates are positive (cf. Murdock and Stiglitz, 1993).

3 Indeed, while some governments have provided explicit incentives to deposit mobilisation (e.g. Korea, cf. Cho and Hellmann, 1993), other countries have failed to provide these incentives (e.g. Tanzania, cf. Krahnen and Schmidt, 1994).

4 The last aspect is very common in developing countries: households hold their wealth in non-monetary forms, such as real assets (life stock, real estate, etc.) and/or gold. It needs some effort on behalf of the banks to convince people to sell these assets in order to get a higher return by depositing the proceeds in the formal sector.

5 A government-owned financial system on the other hand may be even worse, because of government failures and weaker mechanisms to resolve these inefficiencies.

6 A fourth effect discussed in HMS (1995) concerns lending rate controls, and is outside the focus of this chapter.

7 This implies that a pre-condition for financial restraint is that there is a reasonably stable macroeconomic environment, and no heavy direct taxation of the financial sector.

8 It is not necessary for the results presented in this model for us to assume that s becomes perfectly observable after entry – this is only a simplifying assumption. The only necessary requirement for our fundamental result to hold – that entry is under-provided when free entry is allowed – is that a potential competitor's estimation of s improves after entry.

9 The focus of this chapter is on deposit mobilisation, so we ignore any effects an increase in the supply of funds may have on the lending market equilibrium. This assumption may be justified, however, if the volume of savings in any particular rural catchment is small relative to the total volume of funds intermediated. Also, if there is equilibrium credit rationing in the lending market, the lending rate may remain unchanged with an increase in the volume of savings.

10 There is no loss of generality here. We can describe all possible relevant distributions over this support. If $s < L - b$, then a bank with monopoly power will act as if $s = L - b$. This is because the monopoly will choose to serve the entire catchment. If $s > L$, then any bank will lose F, the fixed cost of entry and gain no deposits. We can describe each of these situations with a probability mass on the appropriate extreme of the support.

11 We will assume below that $4 \leq \dfrac{bD}{F} < 8$, which implies that

$$L - \frac{\sqrt{2}}{2} b \leq s^m < L - \frac{1}{2} b$$

12 As we shall demonstrate, when s falls below a critical level, a second bank will enter and both banks will compete with each other for deposits on the margin. If s exceeds that critical level, then the bank will be effectively protected from competition and it will act like a monopolist.

13 We intentionally exclude the case of $8F \leq bD < 9F$. This range of parameters creates a very special case whereby it is feasible for two non-competing monopolists to enter the market. For all other ranges of these parameters ($bD < 8F$ and $bD \geq 9F$), if an additional bank may profitably enter the market, then the banks will compete with each other for deposits.

14 We can show this formally by considering the first order condition of the bank when it competes with another for deposits.

$$\frac{\partial \pi}{\partial r_1} = \frac{D}{b}\left[L - \frac{1}{N} b - r_1 - (r_1 - r_2)\right].$$ In a symmetric equilibrium with ($r_1 = r_2$),

then $\dfrac{\partial \pi}{\partial r_1} < 0$ implies $r_1 > L - \dfrac{1}{N} b$. Thus the bank will lower its deposit rate until

the constraint on s becomes binding.

15 Assuming $G(s^d, \theta) > 0, \forall \theta$.

16 Assuming T is finite and positive.

17 The results with more than two banks are analogous. The only difference is that the probabilities that a household receives more than one message have to be appropriately modified.

REFERENCES

Adams, D. (1978), 'Mobilizing Household Savings through Rural Financial Markets', *Economic Development and Cultural Change*, 26, pp. 547–60.

Caprio, G. and L. Summers (1993), 'Finance and Its Reform: Beyond Laissez-Faire', *Policy Research Working Papers*, Financial Sector Development WPS 1171, Washington DC: World Bank.

Cho, Y. and T. Hellmann (1993), 'The Government's Role in Japanese and Korean Credit Markets: A New Institutional Economics Perspective', *Policy Research Working Papers*, Financial Sector Development WPS 1190, Washington DC: World Bank.

Fry, M. (1988a), 'Financial Development: Theories and Recent Experience', *Oxford Review of Economic Policy*, 6, pp. 13–28.

——— (1988b), *Money, Interest, and Banking in Economic Development*, Baltimore: The Johns Hopkins University Press.

Hellmann, T., K. Murdock and J. Stiglitz (1994), 'Addressing Moral Hazard in

Banking: Deposit Rate Controls versus Capital Requirements', mimeo, Stanford University.

—— (1996), 'Financial Restraint: Toward a New Paradigm', forthcoming in M. Aoki, M. Okuno-Fujiwara and H. Kim (eds) *The Role of Government in East Asian Economic Development: Comparative Institutional Analysis*, New York: Oxford University Press.

King, R.G. and R. Levine (1993), 'Finance and Growth: Schumpeter Might Be Right', *Quarterly Journal of Economics*, 108, pp. 717–37.

Krahnen, J. and R. Schmidt (1994), 'Development Finance as Institutions Building: A New Approach to Poverty-Oriented Banking', Boulder and London: Westview Press.

McKinnon, R. (1973), *Money and Capital in Economic Development*, Washington DC: The Brookings Institution.

Milgrom, P. and K. Roberts (1990), 'The Economics of Modern Manufacturing: Technology, Strategy and Organisation', *American Economic Review*, 80, pp. 511–28.

Murdock, K. and J. Stiglitz (1993), 'The Effect of Financial Repression in an Economy with Positive Real Interest Rates: Theory and Evidence', mimeo, Stanford University.

Shaw, E. (1973), *Financial Deepening in Economic Development*, New York: Oxford University Press.

Stiglitz, J. (1993a), 'The Role of the State in Financial Markets', mimeo, Stanford University.

—— (1993b), 'Some Lessons from the Asian Miracle', mimeo, Stanford University.

Vogel, R. (1984), 'Savings Mobilization: The Forgotten Half of Rural Finance', in D. Adams, D. Graham and J.D. von Pischke (eds) *Undermining Rural Development with Cheap Credit*, Boulder and London: Westview Press, pp. 248–65.

11

THE FINANCIAL SYSTEM AND PUBLIC ENTERPRISE REFORM

Concepts and cases[1]

Aslı Demirgüç-Kunt and Ross Levine

INTRODUCTION

Public enterprise reform is an important component of policy strategies to accelerate economic growth in many countries. Public enterprise (PE) reform consists of two distinct, but complementary, approaches. The private sector development approach to PE reform involves privatising PEs and encouraging private sector development both to enhance economic efficiency and to shrink the relative size of the PE sector. The corporatisation approach involves enhancing managerial incentives and clarifying PE budget constraints, so that PE performance improves without the government relinquishing ownership.

This paper studies the relationship between the financial system and the success of PE reforms. We first develop a conceptual framework that describes the role of three financial services – mobilising resources, evaluating firms, and monitoring managers – in promoting both the private sector development and the corporatisation approaches to PE reform. We then use nine country case studies – Chile, Egypt, Ghana, India, Korea, Mexico, the Philippines, Senegal, and Turkey – to study the linkages between PE reform and both the initial state of the financial system and financial sector reform.

We find that countries with initially relatively well-developed financial systems enjoy comparatively more successful PE reforms than those with comparatively under-developed systems. Furthermore, countries seeking to implement large-scale PE reforms achieve much greater success if they also implement substantial and well-designed financial sector reforms that involve financial infrastructure building, liberalisation, and private financial intermediary expansion.

These conclusions arise after formulating a conceptual framework and studying nine country experiences. Some important caveats should be kept in mind, however. The causal relationship between financial development and

PE reform runs in both directions, and exogenous factors help determine the ultimate success of both PE and financial reform. While this paper argues that financial services promote successful PE reform, we readily acknowledge that public enterprise reform can stimulate financial development and that PE reform and financial reform tend to be mutually reinforcing. Furthermore, we only examine nine country cases. Since many important factors influence PE reform, the number of important explanatory variables probably exceeds the number of country cases. Thus, instead of formal statistical support for our conclusions, we show that the cases are remarkably consistent with our conceptual framework.

The rest of the paper is organised as follows: the first section presents a conceptual approach to the linkages between PE reform and the financial sector. In the second section we evaluate the impact of the initial state of the financial system on PE reform, and the links between financial reform and PE reform are discussed in the third section. The final section presents some policy recommendations.

CONCEPTS

Financial services in a market economy

To exemplify the importance of the financial system in PE reform, consider the role of three financial services in a market-oriented economy. First, the financial system evaluates firms and allocates resources based on these evaluations. Financial market participants research firms, managers, and business trends and choose the most promising and credit-worthy ventures. This includes large financial intermediaries such as banks, mutual funds, pension funds and insurance companies, and small venture capital institutions and individual entrepreneurs. The better financial systems are at obtaining and processing information, the better will be the allocation of capital.

Second, financial systems mobilise capital from disparate savers through banks, insurance companies, pension funds, investment companies, and capital markets. This mobilisation is critical for economic development. Many worthwhile investments require large capital inputs and some enjoy economies of scale. By agglomerating savings from many individuals, financial intermediaries enlarge the set of projects available to society. Furthermore, financial systems that both mobilise savings effectively and select promising firms intensify competition. Currently dominant firms will be less protected from competition if sound financial systems are able to identify and fund competing enterprises.

Finally, financial systems compel managers to act more in the interests of firm claim holders (stock, bond, and debt holders). In large corporations, small equity and bond holders may be unable or unwilling to obtain and process information effectively and oversee the managers. Managers, therefore, may funnel firm resources to themselves or make decisions based on personal as opposed to corporate criteria. Financial intermediaries may be able to improve corporate governance by undertaking the difficult and costly tasks of monitoring managers and obliging them to act in the interests of firm claim holders. Sound corporate governance will encourage more efficient resource allocation by aligning managerial goals with creditors' goals, and more investment by making investors more confident that firms will maximise owner profits and service debt obligations.[2]

Finance and public enterprise reform

This discussion suggests that well-developed financial systems raise the probability of successful PE reform; put differently, countries with poorly functioning financial systems will need financial reforms to support PE reform. The remainder of this section argues that those countries contemplating large-scale PE reform are also likely to be the countries requiring large-scale financial reform; and further exemplifies how the financial system and financial reform facilitate PE reform.

Privatisation and financial reform

Privatising an enterprise signifies a much reduced role for the government in funding the firm. If the financial system is unable to acquire and process information on firms on market principles, resources will be allocated poorly, savings will be mobilised ineffectively, and corporate governance will deteriorate.

Since PE reform and financial reform are both long-run co-dependent reforms, they need to be coordinated. For example, large-scale PE privatisation should be preceded by, accompanied by, and followed by financial sector reforms. Specifically, to initiate financial sector reforms and to begin laying the foundation for future reforms, policy makers should begin liberalizing interest rate and directed credit controls, improving the supervisory, regulatory, and legal systems prior to PE privatisation. During PE privatisation, authorities should continue liberalizing and building a market-oriented financial infrastructure and policy makers should remove impediments to financial intermediary development and initiate the process of privatising some state-controlled banks along with or soon after PE privatisation. Otherwise, PE privatisation with a poorly functioning financial system may prove disastrous.

Unfortunately, but importantly, many countries contemplating large-scale PE privatisation do not have a sufficiently well-developed financial system to support PE privatisation. Not surprisingly, countries with large PE sectors have frequently exerted a strong hand in directing credit to favoured PEs and have often created public banks to facilitate the mobilisation of resources for

PEs. In such an environment, state-controlled banks generally do not research firms carefully and allocate credit on market criteria, nor will state-controlled banks tend to compete aggressively to mobilise resources or exert tight, market-based corporate governance. Thus, the staff of state-controlled financial intermediaries frequently lack market-based financial skills.

This lack of financial acumen may be complemented by a lack of financial and legal infrastructure. Pervasive government interference in financial markets will reduce the development of corporate financial statements and laws concerning collateral, information disclosure, and bankruptcy.[3] Thus, countries with large PE sectors will typically not have the financial and legal infrastructure to support successful privatisation; financial reform may be a necessary condition for successful PE reform.

Privatisation options and finance

A well-functioning financial system broadens the set of privatisation options. First, liquid capital markets make it easier to privatise PEs by selling equity to a broad group of investors. Broad distribution may mitigate criticisms that the government is selling public property cheaply for political or personal advantage or that the government is giving the country away to foreigners. Second, banks and other financial intermediaries may improve the privatisation process. Banks that mobilise savings effectively, assess entrepreneurs, finance purchases of PEs and oversee new management energetically and competently, will expand the number of investors that can participate in the privatisation process, help ensure that PEs go to qualified owners, and compel new owners to act appropriately. Finally, a well-functioning financial system reduces the urgency for breaking up large firms prior to privatisation. Specifically, some large PEs may have market power even though they are not natural monopolies. Under-developed financial markets make entry difficult and therefore allow privatised enterprises with market power to remain relatively immune to competitive forces. On the other hand, a well-developed financial system would help subject even large firms to competition by strengthening the ability of new firms to bring better goods to market.

Finance and adjustment costs

The financial system can also reduce adjustment costs. Newly privatised firms that need to be re-tooled will adjust and grow faster if financial markets can allocate capital quickly to promising firms. Similarly, by redeploying the assets of bankrupt enterprises efficiently, a sound financial system will reduce adjustment costs. Furthermore, by accelerating private sector growth, an effective financial system will indirectly increase labour demand. Since unemployment may be an important obstacle to beginning and maintaining PE reform, the financial system may pacify political pressures emanating

Table 11.1 Privatisation and the changing provision of financial services

	Less reliance on	*More reliance on*

Mobilising resources to finance enterprises	Taxes
	State-owned banks
		Financial intermediaries:
		  banks, investment
		  companies, pension
		  funds, insurance
		  companies
		Capital markets

Allocating resources to enterprises	Direct and indirect
	  government subsidies
	  and guarantees
	State-owned banks
	Private banks compelled
	  by the state
		Financial intermediaries:
		  banks, investment
		  companies, pension
		  funds, insurance
		  companies
		Capital markets

Corporate governance of enterprises	Government or
	  government
	  ministries
		Financial intermediaries:
		  banks, investment
		  companies, pension
		  funds, insurance
		  companies
		Capital markets

from unemployment by boosting private sector labour demand. Table 11.1 summarises the changing roles of the government and financial system in PE privatisation.

Corporatisation

A well-developed financial system also assists PE corporatisation. A market-oriented financial system will oblige newly corporatised firms to compete for financing with private firms. Furthermore, a well-developed financial system will promote private sector development which, in turn, intensifies competitive pressures on corporatised PEs. For corporatisation to succeed, however, banks must be sufficiently strong and independent to reject loan requests from non-creditworthy PEs and the government must credibly quell expectations that it implicitly guarantees loans to PEs, or else banks will funnel credit to PEs instead of to more worthy firms.

Financial system and type of PE reform

As we argued above, a well-developed financial system would assist all types of PE reform, privatisation as well as corporatisation. Thus, in countries with well-developed financial systems, the optimal PE reform strategy will depend on other factors such as political pressures, labour market conditions, the macroeconomy, the legal system, and openness to international trade.

251

By the same token, a very under-developed financial system makes privatisation and corporatisation, which relies heavily on the financial system, relatively unattractive. Under such circumstances the only feasible option becomes corporatisation that consists of improved direct government monitoring of enterprises until the financial sector is further developed.

INITIAL STATE OF THE FINANCIAL SECTOR AND PUBLIC ENTERPRISE REFORM

Measuring financial development

This section examines the relationship between the initial state of the financial system and public enterprise reform in Korea, Mexico, Chile, the Philippines, India, Turkey, Egypt, Senegal, and Ghana. To conduct this examination, we first construct measures of 'financial development'. Each measure is imperfect, but together they provide a useful 'picture' of financial development. We then discuss how financial development compares across regions of the world. Finally, we classify the case study countries into three categories of financial development prior to starting their respective PE reforms.

Financial indicators

We mainly use four indicators to assess the state of financial sector development. The first is a traditional measure of 'financial depth': the size of the formal financial intermediary sector relative to economic activity. We call this indicator DEPTH, defined as the ratio of liquid liabilities of the financial system to GDP.[4] This is an indicator of the degree to which the formal financial sector mobilises domestic savings, so that larger depth should in most cases reflect greater financial development.

The second indicator we use is a measure of stock market development: the ratio of market capitalisation to GDP, MCAP/GDP.[5] Since better developed stock markets make it easier for individuals to price and diversify risk, to raise capital, and to take over poorly managed firms, higher values of MCAP/GDP should reflect greater financial development.

Our third indicator measures the importance of private non-bank financial institutions by computing the share of private non-bank financial intermediary assets in total financial assets. Non-banks complement commercial banks and, more importantly, they often function as effective substitutes for the commercial banking sector when that sector is suppressed by government regulations or taxation. Thus, for many countries, larger non-bank financial intermediaries reflect a broadening and deepening of the financial system.

Finally, our fourth indicator of financial development measures the degree of government ownership of commercial banks.

Comparison across regions

Figure 11.1 gives the 1991 averages of three of our financial indicators for four regions of the world: Sub Saharan Africa (Africa), Latin America (LAAM), Asia, and the OECD. The 1991 GDP per capita figures for Africa, Latin America, Asia, and OECD are $705, $1489, $2611, and $15,016, respectively. As shown in Figure 11.1, moving from poorer to richer countries generally involves greater financial development. Although none of the indicators is perfect, overall they illustrate a distinct pattern. OECD countries lead with the highest level of financial development, since all our indicators, non-banks, MCAP/GDP, and DEPTH have the highest values for OECD. Asian countries follow with high financial depth and stock market capital-ization. The importance of non-bank financial institutions is a distinguishing factor, since for Asian countries our indicator is considerably lower than that of OECD countries. Latin America follows Asia with considerably lower financial depth and stock market capitalisation. African countries have the lowest level of financial development, with lowest non-bank and MCAP/GDP values, although the value for DEPTH is slightly higher than that of Latin American countries. Based on Figure 11.1, these indicators in general provide an intuitively appealing ranking of financial development across countries. Now we turn to evaluating the initial level of financial development in our case study countries prior to their PE reforms.

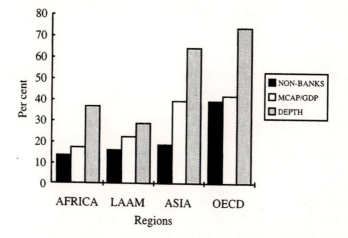

Figure 11.1 Financial structure in 1991

Notes: Non-banks: non-bank financial intermediary assets as a per cent of total financial assets; Depth: M3/GDP; MCAP/GDP: stock market capitalisation divided by GDP

Initial state of financial development

When the financial systems of countries prior to PE reforms are ranked based on the four indicators, DEPTH, MCAP/GDP, the importance of private non-bank financial institutions, and bank independence from government, they fall into three categories along a spectrum (see Table 11.2). Korea, Mexico, Chile II (Chile's second PE reform episode), and the Philippines had relatively well-developed financial systems prior to undertaking PE reforms. Financial depth was over 30 per cent of GDP, and they had relatively significant stock markets. Their private non-bank financial intermediaries had a significant share of financial assets (around 15 to 30 per cent) complementing the commercial banks. Senegal and Ghana are at the other end of the spectrum with under-developed financial systems. They had low levels of financial depth, no stock markets or private non-bank financial institutions in the formal sector, weak banking systems, and generally a very under-developed financial infrastructure. Finally, Chile I (Chile's first PE reform episode), Egypt, Turkey and India are difficult to rank and fall in between, since their financial systems are not as under-developed as Senegal and Ghana, but still less-developed compared to the first group of countries.

Initial financial development and public enterprise reform

The nine countries indicate a strong, positive association between the initial state of their financial systems and the ultimate success of their PE reforms. Galal (1994) reviews these cases in detail and finds that Korea, Mexico and Chile (especially Chile's second PE reform programme in the 1980s) successfully reformed, the Philippines enjoyed some success, while the other countries have thus far been relatively unsuccessful. Table 11.3 briefly summarises PE reform in each country. Table 11.3 shows that all of the most successful PE reform cases started out with relatively well-developed financial systems. Korea, Mexico, Chile II, and the Philippines had higher levels of financial depth, relatively well-developed stock markets, and other non-bank financial institutions prior to undertaking their PE reforms, than the other cases.

Countries that started out with less-developed financial systems (Chile I, India, Turkey, Egypt) or under-developed financial systems (Senegal and Ghana) were not as successful in their PE reforms. These countries had lower financial depth, highly regulated banks, less-developed non-banks, and either insignificant or non-existent stock markets prior to their PE reforms. One apparent exception is Chile's successful corporatisation in its first reform period. However, Chile's corporatisation involved greater government control of enterprise managers, investment and financing decisions, and therefore relied much less on the initial state of its financial sector to provide these services to PEs.

The nine country cases are consistent with the hypothesis that an initially well-developed financial system promotes successful PE reforms.

As discussed in the conceptual overview, a well-developed financial system will tend to assist PE reform by allocating funds to more efficient firms, by forcing other firms to restructure or fail, and by redeploying the assets of these bankrupt enterprises efficiently. While an initially well-developed financial system facilitates PE reform, countries with initially less-developed financial systems should not give up undertaking PE reforms. As we discuss below, financial reform is a long term process that can be synchronised with PE reforms to promote success.

Initial stock market development and public enterprise reform

In our country cases, the initial state of the stock market played a role in influencing the PE reform strategy and the eventual success or failure of the reform process in at least two ways. First, the existence of a well-developed stock market provides different alternatives for privatisation; and second, a well-functioning stock market can be an important source of financing for privatisation transactions.

Privatisation strategy

The extent of the stock market development helps determine available options for privatisation. A well-developed stock market promotes privatisations by enabling public offerings. Using a public offering to obtain widespread public ownership of enterprises requires a sufficiently liquid stock market to be able to absorb the new issues without negatively affecting the market as a whole. In Chile's first reform period, when the stock market was not adequately developed, the government sold controlling stakes of the enterprises in auctions. This concentrated economic power in the hands of a few groups. In the second reform period, however, Chile's stock market was much more developed as a result of the earlier financial liberalisation, the simultaneous strengthening of the regulatory and supervisory framework, and the privatisation of the pension fund system. Thus the government was able to sell small to medium sized packages of shares through the stock market and obtain a broader distribution of ownership.

The existence of a well-developed stock market also makes it easier for governments to privatise, since privatisations that lead to widespread public ownership are often politically more acceptable to the public than sales to a small group of investors – particularly if the investors are foreign. For example, in Turkey block sales of PEs to foreign investors were extremely controversial and led to charges that the government was essentially giving away public assets to foreigners. When the government decided to privatise by public sales through the stock exchange, this change was welcomed by the

Table 11.2 PE reform and the initial state of the financial systems

Country	PE reform period	DEPTH	MCAP/GDP	Share of private non-bank financial institutions	Commercial bank ownership before reform	Bank privatisation
Well-developed financial systems						
OECD	n.a.	72	41	38	Mostly private	n.a.
Korea	I 1981–1983	39	10	30	Mostly public	Banks were privatised 1982–1983, in the first reform period
	II 1983–1985	40	8	32	70% private	
	III 1986–	42	6	33	70% private	
Mexico	I 1983–1987	39	6	15	100% public	Banks were privatised 1991–1992, towards the end of the second reform period
	II 1988–1993	39	6		100% public	
Chile II	1985–1990	38	22	23	Mostly private	Banks were privatised 1975–1977, during Chile I
Philippines	1986–	34	4	16	Mostly private	The share of public banks fell from 28% to 14% of assets, 1980–1990

Less-developed financial systems

Chile I	I	1974–1982	33	5	Some	100% public	Banks were privatised 1975–1977, early in the reform period
Egypt		1980–	57	–	Some	Over 50% public	Just starting. In 1993 one joint venture bank was privatised
Turkey		1980–	32	1	Some	50% public	There are recent plans, but no bank privatisation so far
India		1980–	36	4	None	90% public	No bank privatisation so far

Under-developed financial systems

Senegal		1978–	24	–	None	Mostly public	In 1989, government ownership of banks was reduced to less than 25 per cent in each bank
Ghana		1987–	16	–	None	Mostly public	There are plans but no bank privatisation so far

Notes: DEPTH is the ratio of M_3 (when not available M_2) to GDP obtained from IMF's International Financial Statistics and MCAP/GDP is the ratio of stock market capitalisation to GDP from IFC's Emerging Market Data Base and are averages of five years prior to reform period. Share of non-banks and bank ownership figures are as of beginning of reform period. OECD figures are for 1991

Table 11.3 PE and financial sector reforms

Country	PE reform period	PE reform	Financial reform period	Financial reform
Korea	I 1981–1983	Privatisations. Four state-owned banks and two other PEs were sold through public offerings although government influence remained strong. Programme was reportedly successful in increasing efficiency	1980–	A gradual reform started in 1980 Deposit rates were partially liberalised to establish positive real rates. Preferential lending rates were abolished in 1982 Privatisation of the public city banks started in 1982 and was completed by 1983 Restrictions on non-bank financial institutions were relaxed New domestic entry into the financial system was allowed A gradual opening up to international competition started Capital markets were also gradually opened to foreign participation Lending rates were officially deregulated in 1988. In 1991, government announced a plan to deregulate money market and deposit rates completely by 1997
	II 1983–1985	Corporatisation. Financial performance of PEs improved substantially, although started deteriorating later. The programme was very successful in the short run		
	III 1986–	Privatisations. In 1991, 7 PE subsidiaries and Korea Stock Exchange were privatised. Government is planning to privatise 11 more PEs, while remaining a majority shareholder in 6. It is too early to tell if the programme is successful		
Mexico	I 1983–1987	Privatisation/liquidation of small PEs. Corporatisation of large PEs. 743 small PEs were liquidated or sold. Corporatisation had limited success	1988–	Financial sector reform started in 1988 with liberalisation of interest rates Exchange controls were abolished, forced investment in government securities was eliminated and most of the restrictions on commercial bank activity were lifted during 1989 Regulation and supervision were strengthened during 1989–1990 Bank privatisation started in 1991 and was completed in 1992
	II 1988–1993	Privatisation of large PEs. 192 large PEs were privatised. The privatisation programme is considered to be very successful, both in terms of budgetary impact and increase in efficiency		

Chile	I 1974–1982	Privatisation of small PEs and corporatisation of remaining ones. Most of the privatised PEs were re-nationalised after the 1982 crisis. Corporatisations were successful in improving the performance of PEs
	II 1985–1990	Privatisations. After re-privatisation of firms which had reverted to government control during the financial crisis, larger PEs were also privatised. This led to a significant reduction in the role of the public sector in the economy. The privatisations are viewed as being very successful
Philippines	1986–	Privatisations. Although privatisations are still continuing, government's privatisation efforts are considered to be successful, both in quantity and impact
Egypt	1980–	Reform efforts mostly focused on corporatisation and were unsuccessful. Recently there is revived interest in corporatisation and privatisation

1974–	Financial liberalisation started in 1974 with interest rate liberalisation
	Banks were privatised (1975–1977). Entry restrictions were relaxed, credit ceilings were eliminated, permitted scope of activities were expanded. Pension funds were privatised in 1980
	Restrictions on foreign capital inflows were gradually lifted starting in 1977, and capital account was completely liberalised in 1980 Financial crisis came in 1982 and the government had to clean up and bail out the banks
	After the crisis, prudential regulation and supervision was strengthened, culminating in the passage of a new banking law in 1986
1980–	Financial sector reform focused on strengthening the banking system, reducing taxation and increasing competition
	Banks were allowed to expand into new areas of activity and loan and deposit rates were freed
	The share of public banks in total banking assets was reduced from 28% in 1980 to 14% in 1990
	The reform also started to address institutional features such as the legal framework and bankruptcy laws
1992–	Financial sector reform only started in 1992. Interest rates were liberalised and prudential regulation and supervision were strengthened. Banks were re-capitalised and entry barriers were relaxed. In 1993, one private/public joint-venture bank was privatised

Table 11.3 continued

Country	PE reform period	PE reform	Financial reform period	Financial reform
Turkey	1980–	Although there was limited success with corporatisation initially, generally neither the corporatisation or privatisation efforts have been successful. Recently, there are new efforts focusing on privatisation	1980–	Financial sector reform started with interest liberalisation on deposit and loan rates in 1980. Commercial banks were deregulated and foreign bank entry was allowed. Financial crisis came in 1982. Interest ceilings were re-imposed and a deposit insurance system was established. Later reforms emphasised prudential regulation and improved supervision leading to a new banking law in 1985. Interest rates were partially liberalised in 1988. Recently several state-owned banks were slated for privatisation
India	1980–	Corporatisation efforts have not been successful. There have been new corporatisation and privatisation efforts since 1991	1992–	Financial sector reform started quite late, in 1992. Entry and expansion conditions have been made less restrictive. Interest rates on term loans and most debt instruments were recently decontrolled and increased. Reform efforts to improve prudential and regulatory environment, to recapitalise weak institutions, and to promote greater private sector participation and further financial policy liberalisation are continuing

Senegal	1978–	Corporatisation and privatisation efforts have been unsuccessful so far	1989–	Financial reform programme started in 1989, and included restructuring of public banks, increasing capital requirements, and improving banking supervision. Government ownership in each bank was decreased to less than 25 per cent
Ghana	1987–	Corporatisation and privatisation efforts have been unsuccessful so far	1987–	The financial reform initiated in 1987 included a strengthening of the regulatory framework, liberalisation of government controls, and bank restructuring. Interest rates were liberalised in 1988; 1989 banking law strengthened bank regulation and supervision. In 1990, banks were restructured and government announced plans to privatise banks in 1993

public.[6] Another example is Mexico, where block sales of the PEs have also been criticised for favouring a few investors, who have become very rich as a result of the privatisations.[7]

Rising stock markets can also help decrease opposition to privatisation by making employee or management buy outs feasible. A good example is the privatisation of TELMEX, the Mexican phone company, in which the trade union was offered a 4.4 per cent share of the company for $325 million. Following privatisation, the market value of TELMEX rose to $30 billion, resulting in an increase of 400 per cent over the employees' purchase price.[8] Such gains make it very difficult for trade unions to oppose privatisation, even if it is likely to result in job losses. Chile also relied on share purchases by employees to some extent in its second period of privatisations, when the Chilean stock market was booming.

Conversely, under-developed stock markets may hamper privatisation. For example, Swanson and Wolde-Samait (1989) assert that one of the reasons for failure of the Ghanaian and the Senegalese privatisation efforts was the lack of a domestic equity market on which public share offerings could be floated. Early privatisation efforts in Turkey were also adversely affected by the relatively under-developed state of its equity market. A government announcement in 1987 that it planned to accelerate its privatisation programme through new issues was one of the important factors that caused a sharp fall in the market and stalled the reform programme. Even when there is a well-developed stock market, success of privatisation strategies depends to a large extent on the general stock market environment. For example, Korea also used its stock market in its privatisation programme, but slowed down its efforts, partly due to a down turn in its stock market since 1989.[9]

Financing of privatisation

Stock markets can play an important role in financing the privatisations by complementing the banking system's ability to mobilise savings. For example in Ghana, a number of agreed privatisation transactions could not be completed due to the inability of the purchasers to secure financing.[10] The Mexican privatisation programme used a sealed-bid auction process to sell controlling stakes in each company and therefore the stock market was not the direct mechanism of sale. However, the stock market still provided important support as groups involved in the bidding issued equity to finance their bids. Eight financial groups raised a total of over 4 billion pesos in new equity in 1992, including 2.4 billion pesos domestically, to help finance the purchases of the commercial banks. The ability to attract sizable foreign portfolio investment also enhances the viability of privatisation. Indeed, privatisation programmes in both Mexico and Chile II benefited greatly from an inflow of foreign portfolio investment.

Privatisation and stock market development

Although the existence of a well-developed stock market is important in structuring a successful privatisation, the absence of a highly-developed stock market should not be used as an excuse not to privatise. Privatisation itself can make a major contribution to capital market development. For example, Turkey used bank branches as a substitute for brokerages in the 1988 divestiture of the government's minority stake in Teletas, and in the privatisation of the Bosphorus Bridge and the Keban Dam, which were heavily over-subscribed and sold to a total of 15,000 domestic investors. These banks are now building upon the experience with those sales and attempting to capitalise on the rapid development of capital markets by evolving into universal banks. The Chilean privatisations since 1985 have involved the sale of stock to institutional investors and employees equal in value to nearly 10 per cent of the domestic stock market capitalisation. Again, rather than putting stress on the stock market, the increased capitalisation has strengthened it. In Senegal, the government was even able to sell a small share offering by newspaper.[11]

Initial financial development and corporatisation

Successful corporatisation in Korea and Chile I involved intensified government monitoring of managers and strict enforcement of budget constraints. The government did not abdicate these responsibilities to the financial system. Nonetheless, successful financial reform in Korea helped corporatisation indirectly. By enhancing resource mobilisation, credit allocation, and corporate governance of private firms, financial reforms in Korea contributed to private sector development and thereby indirectly improved 'corporatised' PEs. Specifically, private sector growth seems to have promoted successful corporatisation by intensifying competitive pressures on PEs and increasing labour demand, which eased political pressures on large PEs that were reducing labour to improve financial performance. Similarly, although not ultimately accompanied by successful financial reform, private sector growth during Chile I heightened competition and helped PE corporatisation.

In contrast, PE reform efforts in Senegal and Ghana were less successful than they otherwise might have been because their corporatisation efforts included greater PE autonomy from the government without a sufficiently well-developed and independent financial system to impose a budget constraint and monitor managers. Thus, banks continued to finance PE losses, perhaps because of implicit government guarantees, and did not provide sufficient incentives for PE managers to improve enterprise efficiency. Thus, corporatisation that relies on greater PE autonomy requires a sufficiently developed and independent financial system to impose budget constraints and cultivate market-based incentives, while a well-functioning financial system will bolster corporatisation indirectly, involving intensified government overview by promoting private sector development.

FINANCIAL REFORM AND PUBLIC ENTERPRISE REFORM

This section discusses the linkages between PE reform and financial sector reform.

Countries that successfully implemented large-scale PE reforms

These countries also implemented successful, large-scale financial sector reforms. The financial reforms involved enhancements to the supervisory, regulatory, and legal infrastructure; interest rate liberalisation, reduced directed credit, and less direct government control of financial intermediaries; and a shrinkage of public banks and an expansion of private financial intermediaries through bank privatisation and strengthening of private financial intermediaries. As discussed above, there were three cases of successful large-scale PE reform: Mexico II (the second part of Mexico's PE reform programme), Chile II, and Korea; each of these countries also executed successful financial reforms.

First, consider Mexico II where between 1989 and 1993 the authorities privatised many large PEs. In 1982 there were 60 private financial institutions, including 35 banks. In response to the economic crisis, the government nationalised all but two of these banks in 1982 and reduced the number of state-owned banks to 18 through mergers and closures. From 1982 to 1988, the government tightly controlled the banking system and used commercial banks to finance the government and PEs. Banks faced high reserve ratios, interest controls, and had to lend most of their funds to PEs and favoured sectors at concessionary interest rates. During this period, the non-bank financial sector – primarily brokerages, which were often managed by previous managers of the commercial banks – operated in a much less repressed environment and became important sources of finance for the private sector. By 1987, non-banks held more than 50 per cent of the financial system's assets, and state-controlled banks held less than half.

Financial liberalisation began late in 1988. The government freed interest rates, eliminated forced investment in government securities, and abolished exchange controls, while also strengthening the regulatory environment by imposing capital regulations. The stock market, which had deteriorated in the 1980s, started improving with the liberalisation. Bank lending to the private sector increased from 25 per cent of total assets in 1986 to almost 60 per cent in 1991.

Liberalisation set the stage for privatisation of the entire commercial banking system in 1991–1992. Unfortunately, bank privatisation was not accompanied by consistent monetary and exchange rate policies, which ignited the crises of 1994–1995. Up until that crisis, many observers considered Mexican bank privatisation a success and a model for other countries.

The private banking system helped to finance industrial growth to 1994, including the re-tooling and re-orientation of former PEs. Mexico's financial system is relatively well-developed, with an active securities market (market capitalisation is around 36 per cent of GDP), a diverse set of non-bank financial intermediaries, and a commercial banking industry with financial DEPTH greater than 33 per cent. Financial reform accompanied and seems to have assisted PE privatisation. Even with the crisis, the case of Mexico II is not inconsistent with the view that large-scale PE privatisation will typically require meaningful financial sector reforms to bolster the provision of critical financial services to the growing private sector.

The results from Chile II also support this conclusion. Chile began its second PE reform episode in 1985. The authorities re-privatised companies that were taken over by the government during the 1982 economic crisis and also sold large PEs that had not been privatised during Chile's first PE reform episode in 1974–1982. During Chile II, the authorities also implemented important financial sector reforms and designed many of these reforms to avoid the circumstances that contributed to the 1982 crisis.

During the first reform period, the government implemented many financial reforms. It abolished interest rate ceilings, eliminated credit allocation controls, reduced banks' reserve requirements, freed capital controls, and allowed new entry. The authorities also privatised state banks during Chile I, but without first establishing a sound regulatory and supervisory system. New bank owners used their privileged access to credit to purchase PEs, thus establishing a small number of huge conglomerates. In the absence of effective regulation, this provided an environment amenable for unsound banking practices and contributed to the economic crisis of 1982 that will be discussed below.

Following the 1982 crisis, Chile re-capitalised and re-privatised the banks. Importantly, during this second reform episode, Chile significantly strengthened the role, staff, and funding of prudential supervision and regulation. In addition to its banking system, Chile also has non-bank financial intermediaries, including large private pension funds. Today, Chile's private financial system is quite well-developed and supports a booming private industrial sector. Financial DEPTH is almost 50 per cent of GDP, and the stock market capitalisation to GDP ratio is over 95 per cent. Thus, Chile II is also consistent with the hypothesis enunciated above: large-scale public enterprise reforms benefit from financial sector reforms which include liberalisation, strengthening of prudential supervision and regulation, and privatisation.

Korea also combined effective PE reform with significant financial sector reforms during the 1980s, though Korea's PE reforms focused on corporatisation. Korea's corporatisation involved intensified government monitoring of PEs through a rigorous managerial performance evaluation system.[12] These reforms improved PE performance.

Korea also initiated important financial sector reforms during the 1980s. Early in the reform process Korea liberalised interest rates, reduced directed credits, lowered entry barriers, and formalised the curb market into an important and booming private non-bank financial intermediary sector. Korea strengthened supervisory procedures of both banks and non-banks during the 1980s. Banks were also privatised in 1983, but without cleaning their portfolios of bad loans or re-capitalising the banks, so that the privatised banks remained dependent on the government for subsidies. Later bail outs both of non-financial firms and banks decreased the non-performing loans to less than 1 per cent of commercial banks' assets, but the government still retains significant control over bank lending decisions. While bank lending as a share of GDP stagnated in the 1980s, non-bank credit as a share of GDP has boomed from around 10 per cent in 1976 to close to 40 per cent by the end of the 1980s. Thus, as in Mexico II and Chile II, financial liberalisation, a strengthening of supervision and regulation of financial intermediaries, and development of financial intermediaries, focused on providing market-oriented services, also accompanied successful PE reform in Korea. Although the independent relationship between financial reform and corporatisation is difficult to assess, it is important to establish that successful large-scale corporatisation went hand in hand with substantial financial sector reforms.

Countries that were less successful in reforming PEs

These countries did not implement successful financial sector reforms (including liberalisation of interest rates and credit decisions, enhanced supervision and regulation, improvements in legal codes and enforcement capabilities, and public bank privatisation) along with or before PE reform. As noted above, Egypt, India, Turkey, Ghana, and Senegal have had, on aggregate, much less successful PE reform than Korea, Mexico II, Chile II, and the Philippines. Importantly, these same countries also did not implement comprehensive financial reform and bank privatisation – on the scale attained by Mexico II, Chile II, and Korea – early in their PE reforms. Recent Turkish financial reforms, however, should facilitate future PE reforms.

The remainder of this section reviews financial reform efforts in Egypt, India, Turkey, Ghana, and Senegal. The Appendix provides more details. Reviewing financial reform helps one understand why PE reform has been relatively less successful in these countries and what financial reforms need to be stressed in the future.

Egypt and India

During the 1960s and 1970s, both Egypt and India pursued public sector-led development strategies. Consequently, state-owned banks dominate the financial landscape in both countries. For example, state-owned banks hold over 90 per cent of total banking assets in India and over 50 per cent in Egypt. State banks are used to finance government expenditures and provide subsidised credits to PEs. Furthermore, both countries used pension reserves to finance PEs, public banks and government projects. Prior to the 1980s, there were heavy taxes on banks, stiff barriers to entry, tightly controlled interest rates, and inadequate prudential supervision and regulation. In both Egypt and India, financial reforms started in 1992. Egypt and, to a lesser degree, India have eased interest rate controls, strengthened prudential regulation and supervision, relaxed entry barriers, and capitalised some weak public banks. Reform efforts are continuing in both countries with the goals of reducing domination by state banks and increasing private sector participation. Serious bank privatisation has not yet occurred, although Egypt privatised one public–private joint-venture in 1993. While Egypt and, to a somewhat lesser degree, India are setting the stage for successful PE reform in the future by reforming the financial system, successful large-scale PE reform will probably require a greater willingness to privatise large state banks if they are to break the legacy of state-dominated finance.

Turkey

Turkey initiated PE and financial sector reform in the 1980s. The main focus of the reform programme was on deregulation to increase competition and efficiency within the financial system. The government removed ceilings on interest rates, relaxed restrictions on domestic and foreign bank entry, and expanded the scope of banking activities. Another element of the government's stabilisation programme was a tight monetary policy, which led to high interest rates. While the liberalisation of interest rates was successful in greatly increasing the mobilisation of savings through banks, high interest rates caused difficulties for corporate borrowers. Firms increasingly borrowed to cover interest payments, and poorly supervised banks funded these firms in a failed attempt to save themselves from bankruptcy. This led to the closure of several banks in 1982. Liberalisation without adequate supervision helped foster financial instability.

The crisis shifted the emphasis of the reform programme from deregulation to building a sound regulatory framework. The government reimposed ceilings on deposit rates, enacted the banking law of 1985, which initiated the

267

process of improving prudential regulations, and established the Capital Market Board to regulate and develop securities markets. Interest rates were again liberalised in 1988, although some ceilings still remain.

Turkey's financial system has developed significantly in the last decade. Financial DEPTH is around 32 per cent, stock market capitalisation is almost 20 per cent of GDP, and the number of non-banks is growing. However, financial intermediation is still heavily taxed, both directly and indirectly, through high reserve and liquidity ratios, and state banks have not yet been privatised; the banking system remains 50 per cent publicly owned. Recently, the government slated several state banks for privatisation.

Ghana

In Ghana, PEs play a dominant role in most sectors of the economy, and state-owned banks dominate the financial system. PEs are very heavy users of bank credit, often with government guarantees; and taxes, tariffs, and social security funds all support PEs. Indeed the financial system is best viewed as an extension of the fiscal system, which is used to finance priority PEs. There is little to no systematic monitoring of credit to public enterprises and non-payment by PEs is a huge problem.

Ghana has implemented some financial reforms. In 1987–1988, interest rate controls and sectoral credit target controls (except to agriculture) were eased, and the Bank of Ghana began using indirect monetary control instruments. In 1989–1992, Ghana established the Non-Performing Assets Recovery Trust to re-capitalise seven banks, and efforts were initiated to strengthen accounting, provisioning for bad loans, supervision and legal reforms. Furthermore, Ghana plans to reduce financial intermediary taxes, encourage positive real interest rates, and divest some public sector banks in the future. At present, however, the financial system is still very under-developed with a DEPTH of 19 per cent and stock market capitalisation of around one per cent of GDP.

Senegal

Senegal's PE sector accounted for almost 30 per cent of total investment, about 17 per cent of total employment, and 7 per cent of GDP in 1988. In addition, the government plays a very heavy role in regulating private sector activities and allocating resources. In 1989 Senegal initiated a banking reform. This included a bank restructuring and closure of some distressed banks, privatisation of some of the restructured banks, a reduction in directed credits, elimination of government guarantees of PE borrowing, and a reduction of government ownership of all banks to less than 25 per cent. Although Senegal still has a very under-developed financial system with a financial DEPTH of 25 per cent and no stock market, the financial sector reforms are promising steps. As these financial reforms improve financial development, and if Senegal strengthens existing efforts, the ability of the Senegalese financial sector to provide market-oriented finance will grow and foster more aggressive PE reform.

Countries that implemented modest – though successful – public enterprise reform

Countries which implemented modest PE reform in the presence of an already relatively well-developed financial system did not simultaneously implement large financial sector reforms. The Philippines successfully privatised a limited number of government corporations in the late 1980s. As indicated in Table 11.2, the Philippines already had a relatively deep financial system with a well-functioning capital market, a strong non-bank sector and private commercial banks when it initiated PE reform. Financial reform in the first half of the 1980s helped build a financial system capable of supporting enterprise reform in the second half of the 1980s. Specifically, liberalisation of interest rates in the early 1980s, strengthening of the legal framework, bankruptcy laws, regulations and prudential enforcement capabilities in 1987, and a reduction in the role of public banks from 28 per cent of banking assets to 1.4 per cent of banking assets over the 1980s, helped mould a financial system that was ready to support modest public enterprise privatisation in the late 1980s.

Similarly, Mexico's first PE reform from 1981–1987 was not accompanied by substantial financial reforms. This first reform period focused on privatising and liquidating small enterprises and limiting the losses of large PEs. Although Mexico's banking system was publicly owned, Mexico had a relatively well-functioning capital market and very well-developed non-banks. The experiences of the Philippines and Mexico I are consistent with the view that if the financial system is sufficiently well-developed at the start of the PE reform process, and PE reform is of a modest scale, then substantial financial sector reforms do not have to be implemented to promote successful PE reform.

Effects of unsuccessful financial sector reform on PE reform

Unsuccessful financial sector reform can hurt large-scale public enterprise reform. Chile implemented large-scale PE and financial reforms during its first reform episode, 1974–1982. Out of the 504 firms controlled by the government in 1973, only 109 remained publicly owned in 1982. In all sectors except mining, the government's share of production fell by about 70 per cent. The government also imposed a rigid budget constraint on PEs: PEs had to self-finance projects; any borrowing from banks had to be cleared with officials under strict guidelines; and no government guarantees were issued.

Thus, the private sector grew substantially, and corporatisation improved PE performance.

Chile's financial liberalisation and bank privatisation, however, facilitated the 1982 crisis.[13] Specifically, banks were privatised before non-financial PEs. Business conglomerates – *grupos* – purchased most of the banks with only a 20 per cent down payment and borrowed the remainder from the government. *Grupos* then used loans from their banks to purchase non-financial firms, where the government required only a down payment of between 10 and 40 per cent. This highly-leveraged concentration of industrial and financial power, together with an ineffective, under-staffed, and under-funded bank supervisory system encouraged insider lending, reduced the effectiveness with which banks evaluated clients, and weakened objective bank monitoring of firm managers. When domestic economic problems, external shocks, and inconsistent foreign exchange rate policies caused some non-financial *grupo* firms to flounder, the *grupos* used their banks – with government insured deposits – to support failing firms in a doomed attempt to avoid realising losses. In the resulting 1982 depression, GDP fell by 14 per cent, unemployment soared past 25 per cent, and the government had to take control of enterprises and banks that accounted for 60 per cent of total bank deposits. While changes in world interest rates and inconsistent exchange rate and wage policies would have combined to affect the Chilean economy negatively, with or without the financial reforms of the late 1970s, the lack of sound prudential supervisory and regulatory capacity created a fragile financial system that exacerbated the economic downturn and mitigated the success of Chile's first PE reform episode. Chile's experience suggests that bank privatisation and liberalisation of interest rates and credit controls are not enough. Sound supervision and regulation must also be in place or the financial system will not be able to support aggressive PE privatisation.

CONCLUSIONS AND POLICY RECOMMENDATIONS

We find a striking link between financial development and the success of public enterprise reform: countries which initially had relatively well-developed financial systems enjoyed better PE reform than countries with less well-developed financial systems; and countries that synchronised financial reform with PE reform enjoyed greater success than countries that tried large-scale PE reforms without improving their financial systems. Since we only examine nine cases and focus only on the financial system among many other factors – macroeconomic, political, institutional, labour market, and product market factors – that may affect the success of PE reforms, our conclusions are suggestive. Nevertheless, by highlighting the linkages between the financial system and PE reform we seek to emphasise that once all the other conditions for successful PE reform are met, those reforms that also incorporate financial factors will have a greater probability of success.

Based on our analysis, we make the following tentative recommendations for countries contemplating public enterprise reform:

1 If a country initially has a very under-developed financial system, PE reformers should consider a strategy that relies less on the financial system for its initial success and start developing the foundations for a well-functioning financial system. Specifically, corporatisation that consists of improved direct government monitoring of enterprise managers, firm investment decisions, and PE financing may contain losses and improve performance without relying excessively on the financial system. At the same time, financial reforms, especially liberalisation and improvements in legal, supervisory, and regulatory systems, should be initiated to establish the financial sector basis for more comprehensive, large-scale PE reform involving expanded enterprise autonomy and privatisation and also for more comprehensive and complementary financial reforms involving state bank privatisation and further liberalisation and financial infrastructure building.

2 If a country initially has a relatively well-developed financial system, and the country decides to implement large-scale PE reform, the reform should be synchronised with substantial and well-designed financial sector reforms. Large-scale PE reform involves much greater reliance on the services provided by the financial system. Therefore, a comprehensive PE reform should also involve the reform of public banks that often exist to serve the PE sector. A sound financial reform, which includes bank privatisation, is an important component of any large-scale PE reform and its design is crucial since, just as well-designed financial sector reforms can promote PE reform, poorly designed financial sector reforms can jeopardise the success of the PE reform.

3 If a country initially has a relatively well-developed financial system, and the country decides to implement small- to moderate-scale PE reform, then the reforms can succeed without substantial financial sector reforms. However, unless the PE sector is small to start with, small-scale PE reforms, by definition, will still leave much work for future reform efforts.

4 If a country initially has a relatively well-developed financial system, the country can also choose between different types of reform in addition to choosing the scale of the PE reform. A well-developed financial system will promote all PE reform strategies either directly (privatisation, private sector development, corporatisation with increased autonomy); or indirectly (corporatisation with greater government control). Since these are all feasible choices for a country with an initially well-developed financial system, the choice may be based on other factors such as political pressures or relative sustainability of different options.

APPENDIX

Mexico – Financial sector reforms

	1988	1989	1990	1991	1992
Deregulation of the financial sector					
(a) Ceilings on the issuance of bankers' acceptances were removed.		X			
(b) All interest rate controls and lending restrictions were abolished.			X		
(c) Most restrictions on commercial bank activity were removed.			X		
Strengthening of regulatory, supervisory and legal systems					
(a) Existing laws were amended to strengthen regulation and supervision.			X	X	
Reform of monetary control instruments					
(a) Reserve requirements were replaced by a 30 per cent liquidity requirement which was later abolished.		X			
Restructuring or privatisation of financial institutions					
(a) Commercial banks were privatised.				X	X

Turkey – financial sector reforms

	1980	1981	1982	1983	1984	1985	1986	1987	1988	1989	1990
Deregulation of the financial sector											
(a) Removal of interest rate ceilings on bank deposits and loans.	×										
(b) Restrictions on foreign bank entry eased.	×										
(c) Banks were allowed to expand into new areas of activity.	×										
(d) Ceilings re-imposed on deposit rates.				×							
(e) Istanbul Stock Exchange was re-opened.							×				
(f) Deposit rates liberalised again (with informal CB intervention).									×		
Strengthening of regulatory, supervisory and legal systems											
(a) Capital Market Board (CMB) was established with the power to develop and regulate the securities markets.			×								
(b) Deposit insurance established.				×							
(c) New Banking Law was passed.						×					
(d) Minimum capital base was established for new banks.						×					
(e) BIS capital adequacy requirements were adopted.						×					
(f) Limit of 10 per cent imposed on lending to a single customer.						×					

Turkey – financial sector reforms cont.

	1980	1981	1982	1983	1984	1985	1986	1987	1988	1989	1990
(g) Central Bank supervision and accounting standards of the banking system were improved.							X				

Reform of monetary control instruments

	1980	1981	1982	1983	1984	1985	1986	1987	1988	1989	1990
(a) Limits on extension of credits from the Central Bank.			X								
(b) Establishment of a money market and government securities auctions.							X				

Restructuring or privatisation of financial institutions

	1980	1981	1982	1983	1984	1985	1986	1987	1988	1989	1990
(a) Failure of a leading money-broker precipitated the financial crisis.			X								
(b) Several state-owned banks are slated for privatisation.											X

Egypt – financial sector reforms

	1991	1992	1993

Deregulation of the financial sector

	1991	1992	1993
(a) Capital account opened; interest and exchange rates liberalised.	X		
(b) Foreign bank branches were authorised to engage in local currency business.		X	
(c) Bank specific credit ceilings were removed.		X	

Strengthening of regulatory, supervisory and legal systems

(a) Minimum capital requirements are established and capital adequacy standards are adopted.   ×

(b) Asset classification and provisioning guidelines introduced.   ×

(c) Foreign currency exposure regulations issued and implemented.   ×

(d) Loan exposure limits imposed at 25 per cent of capital to single borrowers.   ×

(e) Limits on equity holdings imposed.   ×

(f) Deposit Insurance Fund was established.   ×

(g) Central Bank powers were strengthened through amendments to the banking law.   ×

(h) Bank supervision and audit practices were improved.   ×

Reform of monetary control instruments

(a) Central Bank staff started training for the implementation of open market operations and indirect methods of monetary control.   ×

(b) Outstanding ratios for reserve and liquidity requirements decreased.   ×

Restructuring or privatisation of financial institutions

(a) Public banks were re-capitalised.   ×

Egypt – financial sector reforms cont.

	1991	1992	1993
(b) Detailed audits of public and other commercial banks.			
(c) Restructuring of problem banks started.		×	
(d) One joint-venture bank (public–private) was privatised.			×

India – financial sector reforms

	1992	1993
Deregulation of the financial sector		
(a) Interest policy somewhat liberalised.	×	
(b) Capital markets were deregulated and their taxation was reformed.	×	
(c) Entry of private banks was allowed, guidelines for entry were issued.		×
Strengthening of regulatory, supervisory and legal systems		
(a) Reserve Bank of India (RBI) introduced new guidelines for income recognition, asset classification, and provisioning requirements.	×	
(b) BIS capital adequacy requirements are adopted with a phase-in period of three years.	×	
(c) Securities exchange board of India started to function as an independent regulatory body.	×	

(d) Legal steps are being taken to improve the loan collection mechanisms for banks.   ×

(e) To modernise supervisory practices a new supervisory body was established under the aegis of RBI.   ×

Reform of monetary control instruments

(a) Incremental 10 per cent cash reserve ratio was eliminated and liquidity ratio was reduced.   ×

(b) RBI introduced 364 day T-bill auctions.   ×

Restructuring or privatisation of financial institutions

(a) Banks are allowed to raise private equity from capital markets while majority ownership will remain public.   ×

(b) Government is prepared to re-capitalise banks. 1993–1994 budget includes an estimate of necessary funds.   ×

The Philippines – financial sector reforms

	1980	1981	1982	1983	1984	1985	1986	1987	1988	1989	1990
Deregulation of the financial sector											
(a) Functional distinctions between different financial institutions were removed. Commercial banks were allowed to operate as universal banks.	×										

The Philippines – financial sector reforms cont.

	1980	1981	1982	1983	1984	1985	1986	1987	1988	1989	1990
(b) Ceilings on long term deposit rates were removed.		X									
(c) Ceilings on long term loan rates were removed.			X								
(d) Ceilings on short term deposit rates were removed.				X							
(e) Ceilings on short term loan rates were removed.				X							

Strengthening of regulatory, supervisory and legal systems

	1980	1981	1982	1983	1984	1985	1986	1987	1988	1989	1990
(a) Reform of the legal framework and bankruptcy laws and strengthening prudential regulations and their enforcement.								X			

Reform of monetary control instruments

	1980	1981	1982	1983	1984	1985	1986	1987	1988	1989	1990
(a) Attempt to give primacy to T-bills in monetary operations.						X					
(b) Reserve requirements were reduced.					X						
(c) Re-discount rate adjusted in line with market rates.				X							
(d) Access to re-discounts were rationalised.					X						
(e) New liquidity window opened for 'normal' needs.				X							
(f) New central bank bills were issued.			X								
(g) There was a shift to base money as intermediate target.			X								

Restructuring or privatisation of financial institutions

(a) Number of financial institutions fell from 1,216 in 1981 to 1,025 in 1986 due to the 1981–1986 financial crisis and subsequent restructuring, merger and failures.

(b) The share of public banks in total banking assets was reduced from 28 per cent to 1.4 per cent in 1990.

Korea – financial sector reforms

	1980	1981	1982	1983	1984	1985	1986	1987	1988	1989	1990
(a)			×	×	×	×					
(b)	×	×	×	×	×	×	×	×	×	×	×

Deregulation of the financial sector

	1980	1981	1982	1983	1984	1985	1986	1987	1988	1989	1990
(a) Transactions in bonds and repos were formalised.	×										
(b) Restrictions on scope of activities were eased.		×	×	×							
(c) New entry of institutions was allowed.			×								
(d) Deposit rates were partially liberalised to establish positive real rates.		×									
(e) Credit ceilings abolished.			×								
(f) Preferential interest rates abolished.			×								
(g) Min/max interest rate ranges were introduced.					×						
(h) Indirect portfolio investment by foreigners was allowed.		×		×		×					

Korea – financial sector reforms cont.

	1980	1981	1982	1983	1984	1985	1986	1987	1988	1989	1991
(i) Most bank lending rates were completely deregulated.									X		
(j) Government announced a plan to completely deregulate money market and deposit rates by 1997.											X
Strengthening of regulatory, supervisory and legal systems											
(a) Supervisory procedures reformed and focus strengthened.				X	X	X	X	X	X		
(b) Over the counter market established for small and medium firms.								X			
(c) Capital market laws were revised.								X			
Reform of monetary control instruments											
(a) Reserve requirements were lowered and unified.		X									
(b) Reliance on directed credit was reduced.				X	X	X	X	X	X		
Restructuring or privatisation of financial institutions											
(a) Public banks were privatised.		X	X								
(b) Bank debts were rescheduled.					X	X	X	X	X		

Chile – financial sector reforms

Deregulation of the financial sector

	1974	1975	1976	1977	1978	1979	1980	1981	1982	1983	1984	1985	1986
(a) Short term money market rates were freed.		X											
(b) Barriers to entry were lowered.			X										
(c) Quantitative credit controls were removed.			X										
(d) Interest rates were liberalised.			X										
(e) Restrictions on scope of activities were eased.				X									
(f) Foreign bank entry was allowed.				X									
(g) Commercial banks were allowed to borrow abroad.				X	X	X							

Strengthening of regulatory, supervisory and legal systems

	1974	1975	1976	1977	1978	1979	1980	1981	1982	1983	1984	1985	1986
(a) Limits were imposed on bank lending to interrelated entities.								X					
(b) Loan classification and provisioning rules were established.								X					
(c) Measures to tighten bank supervision were approved.									X				
(d) A banking law further strengthened prudential supervision.													X

Chile – financial sector reforms cont.

Reform of monetary control instruments

	1974	1975	1976	1977	1978	1979	1980	1981	1982	1983	1984	1985	1986
(a) Auctions of central bank credit and t-bills introduced.		X											
(b) Reserve requirements were lowered and unified.				X									

Restructuring or privatisation of financial institutions

	1974	1975	1976	1977	1978	1979	1980	1981	1982	1983	1984	1985	1986
(a) Commercial banks were privatised.		X											
(b) Pension funds were privatised.			X										
(c) 1981–1983 financial crisis started with a run on a major bank. Authorities had to intervene and took over eight institutions.								X					
(d) Government took over eight more institutions.										X			
(e) Banks were re-privatised.												X	

Ghana – financial sector reforms

Deregulation of the financial sector

	1987	1988	1989	1990	1991	1992
(a) Lending rates were partially liberalised.	X					
(b) Interest rates were completely liberalised.		X				
(c) Government controls over bank fees and charges were eliminated.				X		

Strengthening of regulatory, supervisory and legal systems

(a) Banking law was amended to establish prudential lending limits and capital adequacy requirements. Uniform accounting and auditing standards were also instituted.	X	X	X

Reform of monetary control instruments

(a) A T-bill auction was introduced.	X	

Restructuring or privatisation of financial institutions

(a) Government restructured banks.	X	
(b) Government announced plans to privatise banks in 1993.	X	

Senegal – financial sector reforms

	1989	1990
Deregulation of the financial sector		
(a) Directed credits were reduced.		X
Strengthening of regulatory, supervisory and legal systems		
(a) Bank capital requirements were increased and prudential regulations were strengthened.	X	
(b) Bank supervision was improved.	X	
Restructuring or privatisation of financial institutions		
(a) Banks were restructured. Some institutions were closed.	X	
(b) Government ownership in each bank was reduced to less than 25 per cent.	X	X

NOTES

1 We received very helpful comments from Philip Brock, Gerard Caprio, Ahmed Galal, Michael Gavin, Mark Gersovitz, Niels Hermes, Robert Lensink, Bharat Nauriyal, Steve Saeger, Hemant Shah, Mary Shirley, and Paulo Vieira Da Cunha. The views expressed in this paper are the authors' own and not necessarily those of the World Bank or its member countries.

2 Sound capital markets can assist intermediaries in exerting corporate governance. If capital markets competently obtain and process information, equity and bond prices will reflect managerial performance and thereby influence managerial behaviour. Also, if capital markets effectively mobilise capital and identify inferior managers, capital markets offer motivated groups a vehicle for raising capital, acquiring firms, and changing management.

3 Levine (1996) provides reasons for government supervision and regulation of financial intermediaries. He cautions that care must be taken since government interventions and regulations themselves frequently thwart the stable provision of high quality financial services.

4 Liquid liabilities consist of currency held outside the banking system plus demand and interest bearing liabilities of banks and non-bank financial intermediaries. This equals 'M3'. When it is not available 'M2' is used.

5 Demirgüç-Kunt and Levine (1993) discuss a broad range of stock market indicators.

6 Although complaints arose as soon as the prices of shares started to fall. See Saeger (1993).

7 See *The New York Times*, 27 October 1993.

8 See Tandon (1992).

9 See Saeger (1993).

10 See World Bank (1993).

11 See Gavin (1993) for all these examples.

12 Korean corporatisation also involved greater autonomy of day to day management decisions while keeping management criteria focused on bottom line issues.

13 See Cortes-Douglas (1992), De la Cuadra and Valdes-Prieto (1992), and Edwards and Edwards (1987).

REFERENCES

Cortes-Douglas, H. (1992), 'Financial Reform in Chile: Lessons in Regulation and Deregulation' in D. Vittas (ed.) *Financial Regulation: Changing the Rules of the Game*, Washington, DC: World Bank, pp. 163–94.

De la Cuadra, S. and S. Valdes-Prieto (1992), 'Banking Structure in Chile,' in G.G. Kaufman (ed.) *Banking Structures in Major Countries*, Boston: Kluwer Academic Publishers, pp. 59–112.

Demirgüç-Kunt, A. and R. Levine (1993) 'Stock Market Development and Financial Intermediary Growth: A Research Agenda', *Policy Research Working Paper*, No. 1159, World Bank.

Edwards, S. and A. Cox Edwards (1987), *Monetarism and Liberalization: The Chilean Experiment*, Chicago: University of Chicago Press.

Galal, A. (1994), 'Extent, Performance and Reform of Public Enterprises: A Comparative Analysis', manuscript, World Bank.

Gavin, M. (1993), 'Financial Market Development and Strategies for Public Enterprise Reform', manuscript, Columbia University.

Levine, R. (1996), 'Financial Sector Policies: Analytical Framework and Research Agenda,' this volume.

Saeger, S. (1993), 'The Financial System and Public Enterprise Reform: Case Studies of Chile, Ghana, Korea, Mexico, and Turkey', manuscript, Harvard University.

Swanson, D. and T. Wolde-Samait (1989), 'Africa's Public Enterprise Sector and Evidence of Reforms', *World Bank Technical Paper*, No. 95, World Bank.

Tandon, P. (1992), 'Mexico', in *Welfare Consequences of Selling Public Enterprises: Case Studies from Chile, Malaysia, Mexico, and the UK*, Washington DC: World Bank, pp. 407–515.

World Bank (1993), 'Regional Study on Public Enterprise Reform and Privatization in Africa', Washington DC: World Bank.

12

FINANCIAL LIBERALISATION AND FINANCIAL FRAGILITY

The experiences of Chile and Indonesia compared

Hans Visser and Ingmar van Herpt

INTRODUCTION

Ever since the early 1970s countries in Asia and Latin America, and to a lesser extent in Africa, have moved from inward-looking policies with heavy government involvement in the economy to more outward-looking policies that primarily rely on the price mechanism rather than on detailed government directives, protection and subsidies. The road to a more or less free market economy has not always been smooth. The most radical attempt at liberalisation, the Chilean experiment in the late 1970s, to all appearances foundered in 1982 and it took the Chileans several years to get their liberalisation process on course again. The Indonesian approach by contrast has been much more cautious and so far major crises have been avoided (though in all fairness it should be noted that Indonesia only seriously started her liberalisation process after the 1982 worldwide debt crisis and in addition had very little dollar-denominated debt).

We will first recount the Chilean experience in financial liberalisation in the 1973–1982 period in order to find out what went wrong and next trace the Indonesian liberalisation process. In the short final section, we will try to see what lessons can be learnt from the Chilean and Indonesian liberalisation efforts. Our aim is to discover where Indonesia avoided the pitfalls which bedevilled the Chilean approach and in what respects, if any, the Indonesian authorities failed to pay heed to the lessons the Chileans learned the hard way. The description of the developments in Chile until 1982, with their extreme reliance on the unfettered functioning of markets, is meant as a kind of benchmark with which to contrast the Indonesian experience.

Our approach thus is a comparative-historical one. The theoretical arguments in favour of a market economy and consequently in favour of liberalisation are taken for granted. The transition from a heavily regulated economy to a more market-oriented economy is fraught with difficulties. Deductive logic does not tell us what transition path is best. In financial liberalisation, much will depend on initial circumstances and on the institutional framework. Case studies may help to form a mental picture of the various obstacles on the road to liberalised financial markets and how to deal with them (cf. Trebat, 1991, p. 66). It may be objected that Chile and Indonesia are very disparate countries and that comparisons between very different cases are not very useful. If we start, however, from the premise that people in different countries and different periods of time react in similar ways to similar stimuli, it seems that comparative history can teach us useful things. Moreover, some of the problems facing Indonesia are remarkably similar to those which Chile saw itself confronted with, especially in the field of prudential supervision. Probably no hard and fast rules can be derived by the comparative-historical method, but at least it should help in identifying the areas where liberalisation efforts run a serious danger of getting stuck.

CHILE'S FINANCIAL LIBERALISATION

Chicago macroeconomics

After the overthrow of President Allende and his Unidad Popular regime in September 1973, the new rulers saw themselves confronted with an economy in severe disorder. Inflation had exploded under the Unidad Popular, from 22.1 per cent in 1971 to 487.5 per cent in 1972 and 605.9 per cent in 1973 (figures from Edwards, 1986, p. 245). The new government started on a cautiously liberalising course, but inflation hardly abated after the change of regime: in 1974 it ran at 369.2 per cent and in 1975 at 343.2 per cent. Lacking a clear idea of how to run the economy themselves, the military rulers then turned to the only group with a consistent view on attacking Chile's economic problems, a group of predominantly Chicago-trained young economists. These so-called Chicago kids or Chicago boys took over the management of the economy in 1975 and started to liberalise the Chilean economy at a fast pace. The extremely protectionist and complicated system of import tariffs and non-tariff barriers inherited from the Allende administration was swiftly dismantled (cf. *Euromoney*, 1978; Corbo and De Melo, 1987). Also, export subsidies and cheap credits for special borrowers were abolished.

The opening-up of the economy went hand in hand with a serious, and ultimately reasonably successful, attempt to fight inflation. Fiscal tightness (see Table 12.1) and monetary contraction were introduced, which together with a fall in the price of Chile's main export product, copper, led to a sharp reduction in GNP in 1975. At first, the Chilean government saw the exchange rate as a tool for correcting balance of payments problems (*Euromoney*, 1978). Later on, however, the rate of exchange was primarily deployed to help reduce inflation. In early 1978, the central bank extended the pre-announcement of daily exchange rates one or two months in advance to a schedule (*tablita*) covering the entire year. It was hoped that inflationary

Table 12.1 Macroeconomic data for Chile, 1970–1982

Year	GDP	M_1	M_2	Inflation	Deficit	Exchange rate	Savings
1970	2.1	52	51	34.9	2.9	0.012	21.6
1971	9.0	99	95	22.1	11.2	0.016	17.8
1972	−1.2	96	91	487.5	13.5	0.025	10.4
1973	−5.6	273	286	605.9	24.6	0.360	9.5
1974	1.0	301	279	369.2	10.5	1.87	25.3
1975	−12.9	233	301	343.2	2.6	8.50	8.5
1976	3.5	213	290	197.9	2.3	17.42	15.4
1977	9.9	165	225	84.2	1.9	27.96	10.7
1978	8.2	88	114	37.2	0.9	33.95	11.6
1979	8.3	60	86	38.0	−1.7	39.00	13.7
1980	7.5	58	58	31.2	−0.6	39.00	15.5
1981	5.3	33	89	9.5	−3.0	39.00	7.5
1982	−14.1	−5	−15	20.7	−2.3	73.43	2.1

Sources: real GDP growth from Edwards, 1986, p. 243; 1982 from *International Financial Statistics*; money growth from Corbo, 1985, p. 896; inflation from Edwards, 1986, p. 245; budget deficit from Edwards, 1986, p. 245; exchange rate from *International Financial Statistics*; savings from Edwards, 1986, p. 257 and Marfán and Bosworth, 1994, p. 213
Notes: GDP = percentage real GDP growth; M_1 = percentage growth rate of narrow money; M_2 = percentage growth of broad money; inflation = inflation percentage December–December; deficit = government budget deficit as a percentage of GDP; exchange rate = pesos per US$, end of year; savings = gross domestic savings as a percentage of GDP

expectations would be revised downwards in this way (IMF, 1981). In June 1979 the central bank went one step further and fixed the dollar exchange rate (Cox Edwards and Edwards, 1992). It was, however, not before 1981 that the inflation rate converged to the world inflation rate of 9.5 per cent. In the process, the real exchange rate (defined such that a higher real exchange rate means that domestic goods become cheaper vis-à-vis foreign goods) inevitably fell (cf. Visser, 1993). The fall in the rate of inflation took much longer than expected, probably because of backward indexation of wages which prevented production costs from falling faster, but the capital-import financed boom in the non-tradeables sector will also have played a role (Kiguel and Liviatan, 1994).

What happened can easily be told in terms of the dependent economy model. The Chilean peso underwent a real appreciation, the current account of the balance of payments turned into deficit (to the tune of 13.7 per cent of GDP in 1981; see Corbo, 1985, p. 906), capital inflows soared and the non-tradeable sectors boomed (Corbo and Sanchez, 1985). When capital inflows suddenly stopped in 1982 and the fixed exchange rate could not be maintained, a financial crisis broke out, triggered by bad debts and high dollar liabilities. Even if the opening-up of the Chilean economy had proven quite successful, the liberalisation of the financial sector that went hand in hand

289

with it, ended in disaster. In the next few sections we will try to find out what went wrong.

Financial liberalisation

Under President Allende, the financial sector had been nationalised. The allocation of credit was not based on clear economic criteria. The switch to a market economy, which was the overriding policy aim of the Chicago-trained economists under Pinochet, did not stop at the financial system; on the contrary, its liberalisation was one of their top priorities. This liberalisation included re-privatisation of the banking sector, the lifting of interest ceilings in order to reinstate the market as the allocational machinery for credit with the real rate of interest as the equilibrating mechanism, and encouraging the establishment of new banks and other financial institutions.

Liberalisation had started in 1974 with the lowering of reserve requirements and the permission to establish non-bank financial institutions (NBFIs), so-called *financieras*, which were free of rules as to setting interest rates. In October 1975, the commercial banks also were freed from restrictions as to interest rates. Between 1975 and 1978 furthermore all the banks, except the Banco del Estado and two small banks that were involved in difficulties of a legal nature, were privatised. The public sector was even prohibited to invest in the banking sector (Held, 1990). A number of banks were sold to conglomerates or *grupos* that used the newly acquired banks to finance their own expansion.

International capital flows and the financial sector

The liberalisation of the current account of the balance of payments was not fully matched by a liberalisation of the capital account. Capital controls, in particular controls on external borrowing by commercial banks, were thought necessary in order not to be flooded with capital inflows, which would have made control of the money supply that much more difficult (Sergio de la Cuadra, vice-president of the Chilean central bank, in *Euromoney*, 1978, p. 17). In 1977 the banks were allowed to act as intermediaries for medium and long term foreign capital, provided foreign debt did not exceed 5 per cent of a bank's capital. In 1979 this restriction was lifted and the only restrictions were that foreign debt was subject to a capital–asset ratio of 5 per cent and that capital inflows per bank in any month should not exceed 5 per cent of the bank's capital (Corbo and De Melo, 1987). The latter restriction in its turn was lifted in April 1980. Restrictions on inflows of short term capital remained in force until 1982.

Apparently, the restrictions on capital inflows were insufficient and what happened was what McKinnon had already warned against in 1973 (McKinnon, 1973). Domestic interest rates in Chile rose sharply and exchange rates were believed to remain stable for some time at least. The capital inflows that followed reached a peak of no less than some 25 per cent of GDP in the first half of 1981 and resulted in an inflated non-tradeables sector and a rapidly increasing excess demand in the tradeables sector, i.e. a huge trade deficit (Corbo, 1985). True, when capital import restrictions were partially lifted, capital inflows at first helped to reduce real interest rates sharply in 1979, but in 1981 they soared again (see Table 12.2), probably at least in part because of devaluation expectations (Galvéz and Tybout, 1985), but also perhaps because of an unexpected fall in inflation (Corbo, 1985).

The disappointments of financial liberalisation

Financial intermediation may have undergone multiple expansion, but the hoped-for increase in savings failed to materialise. A plausible explanation is that economic agents anticipated high economic growth and spent heavily on consumer goods. Another contributing factor was that the revenue of the sales of public sector enterprises was used by the government to finance current expenditure (Edwards and Cox Edwards, 1987).

Savings remained at a low level (see Table 12.1), contributing to real interest rates that rose to dizzying heights. Low savings have been attributed to the rise in asset values in the boom period of 1978–1981, which produced a wealth effect on spending (Corbo and De Melo, 1987). There may have been a number of other factors contributing to high interest rates. First of all, there may have been a high demand for loans by firms desperate for funds in order to avoid bankruptcy, and those loans were freely given, especially to firms within the same *grupo*. The squeezing of the tradeables sector resulting from the fall in the real exchange rate will surely have been a contributing factor (Edwards, 1990), but firms had entered the post-Unidad Popular period already seriously undercapitalized (Corbo, 1985). Second, the real estate boom that started with the fixed dollar rate increased the demand for loans, whereas the rise in property prices appeared to provide sound security for lenders (Eyzaguirre, 1993). Third, people may have been willing to pay high interest rates because of devaluation expectations. Both explanations are consistent with the jump in real interest rates between 1980 and 1981 (see Table 12.2; the figures for 1980 do not reflect a jump, but they are an average over the whole year). But they had been high before: the actions of the *financieras* did nothing to restrain the rate of interest. They were subject to fewer restrictions than the banks and paid higher interest rates to depositors, forcing the banks to follow in their footsteps. High real interest rates made life difficult for many firms and contributed to the proliferation of bad loans that plagued the Chilean financial sector. It has been said, probably with good reason, that the high interest rates resulted in adverse selection, because banks did not make funds available for low-risk, low-return investments (Corbo and De Melo 1987; Mirakhor and Villanueva, 1993: the argument stems from

Table 12.2 Real interest rates on fixed-rate 30–89 day loans, 1976–1988

Year	Outstanding loans	Debts
1976	50.9	8.6
1977	46.1	17.3
1978	35.9	22.6
1979	15.8	4.7
1980	11.6	5.0
1981	33.2	25.5
1982	30.6	20.5
1983	14.9	3.9
1984	11.0	2.6
1985	10.6	4.1
1986	7.4	1.5
1987	9.0	3.1
1988	8.0	2.4

Source: Held, 1990, p. 195
Note: 1988 till October

Stiglitz and Weiss, 1981). Ultimately, in November 1981 the central bank had to step in, in order to rescue four banks and four *financieras*, with about one half of the assets of the entire financial system between them (Harberger, 1986).

Prudential supervision

In hindsight, it appears that grossly inadequate prudential supervision is at least partly to blame for the financial crisis that erupted in 1982. Prudential supervision was below par in several respects (cf. Trebat, 1991, pp. 60–61):

(a) requirements for setting up new banks were anything but strict (see Held, 1990, p. 227);
(b) required capital–asset ratios did not take account of the riskiness of different bank assets;
(c) accounting systems were not designed to spot debt accumulation in time;
(d) there was too little legal room for taking action in a crisis situation.

These problems were compounded by the absorption of commercial banks by *grupos*. The *grupos* bought many of the privatised companies from the state, including commercial banks. The government had made an attempt to prevent excessive concentration of economic power by stipulating that individuals were not allowed to hold more than 1.5 per cent of a bank's share capital and companies not more than 3 per cent (Held, 1990). But the government conceded to these rules being circumvented. Moreover, it discouraged foreign banks from taking an interest in Chilean banks (*Euromoney*, 1978). Non-financial companies subsequently were not allowed to hold more than 5 per cent of a bank's share capital. The *grupos*, however, managed to circumvent such rules and at the end of the 1970s 10 big banks, representing 80 per cent of own capital tied up in banking, were directly controlled by *grupos* (Edwards and Cox Edwards, 1987).

The banks attracted dollar loans, which they had to pass on without converting them into pesos. In the three years from 1979 to 1982 the external debt of the banks multiplied from $660 million to nearly $7 billion (Trebat, 1991). Other *grupo* companies, however, contracted dollar loans from the banks and provided peso credits. Meanwhile, capital–asset ratios both in financial and non-financial firms deteriorated. The government could have given the right signals in 1977 when a number of *financieras* and the Banco Osorno la Union failed as a result of bad loans to companies within the Fluxa *grupo*. It took a number of steps, such as increasing the required minimum capital for *financieras* and introducing a temporary deposit guarantee to a maximum of $3,000 for each depositor. All creditors of the Banco Osorno, however, were fully compensated. Economic agents interpreted this government action as a *de facto* unlimited deposit guarantee and in their investment policy disregarded the soundness of the financial institutions. Velasco (1991) notes that if deposits had not been perceived to be guaranteed, there would have been major bank runs, which did not take place. The government was ambiguous in its statements. Central bank vice-president Sergio de la Cuadra told *Euromoney* in 1978 on the one hand that banks had to function in a free market, with all that this implied, and on the other hand that bank failures would have more serious effects than bankruptcies of industrial firms (*Euromoney*, 1978, p. 17). It took the government some years to come to the conclusion that more strict prudential supervision was called for and in the process it created a classical case of moral hazard. Moreover, the monetary authorities failed to deal with the increasingly closer ties between banks and *grupos*. Only in 1980 was a beginning made with the classification of outstanding credits according to risk categories, and in 1981 the banking superintendent gained the right to prohibit some kinds of credits (Held, 1990). But it was too little too late. In 1981 and 1983, banks in trouble were fully bailed out. The sale of bad debts by the banks to the central bank amounted to 28 per cent of their total assets and 18 per cent of GDP in 1985 (Held, 1990).

The aftermath of the crisis

In early 1983 the government saw itself forced to take over the two largest private commercial banks, to close down three banks and to intervene in five others (Eyzaguirre, 1993). During the build-up of foreign debt since 1980 the government had declared that foreign debt contracted by the private sector was not its concern (Edwards, 1986), but it now helped out troubled firms by

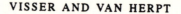

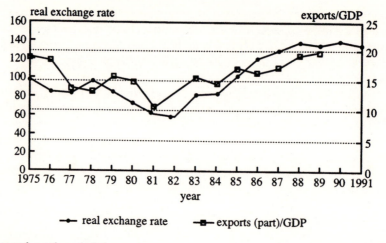

Ores and metals excluded

Figure 12.1 The relationship between openness and real exchange rate (RER) for
Chile, metals and ores excluded
Source: Visser, 1993

selling 'preferential dollars' at a subsidised rate after the 1982 devaluation had
increased the peso value of foreign debt, and it also bailed out the troubled
banks that were saddled with bad debts. It had to give in when, after it had
reiterated its position in 1983, the foreign commercial banks suspended all
credit, including short term trade credit (Meller, 1992). The central bank
bought private banks' non-performing portfolios in exchange for promissory
notes that bore a real interest of 7 per cent, whereas the banks were under the
obligation to re-purchase their debt in the future, against a 5 per cent real
interest rate. Thus, the central bank subsidised the commercial banks (Cox
Edwards and Edwards, 1992; Eyzaguirre, 1993; for more details see Velasco,
1991).

The Chilean liberalisation effort had foundered, or so it seemed even
to well-informed observers (Corbo, 1985; Hanson, 1986). In April 1984
the Chicago-educated minister of finance received his marching orders, and
that looked like the end of it. In 1985, however, free-market economists
were back at the helm and ever since the Chilean economy has been held
up as a shining example of the good that market-oriented policies can do.
The government did not, however, return to the extreme hands-off policy
that had characterised the reign of the Chicago boys (Cox Edwards and
Edwards, 1992). Monetary policy, for example, was aimed at preventing
real interest rates from rising as exorbitantly as in the pre-1983 period.
It is a moot point, however, how much of the success in keeping real

interest rates down was due to monetary policy and how much to increased supply in the credit market, e.g. as a result of the rise of private pension funds (Cox Edwards and Edwards, 1992).

The government also had to give up the fixed exchange rate as from June 1982. It proved possible to depreciate the peso at a much higher rate than the rate of inflation and over the rest of the 1980s the real exchange rate roughly doubled, which went hand in hand with a significant rise in exports as a percentage of GDP (see Figure 12.1).[1]

It was conceded that prudential supervision had been lax, or rather lacking, and steps were taken, *inter alia*, to introduce risk-weighted capital–asset ratios and reduce the (*de facto*) coverage of the deposit guarantee, culminating in the 1986 revision of the banking law (see Ramírez-Villadell, 1991; Eyzaguirre, 1993).

Preliminary conclusions

In the financial climate in the world in 1982, a debt crisis was hard to avoid for any heavily indebted country, and heavily indebted Chile was: the debt–service ratio jumped from 43.1 per cent in 1980 to 71.3 per cent in 1982 (World Bank, 1989). By late 1981 the cracks in the Chilean economy had already become visible, in the guise of non-performing loans (i.e. loans on which interest had not been paid for at least three months) and an extremely high real interest rate (see Table 12.2). Ceilings on foreign borrowing by banks or higher and more effective required capital–asset ratios would have resulted in less foreign borrowing. Also, if there had been no indexing of wages, inflation would probably have fallen faster and the real appreciation of the peso would probably have been less. Furthermore, there would have been less of a financial crisis if prudential supervision had been more effective and if the government had not given *de facto* full deposit insurance. This gave rise to moral hazard problems and it forced financial institutions with a prudent loan policy to pay the same high interest rates to depositors as their more risk-loving brethren.

It took several years before inflation was reduced to single figures. A major contributing factor was backward wage indexation. Severe shocks of other kinds also hit the economy, such as the sale of nationalised firms. The macroeconomic instability was thus compounded by an upward pressure on real interest rates, through an increased demand for credit meeting with a still restricted supply of savings. It is doubtful whether under such circumstances it was a wise decision to leave interest rates completely free (cf. McKinnon, 1988; 1992; Villanueva and Mirakhor, 1990). Apparently, after a shockwise regime change, it may take many years before the economy, and the financial sector in particular, can be left to the discipline of the market.

VISSER AND VAN HERPT

THE INDONESIAN FINANCIAL LIBERALISATION

The underlying philosophy

The introduction of liberalisation in Chile marked an extremely sharp break with the past. In Indonesia too a regime that had allowed inflation to rise to around 1,000 per cent was replaced by a new group of rulers, but the transition was much less of an earthquake, in the sense that Indonesia did not develop into a testing ground for a pure version of some policy approach. After the failed coup of 1965, Suharto assumed power in March 1966 as a member of a triumvirate and only in March 1968 did he succeed Sukarno as president. Again, a group of US-educated people, this time from Berkeley, took over the commanding posts in the area of economic policy, though to all appearances this 'Berkeley Mafia' got much less of a free hand under President Suharto than their Chicago counterparts got under President Pinochet, and they were not such dogmatic laissez-faire proponents anyway. Even if not motivated by such, for the period, extreme free-market principles as the Chicago kids, the New Order government nevertheless energetically attacked Indonesia's economic problems. The Indonesian economy remained strongly regulated, but with technical and financial help from the IMF a Rehabilitation and Stabilisation Programme was drawn up and put into practice over the 1966–1970 period, aimed at reducing inflation, developing the infrastructure and improving the supply of basic goods and services. Inflation fell surprisingly fast and economic growth did not suffer under the anti-inflationary policy (see Table 12.3). One problem the Indonesians did not have to cope with in the first years of their reign, unlike the Chileans, was a precipitous fall in the price of their main export product. Indeed, the opposite happened: the oil price hike of 1973–1974 contributed to a return to double-digit inflation. However, oil prices did fall in the early 1980s, and it was felt that more serious measures were called for to put the economic house in order. Indonesia now started, ever so cagily, on the path to liberalisation (Booth, 1992).

Financial liberalisation

The 1980s started with the Indonesian financial system characterised by severe financial repression. There were hardly any financial institutions outside the commercial banks, which held 95 per cent of financial assets. The five state-owned commercial banks and Bank Indonesia, which acted both as the central bank and as a commercial bank, between them held 80 per cent of all financial assets. The playing field for the state banks and the private banks was far from level: state banks had easier access to Bank Indonesia credit, were allowed a much more extensive branch network and were the only banks where public enterprises could hold accounts. Foreign banks were

296

Table 12.3 Macroeconomic data for Indonesia, 1966–1993

Year	GDP	M_1	M_2	Inflation	Deficit	Exchange rate
1966	2.3	764	743	920	n.a.	–
1967	2.3	132	140	171	n.a.	176/235
1968	11.1	125	137	128	n.a.	277/326
1969	6.0	58	82	16	2.8	277/326
1970	7.5	37	42	12	2.9	340/378
1971	7.0	28	42	4	2.3	374/415
1972	9.4	49	49	6.5	2.4	374/415
1973	11.3	42	43	31	2.0	374/415
1974	7.6	40	46	41	0.9	415
1975	5.0	35	39	19	3.2	415
1976	6.9	26	31	20	1.5	415
1977	8.8	25	18	11	1.0	415
1978	7.8	24	22	8	0.5	625
1979	6.3	33	35	21	0.5	627
1980	9.9	51	49	18.5	2.4	626.75
1981	7.9	29	28	12	1.4	644.0
1982	2.2	10	14	9.5	2.2	692.5
1983	4.2	6	32	12	1.4	994
1984	7.0	13	22	10.5	0.6	1,074
1985	2.5	18	46	4.7	0.3	1,125
1986	5.9	15	6	5.9	2.7	1,641
1987	4.9	9	23	9.2	1.0	1,650
1988	5.8	13	24	8.0	3.2	1,731
1989	7.5	43	39	6.5	2.0	1,797
1990	7.2	16	45	7.4	–0.4	1,901
1991	6.9	12	17	9.4	–0.4	1,992
1992	6.4	8	20	7.5	–	2,062
1993	6.5	–	–	9.7	–	2,110

Sources: GDP growth calculated from *International Financial Statistics*, 1986–1992: from *World Economic Outlook*, October 1994, p. 126 (1993: forecast). Money growth: calculated from *International Financial Statistics*. Inflation: calculated from CPI figures in *International Financial Statistics*. Budget deficit defined as borrowing requirement excluding foreign aid, calculated from *International Financial Statistics*. $ exchange rate: end of year, from *International Financial Statistics*, 1967–1973 rates apply to exports and imports, respectively

even more disadvantaged in that they had no access whatsoever to Bank Indonesia credit and could not open more than two branches. Credit allocation was heavily influenced by all kinds of special programmes. Subsidised directed credit accounted for 48 per cent of all bank lending in 1982 and this so-called 'liquidity credit' would be refinanced at low rates by Bank Indonesia (see Table 12.4). Indeed, refinancing was the main source of funding for the state banks, as they were subject to an interest ceiling for deposits of over three months, whereas the private banks were free to set their own rates. In 1982 state banks paid on average 6.0 per cent interest on six-month deposits, against 18.5 per cent for private banks. Credit allocation was

Table 12.4 Rates on one-year time deposits of state banks in Indonesia, 1968–1989

Year	Nominal rate	Real rate
1968	72.0	−24.0
1969	60.0	35.7
1970	24.0	10.4
1971	24.0	19.2
1972	18.0	10.6
1973	15.0	−12.0
1974	15.0	−18.4
1975	15.0	−3.2
1976	15.0	−4.2
1977	12.0	0.9
1978	9.0	0.7
1979	9.0	−9.6
1980	9.0	−8.0
1981	9.0	−2.9
1982	9.0	−0.5
1983	18.0	5.5
1984	18.3	11.1
1985	15.0	12.8
1986	15.0	0.6
1987	17.5	4.7
1988	18.5	9.6
1989	16.5	9.8

Source: Cole and Slade, 1992b
Note: the real rate has been calculated by deflating the nominal rate by the CPI of the current year

also affected by the credit ceilings imposed by Bank Indonesia on individual banks (on all this, as for the rest of this section, see Hanna, 1994).

Credit allocation was opaque and inefficient, both in the sense that loans did not always reach intended beneficiaries (or that it was well-nigh impossible to judge if the allocation met any intention at all) and in the sense that projects with a low return were financed. This latter effect came about through low, subsidised interest rates and through subsidised credit insurance from a state-owned insurance company, which led to moral hazard problems in that banks had no incentive to monitor projects closely (Hanna, 1994).

The fall in oil income made it imperative to mobilise domestic savings and make more efficient use of available financial resources. A step in the direction of liberalisation was taken in 1983, when directed credit was substantially reduced and interest rates on such credits were increased (Table 12.4). Other interest ceilings were abolished. 'Liquidity credits', though, were not abolished overnight, but were reduced at a very slow pace: they fell gradually from 37.1 per cent of all bank credit in March 1983 to 11.9 per cent in March 1992 (Hanna, 1994, p. 5). Monetary policy, which until June 1983 had relied on credit ceilings for individual banks,

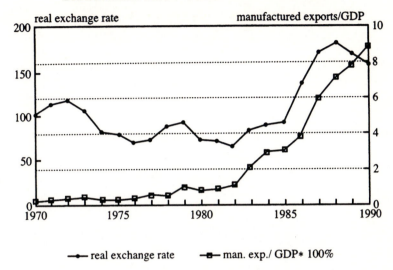

Figure 12.2 Real exchange rate and exports of manufactures, Indonesia 1970–1990

now had to find other instruments. For lack of sufficient government debt, Bank Indonesia introduced Sertifikat Bank Indonesia (SBI), debt issued by themselves, in order to create paper eligible for open-market operations. To the same end, Bank Indonesia stimulated the market for bank acceptances or Surat Berharga Pasar Uang (SBPU) (Sundararajan and Molho, 1988; Binhadi, 1990; see also Van Herpt *et al.*, 1994). Bank Indonesia was, however, handicapped by the shallowness of the market (Woo and Nasution, 1989).

The next step in financial liberalisation again was a reaction to adverse external developments. In 1986 there was another sharp fall in oil prices. With the appreciation of the yen and imports to a large extent coming from Japan, the current account of the balance of payments deteriorated and the budget deficit went up. A substantial devaluation (see Table 12.3 and Figure 12.2)[2] went hand in hand with a substantial liberalisation of international trade. Non-tariff barriers were replaced by tariffs and those tariffs were subsequently lowered. Also, direct foreign investment was made easier. Again, there were no sweeping across-the-board policy changes, but rather a series of measures that followed each other over the years. In the process, the authorities managed, with the help of fiscal tightening, to keep inflation in the one-digit range. Then, in October 1988, a set of reforms for the financial sector was introduced, denoted as PAKTO 27 (the 27 October 1988 package). This included a drastic lowering of entry barriers into the financial sector. Both domestic and foreign banks received more opportunities to increase their branch network, state enterprises henceforth could hold one half of their assets in private banks and both banks and NBFIs were allowed to issue certificates of deposit. Also, the competitiveness of banks relative to NBFIs was improved by a reduction in reserve requirements from 15 per cent to 2 per cent, to which NBFIs were now subject, too. In order to prevent a sharp credit expansion, the Bank of Indonesia required the banks to invest 80 per cent of the funds that became freed through the reduction in SBIs (Binhadi, 1990).

Again, liberalisation measures were taken in a continuous flow, rather than as a shock therapy, and PAKTO 27 was followed by three other packages within 15 months. In March 1989, for example, absolute limits on foreign borrowing by banks were replaced by a limit of 25 per cent of equity to the net open position of banks in foreign exchange. Banks could, under this rule, freely borrow abroad as long as they lent domestically in foreign exchange. January 1990 saw a further reduction in directed credit, with a reduction in the number of priority programmes and interest rates set closer to market levels. The subsidised credit insurance was abolished. Against this, banks were required to make 20 per cent of their loans to small borrowers.

International capital flows

The capital account of Indonesia was liberalised in 1970, with the exception of direct foreign investment and portfolio investment through the domestic capital market (Sabirin, 1993). The main reason seems to have been that the government had little hope that it could monitor and control capital flows effectively (Cole and Slade, 1992b). However, out of a concern about liquidity growth it imposed ceilings for foreign borrowing by banks and NBFIs in 1974, which remained in force until 1989 (Sabirin, 1993). It is curious that a repressed financial system, with real interest rates often negative over the 1973–1983 period, and an open capital account, could go together. It has been suggested that capital flows were not one-way traffic. Both banks and non-bank firms deposited inactive balances abroad, whereas firms that were hit by domestic credit limits borrowed abroad (Cole and Slade, 1992a). A contributing factor was the credibility of the exchange-rate policy, with a fixed dollar exchange rate since 1971. Because of booming oil exports, the current account of the balance of payments did not suffer too badly from the fall in the real exchange rate that occurred as Indonesia still had double digit inflation until 1977. In 1978 the rupiah devalued, possibly with an eye to the increasing unemployment in the export industries, which had suffered from Dutch disease phenomena (Woo and Nasution, 1989, p. 26). The dollar link was replaced by a link with a basket made up of the currencies of the main trading partners. The 1978 devaluation came as quite a shock, but seems, if anything, to have stimulated foreign borrowing, because further steep devaluations were thought to be very unlikely. Non-oil exports reacted very positively to the devaluation and the government let the rupiah depreciate gradually vis-à-vis the currency basket.

One wonders why, with financial liberalisation and real interest rates shooting up, no massive capital inflows followed. One cause probably was the failure of the state oil company Pertamina to refinance $400 million short term debt, which prompted the government to require the state companies to ask permission from the ministry of finance and Bank Indonesia before borrowing abroad. Woo and Nasution (1989) see the Pertamina crisis as a blessing in disguise, as it may well have been a main factor in saving Indonesia from the fate that met Chile in the 1982 developing country debt crisis. Other contributing factors were the limits on foreign borrowing by banks and NBFIs and the fact that only very few non-financial firms were able to borrow abroad. The authorities had kept budget deficits small and there had been no runaway money growth through foreign borrowing. The exchange rate policy had prevented a serious over-valuation of the rupiah and exports were healthy enough to service the foreign debt when oil prices took a tumble in the early 1980s. Also, Indonesia was favourably placed compared with the Latin American countries in that she suffered much less from the dollar apprecia-tion, with only about one third of her debt being denominated in dollars against some 90 per cent for countries such as Mexico or Brazil (Woo and Nasution, 1989). Moreover, much of Indonesia's debt was on concessional terms. Nevertheless, in 1982 the current account ran into deficit to the tune of 6 per cent of GDP (Woo and Nasution, 1989) and capital outflows increased as a result of higher devaluation expectations. Finally, in March 1983 a 38 per cent devaluation was put through.

In 1989 the limits on foreign borrowing by banks were abolished, but as banks were too eager to borrow abroad new constraints were put in place; this time in the guise of a limit to the net foreign liabilities of a bank and a limit of 30 per cent of own capital for short term borrowing (Binhadi, 1993). Borrowers also had to queue. More or less free capital flows forced the authorities to follow credible policies. Fear of devaluations had led to speculative capital outflows in 1987 and 1991 and it was decided that henceforth no sizeable devaluations would take place. Since 1989 the exchange rate has been left to market forces, with Bank Indonesia intervening only to prevent sharp fluctuations (Van Herpt et al., 1994).

The large debt accumulation by Indonesia in the 1980s was to a large part a result of borrowing by the government itself. The political elite that took over after the Sukarno era, imposed a constitutional prohibition of domestic debt finance. The state therefore was dependent on foreign capital to finance its deficits, which averaged roughly 2.5 per cent of GNP over the 1970s and 1980s. The rulers acted out of fear of inflation, but one wonders if they did not realise that foreign-financed deficits swell the money supply as much as domestic credit from the banking sector. The idea probably was that foreign funds were mainly used for development projects with a high import

Table 12.5 Debt–service ratios for Indonesia, 1980–1992

Year	Ratio
1980	13.9
1981	14.1
1982	18.2
1983	20.2
1984	21.4
1985	28.8
1986	37.3
1987	37.0
1988	40.2
1989	35.4
1990	31.0
1991	32.6
1992	32.1

Source: *World Debt Tables 1989–1990*, Vol. 2, Washington DC: World Bank, 1989; and *World Debt Tables 1993–1994*, Vol. 2, Washington DC: World Bank, 1993

component. But the private sector also borrowed abroad, and the debt–service ratio shot up when Indonesia was hit in 1986 by a fall in oil prices and a depreciation of the dollar vis-à-vis the yen (Table 12.5). Exports were largely paid in dollars, whereas imports to a much greater extent were paid in yen and debt also to a large degree was yen-denominated. The current account deficit of 1982 was met by a devaluation, but at the same time by increasing protection. The 1986 near-crisis turned the tables in favour of the more free-trade oriented technocrats centred in the ministry of finance and Bank Indonesia. A 50 per cent devaluation combined with trade liberalisation helped non-oil exports to increase steeply over the next few years, reducing the debt–service ratio again.

The results of financial liberalisation

The liberalisation measures taken in 1983 and 1988 and after have had a great impact on the banking scene, just as finance minister J.B. Sumarlin had expected. His policy objective was to vitalise the commercial banks. Competition by these banks would force the state-owned banks to improve efficiency and the banking system as a whole would get rid of market imperfections. The number of national private banks doubled from 63 to 126 between 1988 and 1991. The branch network of those banks increased from 559 to 2,639, against a small rise from 815 to 960 for the five state banks and a jump from 21 to 53 for foreign banks and joint ventures (Bank Indonesia, 1992). Lending ballooned: whereas total lending rose by 109 per cent, the domestic commercial banks saw their lending soar by 290 per cent and the foreign banks and joint ventures by 345 per cent, which resulted in a fall of the state banks' market share from 65.1 per cent to 52.7 per cent (Bank Indonesia, 1992).

In the scramble for market share, the banks seem to have been less than prudent. As in Chile, huge sums were lent to finance real estate investment and to intra-conglomerate firms. Also, consumer credit rose sharply. Combined with an anti-inflationary restrictive monetary policy, high real interest rates have been the result. If the private banks became saddled with bad and non-performing loans as a result of this fast expansion plus high interest rates, the state banks got their fair share of troubles from politically-influenced credit allocation (the *katabelece* or memo system). The plight of the state banks was such that the World Bank had to provide a $307 million loan which the ministry of finance used to re-capitalise the state banks. It seems, however, that fifteen to twenty times this amount is needed to re-capitalise them fully, according to World Bank calculations (Sender, 1993a).

The private commercial banks were not unaffected either. In September 1990, the board of directors of Bank Duta was forced by Bank Indonesia to resign after it had become known that foreign exchange transactions had cost the bank $419.6 million, or twice its capital, in one year. There are signs of behind-the-scenes manoeuvring which put a big question mark over the levelness of the playing field and the public availability of information in Indonesian banking. First of all, the foreign exchange losses imply a level of foreign exchange transactions far in excess of official limits. Then, Bank Duta was back on its feet in a remarkably short time, after a large capital injection from large shareholders in the form of gifts, the source of which remains somewhat mysterious. It has been suggested that Bank Duta is at least politically strong (Soesastro and Drysdale, 1990). Another shock was the failure of Bank Summa in December 1992, as a result of real estate loans and loans to low-quality borrowers, in particular intra-conglomerate loans. The attempts by the Soeryadjaya family, the main owners of the Summa Group, of which Bank Summa formed part, to save Bank Summa, using the proceeds of the sale of healthier parts of the Summa Group came to grief (though in the end all depositors with a deposit below Rp 10 million were fully compensated). This sent quite a shock wave through the financial community, as it had always been thought that conglomerates were strong enough to save their banks if these landed in trouble.

Prudential supervision

In PAKTO 27, attention was also paid to prudential supervision, with limits to the volume of lending to any individual person, firm or conglomerate. Other measures followed. In March 1991, for example, prudential supervision was made more comprehensive, with, *inter alia*, bank directors having to meet professional standards, restrictions as to the number of relatives of shareholders on the board of directors, and on the loans to shareholders, limits to foreign exchange exposure and the adoption of the Basle Agreement risk-weighted capital–asset ratios foreseen for the end of 1993, later extended to 1994 (Parker, 1991).

All these measures look fine on paper, but it appears that something is lost in the execution. Rules can be circumvented, for example, by granting a loan from a bank's pension fund instead of by the bank itself, and apparently supervision often lacks bite, pointing to a lack of political power of the monetary authorities. This played a role when in mid-1992 the ministry of finance replaced all state bank presidents, with the exception of the president of Bank Bumi Daya, even if Bank Bumi Daya was one of the greatest problem banks (Sender, 1993a). Apparently in the Indonesian political culture it is well-nigh impossible to stamp out the *katabelece* system. One scandal follows another and finance minister Mar'ie Muhammad estimated the volume of non-performing loans at 21.2 per cent of the state banks' outstanding credit (McBeth, 1994).

Against this, the monetary authorities made it clear at the time of the Bank Summa debacle that they did not stand ready to rescue troubled banks or guarantee their debts (Sender, 1993b). Furthermore, under the new bank law of February 1992 insufficient information from the banks' side can be punished with two years in jail and/or a Rp 1 billion fine, and bank activities that are not allowed by the law carry the threat of a 15-year term in jail and/or a Rp 10 billion fine (McLeod, 1992). But even if such measures may help to reduce moral hazard problems and bring down the number of cases of violations of the law, other attempts at shoring up the financial system have been half-hearted. State banks, for example, may under the new banking law issue shares, provided the state retains a majority share. The state banks can in this way try to attract new capital, in order to meet the capital–asset ratios as prescribed by the BIS. Now state bank shares do not look like an attractive investment, given the prevalence of bad loans, and Bank Indonesia subsequently redefined the rules in such a way that the banks, principally the state banks, had less trouble meeting the capital–asset norms (McLeod, 1993).

Preliminary conclusions

Indonesia has not followed a straight course in its liberalisation attempts. Policies seem to have been the outcome of a tug-of-war between various groups, in particular the 'technocrats', including the 'Berkeley Mafia', who favour liberal policies, and the 'technicians', such as technology minister Habibie, who are backed by the army and want to develop high-tech industries, even if that requires stiff protection (cf. Woo and Nasution, 1989). In some markets – cars come to mind – high protection appears to have been the result of ordinary rent-seeking. Abrupt policy turnabouts on the scale that Chile experienced never took place in Indonesia. Its exchange rate policy was not used to restrain inflation, but in so far as it was deliberately used as a policy tool, it was deployed as a means to further non-oil exports, with remarkable success. An element of luck also seems to have been involved, especially as regards the 1982 debt crisis, which left Indonesia relatively little harmed as she happened to have stumbled into the right kind of restraints on capital inflows and had relatively little dollar-denominated debt. On the other side of the ledger, the financial system appears to be quite fragile, not because of deficient legislation but because of lax implementation of the law; good laws do not always make good supervision. Also, foreign debts might throw up problems as soon as export growth is interrupted for whatever reason, although, considering the development of the debt–service ratio, there is no need to start the alarm bells ringing unless a very large shock occurs.

It may be remarked that Indonesia did not follow the conventional wisdom on liberalisation in that the capital account was liberalised before the current account. Capital liberalisation, however, did not amount to full freedom, there was no hands-off policy and the authorities intervened whenever things might get out of hand. Also, the ruling elite was not, and is not, unanimous on the merits of current account liberalisation. Anyhow, high oil export revenues enabled the authorities to liberalise the capital account substantially before the current account. Foreign exchange crises have been avoided, at least in part, by following a prudent exchange rate policy, i.e. by preventing a substantial real appreciation of the currency. With relatively low inflation, positive real interest rates and generally little fear of sharp devaluations, domestic financial assets have remained attractive and wealth holders have had little reason to resort to capital flight. Financial liberalisation combined with restrictive macroeconomic policies have led to very high real interest rates, but the situation might have been worse had not the authorities waited five years after the 1983 liberalisation to remove entry restrictions into the banking industry. This gave banks some breathing space in which to adjust their portfolios and prepare their personnel for a more market-oriented way of operating (see Caprio *et al.*, 1993).

WHAT CAN WE LEARN FROM A COMPARISON?

At first sight, Indonesia seems to have put the cart before the horse in liberalising its capital account before its current account. But there was no quasi-unrestricted freedom as in Chile in 1979–1982. So both the Chilean and the Indonesian experience with liberalisation seem to suggest that full freedom of capital flows is something that should not be a government's first priority: at least the authorities should monitor the capital account carefully. Free capital inflows in times of a domestic boom can all too easily be used to finance real estate investments which push up the relative price of non-tradeables and leave the country without enough means to service its debt once capital imports dry up. A relatively free capital account is possible if a country does not suffer from serious macroeconomic instability. In particular, exchange rate policy and domestic inflation should not conflict.

This brings us to another lesson, that a liberalising country should not use the exchange rate as the main weapon in the fight against inflation, except perhaps for short periods (though it should be conceded that Argentina has been remarkably successful so far; macroeconomic policies, and micro-economic policies as well, have been fully geared to defend the exchange rate, although over-valuation and current account deficits make one wonder how long they will be able to hold out). Both Chile after 1982 and Indonesia provide convincing evidence that inflation can be fought effectively through restrictive domestic macroeconomic policies and that it is possible to engineer a real depreciation. In other words, it is possible to depreciate the domestic currency without provoking a corresponding inflation (for a more positive appraisal of exchange rate-based stabilisations, see Kiguel and Liviatan, 1994).

A common experience has been financial fragility after financial liberal-isation. Apparently markets are far from perfect, and prudential supervision is of the essence. The main problems seem to lie not in devising appropriate laws and regulations, but in implementing them. Also, it may take time to develop the necessary human capital in the banking industry. Furthermore there appears to be a largely un-met need for risk management systems (Caprio et al., 1993). A capital mistake in the Chilean case was the de facto full deposit guarantee provided by the government. The Indonesian govern-ment may have sent the right signals to the market in the nick of time, but the memo system, or old school tie network, is still prevalent. Presumably private banks can more easily resist this kind of pressure than state banks: at least it is easier for the government to deny private banks an implicit full deposit guarantee and thus subject them to the discipline of the market. A deposit guarantee system with premiums geared to the riskiness of a bank's assets would be a good thing.

McKinnon's advocacy of financial liberalisation has been generally accepted, but full liberalisation in one fell swoop may rock the boat too severely, as McKinnon himself acknowledges. High real interest rates lead to adverse selection; low-risk borrowers are driven from the market. If the solvability of the financial sector and non-financial firms is weak to start with, severe shocks can be very dangerous. The financial system may well be the weak spot in any economic transition or regime change, and it should be given a number of years to adjust itself. Indonesia was wise in waiting for five years after liberalising interest rates before it liberalised entry into the banking industry. This may have been one factor in preventing real interest rates rising as high as in Chile. Preventing severe shocks to the financial sector probably is more important than the sequencing of liberalisation. Liberalisation of the capital account before liberalisation of the current account proves to be quite possible, provided a strong real appreciation can be prevented.

When comparing Chile and Indonesia, one thing that strikes the eye is the dogmatic hands-off policy followed by the Chicago economists. To let the market sort things out is irresponsible when it is clear to everybody that the exchange rate policy is bound to founder and that the financial industry is heading for trouble. A government should send unambiguous signals to the market, but it must be flexible enough to adjust its policies if economic indicators take a wrong turn.

Finally, a very general lesson may be that after a severe shock, such as the transition in Chile from the chaotic government interference under the Unidad Popular government (see Visser, 1980) to an extreme free market economy, and even more after a transition from a socialist economy to a market economy, complacency as to the stability of the financial system is completely out of place.

NOTES

1 Note that the figure for exports/GDP for 1982 is missing, which gives the (probably wrong) impression that the curve already starts rising sharply in 1982.

2 The Real Exchange Rate (RER) of Indonesia in Figure 12.2 was calculated as follows. Only trade with the main trade partners, Japan, the USA and Singapore was considered. From imports from and exports to these countries in 1970, 1975, 1980, 1985 and 1990 average trade weights were calculated, summing to 1, which then were applied to the GDP deflators to calculate the average inflation rate of Indonesia's trade partners. From the nominal exchange rate and the Indonesian GDP deflator the RER follows.

REFERENCES

Bank Indonesia (1992), *Indonesian Financial Statistics*, 25 (3), Jakarta: Bank Indonesia.

Binhadi (1990), 'Monetary Policy in Indonesia', paper presented at the 18th SEANZA Central Bank Course, The Indira Gandhi Institute of Development Research, Bombay, 30 November.

—— (1993), 'Deregulation of the Foreign Exchange Market in Indonesia', paper presented at a Seminar on Liberalization of the Foreign Exchange Market in the Asian Countries, Central Bank of the Philippines, 14–15 January.

Booth, A. (1992), 'Introduction', in A. Booth (ed.) *The Oil Boom and After; Indonesian Economic Policy and Performance in the Soeharto Era*, Singapore: Oxford University Press, pp. 1–38.

Caprio, G., I. Atiyas and J.A. Hanson (1993), 'Financial Reform: Lessons and Strategies', in S. Faruqi (ed.) *Financial Sector Reforms in Asian and Latin American Countries*, Washington, DC: World Bank, pp. 67–92.

Cole, D.C. and B.F. Slade (1992a), 'Financial Development in Indonesia', in A. Booth (ed.) *The Oil Boom and After; Indonesian Economic Policy and Performance in the Soeharto Era*, Singapore: Oxford University Press, pp. 77–101.

—— (1992b), 'Indonesian Financial Development: A Different Sequencing?', in D. Vittas (ed.) *Financial Regulation: Changing the Rules of the Game*, Washington, DC: World Bank, pp. 121–61.

Corbo, V. (1985), 'Reforms and Macroeconomic Adjustments in Chile during 1974–84', *World Development*, 13, pp. 893–916.

Corbo, V. and J. De Melo (1987), 'Lessons from the Southern Cone Policy Reforms', *World Bank Research Observer*, 2, pp. 111–42.

Corbo, V. and J.M. Sanchez (1985), 'Adjustments by Industrial Firms in Chile During 1974–82', in V. Corbo and J. De Melo (eds) *Scrambling for Survival; How Firms Adjusted to the Recent Reforms in Argentina, Chile, and Uruguay*, Working Paper, No. 764, World Bank, pp. 83–117.

Cox Edwards, A. and S. Edwards (1992), 'Markets and Democracy: Lessons from Chile', *The World Economy*, 15, pp. 203–19.

Edwards, S. (1986), 'Stabilization with Liberalization: An Evaluation of Ten Years of Chile's Experience with Free Market Policies, 1973–1983', in A.M. Choksi and D. Papageorgiou (eds), *Economic Liberalization in Developing Countries*, Oxford: Basil Blackwell, pp. 241–71.

—— (1990), 'The Sequencing of Economic Reform: Analytical Issues and Lessons from Latin American Experiences', *The World Economy*, 13, pp. 1–14.

Edwards, S. and A. Cox Edwards (1987), *Monetarism and Liberalization; The Chilean Experiment*, Cambridge, Mass.: Ballinger.

Euromoney (1978), 'Chile – A Survey', Supplement to *Euromoney*, July.

Eyzaguirre, N.G. (1993), 'Financial Crisis, Reform and Stabilization: the Chilean Experience', in S. Faruqi (ed.) *Financial Sector Reforms in Asian and Latin American Countries*, Washington DC: World Bank, pp. 127–46.

Galvéz, J. and J. Tybout (1985), 'Microeconomic Adjustments in Chile during 1977–81: The Importance of Being a *Grupo*', *World Development*, 13, pp. 969–94.

Hanna, D.P. (1994), *Indonesian Experience with Financial Sector Reform*, World Bank Discussion Paper, No. 237, World Bank.

Hanson, J. (1986), 'What Went Wrong in Chile?', in A.M. Choksi and D. Papageorgiou (eds) *Economic Liberalization in Developing Countries*, Oxford: Basil Blackwell, pp. 227–32.

Harberger, A.C. (1986), 'A Primer on the Chilean Economy, 1973–1983', in A.M. Choksi and D. Papageorgiou (eds) *Economic Liberalization in Developing Countries*, Oxford: Basil Blackwell, pp. 233–40.

Held, G. (1990), 'Regulación y supervisión de la banca en la experiencia de liberalización financiera en Chile (1974–1988)', in C. Massad and G. Held (eds) *Sistema financiero y asignación de recursos; Experiencias latinoamericanas y del Caribe*, Buenos Aires: Grupo Editor Latinoamericano for CEPAL/PNUD, pp. 171–263.

International Monetary Fund (IMF) (1981), 'Chile's Economic Recovery Reflects a Merging Of Both Demand- and Supply-Oriented Policies', *IMF Survey*, 10, pp. 338–40.

Kiguel, M.A. and N. Liviatan (1994), 'Exchange-Rate-Based Stabilizations in Argentina and Chile: A Fresh Look', in T.J.T. Baliño en C. Cottarelli (eds) *Frameworks for Monetary Stability*, Washington: IMF, pp. 174–75.

McBeth, J. (1994), 'Banking on Friends', *Far Eastern Economic Review*, 157 (25), pp. 25–26.

McKinnon, R.I. (1973), *Money and Capital in Economic Development*, Washington, DC: The Brookings Institution.

—— (1988), 'Financial Liberalization in Retrospect: Interest Rate Policies in LDCs', in G. Ranis and T.P. Schultz (eds) *The State of Development Economics*, Oxford: Basil Blackwell, pp. 386–415.

—— (1992), *The Order of Economic Liberalization*, Baltimore: The Johns Hopkins University Press.

McLeod, R.H. (1992), 'Indonesia's New Banking Law', *Bulletin of Indonesian Economic Studies*, 28 (3), pp. 107–22.

—— (1993), 'Survey of Recent Developments', *Bulletin of Indonesian Economic Studies*, 29 (2), pp. 3–42.

Marfán, M. and B.P. Bosworth (1994), 'Saving, Investment and Economic Growth', in B.P. Bosworth, R. Dornbusch and R. Labán (eds) *The Chilean Economy*, Washington DC: The Brookings Institution, p. 213.

Meller, P. (1992), *Adjustment and Equity in Chile*, Paris: OECD.

Mirakhor, A. and D. Villanueva (1993), 'Interest Rate Policies in Developing Countries', *Finance and Development*, 30 (4), pp. 31–33.

Parker, S. (1991), 'Survey of Recent Developments', *Bulletin of Indonesian Economic Studies*, 27 (1), pp. 3–38.

Ramírez-Villadell, G. (1991), 'Evaluación y clasificación de activos: La experiencia Chilena', in G. Held and R. Szalachman (eds) *Regulación y supervisión de la Banca; Experiencias en América Latina y el Caribe*, Santiago: RSV Impresa for CEPAL/PNUD, pp. 111–67.

Sabirin, S. (1993), 'Capital Account Liberalization: The Indonesian Experience', in S. Faruqi (ed.) *Financial Sector Reforms in Asian and Latin American Countries*, Washington DC: World Bank, pp. 147–61.

Sender, H. (1993a), 'Unhealthy States', *Far Eastern Economic Review*, 156 (13), pp. 75–76.

—— (1993b), 'The Morning After', *Far Eastern Economic Review*, 156 (13), p. 77.

Soesastro, M.H. and P. Drysdale (1990), 'Survey of Recent Developments', *Bulletin of Indonesian Economic Studies*, 26 (3), pp. 3–44.

Stiglitz, J.E. and A. Weiss (1981), 'Credit Rationing in Markets with Imperfect Information', *American Economic Review*, 71, pp. 393–410.

Sundararajan, V. and L. Molho (1988), 'Financial Reform in Indonesia', *Finance and Development*, 25 (4), pp. 43–45.

Trebat, T.J. (1991), 'The Banking System Crisis in Latin America', *Contemporary Policy Issues*, 9, pp. 54–66.

Van Herpt, I.R.Y., C.A.M. Ruhe and H. Visser (1994), 'Liberalisering in Indonesië', *Economisch Statistische Berichten*, 79, pp. 149–53.

Velasco, A. (1991), 'Liberalization, Crisis, Intervention: The Chilean Financial System, 1975–85', in V. Sundararajan and T.J.T. Baliño (eds) *Banking Crises: Cases and Issues*, Washington DC: IMF, pp. 113–74.

Villanueva, D. and A. Mirakhor (1990), 'Strategies for Financial Reforms', *IMF Staff Papers*, 37, pp. 509–36.

Visser, H. (1980), 'Allende, een mythe', *Intermediair*, 16 (44), pp. 13–25.

—— (1993), 'The Exchange Rate as an Export-Stimulation Mechanism', paper presented at the CEDLA-CEPAL conference 'Towards a New Insertion of Latin America in the World Economy', Amsterdam, 12–13 July 1993. To be published in R. Buitelaar and P. van Dijck (eds) *Latin America's New Insertion in the World Economy:Towards Systemic Competitiveness in Small Economies*, New York: St Martin's Press, 1996.

Woo, W.T. and A. Nasution (1989), 'Indonesian Economic Policies and their Relation to External Debt Management', in J.D. Sachs and S.M. Collins (eds) *Developing Country Debt and Economic Performance*, Vol. 3, Chicago: Chicago University Press, pp. 17–149.

World Bank (1989), *World Debt Tables 1989–90*, Vol. 2, Washington DC: World Bank.

13

FINANCIAL REFORM AND FINANCIAL INTERMEDIATION IN CHILE, 1983–1992[1]

Niels Hermes

INTRODUCTION

Chile experienced a deep economic and financial crisis during the early 1980s. These crises had a significant adverse impact on the Chilean economy. In reaction to the crisis, the Chilean government introduced a series of reforms to regain the dynamic process of economic growth before the crisis set in. They recognised that the policy failures made with respect to the liberalisation programme of the 1970s were at least partly responsible for the economic downturn. This especially referred to the exchange rate policies and the financial liberalisation programme.[2] With respect to the latter the government undertook several measures to enhance the process of financial intermediation during the early 1980s to improve resource mobilisation, the efficiency of investment and, ultimately, also economic growth. Important elements were the re-regulations of the banking sector, which aimed at contributing to increased financial stability and to reducing market imperfections based on monitoring and screening problems and asymmetric information. The process of the strengthening of the banking system culminated in the presentation of the new banking law in 1986, which was directed towards improving the framework of prudential regulation. The new banking law was introduced as a reaction to the adverse experiences with weak regulation during the 1970s and early 1980s.

This chapter investigates the impact of the financial reforms directed at strengthening the regulation of the banking system on capital structure and investment choices of the Chilean business sector during 1983–1992. It aims at evaluating whether the reforms have contributed to reducing market imperfections in financial markets. Additionally, it describes the relationship between the reforms and the efficiency of resource allocation through financial intermediation. The analysis uses micro data on balance sheets and income statements of some 200 Chilean firms.

The chapter is organised as follows. The first section reviews the main financial reforms in Chile during the 1980s. The following section describes the changes in financial structures of firms during this period. The third section presents an econometric investigation of the relationship between the financial reforms and the investment decisions of firms. The fourth section then goes on to analyse the relationship between the reforms and efficiency of investment, and is followed by a section which provides concluding remarks.

FINANCIAL REFORM IN CHILE DURING THE 1980S: A BRIEF SURVEY[3]

The 1980s and early 1990s have been quite hectic for the Chilean economy. During the 1981–1983 period it went through a deep economic and financial crisis. The economy experienced the most severe recession since the 1930s. GDP fell by 15 per cent during 1982–1983 and the official unemployment rate rose to 20 per cent in 1982. During the next two years, the economy slowly recovered. During these years, the government implemented several structural reforms to stabilise and reform the economy. The reforms specifically aimed at stimulating and diversifying exports, reducing the outstanding external debt, and increasing domestic resource mobilisation. From 1986, economic growth resumed and remained fairly strong for the next seven years (see Table 13.1). Both saving and investment fell sharply during the first half of the 1980s, but they recovered after 1986.

For the financial sector the 1982–1984 period was especially critical. Financial markets collapsed and the central bank had to intervene to forestall a total financial breakdown. Weak prudential regulation seems to have been a primary factor in triggering the financial crisis (Visser and van Herpt, 1996). In early 1983 the central bank liquidated 14 financial intermediaries, while five others were technically taken over, among them the two largest banks in the country. The loan portfolio of the intervened institutions represented 60 per cent of all loans issued by the financial system (Larraín, 1989, p. 1). Later on, in 1987, these banks were returned to the public sector. To reduce the confidence crisis, the government issued an explicit deposit insurance on deposits held at insolvent intermediaries. The experiences related to the severe financial crisis led the monetary authorities to introduce a new banking law in 1986, which was to prevent the financial sector from collapsing in the future. This new banking law was preceded by several financial reforms during 1981–1985 which were directed at strengthening the regulatory system.

The following brief overview can be drafted, of important financial reforms, implemented by the monetary authorities and related to strengthening the regulatory system during the 1981–1992 period (Walker and Hernández, 1992).

- March 1981: limits on transactions with related individuals or parties; transactions with these individuals and parties have to be notified;

Table 13.1 Macroeconomic developments, average annual growth rates[1]

Year	GDP growth	National saving[1]	Total investment	Unemployment[2]	Trade balance[3]	External debt[4]
1980	7.8	13.9	21.0	10.4	–4.2	12.1
1981	5.5	8.2	22.7	11.3	–10.3	15.7
1982	–14.1	2.2	11.3	19.6	–1.9	17.3
1983	–0.7	4.2	9.8	14.6	2.7	17.9
1984	6.3	2.6	13.6	13.9	–1.1	19.7
1985	2.4	5.4	13.7	12.0	2.8	20.4
1986	5.7	7.8	14.6	8.8	3.8	21.1
1987	5.7	12.6	16.9	7.9	4.1	21.5
1988	7.4	16.2	17.0	6.3	7.2	19.6
1989	10.0	18.0	20.4	5.3	3.6	18.0
1990	2.1	17.5	20.2	5.7	2.9	19.2
1991	6.0	19.0	18.8	5.5	4.9	17.9
1992	10.4	19.6	21.3	4.5	2.1	19.1

Sources: Hermes (1995), tables IIa, IIb and III; Corbo and Fischer (1994), table 1-1; World Bank (1995)
Notes:
[1] Private plus public saving to GDP ratio
[2] Per cent of labour force
[3] Per cent of GDP
[4] Billions of US dollars

- April 1981: loan classification system (introduced in February 1980) extended to the 300 largest debtors;
- August 1981: new law forcing diversification of bank portfolios by changing the definition of an individual borrower;
- December 1981: instalment of loan loss reserves equivalent of 0.75 per cent of loans outstanding;
- February 1982: loan classification system extended to 400 largest debtors; loan loss provisions related to the risk classification scheme;
- November 1986: new banking law specifying new measures for disclosing information by banks on their financial situation; the obligation to publish this information in a regular newspaper; rules dictating diversification of portfolios; measures to privatise the costs of bankruptcy of banks, *de facto* leading to a removal of the explicit government guaranteed deposit insurance (except for small deposit holders) and measures defining a bank closing procedure. The banking law was further modified in May 1988 and August 1989.

The measures implemented before 1982 basically aimed at reducing the possibilities of intra-conglomerate lending. Until the early 1980s, large conglomerates – the so-called *grupos* in which close property ties existed between firms and banks – dominated the domestic economy. The substantial amount of intra-*grupo* lending during the 1970s was held responsible, at least to a large extent, for the growing financial instability during the early 1980s. The measures implemented in the first few years of the 1980s prohibited banks from being the financial heart of the *grupos*, a position they had obtained in the course of the 1970s. The new banking law of 1986 went further and explicitly developed a regulatory system, in which banks were obliged to act risk-averse and in which the public was stimulated to monitor bank behaviour closely. The fundamental objective behind these measures was to improve the process of financial intermediation by improving the quality of bank management and by increasing the confidence of the public in the system. A safer banking system enhances resource mobilisation; it increases the volume of resources available for investment; better monitoring and screening by the management of the bank improves the quality of investment financed; and through higher and more efficient investment, it also raises economic growth.

Note that the government not only took measures related to the banking system, however. It also issued reforms with respect to other parts of the financial sector. Among other things, the pension fund system was privatised in 1981. This gave an important stimulus to trading in financial assets. Moreover, reforms were implemented to increase trading on the stock exchange. Stock trading was furthermore stimulated by the privatisation scheme the government carried out after 1986, as well as by the introduction of the debt–equity swap programme to reduce the country's external debt. While these measures and reforms were important in themselves, their effects on the Chilean business sector are not a central theme of the analysis in this chapter.

The remainder of this chapter investigates the impact of the financial reforms related to strengthening the regulation of the banking system on the financial decision making of firms during the 1980s and early 1990s. It is contended that these financial reforms should have reduced market imperfections in the financial sector and that the provision of financial intermediation should have become more efficient, at least after 1986. This may expose itself mainly through more efficient investment by firms, and decreased segmentation of access to loans by different groups of firms. By looking at changes in financial patterns of firms in the 1983–1992 period, indirect evidence may be provided with respect to whether or not these expected effects have taken place. In particular, the hypothesis tested empirically is that *before* the reforms banks were less able to screen and monitor the projects with the highest expected rate of return, due to externalities related to screening or monitoring borrowers; and that they were restricting their lending activities to particular groups of borrowers and rationed other groups, because of asymmetric information. *After* the reforms of 1986, inefficient financial intermediation may have been reduced. It must be acknowledged that the analysis takes a partial approach, as the influence of other macroeconomic changes and policies on the financial decisions of firms is not directly taken into account. It may, nevertheless, be interesting to investigate the impact of financial reforms on the process of financial intermediation.

THE EFFECTS OF FINANCIAL REFORMS ON CHILEAN FIRMS

In order to be able to evaluate the effects of the financial reforms on the real sector, this section describes the changes in financial variables for a sample of over 200 Chilean firms. The data are provided by the *Superintendencia de Valores y Seguros* (SVS), a government agency that collects information on balance sheets and income statements of a large set of Chilean limited liability companies (*sociedades anónimas*). These firms have to report their financial statement every three months. Data are available for a set of on average 250–300 firms for the 1980–1992 period. For the purpose of the analysis in this chapter, data of non-financial privately owned firms have been used. Firms have been eliminated from the sample when they present information for less than three (not necessarily consecutive) years, when they report zero capital stock and negative values of the stock of equity plus retained profits, and when they are in a state of liquidation.[4] This leaves a sample of time series data for 204 firms.

Below, key statistics on financial variables are presented for different sub-samples of firms in order to investigate whether changes in these variables have occurred for different categories of firms. The sub-samples have been based on criteria of size and age of firms. These criteria have been chosen because looking at variables for firms of different size and age may incorporate information on the presence of market imperfections in financial markets based on information problems. Both the size and age criteria may be useful for identifying firms that have different degrees of problems with communicating private information to financial intermediaries and/or investors. Stated otherwise, these criteria may identify firms for which banks and investors have different problems in monitoring and screening their behaviour. Banks and investors may have fewer difficulties in screening and monitoring the behaviour of larger firms, since the monitoring and screening costs related to lending or investing in these firms are lower per unit of capital due to the fixed cost character of information and due to the fact that the volume of lending to and investing in these firms will generally be larger. Moreover, larger firms generally have more possibilities to provide collateral. Older firms may have fewer problems in communicating private information, since lenders and investors have had longer time to obtain information on their creditworthiness, and since older firms may have shown themselves to be creditworthy and able and willing to pay back their obligations in the past (Chirinko and Schaller, 1995, p. 529). Thus, based on informational difficulties, small and young firms are more likely to be faced by financial constraints. The size sub-samples have been obtained by dividing the total sample of firms in two groups containing an equal number of firms, based on net assets (i.e. total assets minus liquid liabilities) in constant 1985 prices. The age sub-samples have been obtained by classifying firms born less than 21 years ago as being young, whereas firms of 21 years or older have been classified as old.[5]

Table 13.2 shows summary data on key financial variables of firms. The table presents unweighted averages of ratios on the debt structure of all firms in the sample. These ratios include the debt to asset ratio, along with various ratios of components of short and long term debt. All ratios have been scaled by total debt (except for the debt to asset ratio). Short term as well as long term debts have been subdivided into bank loans, loans from related firms and other forms of debt. Other short term debt mainly consists of trade credit. Long term bank loans include long term bank loans falling due within one year. Long term debt includes direct finance from bond issues.

The following patterns emerge from this table. First, it appears that firms generally have reduced their levels of indebtedness. In particular, they have reduced shares of long term debt – and especially bank loans – to total debt. Second, firms have reduced their reliance on direct external finance through corporate bonds. Third, they have increasingly relied on short term bank loans, trade credit and long term debt from related firms. The volume of financial intermediation through intermediaries seems to have been reduced during the 1980s and 1990s. Moreover, short term finance as a share of total indebtedness has increased at the cost of long term finance.

These patterns of change may be related to the financial reforms of the 1980s. First, the reduced volumes of intermediation may simply point out that intermediaries have adjusted their activities from the extremely high levels during the early 1980s to *equilibrium levels*. Moreover, the patterns of change presented in Table 13.2 may also reflect the severity of the financial crisis, which forced intermediaries to reduce their overall levels of intermediation, thus leading to reduced debt to asset ratios for firms. Second, banks seem to have become more risk-averse by shifting from long term to short term finance. Third, while equity markets were growing steadily during the 1980s and early 1990s due to various institutional reforms, the importance of new equity issues as a source of finance did not seem to arise, at least not for the firms in this sample. Finally, the reduction of the share of bond financing may point out that the deepening of financial markets did not really lead to diversification of firm finance. External financing consisted mainly of traditional sources of bank debt and trade credit.

Tables 13.3 and 13.4 present unweighted averages of ratios describing the debt structure of sub-samples based on firm size and on their age, respectively. The following patterns emerge from Table 13.3. When looking at the debt to asset ratio, small firms are more indebted than large firms. The differences

Table 13.2 Debt structure of all firms in the sample (ratios, divided by total debt, unless stated otherwise)

	1983	1984	1985	1986	1987	1988	1989	1990	1991	1992
Debt to asset ratio	0.402	0.341	0.383	0.386	0.356	0.343	0.341	0.329	0.316	0.327
Short term	0.476	0.631	0.545	0.550	0.607	0.625	0.631	0.592	0.586	0.587
Short term bank	0.097	0.154	0.135	0.111	0.141	0.140	0.154	0.128	0.127	0.139
Short term related	0.086	0.097	0.082	0.080	0.065	0.094	0.097	0.058	0.053	0.059
Other short term	0.293	0.380	0.328	0.359	0.401	0.391	0.380	0.406	0.406	0.389
Long term	0.524	0.370	0.455	0.406	0.394	0.376	0.370	0.408	0.415	0.413
Long term bank	0.334	0.197	0.269	0.285	0.246	0.216	0.197	0.203	0.190	0.199
Long term related	0.012	0.050	0.010	0.008	0.021	0.048	0.050	0.076	0.099	0.101
Corporate bonds	0.079	0.023	0.069	0.049	0.040	0.023	0.023	0.026	0.025	0.017
Other long term	0.099	0.100	0.107	0.108	0.087	0.089	0.100	0.103	0.101	0.096

between ratios are relatively small at the beginning of the period, but after 1987 they become more substantial. This is due to the fact that large firms substantially reduce their indebtedness as compared to small firms. The indebtedness of small firms remains relatively unchanged. In general, the composition of debt seems to differ for small and large firms. In most cases, these differences are not reduced substantially over time. Related to this, the patterns of change for some of the more important categories are basically the same. With respect to the composition of debt, the table reveals that small firms have higher ratios of short term debt, and that other short term debt especially – mainly trade credit – is important. Large firms generally have higher ratios of long term debt, of which bank loans are the most important component. With respect to patterns of change of debt categories during the 1983–1992 period, the shares of short term debt, short term bank loans and other short term debt increase for both small and large firms. Long term debt, and especially bank loans, fall for both sub-samples. However, since the fall of bank loan ratios is more dramatic for large firms, these ratios seem to converge slowly over time. Long term debt from related firms rises. This rise is especially pronounced for large firms. Corporate bonds become small as a source of finance for both small and large firms.

Table 13.4 shows data for sub-samples of firms based on age. The table provides the following picture. Old firms have higher debt to asset ratios as compared to young firms, yet the differences between the ratios for the two groups decrease over time, due to falling indebtedness of old firms. The indebtedness of young firms remains relatively the same. The shares of short and long term debt show great similarity for both young and old firms. Short term debt is more important for both sub-samples in most years. The composition of both debt categories diverges significantly at the beginning, but converges towards the end of the period. Young firms have significantly lower shares of short term bank debt and other short term debt, at least until 1988 and 1986, respectively. The share of short term debt to related firms drops significantly for young firms after 1988, whereas for old firms this ratio remains at relatively low levels during the entire period. With respect to long term debt, old firms experience a significant drop in the share of long term bank loans, whereas for young firms this ratio does not change significantly. The drop in long term bank loans is the basic source for the falling debt to asset ratio observed for the old firms. The share of corporate bonds converges for both age groups, due to a significant drop in the shares of young firms.

Table 13.5 provides information on the average values of ratios of equity and retained profits to total assets for sub-samples of firms for the 1983–1987 and 1988–1992 periods. The table shows that equity is more important for both small and young firms and that the equity ratios show little change over time. In contrast, the retained profits to asset ratios are higher for large and old firms. The differences between these ratios for small and young firms on

Table 13.3 Debt structure of firms, size samples (ratios, divided by total debt, unless stated otherwise)

		1983	1984	1985	1986	1987	1988	1989	1990	1991	1992
Debt asset ratio	small	0.399	0.431	0.405	0.393	0.386	0.387	0.390	0.355	0.348	0.371
	large	0.405	0.399	0.362	0.378	0.325	0.299	0.292	0.303	0.284	0.283
Short term	small	0.572	0.602	0.614	0.624	0.686	0.709	0.702	0.697	0.713	0.693
	large	0.380	0.427	0.477	0.475	0.526	0.541	0.559	0.487	0.458	0.478
Short term bank	small	0.119	0.126	0.146	0.109	0.181	0.185	0.164	0.153	0.175	0.176
	large	0.075	0.114	0.125	0.114	0.100	0.094	0.143	0.103	0.079	0.102
Short term related	small	0.090	0.081	0.064	0.100	0.067	0.101	0.112	0.061	0.061	0.066
	large	0.082	0.100	0.100	0.060	0.063	0.087	0.083	0.056	0.045	0.051
Other short term	small	0.363	0.395	0.404	0.415	0.438	0.423	0.426	0.483	0.477	0.451
	large	0.223	0.213	0.252	0.301	0.363	0.360	0.333	0.328	0.334	0.325
Long term	small	0.396	0.354	0.361	0.332	0.273	0.268	0.266	0.267	0.254	0.262
	large	0.562	0.493	0.457	0.482	0.432	0.412	0.396	0.465	0.496	0.473
Long term bank	small	0.428	0.399	0.385	0.376	0.314	0.292	0.298	0.303	0.287	0.308
	large	0.620	0.574	0.524	0.526	0.459	0.459	0.441	0.513	0.542	0.523
Long term related	small	0.005	0.006	0.006	0.000	0.004	0.020	0.020	0.045	0.050	0.054
	large	0.019	0.021	0.014	0.017	0.039	0.076	0.080	0.106	0.148	0.149
Corporate bonds	small	0.046	0.019	0.049	0.051	0.038	0.021	0.020	0.013	0.013	0.016
	large	0.112	0.082	0.089	0.046	0.042	0.024	0.026	0.039	0.036	0.019
Other long term	small	0.106	0.084	0.097	0.078	0.067	0.074	0.079	0.080	0.074	0.064
	large	0.092	0.105	0.117	0.139	0.106	0.105	0.121	0.127	0.128	0.130

Table 13.4 Debt structure of firms, age samples (ratios, divided by total debt, unless stated otherwise)

		1983	1984	1985	1986	1987	1988	1989	1990	1991	1992
Debt asset ratio	young	0.304	0.353	0.288	0.306	0.304	0.295	0.336	0.306	0.293	0.325
	old	0.438	0.435	0.421	0.414	0.376	0.365	0.343	0.342	0.328	0.328
Short term	young	0.476	0.515	0.478	0.562	0.608	0.636	0.579	0.607	0.601	0.561
	old	0.477	0.515	0.569	0.545	0.606	0.620	0.649	0.583	0.579	0.597
Short term bank	young	0.059	0.057	0.068	0.072	0.095	0.077	0.130	0.092	0.138	0.119
	old	0.111	0.141	0.162	0.125	0.159	0.168	0.162	0.147	0.122	0.147
Short term related	young	0.175	0.251	0.172	0.173	0.108	0.157	0.046	0.055	0.036	0.061
	old	0.054	0.038	0.047	0.047	0.048	0.065	0.116	0.060	0.061	0.058
Other short term	young	0.242	0.207	0.247	0.317	0.405	0.402	0.403	0.460	0.427	0.381
	old	0.312	0.336	0.360	0.373	0.399	0.387	0.371	0.376	0.396	0.392
Long term	young	0.524	0.484	0.514	0.438	0.391	0.365	0.422	0.393	0.400	0.439
	old	0.522	0.486	0.433	0.456	0.394	0.380	0.351	0.417	0.421	0.403
Long term bank	young	0.185	0.200	0.162	0.162	0.182	0.135	0.173	0.151	0.143	0.180
	old	0.388	0.369	0.310	0.330	0.271	0.252	0.205	0.231	0.212	0.208
Long term related	young	0.011	0.027	0.019	0.024	0.040	0.083	0.093	0.074	0.089	0.106
	old	0.012	0.009	0.007	0.003	0.014	0.032	0.035	0.077	0.103	0.098
Corporate bonds	young	0.194	0.118	0.209	0.120	0.069	0.023	0.045	0.033	0.029	0.027
	old	0.036	0.028	0.015	0.023	0.028	0.022	0.015	0.023	0.023	0.013
Other long term	young	0.134	0.139	0.124	0.132	0.100	0.124	0.111	0.135	0.139	0.126
	old	0.086	0.080	0.101	0.100	0.081	0.074	0.096	0.086	0.083	0.084

Table 13.5 Equity and retained profits ratios (divided by total assets)

		1983–1987	1988–1992
Equity	small	0.434	0.415
	large	0.372	0.359
Retained profits	small	0.163	0.214
	large	0.254	0.349
Equity	young	0.497	0.470
	old	0.369	0.346
Retained profits	young	0.192	0.219
	old	0.214	0.313

the one hand and for large and old firms on the other hand rise substantially during the 1983–1992 period. Annual data reveal that these differences become really large after 1987.

Next, these patterns of change in the debt structures of different groups of firms may be related to the financial reforms. As is made clear above, one may expect that, in general, banks and investors have more problems in monitoring and screening the behaviour of small and young firms as compared to large and old firms. If this is indeed the case, then one may expect to find that:

- debt to asset ratios are higher for large and old firms, indicating the difficulties small and young firms have in obtaining funds from financial intermediaries;
- short term debt is more important for small and young firms, indicating the fact that if intermediaries have decided to lend to these firms, they want to reduce the risk of non-repayment – which is more difficult to monitor for small and young firms – by shortening maturities;
- bank debt (and especially long term bank debt) is more important for large and old firms; trade credit is more important for small and young firms, which are additional indications for the monitoring and screening problems discussed with respect to debt to asset ratios and short term debt;
- equity to asset ratios are higher for small and young firms, indicating the fact that due to monitoring and screening problems of financial intermediaries, these firms have to resort more often to (more expensive) direct finance.

Moreover, if the financial reforms of the 1980s contributed positively to reducing these monitoring and screening problems, then the differences in debt structures should have reduced, at least from the late 1980s or early 1990s. These expectations are mainly based on assumptions of how bank behaviour may change after the reforms.

Beginning with the expected patterns of indebtedness: these seem to be confirmed only partially by the data. First, as discussed above, small firms have higher debt to asset ratios, in contrast with what might be expected. Second, short term debt is indeed more important for small firms, as was expected. There seems to be no difference between ratios for young and old firms, however. Third, long term bank debt is indeed more important for both large and old firms, again in accordance with what has been hypothesised. Fourth, trade credit seems to be more important for small firms as compared to large firms. In contrast with the expectations, however, these credits are less important for young firms. Finally, equity ratios are indeed higher for both small and young firms, which may be expected. In conclusion, accepting that sub-samples based on size and age may distinguish informationally disadvantaged firms from those without strong informational problems, only some of the expectations formulated above with respect to the composition of financial structures of different groups of firms are indeed confirmed.

Turning to the expectation of converging debt structures, this seems not to be confirmed by the sub-samples based on size, whereas it is only partially confirmed when looking at the sub-samples based on age. As noted, the debt structures of both small and large firms show similar patterns over time, which means that differences in structures between the two samples remain relatively unchanged. However, if the financial reforms had contributed positively to reducing informational imperfections in financial markets, one would have expected converging debt structures.

To conclude, if the analysis of debt structures and their changing patterns during the 1983–1992 period as presented here, is taken as indicative evidence of whether or not the financial reforms may have reduced the existing market imperfections, then it must be concluded that it appears to be difficult to make firm inferences with respect to the hypothesis that the reforms did have a positive impact on reducing monitoring and screening problems on behalf of the financial intermediaries. Note, however, that the observed changes in debt structures of different samples of firms may also have been caused by other factors than those related to the financial reforms of the 1980s. The above analysis does not take these other factors into account properly. It may be useful to try to further analyse the impact of the reforms on the functioning of the Chilean financial markets. The next section analyses how financial reforms may have influenced investment behaviour of different firms.

AN ECONOMETRIC ANALYSIS OF INVESTMENT BEHAVIOUR AND FINANCIAL REFORMS

Did financial reforms in Chile influence the investment behaviour of different groups of firms? In the presence of market imperfections, small and young firms – which are identified as having more problems with communicating information to lenders – may be confronted with financial constraints when financing their investment plans. If these financial constraints are indeed important, it may be expected that they influence investment behaviour. Since these firms have more problems in attaining external finance, fluctuations in their investment spending will be more closely linked to changes in the availability of internal funds. The hypothesis tested is that if the reforms contributed to reducing market imperfections, then financial constraints of both small and young firms are reduced, at least from the late 1980s. This hypothesis may be tested by estimating investment equations, which incorporate variables proxying for internal finance. Before testing this hypothesis, a brief review of the related theoretical and empirical literature is presented below.

Investment and finance constraints: a review of the literature

In a world with perfect markets, firms normally will invest when they have positive expectations about future growth possibilities. Investment may be financed both from internal and external finance. Internal finance consists of (part of) cash flow, whereas external finance may come from various sources of borrowing in financial markets. According to the neoclassical theory of corporate investment behaviour – developed by Modigliani and Miller (1958) – if financial markets are perfect, firms will be indifferent with regard to financing investment with internal or external funds. This means that internal and external finance are perfect substitutes and that, in principle, investment is not constrained by the availability of funds. Firms will invest until the marginal cost of borrowing – which is proxied by the risk-free market interest rate – is equal to the expected marginal rate of return on the investment project. However, financial markets are normally characterised by imperfections related to monitoring and screening problems and asymmetric information. Under these circumstances the Modigliani–Miller proposition no longer holds. In other words, financial constraints may then become important, especially for those borrowers having problems in communicating their private information to financial intermediaries and/or investors.

If financial constraints are important, they may influence the investment behaviour of firms. Since particular categories of firms have more problems in attaining external finance, due to informational problems, fluctuations in their investment spending will be more closely linked to changes in the availability of internal funds. With this framework in mind, it is possible to investigate the hypothesis that the financial reforms in Chile during the 1980s contributed to reducing existing market imperfections.

The first step is to estimate an investment equation which incorporates measures of internal funds such as cash flow, along with other variables, for small and large, as well as for young and old firms. The coefficient for the internal funds variable in the investment equations for small and young firms is expected to be higher as compared to large and old firms in the presence of informational imperfections in financial markets. The higher this coefficient, the more pressing these imperfections are and thus the tighter is the financial constraint for these firms. The second step indirectly establishes the effect of the reforms on the existing market imperfections. To investigate whether there is evidence for the hypothesis that financial reforms succeeded in reducing these imperfections, the same investment equation is estimated for sub-samples and sub-periods, i.e. 1983–1987, or the pre-reform period, and 1988–1992, or the post-reform period. The dividing line of 1987–1988 has been used based on the idea that the major reforms were carried out during the 1981–1986 period, and on the notion that these reforms would need at least one year to have the desired effects on the behaviour of participants in the financial markets. The hypothesis is said to be supported if the coefficient for the internal funds variable in the investment equation for the small and young firms – i.e. those confronted with more severe financial constraints, at least before the reforms – is higher for the pre-reform than for the post-reform period.

The above described method for investigating informational imperfections in financial markets and their impact on access to external funds for different categories of firms has been applied earlier. Fazzari, Hubbard and Petersen (1988) find that younger firms in the United States are more external finance constrained. In investment equations for younger firms they find significantly higher coefficients for cash flow as compared to the equations for more mature firms. Devereux and Schiantarelli (1990) also find evidence for the fact that firms having informational problems do rely more on internal funds, using data from the United Kingdom. Hoshi, Kashyap and Scharfstein (1991) suggest that Japanese firms not belonging to business conglomerates are informationally disadvantaged and therefore have more problems in obtaining external funds. Van Ees and Garretsen (1994) find that relations between bank and firm managers through chief executive officers are important in explaining why Dutch firms differ in their access to external finance. Chirinko and Schaller (1995) look at factors like concentration of ownership and membership of business groups in Canada and conclude that there is strong evidence for the existence of finance constraints for informationally disadvantaged firms, i.e. firms with lower concentration of ownership and/or not related to business groups.

The methodology has also been applied to investigate the impact of financial reforms on investment behaviour of firms in developing countries. Tybout (1983) analyses firm data on investment and access to external funds in the case of Colombia and finds evidence for the fact that after financial liberalisation financial constraints of small firms have been reduced. Atiyas (1992) finds that in Korea small firms are finance-constrained during the early 1980s but these constraints are reduced in the late 1980s, as is suggested by the fact that the coefficient of a stock measure of liquidity drops in investment equations for these firms. For large firms the coefficient of the internal funds variable rises, which may be explained by the fact that after the liberalisations

of the mid-1980s the Korean government significantly reduced its programmes for targeted credits. Before the liberalisation these targeted credits
were more directed towards large firms; after the liberalisation new targeted
credit programmes were introduced, this time focusing on financing smaller
firms. Studies from Harris, Schiantarelli and Siregar (1994) and Siregar
(1995) use data from Indonesian firms and find that in investment equations
of informationally constrained firms, in their case identified as small and/or
non-conglomerate firms, the coefficient for the cash flow variable drops in the
post-liberalisation period of 1985–1988. It must be admitted that these studies
fail to provide direct evidence on the efficiency of finance-constrained versus
unconstrained (or less-constrained) firms before and after the financial
reforms (Fry, 1995, p. 176). With this caveat in mind, the methodology
presented above to test the presence of informational problems in financial
markets and the effects of reforms to reduce them will be applied to the
Chilean case in the next section.

Investment and finance constraints in Chile

In the econometric analysis carried out in this section investment behaviour
is specified as follows. The analysis uses a very simple standard investment
equation based on the accelerator investment model. According to this model
firms adjust their capital stock by investing in response to changes in expected
profitability of their activities. The basic independent variable to incorporate
the accelerator mechanism of investment is the change in sales. Higher
current and past changes in sales may signal possibilities for higher profits in
the near future. The lagged investment to capital stock ratio is added to
account for the stock adjustment process. Next, this investment model is
extended with the cash flow variable to be able to investigate the relation
between investment behaviour and internal finance. Cash flow is defined as
total operational resources which consist of total net profits after taxes plus
depreciation. The cash flow variable indicates the internal funds available to
finance investment. This variable is lagged, since in general a firm will
finance investment in period t, using the cash flow which is generated one
period earlier – i.e. available at the beginning of period t. The problem with
this approach is that cash flow may also proxy for future profitability of the
firm. This may trouble the use of cash flow to indicate the extent of financial
constraints of firms. One solution to this problem is to add a measure for
Tobin's Q to the investment equation. Often, however, this measure is
difficult to use due to lack of data. In the present study, Tobin's Q can be
constructed for a sub-sample of 60 firms only. Therefore, the net profits one
period ahead have been used here to measure for future profitability. This
procedure is suggested by Siregar (1995, p. 45). It assumes that firm managers
have rational expectations. The inclusion of this variable should make it
possible to pick up the variations in investment behaviour coming from the

effect of future profitability. All variables have been scaled by the book value of the capital stock one period lagged to make the data comparable between different firms in the data set.

Summarising the above, the basic investment equation for the estimation procedure can be specified as follows:

$$I_{i,t}/K_{i,t-1} = \alpha_0 + \alpha_1(I_{i,t-1}/K_{i,t-1}) + \alpha_2(Y_{i,t-1}/K_{i,t-1}) + \alpha_3(CF_{i,t-1}/K_{i,t-1})$$

$$+ \alpha_4(PR_{i,t+1}/K_{i,t-1}) + \mu_{i,t'} \qquad (1)$$

where I is total gross investment of firm, defined as the total additions to the capital stock as reported in the profit and loss accounts; K is the capital stock; Y is the change of total sales; CF is the cash flow; PR is the net profits; μ is the firm-specific error term; i is the subscript for firms; t is the subscript denoting time.

The method used to estimate the above model is based on pooled regressions of individual firm data, using the ordinary least squares technique. The investment model has been estimated for the set of 204 firms, for which data were available during the 1981–1992 period. Due to the construction of lagged variables, the estimations refer to the 1982–1992 period.[6] Finally, the estimations have been carried out by taking into account year dummies.[7] These dummy variables have been added to the basic equation. These dummies may capture the impact of macroeconomic shocks and/or business cycles during the 1982–1992 period in Chile.

Table 13.6 shows the results of the estimation outcomes for sub-samples of firms for the whole 1982–1992 period. The table shows that the one period lagged cash flow variable does have a positive and highly statistically significant impact on investment levels for all sub-samples.[8] This implies that for the firms in the data set internal funds are an important source for financing their investment plans. In accordance with what may be expected when it is hypothesised that informationally disadvantaged firms have more problems in obtaining external finance – and thus are more dependent on internal funds to finance their investment – the coefficient for the cash flow variable is higher in the equations for small as well as young firms. Whereas for small firms the coefficient is 0.173, for large firms the coefficient is only 0.104. In the investment equation for young firms, cash flow has a coefficient of 0.184, whereas for old firms the coefficient is only 0.120. In conclusion, these results may indicate that small and young firms are finance-constrained due to informational imperfections, since they do rely more on internal finance when investing.

Did the reforms change the relationship between investment and internal finance for different samples of firms? In particular, is there evidence that financial constraints have been reduced since the reforms were carried out? The hypothesis may be tested whether or not the reforms did contribute to

Table 13.6 Investment and internal finance: estimation results for the entire period, 1982–1992 (dependent variable is the investment to capital stock ratio)

Sample	*1* All firms	*2* Small firms	*3* Large firms	*4* Young firms	*5* Old firms
Observations	1031	485	546	268	763
$IK(-1)$	0.374**	0.312**	0.478**	0.301**	0.461**
$Y(-1)$	-0.008	-0.025	0.017	0.004	-0.007
$CF(-1)$	0.142**	0.173**	0.104**	0.184**	0.120**
$PR(+1)$	-0.008	-0.001	-0.009	0.004	-0.018
Constant	0.082**	0.063*	0.096**	0.097**	0.070**
R^2	0.137	0.134	0.200	0.144	0.176

Notes: All equations have been estimated incorporating year dummies for 1982 to 1992. These dummies have been omitted from the table for presentation purposes
$IK(-1)$ = investment to capital stock ratio one period lagged
$Y(-1)$ = change in sales to capital stock one period lagged
$CF(-1)$ = cash flow to capital stock ratio one period lagged
$PR(+1)$ = net profits to capital stock ratio one period ahead
* = significant at the 5 per cent level
** = significant at the 1 per cent level

reducing informational problems in financial markets. This hypothesis may be confirmed when investment decisions of informationally disadvantaged firms are less dependent on internal finance after the reforms as compared to the period before the reforms. In other words, if the coefficient for the cash flow variable drops for the post-reform period, this may indicate reduced informational problems. Table 13.7 shows the estimation results of investment equations for sub-samples of firms for the pre-reform and post-reform period. Since the number of observations are unequally distributed over the two sub-samples based on the age criterion, the analysis concentrates on sub-samples based on size. The estimation results presented in the table show that the coefficient for the cash flow variable is high in the pre-reform period, amounting to 0.237, but drops significantly in the post-reform period to 0.107. The coefficient for the large firms remains the same and amounts to 0.097 on average over the two sub-periods. Thus, for small firms the dependence on internal finance when financing their investment plans reduces significantly, whereas for large firms this dependence does not seem to change between the pre- and post-reform periods. The value of the coefficients of both small and large firms becomes almost equal for the post-reform period, which may suggest that informational disadvantages for small firms as compared to large firms have been substantially reduced. The outcomes discussed here may indicate that the reforms have contributed to reducing the informational problems which exist in financial markets.

To conclude, based on the econometric investigation presented in this section, informationally disadvantaged firms seem to have been more

Table 13.7 Investment and internal finance: estimation results for the pre- and post-reform period (dependent variable is the investment to capital stock ratio)

Sample	Small firms		Large firms	
	Pre-reform	*Post-reform*	*Pre-reform*	*Post-reform*
Observations	266	219	278	268
IK(−1)	0.261**	0.456**	0.301**	0.652**
Y(−1)	−0.046*	−0.004	0.018	0.027
CF(−1)	0.237**	0.107**	0.096*	0.098*
PR(+1)	0.030	−0.010	−0.008	−0.025
Constant	0.045	0.113**	0.083**	0.087**
R^2	0.125	0.179	0.116	0.229

Notes: All equations have been estimated incorporating year dummies for 1982 to 1992. These dummies have been omitted from the table for presentation purposes
$IK(−1)$ = investment to capital stock ratio one period lagged
$Y(−1)$ = change in sales to capital stock ratio one period lagged
$CF(−1)$ = cash flow to capital stock ratio one period lagged
$PR(+1)$ = net profits to capital stock ratio one period ahead
* = significant at the 5 per cent level
** = significant at the 1 per cent level

dependent on internal finance when financing their investment plans. This may support the hypothesis that informational problems are indeed important in financial markets. Further investigation reveals that the dependency on internal finance for these firms was considerably reduced after the reforms were implemented, which may be taken as evidence for the fact that the reforms did help to reduce informational problems. Small firms seem to have gained increased access to external finance to finance their investments after the reforms were implemented. This outcome seems to indicate that there has been a shift in the pattern of financial resource allocation. Note, however, that this outcome does not provide direct evidence with respect to how this change in access to finance has influenced the efficiency of investment of small versus large firms.

EFFICIENCY AND FINANCIAL REFORM

Is there evidence for improved efficiency of allocation after the implementation of the reforms to be found from the available data? Improving allocative efficiency may be an important channel through which financial intermediation contributes to higher growth rates. A straightforward method to analyse this issue, suggested by Cho (1988), is to look at the changes in the variance of rates of return of firms. If resource allocation has been improved after the reforms, the rates of return of different firms should converge, abstracting from differences in risk premiums and transaction costs (Cho, 1988, p. 106). The reduction of market imperfections should have led to equalising returns. Thus, the variance of these rates is expected to decrease over time, and especially during the post-reform period. Ideally, marginal rates of return on investment should be compared to gain insight into this issue. In practice, it is rather difficult to obtain information on marginal rates of return. To circumvent this problem, Cho proposes looking at average costs of borrowing as a proxy for marginal returns. This is based on the assumption that, in order to maximise profits, firm managers equate the marginal cost of borrowing and the marginal rate of return on investment.

Using this methodology, Cho evaluates the allocative efficiency of the Korean financial reforms of the early 1980s by analysing the average cost of borrowing for different sectors before and after the reforms. To determine whether differences of borrowing costs between firms have decreased, the variance of borrowing costs for 68 manufacturing industries during 1972–1984 is tested. The analysis reveals that the variance of borrowing costs fell during the early 1980s, i.e. after the reforms had been implemented, indicating a positive impact of these reforms on allocative efficiency of the Korean financial system (Cho, 1988, pp. 107–8). Capoglu (1991) uses the same methodology to investigate whether the financial liberalisation of Turkey during the 1980s did have a positive impact on allocative efficiency. Capoglu finds that the liberalisation led to a rise in the variance of borrowing costs for 28 different industrial sectors. One of the important mechanisms causing this outcome was the process of distress borrowing, which has also been observed in Chile after the reforms of the 1970s had been implemented. In both countries, macroeconomic policy inconsistencies led to high interest rates and falling profits and firms borrowed mainly to forestall bankruptcy.

The above approach is also used in the present analysis. The average borrowing costs have been computed from financial statements of the sample of Chilean firms for the 1983–1992 period. These costs are measured by dividing total financial expenses for a particular year by the amount of debt reported for the same year for which interest payments have to be made.[9] Table 13.8 shows that the average borrowing costs fell relatively smoothly – with the exception of 1990 – from 0.150 in 1983 to 0.082 in 1992. This is in line with the observed fall of interest rates during the 1980s and early 1990s. Real interest rates were exceptionally high from the mid-1970s until 1982. From 1983, the monetary authorities were pursuing low and stable interest rates by means of active monetary policy. This policy was relatively successful. Real interest rates on one- to three-year loans fell from 15.6 per cent in 1982 to 8.5 per cent in 1991–1992 (Corbo and Fischer, 1994, p. 32).

Turning to the analysis of the variance of borrowing costs among different firms as a measure of improved efficiency of allocation of resources, Table 13.8 shows that for the main part of the period under investigation, there is not much evidence for falling variances of costs. During 1983–1990, the variance fluctuates and has an average value of 0.120. After 1990, there is a quite substantial fall from 0.128 in 1990 to 0.055 in 1992. The table also

Table 13.8 Average borrowing costs of firms (ratios, divided by debt on which interest payments are due)

	All firms	Variance[a]	Small firms (1)	Large firms (2)	Difference (1)–(2)
1983	0.150	0.136	0.168	0.134	0.034
1984	0.136	0.102	0.171	0.105	0.066
1985	0.140	0.153	0.169	0.112	0.057
1986	0.112	0.071	0.116	0.108	0.008
1987	0.121	0.121	0.122	0.120	0.020
1988	0.117	0.126	0.112	0.121	−0.009
1989	0.114	0.111	0.143	0.093	0.050
1990	0.139	0.128	0.164	0.116	0.048
1991	0.104	0.071	0.108	0.099	0.009
1992	0.082	0.055	0.084	0.073	0.011

Notes: [a]Standard deviation has been used as a measure of the variance of costs; firms reporting borrowing costs to debt ratio of over one have been eliminated from the sample to reduce the effects of extreme outliers on averages

shows borrowing costs for both small and large firms. From these data, it appears that the changing patterns of small firms are more in line with the general interest rate changes for the economy as a whole. Thus, when interest rates dropped quite strongly from 1983 to 1988, this seemed to have mainly reduced the borrowing costs of small firms. Moreover, when the interest rates rose in 1989 and 1990, again this affected the small firms the most. With respect to the differences in borrowing costs between small and large firms, it is difficult to find clear evidence for convergence of costs after the reforms. While for 1988 and 1991–1992 differences are low, they are quite high for 1989–1990 – at levels comparable or higher than those prevailing during the pre-reform period. Comparing the averages of the differences of the 1983–1987 and the 1988–1992 period reveals that differences fall from 0.037 to 0.022. Nevertheless, the conclusion seems to be justified that the data do not provide firm evidence for increased efficiency of resource allocation based on comparing average borrowing costs as a proxy for marginal rates of return on investment.

An alternative test of the efficiency of financial resource allocation after the reforms looks at the variance of average rates of return as a proxy for marginal rates of return for different firms. Cho and Cole (1992) have used this methodology to investigate the impact of the Korean financial reforms of the early 1980s. They find a falling variance of the average rates of return for the 68 Korean manufacturing industries over the 1970–1984 period and interpret this as evidence of an increase in efficiency of allocation (Cho and Cole, 1992, pp. 130–32). Applying this methodology to the Chilean case gives the picture presented in Table 13.9. The table shows data on net profits before taxes to total assets ratio, the same ratio as used in the study by Cho and Cole.[10] The

Table 13.9 Average rates of return of firms (ratios, divided by total assets)[a]

	All firms	Variance[b]	Small firms (1)	Large firms (2)	Difference (1)–(2)
1983	0.003	0.139	–0.007	0.013	–0.006
1984	0.030	0.110	0.015	0.051	–0.036
1985	0.029	0.125	0.011	0.047	–0.036
1986	0.085	0.100	0.070	0.100	–0.030
1987	0.100	0.121	0.075	0.125	–0.050
1988	0.118	0.161	0.087	0.149	–0.062
1989	0.116	0.111	0.110	0.122	–0.012
1990	0.082	0.132	0.079	0.084	–0.005
1991	0.112	0.145	0.131	0.092	0.039
1992	0.099	0.139	0.105	0.093	0.012

Notes: [a]Rates of return refer to profits before taxes divided by total assets; [b]Standard deviation has been used as a measure of the variance of rates of return

data reveal that the variance of rates of return actually increases from the 1983–1987 to the 1988–1992 period. This seems to contradict the idea that the reforms led to improved resource allocation, in which case the variance should have reduced over time. The trends in rates of return for small versus large firms separately show that there is some convergence, though. The rates of both samples increase after 1983, mirroring the economic recovery following the economic reform programme pursued. Yet the recovery seems to have been more important for the small firms. Their rates of return increase from –0.007 in 1983 to 0.110 in 1989, whereas for large firms returns go up from 0.013 to 0.122. Moreover, during 1991–1992 rates of return of smaller firms remain above those reported for the large firms.

To summarise, based on the above analysis it appears difficult to find strong evidence for the hypothesis that strengthening of bank regulation has contributed to increased allocative efficiency. Further research into this issue appears to be needed.

CONCLUDING REMARKS AND FURTHER RESEARCH

This chapter has evaluated the effects of the financial reforms the Chilean monetary authorities implemented during the 1980s. In particular, the analysis has investigated whether the reforms have had a positive influence on reducing monitoring and screening problems of financial intermediaries in Chile, what the impact has been on investment decisions, and whether bank reforms have contributed to increased allocative efficiency. The investigation of how reforms have influenced the functioning of financial markets has followed three different approaches. The first approach looked at changing patterns of debt structures of different groups of firms during the 1983–1992 period. If the reforms had contributed to reduced informational problems, then debt structures of different sub-samples of firms should have converged. The analysis has revealed that no firm evidence is found for such a convergence of debt structures.

This second approach looked at the relationship between investment and financial constraints for different sub-samples of firms. If reforms had contributed to reduced informational problems, fluctuations in investment should have become less dependent on fluctuations in internal finance for firms which were informationally disadvantaged prior to the reforms. This analysis confirms the latter hypothesis, supporting the idea that reforms indeed did contribute to improving the functioning of markets.

The third approach investigated the impact of financial reforms on allocative efficiency of financial intermediaries, based on the analysis of the variance of both borrowing costs and average rates of return. From this analysis it appears to be difficult to find clear evidence for the hypothesis that the reforms have contributed to improved allocative efficiency.

The following factors may explain why it has been difficult to find clear evidence on the positive relationship between financial reforms and improved efficiency of financial intermediation in terms of reduced market imperfections and increased allocative efficiency. First, during the 1980s the Chilean government did in fact introduce many different measures and adjustments, alongside the financial reforms discussed in this chapter, which may have had different effects on the financial position of firms, as well as on their investment behaviour. In the present analysis, these measures and adjustments have not been taken into account. Future analysis may focus on investigating the impact of the economic crisis and the consequences for the access to capital markets of different firms. Moreover, it may focus on what the impact of the successful export promotion policies on the availability of external finance has been. Finally, future research may be directed towards analysing the impact of financial reforms other than those related to bank regulation discussed here.

Second, it may well be that the reforms carried out in Chile need a longer time period to be really effective. A programme of financial liberalisation, which includes abolishing interest rate deregulation, as well as removing credit allocation programmes (see Tybout, 1983; Harris, Schiantarelli, Siregar, 1994; Siregar 1995), does have a more direct effect on changing access to capital markets of different groups of firms. But, changing the bank law, which basically aims at changing the behaviour of bank managers in terms of increased efforts at monitoring and screening, as well as pressing for more risk-averse loan portfolio management, may take longer to achieve the desired effects.

Third, the use of the samples based on size and age may not provide the optimal criteria for identifying firms with and without information problems, restricting their access to capital markets. One important criterion may be whether or not firms belong to *grupos*. Although the reforms of the early 1980s were directed towards reducing intra-*grupo* lending to reduce the risk of bank failure in the future, it may still be important in Chilean financial markets whether or not a firm belongs to a *grupo*, when applying for a loan and/or for other means of external finance. At the time the research for this chapter was carried out no useful information on relations between firms was available. Yet this issue is certainly important for future research with respect to analysing the effects of financial reforms on the functioning of financial markets in Chile.

To conclude, the analysis in this chapter should be appreciated as a first step towards deeper and more thorough analysis of the impact the Chilean financial reforms of the 1980s had on the functioning of financial markets.

APPENDIX: DESCRIPTION OF THE DATA

The econometric investigation in this chapter is based on information from the *Superintendencia de Valores y Seguros* (SVS). The complete data set available consists of information during the 1980–1992 period. The construction of the sample of firms used for econometric investigation has been carried out as follows. First, only firms giving data for more than three – not necessarily consecutive – years for the whole 1980–1992 period have been selected for analysis. Next, firms engaged in financial services, insurance and real estate and business services, as well as firms in the public, recreational, social and household sectors, have been eliminated from the sample. Finally, firms which reported unacceptable and/or inconsistent data have been eliminated. This means that firms in the process of liquidation, and firms reporting zero capital stock, zero sales, and/or negative values for equity plus retained profits have not been taken into account. After these elaborations were made to the data set, the sample consisted of 204 different firms. The number of firms varies annually from 113 in 1987 to 130 in 1983. The next step is to express all the information of the firms into one currency, i.e. the Chilean peso. Although the majority of firms present their financial statements in Chilean pesos, some of them present their information in American dollars. Therefore, data expressed in dollars have been converted into current pesos, using the end of year peso/dollar exchange rate (IMF, 1993, pp. 274–75, line we). Finally, the data have been expressed in real terms. Since no sector-specific price deflators are available, the GDP deflator of 1985 has been used to change the nominal figures into real figures (IMF, 1993, pp. 276–77, line 99bip).

The sample of firms has been sub-divided according to criteria of size and age. Table A13.1 gives details on the number of firms in the different sub-samples. The following criteria have been used to make these sub-divisions:

Table A13.1 Number of firms per annum: total sample and sub-samples

	All firms	Small firms	Large firms	Young firms	Old firms
1983	130	65	65	35	95
1984	118	59	59	29	89
1985	114	57	57	32	82
1986	117	59	58	31	86
1987	113	57	56	32	81
1988	116	58	58	36	80
1989	126	63	63	33	93
1990	120	60	60	42	78
1991	123	62	61	40	83
1992	123	62	61	37	86

- *size*: for every year the total sample of firms has been split into two equally sized sub-samples. Firm size is based on the net assets defined as total fixed assets plus current assets net of current liabilities;
- *age*: firms which were born less than 21 years ago in 1980 are classified as young; firms of 21 years or older have been classified as old.

With respect to the econometric analysis in the section commencing on p. 324, the variables used in the regressions have been constructed as follows:

- *investment*: defined as total gross investment and measured as the total additions to the capital stock as reported in the profit and loss accounts;
- *capital stock*: defined as the sum of land, buildings, machinery and other fixed assets, corrected for technical revaluation and depreciation; measured by the book value of the capital stock;
- *sales*: measured by the total value of sales;
- *cash flow*: defined as total operational resources; measured by total net profits after taxes plus depreciation;
- *profits*: defined and measured as profits before taxes.

NOTES

1 I thank Nanne Brunia, George Coppens, Catrinus Jepma, Ger Lanjouw, Robert Lensink and Hans Van Ees for their useful comments. The usual disclaimer applies.
2 See Visser and van Herpt – Chapter 12 in this volume – for a survey of the Chilean financial liberalisation and its economic consequences during the 1970s and early 1980s.
3 For a broader survey of the financial reforms in Chile during this period, see Hermes (1995).
4 See the Appendix to this chapter for a detailed account of the data preparation methods used.

5   One may question whether this really divides informationally disadvantaged younger firms from better known older firms. Yet, since only a few firms are less than 10 years old, the cut-off point has been set at 20 years to obtain a sufficient number of firms within the sample of young firms.

6   Unacceptable values of the variables in the investment model have been left out of the regression analysis to reduce the impact of extreme outliers on the level of the coefficients found.

7   These dummies have all been constructed in a similar way. The dummy for 1982, for example, has the value 1 for observations in 1982 and zero for observations in all other years.

8   T-values of the coefficients of variables in the estimated models have been used to decide whether or not a variable is statistically significant. This assumes that the residuals of the equations are normally distributed. Closer examination of the estimation results reveals that this assumption is violated. This means that the t-values found may be difficult to interpret. The outcomes of the empirical investigation must therefore be seen as indicative evidence only.

9   The debt for which interest payments have to be made consists of short and long term bank loans and loans from *financieras*, short term trade credit, short and long term bonds, other short and long term liabilities, and short and long term debts with related firms (Mizala, 1985, p. 108).

10 By taking this ratio, returns on real as well as financial investment are compared.

REFERENCES

Atiyas, I. (1992), *Financial Reform and Investment Behaviour in Korea: Evidence from Panel Data*, Paper Prepared for the Conference on the Impact of Financial Reform, Washington, DC: World Bank.

Capoglu, G. (1991), *The Effect of Financial Liberalisation on the Efficiency of the Turkish Financial System: 1980–88*, Paper Presented at the EEA Annual Conference, Lisbon.

Chirinko, R.S. and H. Schaller (1995), 'Why Does Liquidity Matter in Investment Equations?', *Journal of Money, Credit, and Banking*, 27, pp. 527–48.

Cho, Y.J. (1988), 'The Effect of Financial Liberalization on the Efficiency of Credit Allocation: Some Evidence from Korea', *Journal of Development Economics*, 29, pp. 101–10.

Cho, Y.J. and D.C. Cole (1992), 'The Role of the Financial Sector in Korea's Structural Adjustment', in V. Corbo and S.M. Suh (eds) *Structural Adjustment in a Newly Industrialized Country: The Korean Experience*, Baltimore: The Johns Hopkins University Press, pp. 115–37.

Corbo, V. and S. Fischer (1994), 'Lessons from the Chilean Stabilization and Recovery', in B.P. Bosworth, R. Dornbusch and R. Labán (eds) *The Chilean Economy: Policy Lessons and Challenges*, Washington, DC: The Brookings Institution, pp. 29–80.

Devereux, M. and F. Schiantarelli (1990), 'Investment, Financial Factors and Cash Flow: Evidence from UK Panel Data', in R.G. Hubbard (ed.) *Asymmetric Information, Corporate Finance, and Investment*, Chicago: Chicago University Press, pp. 279–306.

Fazzari, S.M., R.G. Hubbard and B.C. Petersen (1988), 'Financing Constraints and Corporate Investment', *Brookings Papers on Economic Activity*, pp. 141–206.

Fry, M.J. (1995), *Money, Interest, and Banking in Economic Development*, Baltimore: The Johns Hopkins University Press.

Harris, J.R., F. Schiantarelli and M.G. Siregar (1994), 'The Effects of Financial

Liberalization on the Capital Structure and Investment Decisions of Indonesian Manufacturing Establishments', *World Bank Economic Review*, 8, pp. 17–47.

Hermes, N. (1995), *Financial Markets and the Role of the Government in Chile*, Capelle aan de Yssel: Labyrinth Publication.

Hoshi, T., A. Kashyap and D. Scharfstein (1991), 'Corporate Structure, Liquidity, and Investment: Evidence from Japanese Industrial Groups', *Quarterly Journal of Economics*, 106, pp. 33–60.

International Monetary Fund (1993), *International Financial Statistics, Yearbook 1993*, Washington, DC: International Monetary Fund.

Larraín, M. (1989), *How the 1981–83 Chilean Banking System was Handled*, Policy Research Working Papers, WPS 300, Washington, DC: World Bank.

Mizala, A. (1985), *Financial Market Liberalization: The Case of Chile 1973–1982*, PhD thesis, Berkeley: University of California.

Modigliani, F. and M. Miller (1958), 'The Cost of Capital, Corporation Finance and the Theory of Investment', *American Economic Review*, 48, pp. 261–97.

Siregar, M.G. (1995), *Indonesia's Financial Liberalization: An Empirical Analysis of 1981–1988 Panel Data*, Singapore: Institute of Southeast Asian Studies.

Tybout, J.R. (1983), 'Credit Rationing and Investment Behaviour in a Developing Country', *Review of Economics and Statistics*, 65, pp. 598–607.

Van Ees, H. and H. Garretsen (1994), 'Liquidity and Business Investment: Evidence from Dutch Panel Data', *Journal of Macroeconomics*, 16, pp. 613–27.

Visser, H. and I. van Herpt (1996), 'Financial Liberalization and Financial Fragility: The Experiences of Chile and Indonesia Compared', Chapter 12, this volume.

Walker, E. and L. Hernández (1992), *Corporate Financial Structure in Chile; Part I: Evidence from Aggregate Time Series Accounting Data (1978–1990)*, Documento de Trabajo, 192–02, Santiago: Pontificia Universidad de Católica.

World Bank (1995), *World Tables 1995*, Baltimore: The Johns Hopkins University Press.

14

RESOURCE MOBILISATION IN THE CARIBBEAN COMMUNITY[1]

George C. Abbott

INTRODUCTION

CARICOM's most enduring feature is its size. As economic communities go, it is very small. The combined area of its members is 271,766 sq kms. Apart from the mainland states of Guyana (214,970 sq kms) and Belize (22,960 sq kms), they range in size from Jamaica (11,424 sq kms) to Montserrat, a mere 102 sq kms. In 1992, CARICOM had a total population of 5.7 million of which Jamaica and Trinidad and Tobago accounted for 64 per cent. Guyana, the largest member, had a population of less than 750,000 and a population density of 4 persons per sq km, and Barbados (432 sq kms) almost 600 persons per sq km.

Similar disparities exist in terms of natural resources. Traditionally, the islands depended on the production and export of agricultural crops for their livelihood, but this has changed. Except for Guyana, services, principally tourism, is now the main foreign exchange earner. In 1992, it accounted for more than two thirds of GDP in Antigua and Montserrat. CARICOM's mineral wealth comes mainly from bauxite in Jamaica and petroleum in Trinidad and Tobago. Guyana has substantial mineral resources, but these remain largely untapped. In brief, CARICOM members are small, open economies with limited resources, high population densities, small domestic markets and diseconomies of scale of production and administration, all of which severely constrain their ability to function as viable and independent states (Abbott, 1991a).

The creation of CARICOM in 1973 was intended to increase trade between the states and encourage coordination of economic policies as well as strengthen and promote regional cooperation and development. However, CARICOM has not lived up to expectations, and after 20 years, there is little to show by way of tangible achievements. The members still largely operate as individual units. A classic example is their approach to the problem of resource mobilisation where members operate independently rather than as a group. There is a vast array of monetary and financial instruments and institutions within the region for mobilising resources. However, the vast majority of these are island-specific, under-capitalised and under-utilised.

This chapter examines the various policies, instruments, structures and institutions which have been devised by CARICOM and its members to mobilise and effectively utilise resources to deal with the region's most pressing economic and social problems. It argues that although more has been done at country than regional (CARICOM) level, the level of activity is low, markets are atomised and the scale of operations too small to allow effective mobilisation and utilisation of the region's resources. Second, there are too many monetary and financial structures and institutions operating in what is essentially a very thin field. There is an urgent need to reduce the number of facilities and rationalise operations on a regional basis. Finally, this chapter assesses the prospects of some of the initiatives and proposals 'making the rounds'.

RECENT ECONOMIC PERFORMANCE

Selected data on the economic performance of CARICOM's members in 1992 are given in Table 14.1. Although the figures are for a single year, they are consistent with established trends; namely,

(a) the smaller members have out-performed the larger, so-called more developed countries;
(b) the disparity in per capita incomes between the smaller and larger members continues to widen. In 1992, per capita income in Montserrat was almost five times that of Jamaica. The disparity is even greater between Antigua and Barbuda and Guyana, CARICOM's poorest member;
(c) inflation is lower in the Organisation of Eastern Caribbean States (OECS),[2] a sub-group within CARICOM. This is due principally to the fact that their governments are not allowed to borrow from the Eastern Caribbean Central Bank (ECCB) to finance budgetary deficits. The larger members borrow extensively from their central banks to finance government expenditures;
(d) member governments are struggling to contain mounting budgetary and balance of payments deficits.

Basically, CARICOM's problems stem from size, the openness of their economies, and dependence on a limited range of exports. In Trinidad and Tobago, petroleum exports account for more than 60 per cent of the country's foreign exchange earnings and about 30 per cent of government revenues. Such heavy dependence on a single commodity clearly carries great risks. Trinidad and Tobago did well out of the two oil crises of the 1970s, only to

Table 14.1 Selected economic indicators for CARICOM members, 1992

	Area (sq kms)	Population (000)	Pop. density per sq km	GDP per cap (US $)	Real rate of growth (%)	Inflation (%)	GDS as % of GDP (1990–1992)	GDI as % of GDP (1990–1992)	Government surplus (deficit) as % of GDP	Current account surplus (deficit) US$ m
Antigua and Barbuda	440	64.3	146	6,769	–	–	31.8	34.6	–0.4	–8.7
Bahamas	13,942	264.4	19	11,570	–	5.7	10.7	21.2	0.5	–110.3
Barbados	432	258.8	599	6,117	–5.2	6.1	18.5	14.9	2.0	137.7
Belize	22,960	199.5	9	2,347	7.4	2.8	26.1	30.9	6.2	–18.8
Dominica	750	71.9	95	2,636	1.7	5.3	31.8	34.6	1.3	–25.2
Grenada	345	95.4	276	2,244	0.6	3.8	16.0	40.0	–2.0	–25.0
Guyana	214,970	749.8	4	500	7.8	–	30.9	38.5	–2.6	–73.0
Jamaica	11,424	2,448.2	214	1,291	1.4	77.2	26.7	27.9	7.0	46.6
Montserrat	102	10.6	103	5,976	4.2	3.4	10.5	53.4	–0.3	–11.6
St Kitts-Nevis	269	42.0	156	3,990	3.0	–	23.4	45.8	–0.1	–21.4
St Lucia	616	135.2	219	3,490	6.5	5.6	13.6	25.0	6.8	22.4
St Vincent-Grenadines	388	109.0	281	2,078	4.7	3.6	15.3	28.2	3.0	–16.7
Trinidad and Tobago	5,128	1,241.6	242	4,383	0.2	6.5	29.6	17.6	0.1	119.3

Source: Caribbean Development Bank, 1993
Notes: – not available (cannot be devised)
GDS: Gross Domestic Saving
GDI: Gross Domestic Investment

suffer badly when the bottom fell out of the international oil market. In 1985, for example, its deficit on current account amounted to $108 million, and reserves were down to $112 million, barely enough to cover one month's imports.

Similarly, the boom in sugar prices during the 1970s encouraged the expansion of production which, in turn, brought considerable hardship when world prices subsequently fell. Barbados and St Kitts, both of which depended on sugar, were particularly hard hit. Barbados has since switched over almost completely from agriculture to tourism. Effectively, therefore, it has switched from a monoculture to a monoservice economy which, given the nature of the international tourist industry, increases rather than reduces its exposure and vulnerability to adverse developments in the international economy.

The OECS members have moved into manufacturing and light industries such as clothing and garments, footwear, food processing and electronic assembly operations in order to lessen their dependence on agriculture. However, notwithstanding generous tax allowances, lower labour costs and preferential access to the US market, these industries remain small-scale operations. Many of them in fact have run into difficulties and folded. The harmonisation of fiscal policy and incentive legislation for industrial development, on which their development and expansion were premised, has not been achieved. Also, the move out of agriculture has increased their dependence on food imports, which currently averages about 20 per cent of their total import bill.

THE DIRECTION OF CARICOM'S TRADE

CARICOM's contribution to the expansion of trade between members is, at best, marginal. Much of the early gains were essentially 'water being drained from the system', and did not represent a fundamental shift in the pattern of trade or lasting efficiency gains. Consequently, when members ran into balance of payments difficulties these gains quickly evaporated. Some imposed import restrictions on intra-CARICOM trade and others reverted to bilateralism. In 1981, for example, Jamaica decided to apply the parallel market exchange rate to all CARICOM goods, thereby making them uncompetitive in the local market. Barbados and Trinidad and Tobago retaliated with a series of measures which resulted in a net loss of about $100 million in Jamaican exports in 1982.

Most of CARICOM's trade is, in fact, with the United States which accounted for 36 per cent of its exports and 41 per cent of imports. The EC, including the United Kingdom, was next with 24 per cent of exports and 13 per cent of total imports. Table 14.2 gives a summary of the direction of trade in 1991.

CARICOM's special regime in favour of its smaller members has helped

Table 14.2 Direction of CARICOM's trade in 1991

	Imports (%)	Exports (%)
Intra-CARICOM	7.1	10.0
United States	41.0	35.7
Canada	3.4	4.5
United Kingdom	5.5	10.3
EC (excluding UK)	7.0	13.4
Other	36.0	25.2
Total	100.0	100.0

to increase their share of intra-CARICOM trade, but the flow of trade has been mainly in one direction. While their exports to the larger members have increased, the latter have tended to concentrate on markets outside CAR-ICOM. Further, their efforts to increase their share of intra-CARICOM trade is constrained by import controls and restrictions in the larger CARICOM countries. They are therefore doubly disadvantaged. They do not have the resource or financing facilities to cater for CARICOM and world markets, so they have concentrated on the former. In the process, they subsidise exports from the larger members in good times, and face stringent import controls when these countries run into balance of payments difficulties. They rely on grants and external capital inflows to cover their balance of payments deficits, but grants have declined, and the cost of attracting and servicing external capital inflows increases their foreign debts which are now a serious problem for them. Between 1980 and 1992, total external debts of OECS members increased from $80 million to $636 million.[3]

CARICOM's domestic markets are small and atomised, and various regional arrangements enable producers to operate in protected markets. Many function as monopolies and pass on their costs to consumers. In the main, they are high cost producers with small volumes and uncompetitive prices. More importantly, they lack the skills and financial resources to penetrate and develop international markets, and have to depend on preferential arrangements such as the Caribbean Basin Initiative (CBI), the Generalised System of Preferences (GSP) and the Lomé Convention to sell their exports on world markets.

TRADE FINANCING FACILITIES

There are a variety of facilities for financing trade in CARICOM countries. These include bank loans, lines of credit, overdrafts, export credits, credit guarantee and/or insurance schemes and a whole range of special funds and facilities financed by multilateral development agencies such as the Inter-American Development Bank (IDB) and the World Bank. Obvious examples include the Re-Discounting Facility, the Rehabilitation Fund and the Export Development Fund, all of which were established in Jamaica. Trade-related finance is also provided by central banks, commercial and merchant banks (Smikle, 1988).

The terms and conditions of these facilities depend on such factors as purpose, period of credit and scale of operations. Practices differ between the member states but, on the whole, one can identify three basic features:

(a) there are more trade-financing facilities in the larger member states, with Jamaica being the most advanced in terms of the number and range of facilities;
(b) in general, the domestic banking system, and in particular, the commercial banks, provide most trade-related finance which contributes to the high cost of trading in CARICOM;
(c) notwithstanding the proliferation of facilities, there is a shortage of managerial skills and funding on appropriate terms to enable CARICOM members to operate an efficient and effective multilateral trade and payments system.

Creditor members are reluctant to extend credit to their debtor counterparts, and imbalances are corrected by restrictions and bilateral deals. The CARICOM Multilateral Clearing Facility (CMCF) which was set up to facilitate trade and payments between members quickly ran out of funds, and had to be wound up in 1983 with debts totalling £100 million. Virtually all of this amount was owed by Guyana, and is still outstanding. Any major initiative for facilitating and increasing intra-CARICOM trade will depend on whether, and how, this debt is settled, and/or what alternative arrangements are made for dealing with deficits and surpluses between members.

CAPITAL MARKETS IN CARICOM

The development of capital markets in CARICOM is still in its infancy, with member states each attempting to provide a full range of private and public institutions and facilities for mobilising domestic savings. These include central banks, commercial and merchant banks, savings institutions such as credit unions and building societies, insurance schemes, pension funds, social security schemes, local development banks, mortgage and finance companies, and stock markets. These institutions operate at different levels of development and efficiency, ranging from Jamaica which offers a more or less complete set of specialist institutions and facilities, to the OECS member states where operations are limited and existing institutions provide a multiplicity of functions. Figure 14.1 gives a schematic presentation of Jamaica's capital market.

Although the diagram in Figure 14.1 refers specifically to Jamaica, there are several features which are characteristic of capital market operations

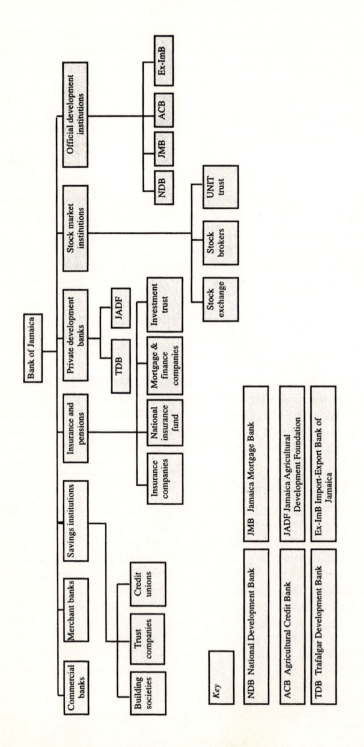

Figure 14.1 A schematic representation of the capital market in Jamaica
Source: Smikle, 1988, p. 20A

throughout the region. First, commercial banks provide between 70 and 75 per cent of domestic savings. For various reasons, firms prefer to borrow from these banks rather than raise equity capital. Consequently, most operations are financed by short term loans at high interest rates which are passed on to consumers in higher prices. There is very little equity participation from outside. Most businesses do not want to dilute ownership and control, so operations are kept small and tend, in the main, to be confined to member country markets.

Second, commercial banks operate principally on the criteria of credit rating, available collateral and ability to repay and restrict their activities to the short end of the market. They seldom engage in medium and long term financing, which is precisely the type of financing these countries need. Third, although there are variations among the members, most commercial bank loans and advances are personal and professional. In recent years the proportion of consumer-oriented loans exceeded 35 per cent of total commercial bank loans in Trinidad and Tobago and the Bahamas. In the OECS, the proportion reached 48 per cent in 1993. Table 14.3 gives the breakdown of commercial bank loans for the group by economic sector activities in 1993.

In all there are 44 banks serving the group. Of these, 24 are foreign owned, principally British and North American. Additionally, there are local branches and offices offering a variety of services, making a total of 100 commercial banking facilities with assets of EC $5 billion (US $1.7 billion). Local banks accounted for 44 per cent of all loans made in 1993.

Apart from the heavy support for personal and professional loans already mentioned, the activities of foreign and local banks seem to be concentrated in different sectors. For example, very few foreign loans went to agriculture, fisheries and financial institutions. Most were for manufacturing, utilities, private businesses, infrastructure and support facilities for the tourist industry in which there is a substantial foreign stake.

The mobility of credit is highly restricted. Very few commercial bank loans are made outside individual member countries, i.e. to other OECS and CARICOM members. Customers in St Kitts, for example, are unable or very unlikely to get a loan in, say, Grenada or Jamaica. Further, interest rates vary enormously throughout the region. In the OECS alone, the prime rate on foreign bank loans ranges from 9 per cent to 11.5 per cent and for local banks from 9.5 per cent to 13.5 per cent. Local banks also tend to pay depositors a higher rate than their foreign counterparts. Consequently, therefore, although the group is well served in terms of the number of banks and the range of facilities, the banking system is fragmented and atomised.

Significant amounts of domestic savings are also held by non-bank financial institutions such as credit unions, pension funds, insurance, building societies, mortgage and finance companies and social security schemes. For various reasons though, most of these funds are governed by legal and other

Table 14.3 Commercial bank loans by economic sectors for the OECS in 1993*
(EC $million)

	Foreign banks	Local banks	Total	Local/total (%)
Agriculture	21.3	92.4	113.6	81.3
Fisheries	2.4	3.5	5.8	60.3
Mining and quarrying	13.0	3.0	16.0	18.8
Manufacturing	92.7	62.7	155.4	40.3
Utilities	86.0	14.1	100.2	14.1
Construction and land development	72.6	65.9	138.5	47.6
Distributive trades	321.2	191.7	513.0	37.4
Tourism (hotels and resorts)	251.9	93.3	345.2	27.0
Entertainment and catering	18.5	18.5	36.9	50.0
Transportation and storage	53.1	47.5	100.6	47.2
Financial institutions	7.6	12.2	19.8	61.6
Professional and other services	76.4	69.5	145.9	47.6
Public administration	118.2	150.9	269.1	56.1
Personal	801.8	700.4	1502.2	46.6
Total	1,936.7	1,525.6	3,462.2	44.1

Source: Eastern Caribbean Central Bank, 1994
*Includes advances, bills discounted, and overdrafts

requirements or earmarked for specific uses, and are not generally available for trade financing or development purposes. To quote Smikle

> a high percentage of these funds must by law be kept liquid and secondly, by custom, trade financing is considered too risky a venture for investing the remaining funds. Consequently, these institutions invest mainly in risk-free ventures such as mortgages, real estate and Government securities.
>
> (Smikle, 1988, p. 3)

Operating at the short end of the market, these non-bank financial institutions are sensitive to the state of the economy and the level of business activity. In Jamaica, the financial sector passed through a rather lean and uncertain time during the 1970s when the country embraced socialism. Liberalisation and re-orientation of economic policy towards the private sector revived it. Credit unions, for example, registered a healthy expansion in membership and total savings, the latter having exceeded J$500 million in 1988 for the first time. By 1993 membership had increased by 25 per cent and total assets had trebled. Credit unions are in fact well-established throughout CARICOM. There are 76 of them in the OECS. The movement is particularly strong in

Dominica where credit unions have extended the range of operations and compete with commercial banks in providing banking and intermediation services for small businesses.

However, the medium and long end of the capital market are poorly served, and there is a shortage of venture and risk capital for private investment. Some venture capital companies do exist, but they are almost entirely financed by external agencies, such as USAID, IDB and the European Investment Bank (EIB), and do not enjoy any tax or fiscal concessions. The Caribbean Financial Services Corporation which was set up in 1984 provides up to 15 per cent of net worth to any one company, or up to US $500,000. The Agricultural Venture Trust established by USAID serves Barbados and the OECS members. It invests up to 49 per cent of the equity in a corporation, or up to 49 per cent of the total capitalisation other than loans in projects for small farmers.

There are several Development Finance Companies (DFCs) and National Development Banks (NDBs) operating at the long end of the market. They provide funds for private sector investment and long term development and are funded partly by central governments, but in the main by bilateral and multilateral financial institutions such as USAID, IDB, EIB and the Caribbean Development Bank (CDB). These institutions do not engage in equity financing. Instead, they provide long term capital finance at low rates of interest.

Examples of DFCs and NDBs include the Trafalgar Development Bank, the Jamaica Agricultural Development Bank, the Trinidad and Tobago DFC and the Barbados Development Bank. A brief review of operations shows that these institutions expanded during the 1970s but have stabilised since the mid 1980s. It is estimated that they provide about 12 per cent of total loanable funds from capital markets. Lack of funding for equity participation is only one of the reasons why they have remained minor contributors to development financing. Other factors include their high administration costs which run to about 30 per cent of total lending costs, a high proportion of bad debts and defaults, inflation and exchange rate variations.[4]

The Caribbean Development Bank (CDB) is a dual-purpose institution, being both a bank and a development agency. Among its many functions, it is required to promote private and public investment, mobilise resources for regional development, encourage the development of regional credit and capital markets, promote regional corporation and development and pay particular attention to the needs of its less developed members. Accordingly, it operates a variety of funds and engages in a full range of financial intermediation and development financing activities.

It has both regional and non-regional members and most of its funds are provided by the latter along with contributions from multilateral financial institutions. It is the largest source of funding within the region. Since its inception, net disbursements have totalled $1.2 billion, of which almost 70 per cent has gone to its less developed members. About 64 per cent of all its loans has been in the productive sectors and social infrastructure projects, while its financial intermediation has been concentrated on four sectors, manufacturing and tourism (37.8 per cent); agriculture, fishing and forestry (35.5 per cent); housing (17.6 per cent); and education (9.1 per cent).

On balance, the CDB has performed well. But it faces serious problems, the most obvious of which is that it is required to do too many things with insufficient funding. It badly needs to increase its capitalisation. Second, it has been more successful in raising loans externally than at home. The regional members need to contribute and invest more in CDB and not regard it primarily as a source of funding. Third, it has engaged in very little equity financing, risk capital and joint venture operations. Its decision not to support these activities may have been justified in the early stages, but cannot now be sustained. Finally, the number of small-scale operations which it undertakes, and the proliferation of NDBs and DFCs particularly in the smaller members to which it on-lends, are uneconomical. Many of its operations need to be rationalised if it is to play a more effective role in mobilising the region's resources.[5]

There are stock markets in Jamaica, Trinidad and Tobago and Barbados catering for the 'deep end' of the capital market. The most sophisticated is the Jamaica Stock Exchange which was established in 1968. It conducts two 45-minute periods of open market trading in 44 listed ordinary securities, and is supported by four brokerage firms which trade as both agents and principals. In 1993, the total volume of trade was 567 million units valued at J$8.4 billion. These figures reflect increases of 43 per cent and 82 per cent, respectively, on 1992 figures.

Although 1993 was a good year, it compares unfavourably with 1984 when 10 million units with a value in excess of J$26 billion were traded. Also, the market has been unsettled in recent months by a number of fiscal and monetary policy changes imposed as part of the country's stabilisation and structural adjustment programmes, such as tight monetary policy to control inflation and stabilise the exchange rate. The out-turn for 1994 is expected to be down on 1993. The market is essentially low volume, uncertain and highly susceptible to domestic and international economic conditions.

These characteristics are also evident in the operations of the stock exchanges of Trinidad and Tobago and Barbados, where volumes and values are even thinner. The Trinidad and Tobago Stock Exchange lists 31 companies with a total capitalisation of TT$1.7 billion. For Barbados, the corresponding figures are 13 companies and BDS$560 million in capital. Table 14.4 shows the amount of cross-border trading between the three exchanges in 1992 and 1993.

The figures show that the value of activities of Jamaican investors in both Trinidad and Tobago and Barbados stock is not only low, but that 1993 was down on 1992. Purchases of Trinidad stock fell from TT$4 million to TT$3.8

Table 14.4 Cross-border activity in CARICOM stock markets, 1992 and 1993

	Volume (000)		Value in local currency (000)	
	1992	1993	1992	1993
Jamaica's purchases in Trinidad	636	783	TT$4,031	TT$3,773
Jamaica's sales in Trinidad	1,649	218	TT$5,256	TT$680
Jamaica's purchases in Barbados	NIL	NIL	NIL	NIL
Jamaica's sales in Barbados	NIL	NIL	NIL	NIL
Trinindad's purchases in Jamaica	83	31	J$1,190	J$150
Trinidad's sales in Jamaica	2	11	J$14	J$354
Barbados' purchases in Jamaica	15	4	J$213	J$18
Barbados' sales in Jamaica	NIL	NIL	NIL	NIL

Source: Bank of Jamaica, 1994

million, while sales dropped significantly, down from TT$5.3 million in 1992 to TT$700,000 in 1993. There were no sales or purchases of Jamaica stock in Barbados in either year. Investments by Trinidadians and Barbadians on the Jamaican market were insignificant, at best, over the two years.

These levels of activity do not speak well for the optimism engendered by the CARICOM Enterprise Regime, which commits each member state to granting a CARICOM enterprise registered in its territory 'terms no less favourable than are accorded to any other similar enterprise of that member state' in areas required for its effective operation. In effect, the CARICOM Enterprise Regime implicitly allows qualified companies to be listed on any CARICOM stock exchange, thereby paving the way for a regional market for equities; a proposal which is being seriously pursued in some quarters (Miller, 1989).

Notwithstanding the disappointing performance of these markets, a proposal to establish a regional capital market to service the OECS member states is also being seriously canvassed. The case is based on the need to encourage and promote the private sector; to mobilise domestic resources more effectively; to create new financial institutions and facilities; on the fact that the smallness and fragmentation of individual members increases overhead costs and imposes serious diseconomies of scale of operations and administration; and on the contribution which the Eastern Caribbean Central Bank (ECCB) has made to regional monetary and financial stability and sound economic performance (see for example Sebastian, 1989).

Superficially, the proposal is attractive. It has certainly caught the imagination of the ECCB which has incorporated it into its Economic Development Strategy, stressing the benefits and requirements of a fully operational capital market and in particular, the contribution which the Eastern Caribbean Enterprise Fund (ECEF) would make to the development of the private sector and the privatisation programme. While the proposal is argued with conviction, it beggars belief, and flies in the face of the experience of other securities markets in the region as well as the practical realities of the OECS member states. In 1991, there were 23 public companies in the ECCB region, with a total capital issue of EC$134 million whose shares could be traded regionally. This is regarded as a viable basis for operations. The experience of the other three equity markets within the region clearly indicates otherwise.

CONCLUDING COMMENTS

Several points emerge from this analysis. First, there is no shortage of monetary and financial institutions and facilities in CARICOM for financing trade and mobilising domestic resources. The region is well-served in terms of numbers and availability of facilities. Nevertheless, each member (counting the OECS as one member for this purpose) seems intent on having its own capital market with a full range of structures and services. There is thus a lot of unnecessary duplication of facilities which, combined with under-utilisation and misallocation of resources, pushes up the cost of capital.

Second, there is no evidence to indicate that existing trade financing facilities have led to an increase in exports or a shift in the pattern and direction of the region's trade. Exports are high cost, marginal and uncompetitive in world markets, and are sold mainly under preferential arrangements. Intra-CARICOM trade remains small and, despite the establishment of a common market, is subject to quantitative restrictions and bilateral deals when members run into payments difficulties. Deficits are financed principally by capital inflows and loans which are a major contributory factor to their growing debt burdens.

Third, while there has been a slight shift in the ownership of capital in favour of domestic savers, this has not been enough to finance long term development or sustain fully functioning capital markets. Net domestic savings, for example, has ranged between 5 per cent and 8 per cent of the region's GDP in recent years. In addition, there has been substantial flight of capital from the region. Although this is notoriously difficult to calculate, it is estimated that almost $2 billion fled the region between 1977 and 1985, mainly from Barbados ($132 million), Guyana ($228 million), Jamaica ($506 million) and Trinidad and Tobago ($1,059 million) (Bennett, 1988). The provision of more financial instruments and institutions would not induce or guarantee a return of this capital. That comes basically from sound economic and financial policies and confidence in the government's management of the economy.

Fourth, the proliferation of capital markets in CARICOM is essentially supply-driven. In other words, they have been established mainly in response to the notion that if markets exist people will use them, and that they are a symbol of independence and economic prosperity, both of which reflect a fundamental misunderstanding of the nature and function of capital markets. It is not the number of structures and facilities, but the quality and range of services, adequacy of resources and profitability of operations which determine their use. They are, in effect, demand-driven. These attributes do not adhere to capital markets in CARICOM. These are poorly capitalised, have high operating costs and low trading volumes. The region cannot in fact support four capital markets, five if the proposal to establish a securities market in the OECS is approved.

Capital markets and stock exchanges depend on high volume and rapid turnover to survive and prosper. To be profitable, therefore, CARICOM markets will have to attract more capital from outside the region. In effect, they will have to compete with well-established, highly capitalised and efficient markets in developed countries. This poses a serious dilemma. CARICOM does not have the expertise, financial resources and technological back-up to compete effectively in world capital markets. These would have to be bought-in or franchised from other financial centres, and would be expensive. The question then, is, should CARICOM set up its own capital markets when the same services can be obtained for considerably less elsewhere?

Presently, the region has too many monetary and financial institutions and facilities, most of which are under-capitalised, inefficiently run and largely dependent on external funds. There is clearly a need to reduce the number of these institutions and rationalise their operations. Those that remain should operate in a regional rather than member context, and should concentrate on promoting and expanding private sector investment, and attracting equity finance, joint ventures and non-debt creating capital inflows.

Greater efforts should be made to reduce regional disparities in the members' economic performance, rates of inflation and exchange rate regimes. The OECS, for example, operate a fixed exchange rate parity of $2.70 (Eastern Caribbean) to $1.00 US. Bahamas, Barbados and Belize also maintain a fixed rate with the US dollar, but at different local currency rates, while Guyana, Jamaica and Trinidad and Tobago allow their currencies to float against the US dollar. Table 14.5 shows the regional variations in exchange rate parities for selected years. These disparities increase the risk and uncertainty as well as the cost of doing business in the Caribbean. They need to be reduced and stabilised particularly in the larger members.

CARICOM would clearly benefit from the establishment of a common currency based on a fixed parity with the US dollar, or some other international reserve asset as well as closer monetary and financial cooperation and/or integration. Among other things, these arrangements would reduce exchange rate variations, discourage 'hot money' and speculative

Table 14.5 Exchange rate parities per US dollar for CARICOM members

Members	Local currency	1980	1985	1990	1993
OECS	EC dollar	2.70	2.70	2.70	2.70
Bahamas	BAH dollar	1.00	1.00	1.00	1.00
Barbados	BDS dollar	2.01	2.01	2.01	2.01
Belize	BZ dollar	2.00	2.00	2.00	2.00
Guyana	G dollar	2.55	4.15	45.00	130.75
Jamaica	J dollar	1.78	5.48	8.03	31.84
Trinidad and Tobago	TT dollar	2.40	3.60	4.25	5.81

capital flows, impose a greater degree of monetary and financial discipline on members and lead to a more effective allocation and utilisation of resources in the region. Farrell and Worrell (1994) have proposed the formation of a common currency and the creation of a monetary union for CARICOM, based essentially on the principles adopted in the Maastricht Treaty for monetary union in the European Community. This union would be created in two stages and become operational by 2000 with most of the cost of adjustment falling on the larger members.

The proposal calls for closer cooperation and coordination of economic, monetary and fiscal policies among CARICOM members. It thus requires a massive leap of faith and commitment to the principle of regional cooperation and integration for which they have shown little enthusiasm. It also presumes that whereas lower and looser forms of regional cooperation have not developed and prospered, monetary integration, which is perhaps the most advanced form of regional cooperation, will not only work but will provide the catalyst which has been lacking.

NOTES

1 The Caribbean Community (CARICOM) is comprised of Antigua and Barbuda, the Bahamas, Barbados, Belize, Dominica, Grenada, Guyana, Jamaica, Montserrat, St Kitts-Nevis, St Lucia, St Vincent and the Grenadines and Trinidad and Tobago. Apart from Guyana and Belize, they form a group of island states and territories which extend over 1,000 miles from Jamaica in the north to Trinidad and Tobago in the south. They share a common history and set of cultural values and traditions in that they were former British colonies, except, that is, for Montserrat which is still a British territory.
2 The members of the Organisation of Eastern Caribbean States (OECS) are Antigua and Barbuda, Dominica, Grenada, Montserrat, St Kitts-Nevis, St Lucia and St Vincent and the Grenadines.
3 For a discussion of CARICOM's debt problem see Abbott (1992).
4 For an account of their contribution to domestic resource mobilisation see Bourne (1991).

5   The role of the Caribbean Development Bank is more fully discussed in Abbott (1991b).

REFERENCES

Abbott, G.C. (1991a), 'Viability and Integration in the Caribbean', *Journal of Commonwealth and Comparative Politics*, 29, pp. 327–45.

——— (1991b), 'The Caribbean Development Bank', in D. Worrell, C. Bourne and D. Dodhia (eds) *Financing Development in the Commonwealth Caribbean*, Basingstoke: Macmillan Education Ltd, pp. 130–52.

——— (1992), 'Debts and Sustainable Development in the Caribbean', paper presented at the INSULA-UNESCO Conference on 'Islands 2000. The World of Islands: What Development on the Eve of the Year 2000?', Taormina-Giardini (Sicily), 19–24 May 1992.

Bank of Jamaica (1994), *Annual Report*, Kingston: Bank of Jamaica.

Bennett, K. (1988), 'External Debt, Capital Flight and Stabilisation Policy: The Experiences of Barbados, Guyana, Jamaica and Trinidad and Tobago', *Social and Economic Studies*, 37 (4), pp. 57–59.

Bourne, C. (1991), 'The Role of Development Finance Corporations in the Commonwealth Caribbean', in D. Worrell, C. Bourne and D. Dodhia (eds) *Financing Development in the Commonwealth Caribbean*, Basingstoke: Macmillan Education Ltd, pp. 153–73.

Caribbean Development Bank (1993), *Annual Report*, Bridgetown, Barbados: Caribbean Development Bank.

Eastern Caribbean Central Bank (1994), *Annual Report*, St Kitts-Nevis: Eastern Caribbean Bank.

Farrell, T. and D. Worrell (eds) (1994), *Caribbean Monetary Integration*, Trinidad and Tobago: Caribbean Affairs, Caribbean Information Systems and Services Ltd.

Miller, J. (1989), 'The Enhancement of the Caribbean Securities Markets: Agenda for Development of National and Regional Markets', mimeo, Commonwealth Secretariat, London.

Sebastian, S.B. (1989), 'The Potential for a Securities Trading System in the OECS', mimeo, Caribbean Development Bank, Bridgetown, Barbados.

Smikle, C.V. (1988), *A Study of Capital Markets and Caribbean Trade*, Economic Commission for Latin America and the Caribbean, New York: United Nations Centre for Transnational Corporations.

INDEX